Understanding Corporate Governance in China

Understanding Corporate Governance in China

Bob Tricker and Gregg Li

HKU
PRESS
香港大學出版社

Hong Kong University Press
The University of Hong Kong
Pokfulam Road
Hong Kong
https://hkupress.hku.hk

ISBN 978-988-8455-70-6 (*Hardback*)
ISBN 978-988-8455-71-3 (*Paperback*)

British Library Cataloguing-in-Publication Data
A catalogue record for this book is available from the British Library.

10 9 8 7 6 5 4 3 2 1

Printed and bound by Paramount Printing Co. Ltd., Hong Kong, China

Dedicated to the memory of Gretchen Tricker (1945–2018), writer, reviewer, and editor of hundreds of articles and books on corporate governance, including this one.

Contents

Acknowledgments   xii
List of cases   xiii

Introduction   1
The advent of corporate governance in China   1
The basis of this book   3
What the book covers   3
Who the book is intended for   3

1. **Corporate Governance: The Basic Ideas**   5
   What is corporate governance?   5
   Corporate governance is not management   6
   The limited liability company   6
   Membership of the board of directors   7
   The role of the board of directors   8
   Classic approaches to corporate governance around the world   8
   Western approach   9
   Eastern approach   10
   References   13
   Case study   14
   Questions for discussion   19

2. **The Chinese Political and Economic History in Post-1980s and Corporate Governance**   20
   An aging population, migration to urban areas, a coastal nation   21
   Domestic drivers of modern corporate governance practices   24
   Deng's drive for modernization of the enterprises in the 1980s   40
   The birth of the private firms   42
   The Chinese modern enterprise system   44
   Conclusion   47
   References   48
   Case study   52
   Questions for discussion   59

3.   The Evolution of Corporate Governance in China   60
     The political history behind the advent of modern China   60
     The corporate governance of SOEs in China   64
     The Chinese government's attempt to reassert control over SOEs   68
     The governance of private companies in China   70
     The development of corporate governance in Hong Kong   73
     One country, two systems of corporate governance   74
     References   76
     Case study   76
     Questions for discussion   80

4.   Culture and Ethics in Chinese Corporate Governance   81
     What culture is and why it is relevant to corporate governance   81
     Modern business ethics in China   83
     The essence of contemporary Chinese business culture   84
     Corporate social responsibility with a Chinese face   85
     The effect of culture in overseas Chinese businesses   87
     Insights into business ethics in modern China   88
     The influence of religion on the development of corporate governance   91
     The proliferation of Buddhist, Confucian, and Daoist thoughts in
     modern China   93
     Comparison of Buddhism with Confucianism and Party ethics   94
     Communist Party ethics   96
     The need for a moral compass in Chinese corporate governance   97
     References   99
     References for the Buddhist section   100
     Case study   102
     Questions for discussion   103

5.   The Ecosystem and Regulatory Framework of Corporate Governance
     in China since 1978   104
     Background of the current ecosystem   105
     Replacing the state as shareholder   107
     Transition into modern corporate governance   108
     The development of private rights in China   110
     Many types of shares in China   111
     Getting ready to pounce   113
     The key participants in the ecosystem   114
     The State-Owned Assets Supervision and Administration Commission
     (SASAC)   116
     The China Securities Regulatory Commission (CSRC)   118
     The 2002 Code of Corporate Governance   120
     China joining WTO and NASDAQ   121

The 2006 Company Law and Securities Law   122
Duties of loyalty and diligence to the company   123
Liabilities of board members   123
Potential criminal liabilities of directors   124
Insurance for director's liabilities and the company's operating risk 124
Other important legislation   124
Current situation   126
References   126
Case study   129
Questions for discussion   139

6. **The Regulatory Framework of Corporate Governance in Hong Kong**   140
    The evolution of corporate governance in Hong Kong   140
    Corporate governance institutions   141
    The Independent Commission Against Corruption (ICAC)   145
    Relevant professions   146
    Nominated advisors (NOMADS)   149
    Some classic corporate governance cases   149
    The Hong Kong Companies Ordinances   152
    Hong Kong Corporate Governance Code   152
    Hong Kong Stock Exchange Listing Rules   159
    Hong Kong Financial Reporting Council (FRC)   159
    Core competencies for an effective director (HKIoD)   160
    Influences for the future   162
    References   164
    Case study   164
    Question for discussion   165

7. **Corporate Governance of Chinese Family Businesses**   166
    The governance of family businesses in China   166
    Key challenges   168
    Growth and succession   174
    Characteristics of Chinese family businesses and family values   178
    The East Asian experience: Ownership, control, and dilution   183
    Conclusion   187
    References   189
    Case study   191
    Questions for discussion   197

8. **The Functions and Practices of the Board of Directors in China** 198
    What boards do: Performance and conformance   198
    Strategy formulation in Chinese companies   203
    Policymaking in Chinese companies   206

Supervising executive activities in Chinese companies   209
Ensuring accountability in Chinese companies   215
Succession planning in China   217
Conclusion   220
References   220
Case study   221
Questions for discussion   227

9. **The Governance of Chinese Companies Abroad**   228
The development of Chinese business abroad   228
Some classic cases of China's investment abroad   229
China's experience of acquisition and merger   235
China's investment in developing countries   237
China's Belt and Road Strategy   239
Keeping governance control   239
The governance of corporate groups   241
Board-level information for diverse groups   243
Transfer pricing, cost allocation, and tax planning   244
Balancing the needs of companies and the state   244
References   245
Case study I   245
Questions for discussion   251
Case study II   251
Question for discussion   252
Case study III   252
Questions for discussion   253

10. **Corporate Governance in China in the Years Ahead**   254
The context for change in corporate governance   254
The basis of power in modern China   256
The future control of Chinese enterprises   256
Drivers of change in corporate governance   258
Forces for change in Chinese corporate governance   262
What the West might learn from Chinese corporate governance   263
Corporate governance as a catalyst for economic growth   269
The new "Xi" era of corporate governance   272
Some final thoughts   275
References   276
Case study   278
Questions for discussion   280

Appendix I: Acquiring and Partnering with Local Entities   281
Appendix II: The Case of the MMMP Saudi Rail Project:
                Building Railroads along the Belt and Road   288
Appendix III: List of Acronyms, Organizations, and Websites   301
Appendix IV: List of Interviewees   307

Index   311
About the Authors   317

Acknowledgments

The authors are most grateful to the many businesspeople, lawyers, auditors, regulators, and others who have shared their experiences of corporate governance in China. Without their input to our research, the book would have been little more than a recital of the legal and regulatory requirements. Some of them wanted to remain anonymous, but the names and affiliations of the others are listed in Appendix IV: List of Interviewees. We want to thank Richard Leung in particular, a seasoned China banker, who has given us exclusive and unique inside coverage of China. We are most grateful to them all. The authors also acknowledge with gratitude the editorial contributions of Linlin Li, Alfred Ho, and Gretchen Tricker, which have greatly added to the readability of the work.

List of cases

Chapter 1: Corporate Governance: The Basic Ideas
Alibaba China and investor relations 14

Chapter 2: The Chinese Political and Economic History Post-1980s
and Corporate Governance
China Baowu Steel Group Corporation Limited 52

Chapter 3: The Evolution of Corporate Governance in China
Huawei China: Rotating CEOs and corporate culture 76

Chapter 4: Culture and Ethics in Chinese Corporate Governance
Foxconn and Apple Computers 102

Chapter 5: The Ecosystem and Regulatory Framework of Corporate
Governance in China since 1978
Vanke: A Chinese conglomerate 129

Chapter 6: The Regulatory Framework of Corporate Governance in
Hong Kong
Hong Kong Stock Exchange: A director's right to know 164

Chapter 7: Corporate Governance of Chinese Family Businesses
Corporate governance at the Wanda Group 191

Chapter 8: The Functions and Practices of the Board of Directors
in China
Corporate Governance at Ping An, China 221

Chapter 9: The Governance of Chinese Companies Abroad
Tencent Holdings Ltd. 245
Teletronic Riches Ltd.: Governance of a joint venture 251
Bright Food (Group) Co. Ltd 252

Chapter 10: Corporate Governance in China in the Years Ahead
Yum China Holdings 278

Introduction

The advent of corporate governance in China

In the 1980s, the People's Republic of China (PRC) began to introduce a market-led economy. The Chinese Communist Party's Central Committee made the decision to bring in a modern enterprise system, the state withdrawing from the central control of state-owned enterprises (SOEs). A new companies law was enacted in 1994 permitting the formation of companies. Many SOEs were subsequently corporatized and their management given greater autonomy. New companies were created; some family firms, others reflecting national, provincial, or local interests.

Among the SOEs were some vast companies in oil, telecom, steel, and finance. In many cases a minority of their shares were floated on stock exchanges in Hong Kong, Shanghai, and Shenzhen (a vast new city close to Hong Kong). A few were floated in London or New York. But governance was needed to oversee those emerging corporate enterprises.

Experts from Hong Kong and the Organisation for Economic Co-operation and Development (OECD) helped to produce a set of corporate governance guidelines. Inevitably, OECD drew on corporate governance practices in countries such as the US, the UK, and Germany. But these countries are democracies with independent judiciaries and a culture of business integrity.

Individual accountability, transparency, governance regulations, or code with regulatory bodies ready to cite non-compliance, which are taken for granted in the West, were not the norm in China. The Chinese culture is one of collective and shared accountability. Opaqueness has been the working norm for many SOEs.

China stands out as a case on its own. Government is an oligarchy, exercising significant central administrative control, with the judiciary serving the state. Nevertheless, the PRC has developed an innovative corporate governance regime, with supervisory boards reflecting the German two-tier board model, but also boards of directors with independent outside directors, somewhat similar to the US and UK unitary board model.

For years governance was left to companies, under the overall supervision of the State-Owned Assets Supervision and Administration Commission (SASAC) and the China Securities Regulatory Commission (CSRC). State involvement at a higher level tended to be distant. Some felt that the Communist Party's leadership had been undermined, so central authorities have recently sought to reassert party influence over the SOEs.

However, corporate governance involves more than company law, governance guidelines, and the rules of the stock exchanges and regulatory authorities. Culture and ethics lie at the core of corporate governance—the culture of the country, the culture of each company, and indeed the culture of every board. In China, the corporate governance culture is still emerging, the ethics underpinning business activity are evolving, and business-government relations continue to change.

Corporate governance in Hong Kong was different. Hong Kong became a Special Administrative Region of China in 1997, after nearly 200 years as a British Protectorate under a lease from mainland China. The roots of corporate governance in Hong Kong were different and deep. Under the British influence, Hong Kong developed its own legislature, an independent judiciary based on English-style common law, and its own currency linked to the US dollar. The Hong Kong Stock Exchange dates from 1891. Institutions for company registration and regulation were created, and strong professions were formed: legal, audit, accountancy, finance, and company secretarial. This infrastructure and these institutions remained after the 1997 handover; as the Joint Agreement between the PRC and Britain put it: "one country, two systems." But as the business worlds of China and Hong Kong grow together, some Hong Kong institutions are coming under China's influence.

To reach its present economic and political significance in the world, China has traveled a unique road. This historical and cultural context means that China has developed corporate governance with a distinct "Chinese face." Exploring and understanding the special features of corporate governance in China and the challenges ahead is the theme of and rationale for this book.

When the authors worked together in Hong Kong, around 20 years ago, they did not imagine that within two decades, China would:

- become the second largest economy in the world
- have some of the most significant companies on the New York Stock Exchange board
- create an affluent, car-owning middle class able to travel to Hong Kong, Europe, and North America
- build many "smart cities" using virtually cashless information technology for their activities
- develop a modern transport network of motorways and railways, and
- formulate a "belt and road" strategy to link China with Europe.

Corporate governance was recognized, at the outset in China, as fundamental to such developments. China has been and continues experimenting with its governance systems. In the process, unlike the West, which tends to think of corporate governance as the method of regulating business, China sees corporate governance as a means of contributing to economic growth for the benefit of the people and the state. This book tells that story.

The basis of this book

To understand corporate governance in China, it is not enough to know the policies and procedures, rules and regulations involved; it is vital to understand how businesspeople and officials act in practice. This book is based on a research project by Gregg Li in 2016 and 2017, in which he conducted in-depth interviews with business leaders, auditors, bankers, lawyers, and others closely involved in corporate governance in China. Some interviewees contributed material based on their unique experiences and insights. The background of interviewees and contributors appears in Appendix IV, although some interviewees preferred anonymity.

This book attempts to understand reality but recognizes that it is only possible to capture slices of the past. Corporate governance practices are evolving rapidly in China. There are many negatives and many positives. What worked in one situation weakened the governance infrastructure of another firm.

The two authors, Gregg Li and Bob Tricker, have extensive knowledge of corporate governance through research, writing, trouble-shooting, and teaching in the subject and through long-standing coaching and consultancy for directors and boards. More biographical information appears in Appendix IV.

What the book covers

The main intention is to provide a practical guide to current corporate governance issues and practices in mainland China and Hong Kong, with an insight into possible futures. Companies involved include private companies and those owned by regional, municipal, or other official bodies such as the People's Liberation Army (PLA), SOEs and their subsidiary companies, and companies with overseas ownership. The governance of companies listed on the Hong Kong, Shanghai, and Shenzhen stock markets, including SOEs, is included. The governance of H-share companies, incorporated in mainland China but increasingly important to the Hong Kong market, is also covered.

Who the book is intended for

The book will interest board chairpersons, company directors, and senior executives, PRC officials at state, regional, and municipal levels, and practicing governance professionals in the, law, and company secretarial fields. Masters-level students studying for an MBA or similar degree, and students working on professional examinations in the accountancy, auditing accountancy, auditing, legal, and company secretarial professions will also find the book useful. Some case studies of actual governance situations have been included for use in courses although practitioners may also find them interesting. Indeed, the book will be valuable to all those around the world who have an interest in China. It is particularly relevant to those sitting on the boards of Chinese companies or foreign companies owned by the Chinese: they need to appreciate the reality of corporate governance in China and the potential for cultural differences.

1

Corporate Governance: The Basic Ideas

Bob Tricker

In this chapter we consider:

- ❖ what is corporate governance
- ❖ that corporate governance is not management
- ❖ the limited liability company
- ❖ membership of the board of directors
- ❖ the role of the board of directors
- ❖ classic approaches to corporate governance around the world
- ❖ the Western approach
  - ➤ the United States unitary board, rule-based model
  - ➤ the UK/Commonwealth unitary board, principles-based model
  - ➤ the continental European two-tier model
- ❖ the Eastern approach
  - ➤ the *keiretsu* model of corporate governance in Japan
  - ➤ the *chaebol* model of corporate governance in South Korea
  - ➤ China's approach to corporate governance

What is corporate governance?

The term "corporate governance" first came into use during the late 1980s[1] and the phrase was soon adopted worldwide. In 1988, Cochran and Wartick, two American academics, published an annotated bibliography of corporate governance: it had 74 pages. Today, Google notes over 57 million references to the phrase. The world's first corporate governance code, Sir Adrian Cadbury's code for the UK, was published in 1992.

But the only thing that is really new about "corporate governance" is the phrase. The practice of corporate governance is as old as trade. Whenever the owners or the members of an organization delegate the responsibility for its running to managers,

---

1. The first book with the title "Corporate Governance" was published in 1984, reporting five years' research at Nuffield College, Oxford, into the practices and procedures of British boards of directors. See Tricker, 1984.

they need a means to ensure that those managers do their job properly and meet the enterprise objectives.

Essentially, corporate governance is about the way power is exercised over corporate entities.[2] It ensures those organizations meet the needs of their members.

All organizations need governing: educational institutions, sports clubs, hospitals, cooperatives and, of course, businesses. In this book we focus on companies incorporated to do things for a profit. We will explore what goes on in and around the boardrooms of businesses in modern China.

Corporate governance is not management

Corporate governance is not the same as management. The management of an organization is in the hands of the corporate executives and other managers who run the enterprise. Management involves planning, controlling, and taking managerial decisions. It is an analytical and logical process. Corporate governance, in contrast, is principally a political process. The governing body is responsible for overseeing the management, ensuring that the enterprise is running in the right direction and meeting its members' objectives. The governing body provides the moral compass for the enterprise, sets its standards, and oversees its ethical approach.

The governing body is frequently called the board of directors though many other names are used—committee, council, or even just the "governing body." For simplicity, we will refer to the board throughout.

The limited liability company

Limited liability companies were a brilliant development of mid-nineteenth-century Britain. To raise capital, company law allowed the incorporation of corporate entities with the powers of an individual trader to do business but limiting the liability of their investors to their shareholding stake. The notion quickly spread around the world, allowing the creation of employment, wealth, and economic growth. The limited liability company now underpins world trade.

Crucial to the concept of the limited liability company is that ownership is the basis of power over that company, allowing shareholders to nominate and elect the directors, appoint the auditors, and receive information about their directors' stewardship of the company. Predictably, over the years, the success of the concept led to immense complexity. In the early days, shareholders were individuals. In most listed companies today, individual "retail" investors are in a small minority, overshadowed by institutional investors, hedge funds, private equity investors, and

---

2. Only a brief insight into corporate governance can be provided in this chapter; for a fuller discussion see Tricker, 2015.

others, including sovereign funds and nationalized state ownership (both relevant to corporate governance in China, as we will see).

Membership of the board of directors

Essentially, there are two distinct types of board member:

- *executive directors*, who are also senior members of the management
- *non-executive directors*, who are not part of the management.

Non-executive directors are often referred to as outside directors. These non-executive directors fall into two significant categories:

- *independent non-executive directors* who have no ties with the company, other than their directorship, who can thus bring independent insights and judgment to board deliberations
- *connected non-executive directors*, who are not members of the management but who do have some connection with the business, such as being a major shareholder, having connections with significant suppliers or customers, or previously being executives of that company and therefore not seen to be able to exercise independent judgment.

Boards vary in size and structure, affecting their operational characteristics. Four possible structures are possible:

The executive board is made up entirely of directors who are also managers in the company. These boards are often found in family businesses, particularly in the first generation, private companies, and on the boards of subsidiary companies within a group of companies.

The majority executive director board has non-executive directors to give advice but they are in a minority, executive directors holding the power. Such structures used to be quite common in companies listed on stock markets around the world. But many corporate governance codes today call for a majority of independent outside directors, so these boards are rarer, except in private companies and some family firms.

The majority non-executive board is now the norm in listed companies, because of corporate governance code and stock exchange listing requirements. Such structures are seldom found in private companies because top management prefers to keep the power over the company in their own hands.

The all non-executive board composed entirely of outside directors is symptomatic of the supervisory board in the two-tier board model, to be discussed shortly. It is also frequently found in the governing bodies of not-for-profit organizations.

The role of the board of directors

The essential role of the board of directors is to direct the company. As we have seen, this is not the same as managing it.

Boards need to look forward and outward at the company in its commercial, competitive, market setting as it *formulates corporate strategies*, in the light of the economic, political and social context. Clearly the board works closely with top management in formulating these strategies although boards vary in the extent to which they initiate strategic changes themselves or discuss and approve strategies proposed by their management.

The board then needs to look inwards to *ensure that policies are in place* for these strategies to lead to appropriate management action. The board *sets the standards* for the entire organization: corporate ethics begins in the boardroom.

Boards also need to look at past and present performance to fulfill their responsibility *to oversee and supervise management*. Reporting on performance against key performance indicators (KPIs) and financial budgets are crucial board information.

Finally, boards have a fundamental duty to *be accountable to their shareholders* and other legitimate stakeholders. Corporate reporting is a fundamental duty of the board, in compliance with company law and other regulations. The classical financial accounts are increasingly being expanded to include integrated reports covering many other aspects of the company's performance, including employee policy, environmental concerns, and social responsibility to stakeholders affected by corporate activities.

Classic approaches to corporate governance around the world

Although the basic intentions of corporate governance around the world are similar, the means of achieving them vary considerably. Evolving history, culture, company legislation and corporate regulation affect the principles and practices of corporate governance in different countries.

Two rather different approaches have emerged in applying corporate governance principles and practices. The Western approach can be divided into three distinct models:

- The United States rule-based model
- The UK/Commonwealth principles model
- The continental European two-tier model

The Eastern approach falls into three basic models:

- The Asia family-based model
- The *keiretsu* model in Japan
- The *chaebol* model in South Korea

As we will see, China has created a unique model, drawing from both the Western and Eastern models. Let us now consider now the basic models of corporate governance that have provided the major influences.

Western approach

The United States unitary board, rule-based model

Companies in the US are incorporated in individual states and are subject to those states' company law and corporate regulation. Investor protection, auditing requirements, and financial disclosure of public companies, however, are federal responsibilities, predominantly overseen by the US Securities and Exchange Commission (SEC), which was created in 1934.

The basic governance model for public companies in the US is the unitary board, with a predominance of independent outside directors. SEC and stock exchange listing requirements also call for mandatory audit, nomination, and remuneration committees of the Main Board.

In the US, governance is regulated by legal statute and mandatory rules, which are inherently inflexible. Litigation levels are high. Directors face legal penalties for non-compliance. The 2002 Sarbanes-Oxley Act strengthened this emphasis on governance under penalty of law, with disclosure requirements that proved more expensive and burdensome than expected. The US financial markets are still among the best regulated, as well as being the largest and most liquid in the world; but that lead is being eroded.

The UK/Commonwealth unitary board, principles-based model

The law that recognized the incorporation of the joint-stock shareholder limited-liability company originated in the United Kingdom in the mid-nineteenth century. Membership of the old British Empire, in the later nineteenth and early twentieth centuries, meant that UK company law influenced the development of company law in Australia, Canada, Hong Kong, India, New Zealand, South Africa, Singapore, and indeed throughout what is now known as the Commonwealth.

Company law in the UK/Commonwealth model is based on common law, rooted in legislation, which is reinforced as the courts decide specific cases. However, by contrast with the US model, in the UK and in Commonwealth countries, corporate governance is "principles-based." Codes of corporate governance principle or good practice determine board responsibilities, not legal doctrine. Companies are required to report that they have followed the governance principles laid down in the codes or to explain why they have not. Consequently, this model is often referred to as the "comply or explain" approach to corporate governance. Self-regulation by each company, not the rule of law, is the underlying theme.

Compliance is voluntary, the sanctions being the exposure of corporate govern-ance failings to the market and, ultimately, delisting from the stock exchange. Stock exchange regulations and company regulators ensure that investors and potential investors have accurate information on which to base their judgments.

Throughout the Commonwealth, corporate governance codes for listed com-panies; although differing slightly in detail, all call for independent non-executive or outside directors, audit, remuneration, and nomination committees of the board, and high levels of transparency and accountability. The codes also call for a separa-tion between chairperson and CEO.

The Hong Kong approach to corporate governance mirrors the UK's unitary board, principles-based model, as we will explore in Chapter 3.

The continental European two-tier model

In the two-tier board model a supervisory board, with no management members, sits above the executive board, which comprises entirely executive (management) members. As the name suggests, the supervisory board oversees the work of the executive board and can hire and fire its members. Two-tier boards are required in Germany and The Netherlands and are found in France and Italy. In Germany, large companies are seen as a quasi-partnership between capital and labor. Reflecting this idea of social democracy, German co-determination laws require one half of the supervisory board to represent labor, the employee representative directors elected through the workers' trades unions; the other half, representing capital, is elected by the shareholders.

Typically, members of top management attend and report to their supervi-sory board. Critics of the two-tier model of corporate governance argue that the supervisory board is often dominated by top management and lacks the informa-tion inputs, advice, and wise counsel that can be provided by outside independent, non-executive directors in unitary boards. Other critics question the effectiveness of supervisory boards, their lack of real power, and their ability effectively to control the management board. Some also argue that the representative character of the supervisory board produces conflicts of interest.

For a while, countries that employed the two-tier board believed that this was a superior model to the unitary board. Indeed, the European Union once tried to impose the two-tier model on all companies in member states—a proposal that was strongly resisted in the unitary board countries.

Eastern approach

- The Asia family-based mode
- The *keiretsu* model in Japan
- The *chaebol* model in South Korea

The Asian family-based model[3]

Chinese businesspeople play a fundamental part in the business life of Southeast Asia, as a result of the Chinese diaspora from the Mainland over the years. Many companies in the significant Asian economies—Singapore, Taiwan, Malaysia, Thailand, Indonesia, Hong Kong, and the Philippines—are in the hands of Chinese families. For example, nearly half of the share capital invested in Malaysian companies is owned by Chinese residents.

In the governance of overseas Chinese companies, the board tends to play a supportive role to the real exercise of power, which is exercised through relationships between the key players, particularly between the dominant head of the family and other family members in key top management positions. Some of these companies are quite diverse groups with considerable delegation of power to the subsidiary units, but the owner-manager, or a family-orientated small group, still holding a strategic hand on the tiller.

Research into the management of companies owned by overseas Chinese has suggested some distinguishing characteristics about their management and governance. Such firms tend to be:

- family-centric with close family control;
- entrepreneurial, often with a dominant entrepreneur, so that decision-making is centralized, close personal links emphasizing trust and control;
- family inclusive with family members working in the family business;
- paternalistic in management style, in a social fabric dependent on relationships and social harmony, avoiding confrontation and the risk of the "loss of face";
- strategically intuitive, the business seen as more of a succession of contracts or ventures, relying on intuition, superstition, and tough-minded bargaining rather than strategic plans, brand creation, and quantitative analysis.

Where such companies are floated on the stock market, the outside shareholders are often in the minority. Consequently, regulatory authorities tend to emphasize the importance of disclosure and the control of related-party transactions. Although many corporate governance codes require independent non-executive directors, the independence of outside directors is less important to the owner than are their character, trustworthiness, and overall business ability. Of course, corporate governance problems exist in Chinese and overseas Chinese companies: corruption, insider trading, unfair treatment of minority shareholders, and domination by company leaders, to name a few. But these are unfortunate attributes of corporate governance that reflect human behavior everywhere.

---

3. For more information on the business methods of overseas Chinese, see Redding, 1993.

The keiretsu *model of corporate governance in Japan*

In Japan, the *keiretsu* are networks of companies connected through cross-holdings and interlocking directorships. Member companies tend to inter-trade extensively. Frequently, the network includes a financial institution. The classical model of the *keiretsu* reflects the social cohesion within Japanese society, emphasizing unity throughout the organization, non-adversarial relationships, lifetime employment, enterprise unions, personnel policies that encourage commitment, initiation into the corporate family, decision-making by consensus, cross-functional training, and promotion based on loyalty and social compatibility as well as performance.

In the classical *keiretsu* model, boards of directors tend to be large and are, in effect, the top layers of the management pyramid. People speak of being "promoted to the board." The tendency for managers to progress through an organization on tenure rather than performance means that the mediocre can reach board level.

Japan's 2016 Corporate Governance Code overcame decades of resistance to the inclusion of independent outside directors on Japanese boards. The code took a pro-investor stance and emphasized that corporate governance should add to the long-term growth of the company. Two governance models were offered—one with a supervisory board, the other with an audit committee of a unitary board—both to have independent outside directors. A nomination committee and a nomination committee of the main board were also required.

Many Japanese still do not see the need for such intervention. Indeed, they have difficulty understanding how outside directors operate. How can outsiders possibly know enough about the company to make a contribution, they question, when the other directors have spent their lives working for the company? How can outsiders be sensitive to the corporate culture? They might even damage the harmony of the group.

The chaebol *model of corporate governance in South Korea*

Chaebol groups in South Korea developed following World War II, when the government advanced loans on attractive terms to family-based firms to stimulate economic revival. Over time, some of these family firms prospered and became large groupings of associated companies. Even *chaebol* companies that are listed are often still controlled by the dominant owner-family interests. Even though companies attracted outside capital, family domination was maintained predominantly through insider boards and cross-ownership with subsidiary companies.

Attempts to introduce independent outside directors into South Korean boards have had only limited effect against the entrenched power of the existing block owners. At times, this has led to protests from employees and social unrest. In recent years, the South Korean government sought to reduce the power of the *chaebol* by requiring them to divest some of their interests. But before the financial and economic crisis of 1997, success was limited. Subsequently, the *chaebol* found it increasingly difficult to compete with other Asian producers, because of their tradition of lifetime employment and militant trade unions, and governance changes were forced on them.

The governance of companies in Southeast Asia has its own distinctive characteristics. The significance of the cultural context—the history, traditions, business methods, and law—is apparent. This is a key feature in understanding corporate governance in China.

China's approach to corporate governance

The Chinese approach to corporate governance is different. China has evolved a unique form of governance for both its SOEs and independent companies, as we will see in the following chapters. In the early stages of the market-orientated reforms, ideas were borrowed from the experience of Western countries, encouraged by the World Bank, the OECD, a club of mainly rich countries, and well-meaning US institutional investors.

But over the past 20 years, China has developed its own form of corporate governance, appropriate to a country in which the law, the judiciary, and the courts serve the state and are not an independent check on the legislature as in most democracies, as will be explored in depth in Chapter 3. Moreover, Chinese corporate governance has become a fluid learning system, not a set of laws, rules, and voluntary codes as is typical in many other countries. We will argue that the West now has something to learn from China.

References

Clarke, T. (2004). *Theories of corporate governance: The philosophical foundations of corporate governance*. New York: Routledge.

Leblanc, R. (Ed.). (2015). *Handbook of corporate governance*. San Francisco: Jossey-Bass.

Mallin, C. (2016). *Corporate governance* (4th ed.). Oxford: Oxford University Press.

Monks, R. A. G., & Minow, N. (2001). *Corporate governance* (4th ed.). Chichester: Wiley.

Redding, S. G. (1993). *The spirit of Chinese capitalism*. Berlin: Wakter de Gruyter.

Stiles, P., & Taylor, B. (2001). *Boards at work: How directors view their roles and responsibilities*. Oxford: Oxford University Press.

Thomsen, S. (2008) *Introduction to corporate governance*. Copenhagen: DJOF Publishing.

Tricker, R. I. (1984). *Corporate governance: Practices, procedures and powers in British companies and their boards of directors*. Aldershot: Gower.

Tricker, R. I. (2015). *Corporate governance: Principles, policies, and practices* (3rd ed.). Oxford: Oxford University Press.

Turnbull, S. (2000) *Corporate governance: Theories, challenges and paradigms*. Sydney: Macquarie University.

Case study

Alibaba China and investor relations

Alibaba Group Holding Ltd. is China's largest e-commerce group and processes more transactions each year than Amazon and e-Bay combined. Alibaba is a global leader in Internet-based businesses, offering advertising and marketing services, electronic payment systems, cloud-based computing, network services, and mobile communications. The group also provides wholesale and retail online markets. Gross revenues (excluding investment income) for the year to March 31, 2016 was RMB 10,143 million, or US$15,686 million.

The Alibaba Group was listed in New York in 2014 raising US$22 billion, the largest initial public offering on record; bankers handled the float claiming they had orders for more than 10 times that amount.

Alibaba has a strategic alliance with Ant Financial Services Group, to provide MYbank, one of China's first privately owned online banks; Sesame Credit, a credit-scoring service; and Koubei, which provides financial services to the China market. The Alibaba Group also has a strategic alliance with Suning to build on synergies in e-commerce, logistics, and online-to-offline (O2O) commerce, which draws potential customers from online channels to physical stores. Alibaba also runs DingTalk, a mobile group messaging tool for SMEs, and owns the Hong Kong English language newspaper *The South China Morning Post*. The hub of the group's European operations is in London. The international headquarters of Alibaba Cloud is in Singapore.

Cainiao is the Alibaba Group's logistics company, formed in 2013. It provides a China-wide parcel delivery system and offers next-day delivery in 50 cities for goods ordered from Alibaba's online marketplaces.

For more detailed information on the businesses of the Alibaba Group, see www.Alibaba.com.

The origins of Alibaba

Alibaba was founded in 1999 by Jack Yun Ma, a teacher of English from Hangzhou, the capital of Zhejiang Province on China's east coast. Ma created a website for the rapidly growing number of entrepreneurial, but relatively small, Chinese manufacturers, retailers, and exporters to sell their goods around the world. At the time Alibaba had 18 employees.

The founders saw that that the Internet could be used by smaller enterprises to compete in the global as well as the Chinese market against larger companies with well-established supply chains, distribution networks, and marketing outlets. Users of the Alibaba Internet services could apply their innovation, technology, and entrepreneurial skills more effectively.

In 2005, Alibaba acquired the China operations of US-based IT company Yahoo for a 43% stake in Alibaba. Prior to the New York listing in 2014, 43% of Alibaba shares were held by Yahoo, 28% by a Japanese IT company, Softbank, and 29% by Jack Ma and colleagues in top management.

At the time, Yahoo was losing market share in its American and other worldwide operations, so Alibaba became a jewel in its crown.

The Alipay saga

A significant component of the Alibaba Group was a business called Alipay, which was launched in 2004, to provide the online payment portal for transactions on Alibaba.com. It became the world's largest online payment system.

But in 2010, the Chinese government ruled that all Internet payment systems should be wholly owned by Chinese interests. Alipay did not qualify, because Alibaba was 71% foreign owned. Alipay risked losing its license to operate, which would destroy its business. Jack Ma then made a unilateral decision to transfer ownership of Alipay to a new entity—Zhejiang Alibaba e-commerce Ltd—which he and Shihuang Xie, his co-founder, controlled. Apparently, neither the Alibaba board nor Yahoo was informed at the time.

In March 2011, Yahoo and Softbank were told officially that Alipay had been spun off from Alibaba. Yahoo shareholders found out in May 2011 from an SEC filing, and the share price fell 10%.

When asked why he had bypassed the board, Ma apparently said that the Alibaba board seldom met formally and taking the matter to the board might have meant a delay, the loss of the license, and the end of Alipay. Alipay did obtain a license to operate as a Chinese-owned company in May 2011.

A formal agreement was ultimately signed between Alibaba, Yahoo, and Softbank for the transfer out of the Alipay business, involving a capital sum, an agreement on sharing profits, and licensing agreements.

The Alibaba Group's mission, vision, and values

Today the company has a clear mission statement:

> To make it easy to do business anywhere

Which it achieves by providing:

> the fundamental technology infrastructure and marketing reach to help merchants, brands and other businesses that provide products, services and digital content to leverage the power of the Internet to engage with their users and customers. Our businesses are comprised of core commerce, cloud computing, digital media and

entertainment, innovation initiatives and others. Through investee affiliates, we also participate in the logistics and local services sectors.

The company reinforces its mission statement with its vision that:

> We aim to build the future infrastructure of commerce. We envision that our customers will meet, work and live at Alibaba, and that we will be a company that lasts at least 102 years [thus covering three centuries since its creation in 1999]. We enable hundreds of millions of commercial and social interactions among our users, between consumers and merchants, and among businesses every day. We empower our customers with the fundamental infrastructure for commerce and data technology, so that they can build businesses and create value that can be shared among our ecosystem participants. We strive to expand our products and services to become central to the everyday lives of our customers.

The group emphasizes the importance of its values and publishes a code of ethics, stating that "the conduct of all employees should reflect Alibaba Group's values and promote a work environment that upholds and improves Alibaba Group's reputation for integrity and trust." For details of the code of ethics, go to: http://alibaba-group.com/en/ir/governance.

Corporate governance of the Alibaba Group

Alibaba is today a leader in its approach to corporate governance, not the least because it has to meet the demands of the US SEC and the listing rule of the New York Stock Exchange (NYSE). (For the latest SEC filing, go to http://www.alibaba-group.com/en/ir/pdf/agm160524_ar.pdf.)

The board has established corporate governance guidelines describing the principles and practices that it follows in carrying out its responsibilities. The corporate governance guidelines cover:

- The role and responsibility of the board
- Board composition, structure and policies
- Board meetings
- Committees of the board
- Expectations of directors
- Management succession planning
- Evaluation of board performance
- Board remuneration
- Approval of related-party transactions
- Equity incentive plans
- Communications with shareholders

To explore these guidelines more fully, go to: http://alibabagroup.com/en/ir/governance_1.

The **Board of Directors** currently has 11 members:

six executive or connected directors:

- Jack Yun MA Executive Chairman
- Joseph C. TSAI Executive Vice Chairman
- Daniel Yong ZHANG Director and Chief Executive Officer
- J. Michael EVANS Director and President
- Masayoshi SON Director
- Eric Xiandong JING Director

and five independent directors:

- Chee Hwa TUNG
- Walter Teh Ming KWAUK
- Jerry YANG
- Börje E. EKHOLM
- Wan Ling MARTELLO

Detailed biographies of each of the directors can be read at: http://alibabagroup.com/en/ir/governance.

The board has three standing committees:

- audit committee
- compensation committee
- nominating and corporate governance committee

Each committee has a published charter, which can be read together with details of the committee membership at: http://alibabagroup.com/en/ir/governance.

The corporate governance guidelines are reviewed periodically by the nominating and corporate governance committee to ensure that they continue to promote the best interests of the company and its shareholders and that they comply with all relevant laws, regulations, and stock exchange requirements and are in line with the company's memorandum and articles of association.

The Alibaba Group held its 2017 annual general meeting in Hong Kong to elect three directors and auditors. To encourage shareholders around the world to participate, the company provided a virtual shareholder meeting over the Internet. The company explained to its shareholders: "you can attend the meeting, view materials, and ask questions without leaving the comfort of your home."

Exercising governance power over the Alibaba Group

Shareholders do not own Alibaba directly. Ownership is covered by legal agreements with a company incorporated in the Cayman Islands. Power over that company is exercised by a somewhat opaque entity called the Alibaba Partnership.

Shareholders in Alibaba Group Holding Ltd. have few powers over the governance of their company. Their interests are sidelined; in the words of the *Economist*: "ordinary shareholders are supine." The Hong Kong Stock Exchange (HKSE), which was approached first to list Alibaba, turned down the opportunity because of its listing rules, which require all shares to carry equal voting rights. Dual-class shares, one class able to maintain control even though they represent a minority of the equity, are not allowed.

New York has no such restriction. Indeed, many prominent US public companies, including some in Silicon Valley, have dual-class shares, with the founders owning shares with enhanced voting rights to maintain their control.

The Alibaba Group justifies the use of the Alibaba Partnership as the vehicle for exercising governance power over the company as follows:

> Our partnership is a dynamic body that rejuvenates itself through admission of new partners each year, which we believe enhances our excellence, innovation and sustainability.
>
> Unlike dual-class ownership structures that employ a high-vote class of shares to concentrate control in a few founders, our approach is designed to embody the vision of a large group of management partners. This structure is our solution for preserving the culture shaped by our founders, while at the same time accounting for the fact that founders will inevitably retire from the company.

The company further explained that, in the early days of Alibaba, the directors realized that their new business, built on innovation, technology, and harnessing of the Internet, had also created a distinct culture. As the company grew larger, more complex, moving into new businesses, the directors wanted to maintain this distinctive culture, because they felt it was fundamental to the group's success.

From the outset, the company explained, directors and management had acted in a spirit of partnership, to serve their customers, develop their employees, and deliver long-term value to their shareholders. To preserve this spirit of partnership and to ensure the sustainability of the group's mission, vision and values, the founders formalized the Alibaba Partnership.

The Alibaba Partnership currently has 32 members: 24 members of senior management, 7 members of management from Ant Financial Services, and 1 member of management from Cainiao Network. The number of partners is not fixed and can change from time to time. All partnership decisions are made on a one-partner-one-vote basis. The partnership is governed by a partnership agreement and operates under principles, policies, and procedures that have evolved with the business.

The group believes that the peer nature of the partnership enables senior managers to collaborate and override bureaucracy and hierarchy.

Questions for discussion

1. The Alibaba Group appears to meet the norms of good corporate governance, with one exception: shareholder rights. Is the Alibaba arrangement using the Alibaba Partnership to exercise governance control acceptable?

2. Do you believe that "one share one vote" should apply to investment in all companies listed on stock markets?

3. The HKSE does not allow companies with dual-class, different voting rights to list. Discussions continue on whether allowing companies with dual-class shares to list would encourage founders of successful start-up companies to make an IPO (initial public offering). Should the HKSE change its rules?

4. Is a shift towards protected insider rights likely to be a trend?

5. If you were on the board of the HKSE, how would you introduce dual-class shares in Hong Kong? (The HKSE introduced a trial of the weighted voting shares in latter 2018. Please refer to their latest webpage for more information. http://en-rules.hkex.com.hk/en/display/display_main.html?rbid=4476&element_id=5103.)

2

The Chinese Political and Economic History in Post-1980s and Corporate Governance

Gregg Li

In this chapter we consider:

- ❖ an aging population, migration to urban areas, a coastal nation
- ❖ domestic drivers of modern corporate governance practices in China
  - ➤ leadership and the direction of the political wind
  - ➤ sense of urgency and fear of the loss of control
  - ➤ a reference for history, culture, religion, philosophy, and ethics
  - ➤ the uncompromising drive against corruption
  - ➤ the strong push for innovation, entrepreneurship, and smart cities
- ❖ Deng's drive for modernization of the enterprises in the 1980s
- ❖ The birth of private firms
- ❖ The Chinese modern enterprise system

To understand China one has to begin with an appreciation of the rich and long history of China. Today, Chinese bureaucrats think in decades, not years, and in systems that can cater to billions of people, not thousands. Chinese leaders, made wiser with an understanding of history, also have realized that nothing is everlasting and anything can be changed with time and patience. A history of turbulence, politically and economically, since 1949 and leading up to the 1980s, has refined a leadership rank that favors political stability and continual economic growth over other priorities. Central to this is a working system of sound corporate governance for their modern Chinese enterprises because those systems can properly answer and balance authority, decision rights, incentives, and ownership; but China is still a communist country, or a socialist country with Chinese characteristics for that matter. Shared ownership is still the spirit, and decisions and accountability should be determined collectively, not individually. Chinese leaders see and understand interdependency and interconnectedness. That is why the discussions and feasible practices of corporate governance are so important, and different, and why the authorities are willing to experiment.

China is a land of contradictions, mystery, paradoxes, and inconsistencies. Politics and political awareness underpin nearly all facets of life, and sometimes, the same "capitalist roaders" that have promoted ownership under capitalism in China may appear more "red" than most socialists and reformers today. Chinese history is a history of a people trying to manage conflicting self-interests, limited and unfair allocation of resources, proud traditions, deep philosophical beliefs, and the continuing exercise of power to work with nature, to overcome themselves, and to overcome adversities. No one is ever alone in China. China is mysterious because this is a land that is not known to have information readily available to anyone. It is a big black box, and by association, the board of directors is a big black box. The walls of bureaucracy are thick and often invisible so as to protect the incumbents. Being explicit with ideas, concepts, roles, or functions assumes these do not change. Asking for certainty and clarity assumes, as most Westerners would tend to do, the world remains the same. The history, culture, language, people, and geography of China have had a definitive impact on how corporate governance and its various forms for the many different types of ownership structures in China have been formed, constituted, and sustained today, and these factors will continue to have an influence.

The focus of this chapter will be mainly about some of these attributes that have given rise to the current ecosystem of corporate governance we see today. As much as possible, these attributes will be explained with a backdrop during the time of China's drive to modernization from the 1980s. Although growth in GDP has been phenomenal, such a pace also has produced a wide range of imbalances. We see that many firms have installed a range of input parameters that would improve their corporate governance. Others have great governance processes. A few may even exhibit outcomes that resonate with sound governance but have paid only lip service to internal control. Also fundamental to the topic of corporate govern-ance in China is the discussion and evolving practices and alignment of incentives, ownership, transparency, responsibility, diversity, ESG (environment, sustainabil-ity, governance), ethics, and accountability, which are the very essence of corporate governance. When the Chinese government got certain of these elements to align, the number of enterprises blossomed because they have worked well in the Chinese ecosystem. In this chapter we will explore these and other related issues, in light of the chaotic and turbulent history of modern-day China that had provided the context.

An aging population, migration to urban areas, a coastal nation

In China today, many would simply describe China this way: "everything is possible but nothing is easy." Developing China into a prosperous nation is not only difficult but also impossible to be consistent. China is still a poor nation by any standard, but we are seeing more pockets of wealth, mostly in the coastal areas. China is a populous nation as well, and with rapid urbanization and an increasingly wealthy middle class.

China is a nation of many ethnicities, the majority belonging to the Han,[1] and most Chinese live on the east and coastal regions of the nation. Many Chinese do see themselves as multiracial but with centrality as Han.[2] China claims it has 56 ethnic groups although Han accounts for over 90% of the population.

Much of the 1.4 billion people are crowded into just 40% of the land that is viable. Over many years, these eastern and coastal zones have provided sufficient protection against barbarians, as the Great Wall had once against the barbarians from the north, even though the true invaders came from the coast and from the south. Xinjiang is mainly Islamic, and Tibet mostly Bon and Tibetan Buddhists, and both places have extremists eager to separate from the motherland. The coastal regions are richer, but generally China is a poor nation, the majority of its population earning less than US$3.10 a day for each household.[3]

China is an aging nation. By 2050, more than 25% of the population is projected to be 65 years and older; in Hong Kong, that percentage rises to 33%. For China, 25% of 1.4 billion translates to over 300 million people. That's a huge burden for the next generation to look after.[4] The social impact of China's old one-child policy[5] means potentially an adult may have to visit a set of parents and two sets of grandparents over a typical weekend. This problem is compounded by the fact that most good jobs are in the cities, and migrating to cities from rural China to seek employment has placed massive stress on the cities' social infrastructure. We have to understand that China was primarily an agrarian country after 1949, nearly 80% of the population in agriculture.

China has been rapidly urbanizing, and by the end of 2015, more than 56% of the population was living in cities.[6] Along with the modernization drive, the *hukou* system of control that required the registration of migrants into urban areas was largely substituted with incentives for registered urban dwellers. But this did not stop migration. We are now looking at millions of young people, mostly from the rural areas, on the move, in search of a brighter future while leaving their parents and grandparents behind.[7] Surplus agricultural workers, displaced by the agricultural responsibility system and the dismantling of the communes after the 1980s, were the army that allowed China to employ cheap laborers for the world's manufacturers that is China. Although the size of migration is falling due to a shift in economic activities, the National Bureau of Statistics put the number of people working outside their hometowns for at least six months at 278 million in 2014. That is the population size of the United States moving into cities for employment each year. By

1. 92% of the Chinese population is Han. There are 55 ethnic groups in China, recognized by the government. See List of ethnic groups in China and Taiwan. Retrieved April 30, 2018 from https://en.wikipedia.org/wiki/List_of_ethnic_groups_in_China.
2. Jacques, 2009.
3. Mauldin, 2016.
4. Bailey, Ruddy, & Shchukina, 2012.
5. Abolished in 2015.
6. Sun, Wenyu, 2017.
7. Xu, 2012.

2015, however, that number began to drop by 5.68 million, and indications showed that rural economies were improving.[8] Planning and establishing employment in the rural communities should continue to relieve this pressure.

Other than moving in and out of cities, people are visiting other provinces and other countries. The Chinese middle class, estimated to be a third of the population, can mean an explosive impact on the retail market when they begin to shop and travel.[9] McKinsey estimated that by 2022, more than 75% of the urban consumers would earn between RMB 60,000 (US$9,000) and RMB 229,000 (US$34,350). These middle-income earners are traveling more and looking for consumer items like laptops and digital cameras. Though the overall population in China is aging, the middle class is actually younger, nearly half the people under 35. Young people everywhere have a different attitude and this is true in China. According to academic research reference by Blau,[10] these young and middle-class individuals have less trust in institutions, the police, and the local government, and these income earners are mostly urbanites.

Chinese tourists have visited Europe and Asia, and reportedly a Chinese passport holder can visit 56 countries without a visa, compared with 155 countries for a US passport holder. Without a doubt, the Chinese people are on the move. Having a huge middle class of 116 million people, China has dropped its restriction on travel. In 2011, Chinese traveling abroad took more than 70 million trips.[11] In the US alone, more than 300,000 Chinese students flooded university campuses in 2011; and by 2019 and beyond, 700,000 are expected to be traveling to the US and elsewhere.[12] Richer Chinese have meant more traveling tourists, and their movement sometimes has saved a few economies, such as that of Hong Kong immediately after the handover in 1997. These tourists have brought a massive amount of foreign currency. Mainland tourists into Hong Kong on average spent from HK$7,105 (US$911) to HK$9,000 (US$1,154) per person in 2016.[13] Nearly 4 million mainlanders visited Hong Kong during December 2016 alone.[14]

The Chinese are on the move, physically. A more affluent middle class means a higher level of disposable income, and traveling for leisure is preferred these days by many Chinese. The Chinese authorities understand this. They have learned to leverage on this windfall to bargain with countries frequented by Chinese mainlanders that have included students, tourists, and of course, potential buyers of foreign companies.

---

8. Wildau, 2015; Holodny, 2016.
9. Barton, Chen, & Jin, 2013.
10. Blau, 2016.
11. Trilling, 2016.
12. China National Bureau of Statistics. Also, Luo (2017, March 21).
13. Sun (2016, October 3). Hong Kong tourist numbers up, but no cash bonanza for retailers as Chinese visitors spend less and leave sooner.
14. HKTB, 2017.

Domestic drivers of modern corporate governance practices

Let's now go back about a hundred years and put this locomotive, China, into proper perspective and study the tracks that have been laid, to see how modern corporate governance as we know it today has evolved and grown. To do this properly, we will use the concept of "drivers." That is, this train of modernization of corporate governance has had many domestic and internal drivers. These drivers worked together mostly, but sometimes one driver took the lead. Depending on which driver held the steering wheel, this train would head and accelerate in a certain direction. Actually, it is the culmination of the influences by these drivers that have determined the speed and direction of the train. Each driver or a combination of drivers took turns, and the train lunges forward or slows down. China is a complex and complicated entity, and we believe this driver concept is a more useful way to help the reader understand the building blocks of development, biases, and tendencies of changes to corporate governance practices as this train meanders down an increasing chaotic and complex international business ecosystem.

We have been able to identify a handful of internal drivers. When asked about corporate governance in China, a teacher won't be wrong by focusing on issues around the three big Cs: capital, corruption, and control. But these are only superficial answers because the China is much more complex than this, and China's corporate governance future has become more uncertain, volatile, ambiguous, and chaotic. With so many uncertainties, Chinese leadership appeared to want to have more control over the pace and change of these drivers. In the following section we will give a glimpse to the readers why these, and many other factors, have contributed, and will continue to be contributing, to the development and evolution of corporate governance in China.

We first describe each driver with its section heading:

- Leadership and the direction of the political wind
- Sense of urgency and fear of the loss of control
- Culture, religion, philosophy, and ethics
- The uncompromising drive against corruption
- The strong push for innovation, entrepreneurship, and smart cities

Leadership and the direction of the political wind

We believe that a key and important factor that affected the pace of reform in corporate governance was the position and influence of the Deng camp of reform versus those of his detractors—including staunch believers of the ideals behind communism and socialism. Understanding the political wind or the struggle for political control is important; and this understanding may have nothing to do with greed, market economy, or private ownership, or any of the unintended consequences that capitalism would bring. Today, Xi Jinping and his camp are in charge, and they are pro-market and willing to experiment with capitalism. Today, the wind of politics is not blowing as hard. But this may not be true for the future leadership.

In China, politics and economics go hand in hand; this also extends to corporate governance or the working life of workers. China was nearly bankrupt by the turn of the last century, according to some economists, and needed new land reform practices, new means to incentivize workers, new ways to guarantee worker's rights and avoid exploitation by the "foreign" capitalists, new means to educate and professionalize workers.[15] To institute any form of change and to seed the development of the economy, Chinese leaders needed political clout and control. Like Siamese twins, China's economy is linked with its political institutions and bureaucrats. **The Chinese economy, in fact, can be interpreted as being led by political power, and the output we are seeing in the form of corporate governance is the exercise of political power by the country's top leaders.** "Power comes from the barrel of the gun," remarked Mao, as he injected the might of politics into everything Chinese.

Chinese leadership often marvels at the smooth transition of power in the US, as when Obama gave way to President-elect Donald Trump, on January 20, 2017. No one died. Power transfer is not an easy task in China. Since the placement of Jiang Zemin into position of power as general secretary of the party in 1993, the transfer of political power has been relatively bloodless, partly because those who were in power had had a firm grasp. When Deng assumed power after the death of Mao and Zhou Enlai at the end of the Cultural Revolution in 1976, his power base was tenuous. Deng, a protégé of Zhou Enlai, took on a refined Zhou's idea of modernization.

But Deng's reemergence was dramatic, opportunist, and timely. By 1992, his power base was stronger but not dominant. As a demonstration of publicity and to justify having Shenzhen as a successful experiment in "capitalism with socialist characteristics," Deng visited Shenzhen in 1992, with much fanfare. That visit marked a turning point in how control over companies could be tuned to the market. He needed to demonstrate to the hidden powers that his foray into capitalism worked. During his visit, he declared that Shenzhen was the model of economic development for the rest of China, that China needed to speed up its economic steam engine to 12% annual growth, and that more changes in political power were to be expected. When he returned to Beijing, he put Zhu Rongji, the former dean of the School of Business at Tsinghua University, in charge as premier and economic czar and reorganized the powerful Standing Committee of the Politburo.[16]

To put things in the proper perspective, we have to remember that his detractors and skeptics had run the gamut from pure Marxists to Maoists to Leninist-Marxists to anybody who wanted to bring back the old dynasty or anyone who would blame Deng for ridding them of their jobs during restructuring and downsizing. In a country so large and with so much history, changing tradition and

---

15. Hinton, 1991.
16. Vohra, 2000, p. 288.

people's mindset required a strong burning platform. Deng was the torchbearer on this burning platform, and rapid change ensued. He was heavily scrutinized from all angles, as unemployment began to soar due mainly to economic restructuring. Major restructuring and structural dislocation had led to huge discontent in the society, and the Tiananmen Square incident of 1989 was a visible outcome of those policies. Between 1995 and 2001, more than 49 million workers were laid off. Any misstep would have been disastrous for him and his economic policies, which were being labeled the Deng Xiaoping Theory. Deng needed to demonstrate quick and sustainable wins, to which double-digit economic growth appeared to be the evidence he needed to silence his critics. On a visit to Shenzhen today, one can still see huge posters with Deng showcasing Shenzhen as the next big thing for China. Politically, the presence of these posters signifies in one small aspect that his ideas and his protégés are still in charge. Reformers beware!

The free market pushed for rapid economic growth, but it also created a series of dilemmas and dislocations. As the markets became less regulated, it also created massive pockets of unemployment and huge influx and movement of workers. The "iron rice bowl" was no longer a sure thing for the high percentage of unskilled workers, whereas in the past employment was a sure thing and one would always have rice in one's rice bowl. You could drop your bowl and it would not break; hence, having an iron bowl meant one would always be employed. In the past, the state had always provided. Under the Four Modernizations, since not everyone was an entrepreneur or be in any position to be one, those who couldn't perform at a market rate were displaced. Not all sectors grew at the same rate. Some continued to produce despite the unattractiveness of their goods and services. Protectionism rose. Rapid growth created excessive demand, and sometimes to get around bureaucracy, bribes had to be paid. As a result of market failures and the inability of any plan to catch up, inflation rose. Life got tougher during this transition period. To placate discontents, Deng took a step backwards and continued to advocate "socialism," claiming that such free market moves were only temporary. Deng told his following that the government would continue to control the large and medium SOEs and rural enterprises; thus capitalism wouldn't get out of hand. At the time, the large and medium SOEs were in fact quite inefficient and had contributed to the malaise of the economy.[17]

From 1993 to 2003, China was transitioning into modern corporate governance. By 1999, more than 1,200 companies had been listed and most began as SOEs. Eighty percent of the smaller and medium-sized firms were turned into non-state enterprises. By 2001, the number of industrial SOEs had dropped from a high of 85,000 in 1994, to just 47,000.[18] Deng needed to stabilize his base and placate his critics, so he delayed the reform of these enterprises to a later period, possibly to a

---

17. "In 1990, nearly two-thirds of the 200,000 SOEs reportedly were losing money. Nearly one-third of the government's revenue went into subsidizing the SOEs." See Vohra, 2000, p. 291.
18. Fewsmith, 2008; Jefferson & Su, 2006.

time when he would have more control over the economic development and when the proper legislation had been installed. Starting from the year 2000, a host of new legislations had been introduced that would complement the integrity of the corporate governance system. They ranged from the new Accounting Law (2000), the Code of Corporate Governance for Listed Companies (2002), to the Rules on Shareholders' Meetings of Listed Companies (2014). Underpinning this blossoming of new legislation and regulations was the implicit collective approval by the political power. One could even argue that the weakness of the corporate governance system at that time was due mainly to the lack of proper legislation and enforcement.

In early 2017, the political wind was quiet, but one can easily hear the silence. Open debate was being curtailed once again. The Unirule Institute of Economics, which has been forthcoming with open seminars and discussions ranging from pegged to free-flowing exchange rates in Beijing, has been unusually quiet these days. Unirule was founded in 1993 and has been one of China's most prominent think tanks. Some believe this is a sign that the liberals in the party have begun to self-censor. Hardliners reportedly have taken over a monthly magazine called *Yanhuang*, which has been pro-reform. Its founding publisher, Du Daozheng, has been purged. In contrast, websites run by diehard Maoists were still up and running.[19] Reform was quietly under threat. *In other words, the pace of economic development, particularly the modernization of corporate governance, will be subject to the pace of political governance reform in China.*

The pace of reform has always been moderated by political wind. By the early 1990s, as the economy began to show positive signs, the calling for SOE reform, once quiet, became louder. Pilot programs to streamline the SOEs began to show good results by 1995, and the need to introduce the "Modern Enterprise System" was in play. But Deng had to wait until the market economy was sufficiently robust to absorb the many workers who had been laid off by the SOEs. Corporate governance changes moved into a higher gear from 1993, after Jiang was in charge. The tax system was simplified and successfully restructured. China replaced the Enterprise Accounting Standards (EAS) with the International Accounting Standards (IAS), introduced company law; independent directors; and property rights. Beginning in 1994, purchasing private housing began to take shape. Private property finally became a reality. By 2001, China joined the WTO, reduced import tariffs, and stopped devaluing its currency.[20]

Sense of urgency and the fear for the loss of control

China slowly began to settle into a state of political stability after Deng took power, and that was critical and necessary for both long-term reform in politics, economics,

---

19. An illiberal dose, 2017, pp. 27–28.
20. So & Chu, 2016.

and corporate governance towards modernization. Stability was needed. By the end of the nineteenth century, China came out of decades of national and civil wars, and three decades of socialist construction which wreaked havoc. By the turn of this century, it was sufficiently impatient and wanted to introduce and explore deeper and wider form of shareholders and ownership reform that could work. China needed and wanted to catch up with the rest of the modern world in how institutions could be governed.

There was a sense of urgency, and this sense is still pervasive. When we teach Chinese students in China or speak with government and business leaders, we can sense this urgency. There is this pressure to "catch up" and to do so quickly in their tone and action, partly because they can sense this stable window of opportunity may close very soon, and partly because other businesses and nations are rapidly transforming themselves. This climate of experimentation and rapid prototyping permeates the air today, along with the thick smog in Beijing and Shanghai. Every breath of foul air the city citizens breathe is a reminder.

Entering the twentieth century, China was predominantly a peasant economy, over 80% of its population in agriculture, lacking any experience in business management and governance. It was poor and barely had enough to eat. In 1952, the population was just 588 million and per capita income was only RMB 116 (US$17.4).[21] With massive unemployment into the tens of millions, transiting into the "Factory of the World" was a strategy that the country had to own. It took advantage of its cheap labor and attracted foreign capital, built large factories and manufacturing bases of consumer goods and textile mills where unskilled workers would be readily employed. But the tradeoffs by many, knowingly and unknowingly, had had a detrimental impact on the environment, a hugely unbalanced economy, and visible income gaps between the rich and the poor.[22] Labor substitution, export-led economic development strategy, and the attraction of foreign investments through concessions were the prime economic development strategies leading up to the period of modernization for China. Consumption for its own people was not a part of the strategy at the beginning of the twenty-first century.

The long view

Long-term control has been the mindset and large-scale economic planning has been the modus operandi under the Communist rule, which China had borrowed from the Soviets. Such levels of control measures, however, have slowly given way to a more decentralized and market-based economy, with the introduction of Deng's policies and these policies needed time to be put in place. To have such an extended

---

21. So & Chu, 2016, p. 32.
22. China's income inequality is now one of the world's worst, the richest 1% of households owning a third of the country's wealth, according to a study by Peking University. Only South Africa and Brazil are higher, and the US is about the same. Wildau (2016, January 14).

period of experimentation has meant the need for a strong, consistent, and pro-longed period of control against unintended disruption. Perhaps this has given this sense of urgency that the longer one side is in power, the more likely is the chance the opposition will surface to challenge the status quo. In other words, maintaining a strong growth, and not just simply growth, appears to be necessary to legitimatize governance.

From 1953 to 1957, China implemented the first five-year plan, which amended all the major economic sectors and focused the economy on large-scale production in heavy industry. The agriculture sector was left to continue with its inefficient small-scale operations. The aim of the first five-year plan was to move the country forward economically but in a planned way. At that time, the government created a large number of SOEs and industrial enterprises in key economic sectors. By the 1980s, China had more than 1,000 large SOEs and 580,000 SMEs.[23] Building a nation was the calling, and the Chinese modeled their efforts to building a great nation after the Soviet centrally planned economy.

At the beginning of 1958, Chairman Mao initiated the Great Leap Forward and the call was to make the country self-sufficient. This massive effort and control did not work, however. The ideas of having enough to eat, enough to build, and not a puppet of any nation's agenda were the driving force. Being "red" was more impor-tant than being "right" (even technically), as politics should underpin all major decisions, as advocated by Mao. Millions of farmers, peasants, and city workers were commanded to leave their posts and were asked to raise production. At times they were asked to produce steel, albeit most was low quality and highly inefficient, and the backyard furnace industry was born (readers may want to refer to the case of the Baowu Steel Plant). However, the lack of expertise, not only in steel making but nearly in everything else—and inefficient agricultural production coupled with natural disasters such as floods and droughts during the latter period—caused serious famines. Millions perished. Massive economic dislocation also caused fun-damental economic problems during that period and demonstrated to many that the Great Leap Forward was a backward leap instead.

Under the pressures of unemployment, worsening economic fundamentals, and political cleansing, the Cultural Revolution began in 1962 and lasted until 1976. A part of it was to purge those who disagreed with the direction of reform, and Mao needed more power to push his economic promises. It wasn't his ideas that were failing, he thought. The plans were failing because there were simply too many "revisionists."[24] Many so-called "intellectuals" were sent to labor camps to be reedu-cated. Riots overflowed into Hong Kong, where some elements were aiming to turn Hong Kong into a communist satellite in 1967. Deng was purged and stripped of power. Being politically correct was more important than ever than being efficient. Communes were reorganized in China. SOEs began to grow into bigger and huge

23. So & Chu, 2016, p. 37; Nolan & Ash, 1995, p. 993.
24. Dikötter, F. 2016.

bureaucracies, the majority incurring the need for continued and massive amounts of state subsidy. China closed its door to the world during this time and because of this, allowed Hong Kong to become the gateway of goods and services into and out of China. Hong Kong became the "Goose that would lay the golden egg" for China.

Many today still bear the scar and pain of those reforms. This long period of bitterness, which some people would say was done with the best intentions, has not disappeared but has become a part of the psyche of many Chinese. Deep scars remain today. In one respect, some families and clans became closer, as one can always rely on family and close friends. This famous Chinese term *guanxi* became vernacular vocabulary of this evolving civilization.

From this short detour on history, we have to move further backwards in time to sense the contribution of philosophy and culture that has formed the psyche of many Chinese. Many scholars over the years have touched on this topic, that of being Chinese. What does this mean? Many living in Hong Kong today would categorically state that they are as different from the mainlanders as they are from the Japanese. China is one of the few nations that define its citizenship as Chinese in passports.

The sense for control has been tested by the onslaught and ubiquitousness of the Internet. In a case of global ethical standards against national law, Google was put in a position that it had to give up the China market because it felt it could not reasonably balance the two, standing by its ethics or giving in to control.[25] Google entered China in 2006, when it launched a Chinese website. At that time, it agreed to be in compliance with the local law to eliminate links that the authorities found objectionable. But doing so meant Google had to play down its ethical belief that no nation may censor its contents. The Chinese authorities were reluctant to allow Google to enter China, as the disruption could potentially bring new elements into play that might interrupt the pace or depth of reform. Giving in to Google's demand for no censorship would mean losing control and possibly bringing in unintended consequences. Both sides finally parted company in early January 2010. Since then, Gmail accounts are no longer accessible. Starting in 2017, Facebook's WhatsApp was no longer accessible in China.

A reference for history, culture, religion, philosophy, and ethics

Culture is a powerful driver in corporate governance, and culture is not something that can be easily described. China is a land of deep and continuous history and evolving culture. Perhaps this vast expanse of time has given the people a sense of patience and respect for tradition and legacy. In China, the Communist Party plans in decades, a timetable that business today can hardly contemplate. Modern companies in contrast, hardly use any long-term five-year plan and are moving

---

25. Heineman, 2010.

towards the other direction, to do less planning but more analysis. How Chinese interpret time is a separate subject and far beyond the purpose of this book. For this section, we are suggesting that history, culture, ethics, religion, and mindset have all served to slow down or speed up the pace of modernization of corporate governance in China. A brief introduction to these factors is necessary before the reader can understand why foreign corporate governance practices have often been copied, applied, changed, and "sinophiled." Buddhism, originally from India, took on a religion with Chinese characteristics, and Zen Buddhism was born. Even Kublai Khan, the great Mongol conqueror from the north, became more civilized and instituted Chinese governing practices in order to govern the Chinese. And even today, the American business model of eBay worked better with a slight twist, through Alibaba's e-commerce model, because Chinese consumers behave differently and want different things. (By 2012, Alibaba had eclipsed Amazon and eBay combined in merchandise volume.)[26]

Although communist ideals have no room for religion in Chinese society, China has been deeply ingrained by the religions and philosophies principally of Buddhism, Confucianism, and Daoism, and it is impossible to remove them completely. Mao tried, but that didn't work with his Cultural Revolution. Those systems of thought laid the groundwork for the acceptance of "foreign" practices and will affect how outside practices of control and transparency under modern corporate governance can be adapted and assimilated. These combined systems of thought have always been about harmony, integration, and reality. China has been a huge melting pot of things that work. It assimilates. Sustainability is made stronger through practice. The Chinese authorities have studied corporate governance practices around the world, adopting only those that would work. But in so doing, they also had to recognize the operating principles that have been ingrained through years of practice. Patriarch governance or respect to the head of family, collective decision-making, collective accountability, and privacy are just a few of those principles.

The Chinese culture is not one that is based on monotheism and talk of metaphysics, the next life, and afterlife. Pragmatism, a term later hijacked by Deng, is probably most apt to describe the Chinese culture. The Chinese people are very

---

26. Today, "sinophiled" means the following trend in China, according to Elaine Ann (2018), an innovation evangelist in China and a director of Invotech:
    - Segway is now a Chinese company thanks to Ninebot and Xiaomi;
    - Later entrants like Tencent, Alibaba, and Baidu replaced first movers like Facebook, Amazon, and Google;
    - Douban, Weibo, WeChat replaced LinkedIn, Twitter, and Yahoo;
    - Alipay replaced PayPal;
    - InTime replaced JC Penny;
    - Kanbox replaced Dropbox;
    - Lyft and Kauide replaced Uber;
    - Taobao replaced eBay;
    - Tmall replaced Amazon;
    - Xiami replaced Spotify;
    - Youku and Toudu replaced Hulu.

practical. If it doesn't work, they discard it. This is a culture, with morals and ethics that have focused on humanism, on nature, on human welfare, on compromises, and on the present. Gods and afterlife, however little impact these have had, were first introduced by Buddhism. The teaching of Karma from Buddhism is ingrained in the Chinese psyche: everyone is ultimately held responsible for his or her own action and one cannot justify that with a divine will. The Confucian philosophy of life is confined to this life, and it teaches everyone to participate in life and contribute to his society—with order, hierarchy, harmony, compassion, and respect of the family. The Daoist thought and practices of sustainability, respect for nature, duality, change, and resilience have permeated Chinese society as well. Finally, the Buddhist ideal of impermanence, Karma, moral precepts, interdependency, compassion, and the cultivation of one's mind have remained the mainstream thinking of many Chinese today. As they have done for thousands of years, these religions and philosophies, and the moral principles that they have endorsed, will continue to exert their influence on how foreign practices could be adopted in China.

Fundamental to the topic of corporate governance in the business world is how trust is shared and respected by the many societies that exist throughout China.[27] In areas where societal trust is lacking, institutional arrangements, contracts, and even familial relationship have been used to work around such gaps, and these have taken on unique characteristics in China. In today's China, due to new Fintech innovations, one can easily open a bank account within the same day, through a machine, while it would take nearly a year to do the same in Hong Kong where KYC[28] and diligence requirements are much more stringent. Travelers into Shenzhen will instantly notice the absence of cash, and literally everything can be paid through WeChat or Alipay, using one's smartphone. In comparison, in today's Hong Kong, only the Octopus card, an old technology by today's standard, has this level of coverage. The sophistication and relevance of corporate governance inevitably is dependent on a platform made real by history, culture, ethics, mutual trust, and the people of a society.

According to our interviews with many expatriates who are working in China, the standard of ethics varies considerably in China as viewed through their lenses, partly due to the excesses of the Cultural Revolution and partly to the need of expediency, lack of independent audit, and years of living in a shared economy without any sort of moral code since religion is taboo. As one Communist Party official whom we had interviewed would put it, "the ethical standard in China has been tested continually by the negative trade-offs of capitalism." In some parts of China, notably Wenzhou, an aura of "greed" fills the air.[29] China is not a transparent

---

27. Undoubtedly, trust between peers as in the case of peer-to-peer banking, with government authorities, with other members of the society, is undergoing rapid change as well in modern China.
28. KYC stands for "knowing your customer." Banks must establish verifiable and traceable procedures on new customers and the source of their funds, as a part of their corporate governance and risk management requirements. See Basel III for more details.
29. Tsia, 2004.

society, and rules and procedures in this empire are often inexplicit, difficult to locate, and hidden. The stronger is the presence of excessive and hidden profit, with bureaucrats as gatekeepers, the higher is the tendency to work around company safeguards for the sake of quick profit. Chinese officials are not well paid, by any standard. This has further fuelled the urge for many bureaucrats to look for other ways. Although many top executives at SOEs reportedly have "unlimited" entertainment budget before Xi Jinping's crackdown on corruption that started in 2015, their total compensations were relatively sparse by international standards. Later, we will further discuss how the varying levels and practices of ethics throughout China have been testing the strengths and robustness of corporate decision-making systems in China.[30]

The uncompromising drive against corruption

When one talks of ethics and corporate governance in China, one is instantly reminded of corruption, and these days, the war on corruption. This business practice has permeated many businesses and institutions, partly because these facilitation payments have been frequently and easily applied, like natural oil being sprayed to loosen bureaucratic gears. This drive, like many things in China, should not be viewed as equally intense across all industries. Any generalization for China is bound to be wrong. For some companies, the drive against corruption may even reach into their suppliers. Huawei for example, has been known to demand their suppliers inform on the ethical improprieties of Huawei's employees.

The drive against corruption is not new and has been around since there was government. But the recent pace and intensity, as started by Xi Jinping in 2012, is. Xi vowed to crack down on "tigers and flies" and by 2016 had netted over 120 high-ranking officials including powerful Politburo Standing Committee member Zhou Yongkang, military leaders such as Xu Caihou, Guo Boxiong, and even Bo Xilai, who has been known to be staunchly and visibly "Red."[31] The pace and intensity of this drive carries a special significance because the very foundation of the mandate to rule by the Communist Party has been put to question. History has a tendency to repeat itself, and with a respect for history, Chinese are quick to reference stories and historical anecdotes. The fall of the Nationalists in the 1940s, due mainly to corruption and the invasion of the Japanese empire, has been one reminder for the Communist Party. The last dynasty had to go, because it was too corrupt, as Dr. Sun Yat-Sen, the founding father of modern China, so aptly described in 1911.

---

30. Chen, 2016.
31. For an ongoing update on the results of this anti-graft campaign, go to South China Morning Post Topics (2018): Xi Jinping's Anti-Graft Campaign. Retrieved April 30, 2018, from http://www.scmp.com/topics/xi-jinpings-anti-graft-campaign.

The Nationalists fell from grace due to a number of detrimental factors, of which the pervasiveness of corruption was key.[32] That level of self-interest and corruption has left an indelible mark on the mindset of the present-day governors, which also serves to remind those in power of the fragility of the present Communist regime, should corruption continue to go unchecked. Before Xi consolidated his power, we had included corruption as a key issue in any discussion of corporate governance, as it was pervasive and endemic. It was a part of doing business in China, and knowing how to avoid or manage it has been an art of corporate governance.

There have been numerous other cases of unethical business behaviors in China. China has had its share of Enrons. Unethical companies do not exist in the US alone. The notable ones probably include some of these forms of fraudulent activities:

- **Yinguangxia** (银广夏): In 2001, a local business publication, *Caijing Magazine*, unveiled the Yinguangxia Chinese RMB 745 million fraud, the biggest economic scandal in mainland China's history since 1949. The case of Yinguangxia has drawn a good deal of public attention, and a considerable number of reviews have been published.
- **Minsheng Bank** (民生银行): On April 21, 2005, this bank admitted that one of its employees committed an RMB 300 million loan fraud. The bank is China's so-called private bank and reportedly one of the better run.[33] Banking has been a major challenge for the PRC, and in the early stages it was difficult to evaluate the quality of bank listing since many did not even have credit control or risk management systems in place. Imposing tight deadlines on the establishment of BASAL II control appears to have helped.
- **Chundu** (春都): This meat processor and producer of pork sausages once accounted for 70% of the market in China with assets reportedly over RMB 2.9 billion. In 1997, it was one of the 120 national SOEs. Overexpansion, intense competition, loss of market leadership, increasingly higher risk exposure, excessive diversification, and lack of working capital were attributed to its downfall in 1998.[34] This is one of the few cases where fraud was not the key contributor.
- **Monkey King** (猴王): Following its listing in 1999, accounts revealed increasing debts of unknown origin, and by 2001 its major connected shareholder, Monkey King Holdings, went into bankruptcy, leaving behind a shell company.[35]

---

32. Some Chinese business leaders today, through our interviews, cynically believed that, particularly in today's China, corruption has been so ingrained as a means of getting things done that it has become a business norm and would take an act of God to eliminate.
33. Sun, 2005.
34. Wang, 2005.
35. Ibid., pp. 135–137.

- **Zhengbaiwen** (郑百文): Listed in 1996, it quickly became the best-performing stock in the Shanghai and Shenzhen stock markets. But it became the worst performing by 1999, as increasing evidence pointed to fraudulent accounting, many parties contributing to the problem: the bank providing collateral-free loans, the local government acting as sponsor, employees falsifying revenue, and an absentee board of directors.[36] Here we have fraud brought on by ineffective governance.

- **Guangdong Kelon Electrical Holdings Co.** (广东科龙): Kelon, China's biggest refrigerator maker, had inflated sales and embezzled at least RMB 592 million (US$73 million). Its new auditor, KPMG, found sales were inflated by transactions with affiliates controlled by former Chairman Gu Chujun. The authorities fined Kelon RMB 600,000 (US$75,000) for fraudulent accounting between 2002 and 2004. The company's top management was also given fines of between RMB 50,000 (US$6,250) and RMB 300,000 (US$37,500). Hisense Group, China's sixth-biggest electronics company, bought control of Kelon in September, after Gu was arrested and fined.[37]

- **China Aviation Oil (listed in Singapore)** (中国航空石油): According to The New York Times, this once high-flying company is a complete failure of corporate governance. A key subsidiary of China Aviation Oil Holdings Co. (CAOHC), an SOE in China, violated Singaporean laws and ignored the relevant regulations issued by the Chinese authorities. In this case it was a lack of understanding of derivative trading and a slow reaction to initial losses that attributed to the downfall. The company reportedly lost US$550 million in derivatives trading.[38] (This followed a similar loss by another trader in 1997, when Zhuzhou Smelter Group, a state-owned smelter, incurred US$175 million in losses due to speculative futures trading. After that incident, China temporarily suspended offshore futures trading.)

The Chinese authorities have been working very hard to stamp out fraud at all levels. The recent attack on corruption in China is a strong indication that they are clamping down on the problem and indirectly telling the world that they are on top of the situation. China has been quite harsh when it comes to punishment. In July 2000, a senior official of the government, the National People's Congress Vice Chairman Cheng Kejie, was sentenced to death for his role in probably one of the biggest corruption cases in China's history. Thus far, the government is winning the war against corruption; however, this is a long, drawn-out war.

The high number of Chinese knockoffs, or fake goods with similar-sounding brands, produced by millions of Chinese factories, also is reflective of the state of low business ethics in China. Just recently Alibaba and Tencent have been cited,

---

36. Ibid., pp. 138–140.
37. Yan (2006, January 24).
38. Arnold (2004, December 9).

again, as having an "unacceptably high" number of fake goods on their sites.[39] In that report, one large motor vehicle manufacturer reported that at least 95% of the merchandise with its name and trademark found on Alibaba's platform was suspected to be counterfeit.

Fakes are made and sold everywhere in China. The problem may be due to the disparity in income and opportunity, coupled with a young regulatory and compliance infrastructure. But, it is most likely due to a lack of understanding of what is ethical. "Corruption is sadly becoming a norm," said one trader. Many entrepreneurs we have spoken with cited a general tendency for many of their employees to "copy" then rebuild a product using their own network. "In the early days, it was not uncommon to find senior executives opening a copycat factory just miles down the road from your factory," retorted a retired factory manager from Hong Kong. "Ten years ago, I could even negotiate with the tax authorities on how much taxes I would need to pay, but not today."[40]

The concern is not only with the pervasiveness of fraudulent and unethical practices but with the intensity and depth. The cases of melamine-tainted milk scandal in 2008, in which more than 300,000 babies in China were sick from contaminated milk,[41] destroyed the reputation of China's food export. More importantly, such incidents again called into question a fundamental belief that the protection of humanity was ignored by unscrupulous money-hungry capitalists and simultaneously attacked the party's system of governance, which should have protected its citizens.

Perhaps introducing more Buddhist and Confucian ethical practices would be in line with the aim of the Communist Party to reduce corrupt practices throughout China. Control through belief systems can be a much more powerful means for governance than can rules and regulations alone.

The strong push for innovation, entrepreneurship, and smart cities

Another important driver for the state and sophistication of corporate governance is the impact of innovation. Like Japan, that in the beginning produced cheap goods but now has a reputation of quality, China started in knockoffs and now is building a reputation for innovation. China has put a top priority on introducing innovation and fostering entrepreneurship, and this will have a major impact on the sophistication and variety of corporate governance practices to come, including the introduction and acceptance of venture capital. By comparison, China has fallen far behind in technology and innovation. According to a study in comparative innovation by Booz Allen (2013), China added just 15 companies to the list of 1,000 global top spenders in R&D after the turn of the century. Since 2008, the number

---

39. Pham, 2016.
40. The government simplified the tax structure in Jiang's time, circa 1993.
41. Huang, 2014.

of Chinese companies in the Global Innovation 1,000 has risen from 10 to 75, and the total amount spent on R&D by Chinese companies on the list rose from $1.7 billion in 2008 to $20.5 billion in 2013. A good attempt but pales in comparison to what other countries are doing. By 2016, still, none of the top 20 slots belonged to a Chinese company.[42] China overall had invested just 1% of its revenue, while for North American companies that figure stood at 5%. Not Alibaba, Tencent, Baidu, nor Huawei belonged in the ranks of Apple, Alphabet, or Samsung as the top most innovative companies in 2016, according to the PwC (2016) study.

But this is changing as well. By 2012, China had planted the seed for 22 Silicon Valley-like innovation hubs. Its R&D was US$198.9 billion, compared with that of the US at US$436 billion, or roughly 46% of the US. By 2015, China was at US$396 billion, compared with the US at US$514 billion, or roughly 77%. The more notable number is the size of R&D, which is looking to match the investment by the US government by 2020.[43] Haour[44] predicted that by 2020, China's investment in R&D will reach 3% of its GDP, the same level as that of the US.

Stronger need for capital is a good incentive to push the frontier of corporate governance. In late 2013, as a means to raise more capital, Alibaba petitioned the HKSE to allow the firm to issue dual-class shares[45] for its IPO so that its minority directors could control the board.[46] In late 2013, this request pushed the authorities in Hong Kong to debate the pros and cons for over a year, and market participants finally voted to put a moratorium on this debate and under pressure by the SFC (Securities and Futures Commission (Hong Kong)), the exchange gave up on the idea by October 2015.[47] This effectively put a damper on efforts in Hong Kong to attract high-profile technology companies in China to list in Hong Kong. If Hong Kong really argued the multiple voting right issues in depth, and acted on the

---

42. PwC, 2016.
43. World Bank, 2016.
44. Haour, 2012.
45. Dual-class has been used in many countries and historically families have used it to keep control for themselves and sold restricted-voting shares to the public. As a company grows, controlling shareholders may opt to move to more equitable voting structures in a bid to build a larger investor base. Some dual-class shares have performed well—Warren Buffet's Berkshire Hathaway, Facebook, Groupon, Manchester United, Zynga, Baidu, and Google—others, not quite. Those arguing for dual- (or multi-) class shares would cite the very successful US listed companies that have unequal voting rights. But not everyone in the US is comfortable with varied voting rights. Some institutional investors have been lobbying for the US exchanges to ban the practice, like Hong Kong. Their argument is that dual-class shares are used by dominant owners to avoid the discipline of the market by removing the threat of hostile bids—and of course preventing the institutional investors making a fortune from M&A activity. There have been cases like Conrad Black or Murdoch where abuses by the dominant and entrenched shareholders have been detrimental. Nonetheless, there are many single-share companies that have been disastrous. Again, it is the debate that is important. Corporate governance needs to evolve. Corporate governance, after all, is an art, and those who can master it define the quality of the art.
46. The US markets has given exception to the one-share-one-vote since the 1940s, and dual share became more prominent in the 1980s. By 2000, more than 300 listed firms in the US had chosen dual shares.
47. Hughes & Noble, 2015.

conclusions, it could lead the world in developing corporate governance thinking and practice. Sadly, this did not happen, and a golden opportunity was lost.[48]

As a final note, Alibaba ultimately listed outside Hong Kong. Its headquarters in Hangzhou, it was listed on the NYSE on September 19, 2014. At that time, it was the largest IPO in the world in funds raised.

China hopes to ignite and to encourage more of its citizens to wealth. It has one of the highest Gini coefficients[49] in the world, and to manage the dichotomy between the rich and the poor, the perception that anyone can ultimately become well off has to sit center stage. With smart city, this may work. But smart city and the technologies that accompany it will test the framework of corporate governance and may even introduce new pillars, such as the ownership of a buyer's behavioral data.

Smart city has been viewed as a key strategy to promote industrialization, informatization, citizen participation, and urbanization. This concept was developed globally around 2008. Underpinning smart city includes Radio Frequency ID (RFID) sensors, wireless connectivity, electronic payments and cloud-based computing. Smart city inevitably would include new smarter firms that can move much faster, using leaner and cleaner decision-making corporate governance architecture. For example, firms that operate in this space hardly have traditional means to discuss strategy. Yahoo does not operate on a three-year strategic plan, as the industry and the competition are evolving by weeks, not years. Now directors and executive directors in particular need to act and respond to such high-speed decision-making. As innovation becomes an essential value contribution, the role and responsibility of directors will have to include an understanding and mastery of this mindset.

Apple has done it. And Google and Facebook are doing it. Apple and Google are contributing to building new and smarter cities around the world. In China, Chinese giants like Tencent, Baidu, Alibaba, and Huawei are being called upon to play their part. Inevitably, they will have to find their own way to get the most value from their board of directors. The action may include a complete revamp of their board, the governance structure, and the many linkages that had allowed the old system of governance to work.

---

48. All was not lost apparently. The HKSE quietly rekindled talks of dual-class shares in early 2017. Yiu (2017, January 19).

49. Gini coefficient is a statistical measure and often used as a gauge to imply a certain level of discontent in a society based on income inequality. It is a number between 0 and 1 and corresponds with perfect equality (at 0) when everyone has the same income, to perfect inequality (near 1).

Case: Chinese Googles

Because of the size of the Chinese market, great business models that have worked elsewhere can be introduced into China but only after these have been sinophiled. These models cannot be replicated exactly, as the ecosystem in China is vastly different.

The Chinese version of eBay and Amazon is Alibaba. For Google, it is Baidu. For Cisco, it would be Huawei. For Apple, probably Xiaomi.

Today, **Alibaba**[*] has become the world's largest e-commerce platform. Over 420 million people have purchased some form of products through its platform. It was founded by Jack Ma, a schoolteacher of English who loves the Internet. Today, it has three main sites: Taobao, Tmall, and Alibaba.com. Transactions in 2016 reached a total of US$248 billion, according to The Wall Street Journal, more than eBay and Amazon combined.

Baidu Tieba,[†] is China's largest communication platform with a search engine called Baidu. The company was set up in 2003 by Robin Li. Baidu is China's Google. More than 731 million users were reported as of December 2016, so China has the world's largest Internet user base. Baidu was funded by Silicon Valley money, raising US$1.2 million, and went public on Nasdaq in 2005. Baidu's model allowed advertisers to bid for ad space.

Huawei,[‡] would be the Cisco equivalent in China. It is a telecommunication equipment, network servicing, and switching company in China, now operating around the world, unlike Baidu, which is mostly domestic. The company was founded in 1987 by Ren Zhengfei, a former engineer in the PLA. It also makes mobile phones and hence competes directly with Apple. It reported a revenue of RMB 395 billion (US$6 billion) in 2015.

Xiaomi[§] is a private mobile phone company, started in 2010 by Lei Jun. It has cheaper phones than Apple's and has reached into India, Indonesia, the Philippines, and South Africa. In 2014, it was the largest provider of mobile phones in China. In 2016, it became the world's fourth largest mobile phone maker.

[*] Retrieved from http://projects.wsj.com/alibaba/.
[†] Retrieved from http://ir.baidu.com/phoenix.zhtml?c=188488&p=irol-homeprofile. See also https://www.searchenginejournal.com/18-things-know-baidu/119219/.
[‡] Retrieved from https://en.wikipedia.org/wiki/Huawei. See also http://www.huawei.com/hk/.
[§] Retrieved from https://en.wikipedia.org/wiki/Xiaomi. See also http://www.mi.com/en/.

The rapid development of smart cities in China would require the cooperation between IT companies, citizens, and the government. When Hong Kong was starting to investigate the idea of a smart city in 2013, China declared it would start planning with 200 smart cities in China. By 2017, as Hong Kong was still designing its blueprint for a smart city, Beijing declared more than 300 cities were already being put in place. According to the China-Britain Business Council, by April 2015, there were well over 285 pilot smart cities in China.[50] The National Development and Reform Commission (NDRC) even formed a Smart City Development Alliance as early as 2014. This is important because much of the technology will be introduced by the private sector, because smart city involves the development of an emerging collection of technologies. For example, what is expected to happen in Yinchuan, the capital of Ningxia Province? In the near future, a person's face is sufficient to authenticate his or her identity in this pilot smart city for China.[51] For this to work, the payment gateways would allow the participation of merchants and shoppers to log onto their systems. The speed required to make decisions will need to be raised to an unprecedented level. The old archaic system of decision-making cannot and will not survive the onslaught of the digital age.

The above are a few internal drivers that have continued and will continue to have a dominant influence on the pace and depth of corporate governance reform in China. In later parts of this book we will look at other drivers, including external opportunities that would attract new changes and adoption of new corporate governance practices in China.

We next move to a discussion about the general economy, particularly focusing on the Four Modernizations that gave birth to the development of China's modern corporate governance infrastructure, policies, and practices. China began to move from a state-controlled economy to a market-led economy in the late 1980s. Until 1978, most enterprises were stated-owned; governance was "administrative." The modernization of corporate governance in China effectively began during the onset of the Four Modernizations in the 1980s. We begin our focus of this book starting from this period.

Deng's drive for modernization of the enterprises in the 1980s

Following the death of Mao and Zhou Enlai in 1976, and the removal of the Gang of Four that signaled the end of the Cultural Revolution, China was prime for a change under a new leadership. That came in the form of Deng Xiaoping, a protégé of Zhou Enlai. Deng, as the elder cadre, had more influence than he had official titles, and took on China's political and economic crisis. In 1978, he introduced the

---

50. CBBC, 2016.
51. Carrington, 2016.

Four Modernizations: modernization of the fields of agriculture, industry, national defense, and science and technology. Deng, a pragmatist, felt the way to growth and prosperity was less a class struggle and more towards some form of market competition and introduced targeted industrialization. The biggest reform began when Deng Xiaoping was able to convince the political infrastructure to accept the market economy, albeit with a "socialist" flavor. He opened the doors and invited Europeans and Americans to invest in China. He looked into how best to harmonize China's own systems with those of the West. A better form of corporate governance inevitably would have to be considered, and his modernization efforts paved the way for the modern corporate governance in China that we see today.

China opened its doors wider to the world after the "ping-pong diplomacy" period with Richard Nixon in the early 1970s, which was favorably received. Deng's Four Modernizations campaign gave farmers the incentive to increase agricultural production and allowed the development of other forms of enterprise. It is only since then that private businesses have reappeared in rural areas. These include small individual businesses and the privatization of agriculture collectives.

Collective agriculture was reorganized in 1980, and the first goal of the modernization efforts was to modernize the agricultural practices. Here, the "Family Contract System" or "Household Responsibility" system was introduced on an experimental basis.[52] Under this system, a family could keep any excess over its required quota to its brigade and sell to the market. It was one form of an incentive system, and it worked wonderfully. Higher yields resulted, and China reportedly became one of the largest agricultural producers in the world. Responsibility, accountability, and reward were much more closely aligned.

Along the line of incentive adjustments, from 1984 to 1993, a transitional model of governance for SOEs was introduced to give workers greater autonomy and to increase productivity and profitability. The second aspect of the Four Modernizations was about improving the core industries. In addition to encouraging foreign investment, the government formally encouraged other ownership structures such as the establishment of collectives and private ownership. This also worked and the economy grew steadily.

When private ownership was introduced under Deng, however, it was viewed with skepticism at first. One needs to understand that when the Communists took power in 1949, they confiscated all property, and land was one of the most valuable. The confiscated land has threatened the foundation of capitalist ideals ever since. Despite the initiatives of Mao and others in introducing some form of private ownership, initial uptake was slow at first. But even this last barrier collapsed, and private ownership slowly took its rightful place as a key pillar in economic development.

The Four Modernizations was probably one of the most successful economic transformations and economic development miracles in recent history. According

---

52. Hinton, 1991, p. 13.

to Vohra[53] using *Far Eastern Economic Review*'s statistics, during the period from 1992 to 1997: "the Chinese population grew from 1.158 billion to 1.2 billion; annual per capita GNP nearly doubled, from $370 to $620; foreign trade from $137 billion to $278 billion." The transformation took so many people out of poverty, unprecedented in any history and in comparison with any form of economic development model. More than half a billion people came out of poverty.[54] When China started on its ascent in 1978, per capita income was at low-income status, about one-third of that of Sub-Saharan Africa. In three decades, and following an average annual growth rate of 10% in GDP, China's per capita income had reached that of upper-middle-income status.[55]

In so doing, this drive to modernization also created a hybrid form of capitalism.

The birth of the private firms

Private ownership in China can be a touchy topic and is a recent phenomenon in respect to the long history of China. When Communism was formally introduced, private enterprises went into hiding. Capitalists were persecuted during the early days of Communist China. Political capital was superior to financial capital.

Let's take a step back about a hundred years, to the beginning of the Communist Party in China and that of shared ownership. Some of us remember that the Communist revolution started in August 1927,[56] and we can use that as a starting point. Between 1927 and 1949, the Communists slowly won control over the Nationalist regime, and the Communist Party has been in charge of China ever since. Communism proclaimed public ownership, and this was one of the guiding principles in China since 1949, when the People's Republic of China was founded under Communism. The idea of "no property, no assets, and no companies" was widely promoted by the Chinese leaders at the outset. But adhering to this concept of public ownership didn't really work.

Premier Zhou Enlai at one stage spoke out against private ownership and even declared that these "bourgeoisie" wanted only profit, benefiting at the expense of others. According to Carolyn Hsu[57] in the early days, those who would seek profit for self were easily labeled the bourgeoisie class, or exploiters of the masses. The public narrative at that time was egalitarian, and not private ownership. Private businesses never completely disappeared, however, but they were being viewed with

---

53. Vohra, 2000, p. 289.
54. Schellekens, 2013.
55. Schellekens, 2013, p. 1.
56. If you travel to Xintiandi in Shanghai, you will be introduced to a house where the revolutionaries first met and developed the plan for Communism, which effectively gave birth to Communism in China. Xintiandi is a mixture of old and new architecture and in its own way presents the microcosm that we are seeing of corporate governance in China, a mixture of tradition and new.
57. Hsu, 2007, p. 40.

disdain and operated at the margin. By 1975, workers in urban private businesses reportedly had dropped to less than 0.01% of the total workforce.

Once Deng took control, he slowly and carefully introduced some form of private ownership, carefully because detractors and pure socialists would see such practices as blasphemous to Communism (and a shared economy). Even today, one has to be extra careful with this concept of private ownership. Public ownership, and not private ownership, has been the basis of the so-called Scientific Socialism endorsed by Karl Marx and Friedrich Engels.[58]

Since the early 1990s, the number of registered private firms began to surface and grew from a total of 108,000 in 1991 to 960,000 in 1997.[59] During this period, the modern enterprise system was introduced to further promote the modernization of China. The modern enterprise system, which was geared for the SOEs as defined under the Corporation Law of China, took effect in 1994, and implementation began in 1995.

This 1997 enterprise reform then included:

1. the transformation of the SOEs into corporations by defining the ownership clearly;
2. the setting-up of the board of directors to represent owners' interest; and,
3. the use of independent non-executive directors on the main board and a supervisory board to oversee the management board.

The government also gradually stopped providing subsidies to private enterprises and only allowed them one percent of the bank credits that they had. In accordance with the 15th Party Congress, the Chinese government announced the clarification on property rights, the separation of ownership and management, and the privatizing strategy for most of the SMEs under the SOE reform.[60] Subsequently, discussions on this topic during July 1997, under the banner of "Senior Experts meeting organized by the OECD and the Development Research Center (DRC) of the State Council of the People's Republic of China" produced a set of corporate governance directives for SOE reform:

Rule One
- Adoption of a clear, flexible legal framework for property rights (including intellectual ones), their exchange through contractual arrangements and their use as collateral
- A set of rules that allow the rapid establishment, smooth, and transparent functioning and orderly exit of commercial companies
- A predictable and level playing field for the requirements of entry into markets and sectors (through licensing) and for the terms of competition with other firms

---

58. Xi, 2014, p. 26.
59. Gregory & Tenev, 2001.
60. Huchet & Richet, 1998.

Rule Two
- The resolution of disputes between private parties or between private parties and the state
- The allowance for transparent private dispute resolution so as to enforce property rights regime and increase investor confidence

Rule Three
- The focus on fighting corruption and economic crime

Transition was not easy. The problems of SOEs and the challenges faced in corporate governance could not be resolved with just the above directives and initiatives. Resistance ran high, as expected. A quote from China's state newspaper, *The People's Daily*, should shed some light on the subject at that time. According to China's *People's Daily* online news in May 2001:

> Currently, the government owns around 70 percent of most state-owned listed companies and those shares are not publicly traded. Any move to sell off government-held shares would hugely dilute market liquidity.[61]

The changes and improvement to the governance arrangement has taken considerable time and effort. Due to a long history, vast population and insufficient capital, such changes have taken time, and there's still much work ahead.

The Chinese modern enterprise system

How ownership would be changed in order to align responsibility, accountability, and reward had continued following Deng's successful modernization drive. In 1994, a new corporate law provided for the restructuring of traditional large and medium-sized SOEs as legal entities, establishing a modern corporate enterprise system. Some of the reformed corporate entities were floated on the China stock markets in Shanghai and Shenzhen. Other Chinese companies were listed in Hong Kong and other stock exchanges around the world, after due diligence studies on their financial standing. Some listed "through the back door" in Hong Kong, by acquiring a listed company and backing a China business into this shell.

China's drive to modernize its enterprises officially began in 1993. The state officially gave more power and control to individual enterprises. Enterprises would be provided with clear property rights, clear powers, and clear responsibilities. A clear demarcation was put in place between the state and the enterprises (but not between the party and the enterprises). By the end of 1999, of the 2,473 SOEs that had been selected for reform, 2,016 or 82% had been converted into limited liability

---

61. Shanghai Stock Market Sets New Record (2001, May 18).

companies, as defined by the 1994 Corporate Law.[62] The process of enterprise reform looked to be unstoppable.

The introduction of a new mindset in modern enterprise had meant a complete rethink from corporate governance to operations. A modern enterprise has a self-governing system of checks and balances. Its shareholding base would be much more diversified, ideally with more outside shareholders and investors. Shareholders rights would be protected. Modern management methods including scientific management would be encouraged. Incentives would have to be redesigned to encourage self-initiation and accountability and less with paying everyone the same regardless of performance. Those were the expectations then.

By 2011, the range of the types of enterprises permissible by law grew to encompass nearly all the possible forms in any modern economy. Table 2.1 has the definition of the key ownership types in China during the period from 1979 to 2011.[63]

Type of Ownership	Definition
State-Owned Enterprises (SOEs) (*Guoyou qiye*)	"There are many possible definitions of what constitutes an SOE. The World Bank defined SOE as government-owned or government-controlled economic entities that generate the bulk of their revenues from selling goods and services. This definition limits the enterprises we consider to 'commercial activities' in which the government controls management by virtue of its ownership stake. It encompasses enterprises directly operated by a government department or those which the government holds a majority of the shares directly or indirectly through other SOEs" (World Bank, 1995a). Since the state rarely gets involved in the day-to-day management work, SOEs are set in place by policy and the state typically does not interfere in its management. SOEs are supposed to provide complete social security from cradle to grave, in contrast with other forms, which often do not. State-owned typically refers to industrial enterprises, but we suspect this may encompass new digital enterprises under the new economy.
Collectives (*jiti qiye*) or Collectively Owned Enterprises	These are enterprises in which the means of production are owned collectively. Typically, these are set up by low-level administrative organizations (The World Bank (1995b). Most are subsidiaries of SOEs, which provided their start-up capital and employees (Gregory & Tenev, 2001).

---

62. China's SOEs Embrace Modern Enterprise System (2000, October 16)
63. World Bank, 1995, p. 73; Yueh, 2011, pp. 328–330.

Type of Ownership	Definition
Town and Village Enterprises (TVEs)	TVEs are collective enterprises owned by the town and villages, most of which are effectively owned by township or village governments. TVEs have been responsible in many areas for the rise of standards of living. Ongoing problems center on having TVEs pay proper taxes, copying other people's products and ideas, and ensuring they don't violate copyright laws. TVEs typically do not have as deep pockets as the SOEs have, and this has meant social security is not a top priority. Comparatively, TVEs have tighter budget constraints than do SOEs, which have been selected as key enterprises, thus, a higher level of subsidy.
Communes	During the 1950s, the Communists *collectivized* China's agriculture; that is, farm ownership was transferred to the state. They organized peasants to farm the combined piece of land cooperatively in units called *communes*. Communes do not exist in practice today.
Conglomerates (*jituan*)	Known as *jituan* in Chinese, the group is really not a legal entity. A group of companies, typically state-owned, is formed around a core and the core is a legal entity. The group pays a management fee to the core and has the added advantage of shared services (Peverelli, 2006).
Limited Companies	Most newly established companies are limited companies. A recent development and reportedly different variants have spun up through a different mix of ownership. Chinese called this "People-Operated" or *minying*. Many new IPOs before 2006 were former SOEs, converted into now limited companies where the state can own less than 100%.
Foreign-Invested Enterprises	Following the Cultural Revolution, due to China falling drastically behind the West in technology, the state began to invite foreigners to set up joint ventures (JV) after 1979, in which foreigners may participate on a partial ownership status. As a result of a WTO agreement slowly being introduced in the early 2000, China has now begun to allow wholly owned (100%) foreign invested enterprises to be set up: these are called WOFEs. Sometimes these foreign invested enterprises are labeled as foreign-funded enterprises.
Joint-Stock Cooperative Enterprises	These are enterprises set up on a cooperative basis with start-up capital from members and from outside investors. The members are executives and management.
Limited Liability Corporations	The LLCs are enterprises that have more than 1 but fewer than 49 investors and each is limited in their liability.

Type of Ownership	Definition
Private Enterprises or Private-Owned Enterprises (POE)	These are privately owned businesses that engage employees. These are for-profit entities. Private limited liability corporations, private shareholding corporations, private partnership enterprises, and private sole proprietorships are all included in this category. Private-owned enterprises (POE) nearly disappeared after 1949. Since 1979 however, POE recovered gradually. By 1989, the total number of POE was 90,581. By 2003, it exploded to become one of the largest types of enterprises, just over 3 million enterprises. (Feng, 2006).
Incorporated Companies	These are companies that have been listed, and their total registered capital has been divided in equal shares and has been raised through the issuance of stocks. Each shareholder has limited liability. Companies would have been first registered collectives, jointly operated enterprises, JVs, private enterprises, and any other type in which the company can be classified as a legal person.

Throughout the rest of this book, we will be including a selection of relevant case studies on a range of modern enterprises. Any blanket statement on the successful or unsuccessful transition of these enterprises on their path towards modernization simply based on a change of governance or ownership would be incomplete or probably wrong. There are simply too many variables to consider in analyzing the health, performance, or success in any business entity. A good firm can still fail if it is in the wrong industry, or in the right industry but at the tail end of a business cycle. We will need to study and analyze both the governance and management aspect of each company in relations to its context, its competition, and its culture.

Conclusion

China is one of the world's oldest civilizations, with a turbulent history and incredible economic growth and social change over the past 20 years. In this chapter we saw how massive industrial expansion led to a huge migration from villages and towns to urban conurbations along the eastern seaboard, heralding significant social change.

The centralized political system, fearing the loss of control, responded with strong leadership and a sense of urgency. The government pushed for innovation, entrepreneurship, and the development of smart cities based on information technology. Government also launched an uncompromising drive against corruption.

The chapter showed the significance of Deng's 1980s' drive for the "modernization of the enterprises," the corporatization of SOEs, and the birth of private firms, leading to today's Chinese enterprise system. The rate of change emphasized the need for a renewed sense of history, culture, religion, and ethics, which were being lost. Overall, the economic, social and political context provided the basic drivers for the modern corporate governance practices in China today.

References

2016 Global Innovation 1000 Study. (2016). *PwC*. Retrieved January 20, 2017 from https://www.strategyand.pwc.com/media/file/2016-Global-Innovation-1000-Fact-Pack.pdf.

An illiberal dose; intellectual debate. (2017, February 18). *The Economist* (US), 27–28.

Ann, Elaine (2018). China vs West Tech and HK's role. *Invotech: Smart City Series*. Jan 28, 2018. Hong Kong.

Arnold, Wayne. (2004, December 9). Singapore Oil Company chief arrested in trading losses. *The New York Times*. Retrieved April 30, 2018, from https://www.nytimes.com/2004/12/09/business/worldbusiness/singapore-oil-company-chief-arrested-in-trading.html.

Bailey, D., Ruddy, M., & Shchukina, M. (2012, September 19). Ageing China: Changes and challenges. *BBC News*. Retrieved March 28, 2018 from http://www.bbc.com/news/world-asia-19630110.

Baosteel History. (2017). Retrieved April 30, 2018 from http://bg.baosteel.com/en/contents/3668/65054.html.

Baowu Group Company Profile. (2018). Retrieved April 30, 2018 from http://www.baowu-group.com/en/contents/5273/102759.html.

Baowu Webpages (2018). Memorabilia. 大事记 Retrieved April 30, 2018, from http://www.wisco.com.cn/dsj/723.jhtml.

Barton, D., Chen, Y., & Jin, A. (2013, June). Mapping China's middle class. McKinsey Quarterly. Retrieved March 28, 2018, from http://www.mckinsey.com/industries/retail/our-insights/mapping-chinas-middle-class.

Blau, Rosie. (2016) Chinese society. The new class war. *The Economist*. Jul 9, 2016. http://www.economist.com/news/special-report/21701653-chinas-middle-class-larger-richer-and-more-vocal-ever-threatens.

Booz Allen. (2013) Booz & Company's 2013 Global Innovation 1000 Study. http://innovationexcellence.com/blog/2013/10/22/booz-companys-2013-global-innovation-1000-study/. For a better comparison from 2005 to 2016, refer to PWC's website. http://www.strategyand.pwc.com/innovation1000#VisualTabs2. Date accessed. Jan 20, 2017.

Chinese Society: The new class war. (2016, July 9). Retrieved March 28, 2018 from http://www.economist.com/news/special-report/21701653-chinas-middle-class-larger-richer-and-more-vocal-ever-threatens.

Carrington, D. (2016, October 11). In Yinchuan, China, your face is your credit card. *CNN*. Retrieved March 28, 2018 from https://edition.cnn.com/2016/10/10/asia/yinchuan-smart-city-future/index.html.

China's SOEs Embrace Modern Enterprise System, *People's Daily*, Oct 16, 2000. http://en.people.cn/english/200010/16/eng20001016_52748.html.

Chen, Zongshi. (2016) *The revival, legitimization and development of private enterprise in China*. Palgrave Macmillan.

CBBC. (2016). Smart cities in China. *China-Britain Business Council.* London. Jan 2016. http://www.cbbc.org/cbbc/media/cbbc_media/KnowledgeLibrary/Reports/EU-SME-Centre-Report-Smart-Cities-in-China-Jan-2016.pdf.

Chen, Z. (2015). *The revival, legitimization and development of private enterprise in China: Empowering state capitalism.* New York: Palgrave Macmillan.

China's SOEs embrace modern enterprise system. (2000, October 16). *People's Daily.* Retrieved February 21, 2017, from http://en.people.cn/english/200010/16/eng2000 1016_52748.html.

Chinese steel companies are facing over capacity. (2016). 中国钢企每生产1吨钢要亏损100多元，产能全面过剩 *Sina News.* Retrieved April 30, 2018, from http://finance.sina.com.cn/roll/2016-04-10/doc-ifxrcizs7160144.shtml.

Clover, Charles. (2017, January 18). China's Baosteel posts eightfold surge in full year profit. *Financial Times.* Retrieved April 30, 2018 from https://www.ft.com/content/eb284a18-dd50-11e6-9d7c-be108f1c1dce?mhq5j=e6.

Dikötter, F. 2016. The silent revolution: decollectivization from below during the Cultural Revolution. *The China Quarterly.*

Feng, Qiaobin (2006). China's private-owned enterprises—economic performance, political action & fiscal consequences. *Journal of the Washington Institute of China Studies,* Fall 2006, Vol. 1, No. 2, pp. 118–132. Retrieved on August 16, 2018 from https://www.bpastudies.org/bpastudies/article/view/5/5.

Fewsmith, J. (2008). *China since Tiananmen from Deng Xiaoping to Hu Jintao.* Cambridge: Cambridge University Press.

Gregory, N., & Tenev, S. (2001). China's home-grown entrepreneurs. *The China Business Review,* January.

Haour, G. (2012). The shifting geography of innovation: China and India surging ahead. IMD. Retrieved March 28, 2018 from https://www.imd.org/research/challenges/upload/the_shifting_geography_of_innovation.pdf.

Heineman, B. (2010, January 13). The Google case: When law and ethics collide. *The Atlantic.* Retrieved February 6, 2017 from https://www.theatlantic.com/politics/archive/2010/01/the-google-case-when-law-and-ethics-collide/33438/.

Hinton, W. (1991). *The privatization of China: The great reversal.* London: Earthscan.

HKTB (2017). *Total Visitor Arrival by Country Arrivals.* Retrieved August 16, 2018 from https://partnernet.hktb.com/filemanager/intranet/pm/VisitorArrivalStatistics/ViS_Stat_C/ViS_C_2016/Tourism%20Statistics%2012%202016.pdf.

Holodny, E. (2016, May 4). There's one big problem with China's plan to transform its economy. *Business Insider.* Retrieved March 28, 2018 from http://www.businessinsider.com/chinese-migration-flow-to-cities-slowing-down-2016-5.

Hong, Tao. (2005). 国企董事会拯救央企 [Setup of Board of Directors will save SOEs]. *People's Daily.* Retrieved April 30, 2018 from http://www.people.com.cn/GB/paper81/16279/1437704.html.

Hsu, C. (2007). *Creating market socialism: how ordinary people are shaping class and status in China.* Duke University Press. Durham, NC.

Hu, X. (2012, January 4). China's young rural-to-urban migrants: In search of fortune, happiness, and independence. *Migration Policy Institute.* Retrieved March 28, 2018 from http://www.migrationpolicy.org/article/chinas-young-rural-urban-migrants-search-fortune-happiness-and-independence.

Huang, Yanzhong. (2014, July 16). The 2008 Milk Scandal revisited. *Forbes*. Retrieved August 14, 2018 from https://www.forbes.com/sites/yanzhonghuang/2014/07/16/the-2008-milk-scandal-revisited/.

Huchet, J. F., & Richet. X. (1998, March). China in search of an efficient corporate governance system in a globalized world economy: International comparison and lessons for China. Paper given at the conference on Chinese Economic Reform: Comparative Perspectives, University of Hong Kong.

Hughes, J., & Noble, J. (2015, October 5). Hong Kong exchange gives up on dual-class share plan. *Financial Times*. Retrieved January 20, 2017 from https://www.ft.com/content/0bc597ee-6b42-11e5-aca9-d87542bf8673.

Jacques, Martin. (2009). *When China rules the world*. London: Penguin Books

Jefferson, G. H., & Su, J. (2006). Privatization and restructuring in China: Evidence from shareholding ownership, 1995–2001. *Journal of Comparative Economics*, 34(1), 146–166. doi:10.1016/j.jce.2005.11.008.

Leadership of China Baowu Group. (2016). 中国宝武钢铁集团有限公司主要领导配备 Retrieved April 30, 2018, from http://www.baowugroup.com/contents/5173/97528.html.

Luo, Wangshu. (2017, March 21). More Chinese students set to study overseas. *The Telegraph*. Retrieved August 13, 2018 from https://www.telegraph.co.uk/news/world/china-watch/society/more-students-to-study-overseas/.

Mauldin, J. (2016, February 25). 5 maps that explain China's strategy. *Forbes*. Retrieved March 28, 2018 from http://www.forbes.com/sites/johnmauldin/2016/02/25/5-maps-that-explain-chinas-strategy/#2a9825ae202d.

Neil Gregory and Stoyan Tenev. (2001) China's home-grown entrepreneurs, *The China Business Review*, Jan edition.

Nelson, C. (2014, June 17). Smart city development in China. *China Business Review*. Retrieved March 28, 2018 from https://www.chinabusinessreview.com/smart-city-development-in-china/.Nolan, P., & Ash, R. F. (1995). China's economy on the eve of reform. *The China Quarterly*, 144, 980. doi:10.1017/s0305741000004690.

Peverelli, P. J. (2006). *Chinese corporate identity*. London: Taylor & Francis. [This book provides a good context to the background to corporate governance in China.]

Pham, S. (2016). Alibaba points to politics after US puts it back on fake goods blacklist. CNN Tech. December 22, 2016. Retrieved August 14, 2018, https://money.cnn.com/2016/12/22/technology/alibaba-notorious-markets-fake-goods-us-trade/index.html.

PWC. (2016). 2016 Global Innovation 1000 Study. http://www.strategyand.pwc.com/innovation1000. Date accessed 20 Jan 2017.

Reform of SOEs: Board of Director in SOEs cannot be shaped as a vase. (2015, December 14). "国企改革：董事局，不能当"花瓶"" Retrieved April 30, 2018, from http://www.gov.cn/xinwen/2015-12/14/content_5023344.htm.

South China Morning Post Topics (2018): Xi Jinping's Anti-Graft Campaign. *SCMP.com* Retrieved April 30, 2018, from http://www.scmp.com/topics/xi-jinpings-anti-graft-campaign.

Schellekens, P. (2013, May). A changing China: Implications for developing countries. World Bank.

Shanghai Stock Market Sets New Record. (2001, May 18). *People's Daily*. Retrieved April 30, 2018 from http://english.peopledaily.com.cn/200105/17/eng20010517_70212.html.

Speech on pilot of Board of Directors in Baosteel. (2005). 在宝钢集团有限公司董事会试点工作会议上的讲话 Retrieved April 30, 2018, from http://old.sasac.gov.cn/gzjg/xcgz/200510180005.htm.

So, A. Y., & Chu, Y. (2016). *The global rise of China*. Cambridge: Polity.

Steel Industry Adjustment Plan (2016–2020). (2016). 钢铁工业调整升级规划（2016–2020年）Retrieved March 28, 2018, from http://www.ndrc.gov.cn/fzgggz/fzgh/ghwb/gjjgh/201706/t20170621_851923.html.

Sun, Min. (2005). Minsheng Bank reveals property scandal. *China Daily*. Retrieved April 30, 2018 from http://www.chinadaily.com.cn/english/doc/2005-04/22/content_436546.htm.

Sun, Nikki. (2016, October 3). Hong Kong tourist numbers up, but no cash bonanza for retailers as Chinese visitors spend less and leave sooner. *South China Morning Post*. Retrieved April 30, 2018 from http://www.scmp.com/news/hong-kong/economy/article/2024639/hong-kong-tourist-numbers-no-cash-bonanza-retailers-chinese.

Sun, Wenyu (2017, July 13). China's permanent urbanization rate hits 57.4 per cent. People's Daily. Retrieved April 30, 2018 from http://en.people.cn/n3/2017/0713/c90000-9241304.html.

The plan of restructuring of Baowu will be published in two days. (2016, September 20). 宝武重组方案最快两天面世，"46"号文揭开钢铁产业路线图. *eeo.com.cn*. Retrieved September 20, 2018 from http://www.eeo.com.cn/2016/0920/292076.shtml.

Thrilling, D. (2016, December 5). China's tourists: Economics, the environment and what they want. *Journalist's Resource*. Retrieved March 28, 2018 from https://journalistsresource.org/studies/international/china/china-tourist-economics-environment-research.

Top steel-producing companies 2017 (2017). *Worldsteel Association*. Retrieved April 30, 2018 from https://www.worldsteel.org/steel-by-topic/statistics/top-producers.html

Tsai, K. (2004). *Back-alley banking: Private entrepreneurs in China*. Ithaca, NY: Cornell University Press.

Vohra, R. (2000). *China's path to modernization: A historical review from 1800 to the present* (3rd ed.). Englewood Cliffs, NY: Prentice-Hall.

Wang, G. C. (Ed.). (2005). *Case Studies of Corporate Governance* (pp. 103–107). Beijing: Economy and Management Publishing House.

Wildau (2016, January 14). China income inequality among world's worst. *Financial Times*. Retrieved April 30, 2018, from https://www.ft.com/content/3c521faa-baa6-11e5-a7cc-280dfe875e28.

Wildau, G. (2015, May 4). China migration: At the turning point. *Financial Times*. Retrieved March 28, 2018 from https://www.ft.com/content/767495a0-e99b-11e4-b863-00144feab7de.

World Bank. (1995a). *Bureaucrats in business: The economics and politics of government ownership*. Oxford: Oxford University Press.

World Bank. (1995b). China growth rates by ownership type. *Bureaucrats in business—A World Bank Policy Research Report*. Oxford: Oxford University Press.

World Bank (2016). Doing business ranking. See http://www.doingbusiness.org/Rankings.

Xi, J. (2014). *The governance of China*. Beijing: Foreign Languages Press.

Xu, Xiaochu. (2012). *China's young rural-to-urban migrants: in search of fortune, happiness, and independence*. Jan 4, 2012. Migration Policy Institute. http://www.migrationpolicy.

org/article/chinas-young-rural-urban-migrants-search-fortune-happiness-and-inde-pendence.

Yan (2006, January 24). Kelon executives embezzled US $73 million. *New Guangdong*. Retrieved April 30, 2018 from http://www.newsgd.com/business/enterprise/200601240031.htm.

Yiu, Enoch. (2017, January 19). HKEX rekindles plans for dual-class share structure in Hong Kong. *South China Morning Post*. Retrieved April 30, 2018 from http://www.scmp.com/business/china-business/article/2063569/hkex-rekindles-plans-dual-class-share-structure-city. The practice of weighted voting shares finally was instituted at the HKSE during early 2018.

Yueh, Linda (2011). *Enterprising China: Business, economic, and legal developments since 1979*. Pages 328—330. Oxford: Oxford University Press.

Zhang, Weiying. (2014). 国企不可能建立有效公司治理 [SOEs can't establish effective corporate governance]. *Phoenix*. Retrieved April 30, 2018 from http://finance.ifeng.com/news/special/caizhidao198/.

Case study

China Baowu Steel Group Corporation Limited

China's Baosteel, now known as Baowu Steel, is one of the oldest and largest SOEs in China and is now China's largest steel plant, after merging with its rival, Wuhan Iron and Steel (Wisco). In fact, it is the world's second-largest steel maker after ArcelorMittal.

Due to its massive size and bureaucracy, Baosteel had been laden with problems from the start. As a result of competition increasing from abroad and the slowing global economy, Baosteel became a political hot potato domestically and a poster child for unfair trade practices internationally. US Steel at one stage had accused Baosteel of stealing its commercial secrets, which led to an investigation by the International Trade Commission in 2016. In the same year, and along with South Korea, Taiwan, and India, China and Baosteel was accused by developed nations of dumping cheap steel, apparently to gain a market share and to cover up its excessive production.

To reassure its accusers, the Chinese government employed the strategy of acquisition and merger to restructure the company. At one stage, Baosteel had even acquired a controlling stake of Guangdong Shaoguan Iron and Steel Corporation from the Guangdong branch of SASAC. As a result of the latest merger with Wisco, Baosteel took over control of Wisco, which became a subsidiary. Interestingly, the chairperson of Wisco became the chairperson of the new entity.

The steel industry in China

After a roaring pace of growth for over 10 years, the steel industry began to slow in 2015. Overall, the industry had employed over 4 million people and contributed to over RMB 241.6 billion in taxes.[64] But by 2015, 51% of the SMEs in the steel industry had begun to suffer huge losses. China was facing an issue of overcapacity.[65] Major restructuring had to be introduced into the industry and would involve other related industries such as coal. Vertical and horizontal integration may further improve efficiency of the steel industry. These huge SOEs needed reform and a better way then was to merge two giants.

China Baowu Steel Group Corporation Limited

Interestingly, Baosteel was no longer officially called Baoshan (Baoshan is the listed vehicle of the Baosteel Group) or Baosteel. The new name is the China Baowu Group Corporation (Baowu), which is a name created from the amalgamation of Baosteel Group Corporation with Wuhan Iron & Steel (Group) Corporation, in December 2016. (Perhaps this new name will help shed the reputation it has had, but the foreign press still referred to it as Baosteel.)[66] After this latest merger, China Baowu became the largest steel and iron producer in China with registered capital of RMB 52.79 billion and 228,000 employees.[67] In 2016, China Baowu ranked as the second-largest steel producer in the world,[68] having crude steel production of 63.81 million tons and RMB 7.02 billion in profit.[69]

But such ranking is misleading because, like everyone else, Baowu has been seeking to reduce production in a period of slumping demand and excess production. There have been rumors that the Chinese government forecast that 60%–70% steel production in China, by 2025, would be produced by just 10 domestic companies.[70] Industry consolidation is more the reality these days. Reportedly, the Chinese government has had goals to reduce production of steel in China by another 50 m metric tons in 2016 and even more in 2017.[71]

History of the two companies

Wisco is even older than Baosteel. Wisco was the first steel production plant, established after the founding of the PRC in 1949. Wisco began production in 1958, when China was deep in the period the Great Leap Forward and when making more steel was a sign of industrial might. Since Mao Zedong ignited the first blast furnace,

64. Steel Industry Adjustment Plan (2016–2020) (2016).
65. Chinese steel companies are facing over capacity (2016).
66. Clover (2017, January 18).
67. In headcounts, this is not the largest group in China. China National Petroleum, China Post, Sinopec, and the Agricultural Bank of China have more employees. For comparison, Walmart in the US has 2.1 million employees.
68. Top steel-producing companies 2017 (2017).
69. Baowu Group Company Profile (2018).
70. The plan of restructuring of Baowu will be published in two days (2016, September 20).
71. Clover (2017, January 18).

it has been known as "the eldest son of the steel industry in China," a pride of the nation. After the Cultural Revolution, Deng Xiaoping paid a site visit to this Wuhan Group and wanted to enhance its autonomy. (Like his visit to Shenzhen, Deng's visit is symbolic and carries a key political message for party members.) Thus, the Wuhan Iron & Steel Company was listed in 1999. By 2005, Wisco's revenue was RMB 53.3 billion, with RMB 7.1 billion profit, and contributed RMB 11.2 billion in taxes.[72]

Unlike Wisco, Baosteel Group started from the Baosteel Project at the beginning of the Four Modernizations in the 1980s. Allegedly, Deng Xiaoping wanted China to build an iron and steel company like that in Japan, having been impressed by such a plant in Japan. As a result, the Baoshan Iron and Steel or Baosteel was born with the assistance and modern technology of the Japanese. The Baosteel Project construction ceremony was held the day after the Third Plenary Session of the 11th Central Committee of the Communist Party of China (CPC). The years 1985 and 1991 witnessed the ignition of the first and second blast furnaces at the Baoshan District, a suburb of Shanghai. The site was chosen because it was closest to the Port of Shanghai, and China needed a large integrated steel production facility near the port.

The original Wuhan Iron & Steel Co. Ltd. was the backbone and listing vehicle of Wisco. It had suffered RMB 7.5 billion in losses in 2015, and RMB 1.29 billion in losses in the first half year in 2016. On June 27, 2016, the stock of the Wuhan Co. was suspended from trading, due to the restructuring with Baosteel. On September 22, SASAC, Baosteel Group, and Wisco simultaneously announced that, after the approval of the State Council, Baosteel would absorb the stocks and assets of Wuhan Steel and the Baowu Group would be the new name for the merger of Baosteel and Wisco. The old Wuhan Iron & Steel Co. Ltd. would become a wholly owned subsidiary of Baowu. On January 23, 2017, the Wuhan steel company was delisted.

Since its foundation 30 years ago, Baosteel has merged with several steel companies in China, such as the Shang Metallurgical Holding Group, Shanghai Meishan Group, and Shaoguan Iron & Steel Company.[73]

Governance overview of China Baowu

Based on the orientation of the state-owned capital investment company, China Baowu follows the so-called "One Body, Two Wings" strategy in which steel is the main body and core business. Smart manufacturing of green premium products and platform-based services for steel ecosystem are the two wings. It has since diversified into four segments:

- Steel and relevant manufacturing sector;

---

72. Baowu webpage (2018).
73. Baosteel History (2017).

- Steel and relevant services (to enhance service competitiveness of the steel industry);
- Finance related; and
- Real estate and new urban industries that would help with taking up the slack employment of the steel industry (in line with the reduction of steel production).

Of all the subsidiaries, only a few have been individually listed and are still grouped under China Baowu:

- Baosteel,
- Bayi Iron & Steel,
- Shaoguan Iron & Steel,
- Baosight Software, and
- Baosteel Packaging.

The various subsidiaries under Baowu:

Figure 2.1

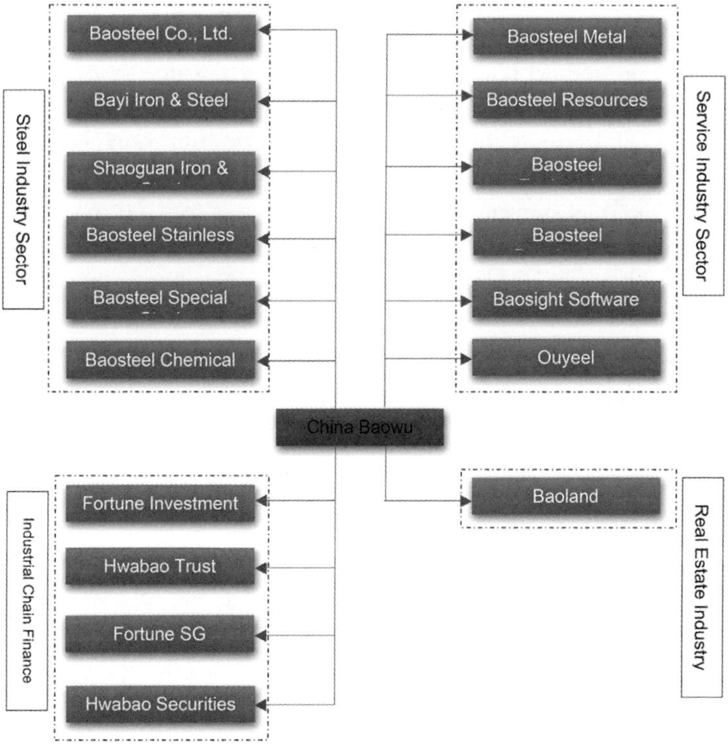

Source: Business Sector of China Baowu. Adapted from "Business Perspective." Retrieved November 16, 2017 from http://www.baowugroup.com/en/contents/5279/102786.html. ©2016 by China Baowu Steel Group Corporation.

SOE Reform: Establishment of the first board at the Baosteel Group

With China's company law established as a foundation of modern governance system, setting up a board of directors was on the agenda of reform for SOEs. In the 3rd Plenary Session of the 16th Central Committee in 2003, the framework of a modern corporation system for SOEs had required the setting-up of shareholder meetings, board of directors, supervisory board, and executive management. In April 2005, the State Council stated that furthering the reform of China's economic system would rely on the establishment of board of directors and the improvement of corporate governance structure.[74] As such, during October 2005, the first meeting of the board of directors of the Baosteel Group (a pilot enterprise for governance reform) was held. **Piloting has been a very successful means to test and explore the adoption of foreign governance practices, including the inclusion of independent outside directors.**

In setting up their first board, Baosteel Group adopted the pattern of "4+5." Four directors were from the organization and five from outside. As the one and only shareholder of the Baosteel Group, SASAC could nominate five outside directors, and two of them were foreigners, ideally those who could speak Putonghua. Moreover, the board office and board secretary needed to be established to ensure the proper functioning of the board. The board held meetings twice a year. SASAC delegated certain authority to the board, including the power to select professional managers, assess their performance, decide their remuneration, and make major investment decisions. The board was required to submit an annual report to SASAC.[75] After approval by the CPC'S Organization Department, Mr. Ma Guoqiang assumed the chairmanship and became the secretary of the CPC in China Baowu. Upon approval of SASAC, Mr. Chen Derong was named CEO and vice secretary of the CPC.[76] All senior leaders typically take on one position as an executive and another on behalf of the CPC.

---

74. Speech on pilot of Board of Directors in Baosteel (2005).
75. Hong, 2005.
76. Leadership of China Baowu Group (2016).

Table 2.2: Board of directors of Baosteel Group, before its merger

Position	Board Member of Baosteel
Chair	Mr. Xie Qihua
Director, Secretary of CPC	Mr. Liu Guosheng
Director, CEO of Baosteel	Mr. Xu Lejiang
Outside Director, Professor	Mr. Xia Dawei
Outside Director, Chairman of Li & Fung Group	Mr. Fung Kwok-king
Outside Director, Chairman of PSA	Mr. Stephen Lee CY
Outside Director	Mr. Wu Yaowen
Outside Director	Mr. Yang Xianzu
Employee Director, Chairman of Labor Union	Mr. Wang Jinde

When the pilot scheme was under discussion, many people were skeptical about the role and influence of outside directors. According to official explanation, the objective of appointing outside directors to the board was to oversee internal control and to bring an independent mindset. To allay fears, managers were allowed to sit in and observe the first board meeting. But skeptics remained. The board's effectiveness was called into question by Western critics, as the directors were really not held accountable for the performance of SOEs, and they were just government officials.[77] These critics saw that individual accountability was more important than empowering group accountability and collective decision-making. Some other skeptics felt the board of SOEs was just a rubber-stamp mechanism and lacked purpose.

But the government persisted because it knew the many problems of corporate governance had to be considered on a broader scale. Since the corporate governance ecosystem of China's SOEs would involve the Party Committee of the Communist Party, the actual power and relationship of the players in this ecosystem (the board of directors, the supervisory board, and management) would have to be considered in this light. Individual accountability was very much a Western concept and needed to be adapted slowly.

The power of the board was quite limited at first, as certain powers had already been taken away. A chairperson from another SOE commented that, for such pilot projects, many government departments had been involved. For example, reform and investment decisions were managed by the NDRC, SASAC, and the Ministry of Industry and Information Technology (MIIT). Personnel selection and nomination was being handled by SASAC. Payroll was managed by the Ministry of Human Resources and Social Security.[78] In this regard, the delegated authority of the board was limited, and the experiment allowed the Chinese authorities to devolve control gradually for other SOEs.

---

77. Zhang, 2014.
78. Reform of SOEs: Board of Director in SOEs cannot be shaped as a vase (2015, December 14).

China Baowu's vision and mission

"To be a leader in steel technology"

Corporate governance architecture

Figure 2.2

Source: Corporate Governance of China Baowu. Adapted from "Management Structure." Retrieved November 16, 2017 from http://www.baowugroup.com/en/contents/5274/102760. html.
©2016 by China Baowu Steel Group Corporation.

Table 2.3: Board of directors of China Baowu (after the merger and name change)

Position	Board Member of Baosteel (2012–2016)	Board Member of China Baowu (2016–present)
Chair, Secretary of CPC	Mr. Xu Lejiang	Mr. Ma Guoqiang*
Director, Vice-secretary of CPC	Mr. Chen Derong	Mr. Chen Derong
Outside Director	Mr. Wang Xiaoqi	Mr. Wang Xiaoqi
Outside Director	Mr. Bei Kewei	Mr. Bei Kewei
Outside Director	Mr. Wang Fucheng	Mr. Wang Fucheng
Outside Director	Mr. Lin Jianqing	Mr. Lin Jianqing
Employee Director	Mr. Zhu Yiming	Mr. Zhu Yiming

* Mr. Ma is now the chair of this new company.

Questions for discussion

1. Do you think such setup of the pilot board has been successful in China? What components do you think would be needed in order to improve the effectiveness of the piloted board of directors?

2. What are the roles of the CPC and SASAC in the corporate governance of SOEs? Are their roles justified?

3. "There is no real board of directors in SOEs." What do you think of this statement? Since some functions of the board are being performed by other parties, like SASAC, or by their supervisory board, should the power and scope of the board of directors be reduced? Please itemize them.

4. Would the intervention of government reduce or enhance the benefits of the non-government shareholders?

5. The chairperson of the new entity, Baowu, actually was the chairperson of Wisco.

   Apparently this person was sent into Wisco to help turn it around. As a token reward, he was given the helm of Baowu. Which party, SASAC or NDRC, would have such authority to move board members?

3

The Evolution of Corporate Governance in China

Bob Tricker

In this chapter we consider:

- ❖ the political history behind the advent of modern China
- ❖ the corporate governance of SOEs in China
- ❖ the Chinese government's attempt to reassert control over SOEs
- ❖ the governance of private companies in China
- ❖ the development of corporate governance in Hong Kong
- ❖ one country, two systems of corporate governance

The political history behind the advent of modern China

As we saw in Chapter 2, the history, culture, and politics of mainland China created a unique context for the development of corporate governance with "Chinese characteristics." In this chapter, we review the evolution of corporate governance in SOEs and private companies in China and contrast that with the development of corporate governance in Hong Kong. In subsequent chapters we will explore the reality of governance practices, review the state of play in all types of corporate enterprise in China, recognize the significance of board-level abilities and attitudes, and identify some ethical challenges. But first, we need to remember the immense political and economic changes that have occurred in China in just half a century.

The PRC was established in 1949, by Mao Zedong following the defeat of the Nationalist Army under Chiang Kai-shek and its retreat to Taiwan after the civil war of 1946 to 1949. Mao founded the PRC and remained chairman of the CPC from 1949 until his death in 1976.

Over that period, the state proclaimed ownership of the means of production, prohibited private property, and banned incorporated companies. In 1958, Chairman Mao initiated the Great Leap Forward, relocating millions of farmers, peasants, and city workers. Massive economic dislocation and famine resulted. The Cultural Revolution began in 1966 and lasted a decade. Communes were reorganized and SOEs were created, most relying on state subsidies.

In the 1970s, Mao's successor as paramount leader, Deng Xiaoping, introduced a pragmatic form of market economy while maintaining an orientation towards a centralized communist state. The industrial SOEs, which were large bureaucracies, continued to receive their production and distribution orders from state planners. Employees of the SOEs received housing, medical care, and schooling for their children. Foreign investment in China was now permitted.

Deng stood down in 1989 and is now recognized as the initiator of the changes that led to the subsequent incredible economic growth up to the present day. His successor, Jiang Zemin, assumed power following the Tiananmen Square protests and continued until 2002, overseeing the return of Hong Kong and Macau to mainland control. Jiang continued the economic reforms. Between 1984 and 1993, the SOEs were given more autonomy, with a transitional model of governance to improve their productivity and profitability.

During the tenure of Hu Jintao, who was paramount leader from 2002 to 2012, economic growth continued, bringing China into the top rank of world economic powers. Hu was a conservative and tightened controls on some SOEs, which the previous administration had tended to relax. Hu was succeeded by Xi Jinping in 2013.

In 1988, the State Council of the PRC, advised by experts from the OECD, produced a set of corporate governance directives for SOE reform. In September 1999, the Fourth Plenary Session of the 15th Chinese Communist Party's Central Committee made a vital decision on enterprise reform, in what was termed a "strategic adjustment" of the state sector, agreeing that the state should be "withdrawing from what should be withdrawn." Interestingly, corporate governance was recognized as being at the core of the modern enterprise system.

A new companies law was enacted in 1994, which was revised in 2006. Two types of company were created:

- a "limited liability company" (LLC), with at least 2 and no more than 50 shareholders, somewhat similar to private companies in other jurisdictions
- a "company limited by shares," in other words a joint stock company (JSC), with some similarities to public companies in other jurisdictions.

Both types of company were defined as legal persons with property rights as well as civil rights and duties. Shareholders' liability for corporate debts was limited to their investment. Each company's articles of association defined its name and domicile, the scope of its activities, the structure of its share capital, and shareholders' rights.

Companies were given autonomy to run their businesses according to the market in order, as the Companies Act said: "to raise economic efficiency, improve labor productivity, and preserve and increase the value of assets." Companies were also called on by the new law "to conduct their business activities abiding by the law and by business ethics, strengthen the construction of socialist spiritual civilization and accept the supervision of the government and the public." Companies were allowed to invest in other companies and to create groups of companies with subsidiaries and branches.

The governance of companies under the act was through meetings of:

- the shareholders
- the board of directors
- the supervisory board

According to the act, meetings of shareholders could:

- elect and replace directors
- decide on matters related to directors' remuneration
- decide on the company's operational policies and investment plans
- elect and replace shareholder representatives on the board of supervisors
- decide on matters related to supervisors' remuneration
- examine and approve reports of the board of directors
- examine and approve reports of the board of supervisors
- examine and approve the company's financial accounts and proposed budget,

and on major strategic issues:

- decide a merger or change in corporate form
- decide on the dissolution of the company.

The act provided for a company to have a board of directors appointed by the shareholders. A company limited by shares should have a board of between 5 and 19 members. The board of directors should appoint a manager (chief executive) to run the operations, who reports to the board. The manager attends meetings of the board of directors. Where a limited liability company was formed by two or more SOEs, the board should include "representatives of the staff and workers chosen by democratic election."

Companies with "a relatively large scale of operation" were also required to have a **board of supervisors**, with not less than three members, made up of representatives of the shareholders and a "reasonable proportion" of representatives from the company's staff and workers, again chosen by democratic election, as provided for in the company's articles of association. The board of supervisors had the power to:

- inspect the company's financial position
- exercise supervision over the acts of the directors and managers
- call for a shareholders' meeting

According to the act, members of the supervisory board could attend meetings of the board of directors.

A company could be set up, and its boards of directors and supervisors appointed, once the promoters satisfied the Company Registration Authority by providing the company's articles of association and other approval documents. Before a company could offer shares to the public, including investors outside China, approval was required from the Securities Administration Authority of the State Council.

An element of industrial democracy was provided for in the act:

> When considering and deciding on wages, welfare, and production safety of staff and workers and labor protection, labor insurance and other issues involving the personal interests of staff and workers, (and major issues relating to the company's production and operations) the company shall first solicit and consider the opinions and proposals of the company's trade union and the staff and workers, and shall invite their representatives to attend the relevant meetings.

The act required companies to establish financial and accounting systems and to prepare financial statements for each fiscal year "according to the law and the regulations of the responsible finance department of the State Council."

The 16th Congress of the party called for a joint-stock system with outside investors. Some SOEs were restructured prior to stock market listing although the state maintained control of critical enterprises. Some of the reformed corporate entities were floated on the two Chinese stock markets, in Shanghai and Shenzhen, which had been set up in 1991 and 1992 respectively. Other SOEs continued their corporate reforms. Many small and medium-sized firms were transformed into non-state-owned enterprises

Although the company laws enabled traditional large and medium-sized SOEs to be restructured as legal entities, incorporating an SOE was a complex process. Previously many SOEs were, effectively, towns providing employees' housing, medical facilities and hospitals, schools, and social facilities. Now boundaries had to be drawn around the new company's assets and liabilities, which had to be valued to create a balance sheet. Accounting firms from Hong Kong provided some of the necessary expertise. As corporate entities, SOEs could now be incorporated as a company, valued, listed on a stock exchange, and its shares bought and sold.

In a country with strong central control, in which the Communist Party, the State Council, the National People's Congress, the Politburo Standing Committee, and the Central Military Commission (the PLA) play significant roles, share ownership is not the obvious basis for exercising governance power over state-owned companies, even if they had been listed on a stock exchange. The governance of newly emerging private companies in China presented a different range of challenges. Yet the PRC developed an innovative corporate governance regime, to become one of the world's leading economies.

> *Private entities and SOEs cannot be discussed with the same breath.*
>
> An investment banker of a financial institution in China for over 10 years commented that:
>
> "To really understand corporate governance in China, one has first to clearly distinguish private entities and SOEs. They cannot be discussed in the same breath."
>
> "On the private side we have a wide range and the most diverse types of companies, with both good and badly governed ones. Of course, the present situation is quite different from what it was ten years ago."
>
> "Corporate governance in SOEs is very different from that of the private sector. On the surface, it may appear that SOEs are sophisticated with two-tiered boards. In reality, much is superficial. There are too many systems and bureaucracy is everywhere. The CEO is all-powerful. No such thing as checks and balances. He alone holds all the power."

The corporate governance of SOEs in China

When SOEs incorporated as companies, the state, at the national, provincial, or sometimes local level, maintained ownership. Lines of control from various state authorities could be numerous. The State Council, the People's Bank of China, the ministry responsible for the industry in which the company operated, tax offices, and other state and provincial officials might act in what they saw as the interests of the state and the people; for example, by regulating supplies and prices, by taking action to avoid unacceptable economic or social stress including unemployment, bankruptcy, corruption, or financial pressure on the state economy, or undesirable competition between state enterprises.

If the shares of an SOE were listed on a stock exchange, the state kept the majority of the voting shares and thus control. In the earlier years, these majority shareholders typically nominated the directors, expecting other shareholders to accept them. The major shareholders often controlled and dominated shareholders' meetings.

Initially, control by insiders was a widespread problem. The roles and responsibilities of key players were often unclear. Board activities could be dominated by management. Since the duties of the board and top management were often vague, the chairperson might usurp the chief executive's role, and the chief executive might encroach on the work of the chief operations officer and divisional heads.

Internal control systems were not well established. In some cases, information was manipulated, delayed, even falsified. Performance assessment of individual directors was immature and not necessarily linked to incentives. Reviews of the performance of the board and its committees were seldom undertaken. The supposedly independent audit firms were not experienced and not always independent. Claims were made that financial problems had been hidden rather than disclosed.

The State-Owned Assets Supervision and Administration Commission (SASAC) of the State Council holds the China government's shareholding in all China's listed companies (other than those in the finance sector). SASAC is the largest institutional shareholder in the world, holding 8 of the world's top 500 companies in the Fortune 500 list. SASAC ensures that the state's interests are represented in the activities of China's listed companies, including the appointment of directors and top executives to state majority-owned companies. In 2013, the head of SASAC, Jiang Zemin, was investigated for "serious disciplinary violations," which usually refers to corruption-related issues. But no further information became public.

The China Securities Regulatory Commission of the State Council (CSRC) is the Chinese government's corporate regulator. The CSRC issues the Corporate Governance Code and other corporate governance regulations and publishes regular reports on corporate governance reform and performance in China. The CSRC also liaises closely with the management of the stock exchanges in Shanghai and Shenzhen, and with those exchanges overseas that list Chinese stock.

In 2001, the CSRC formulated some basic norms of corporate governance, promoting the separation of listed companies from controlling shareholders. At least one third of the board was required to be independent directors, including at least one accounting professional. Unfortunately, the concept of independence was not well understood and there was a lack of suitable people. These independent directors could be nominated by the board of directors itself, the board of supervisors, or any shareholders holding 5% of the shares. Also in 2001, China became a member of the WTO.

In 2001, a code of corporate governance for listed companies[1] was formulated, which included:

- basic principles for the rights of shareholders
- rules for shareholder meetings
- controls on related party transactions
- the behavior of controlling shareholders
- the independence of the company from controlling shareholders
- directors' election, duties, and responsibilities
- the composition, duties, rules and procedures of the board of directors

Significantly, the corporate governance code called for the appointment of independent directors to the boards, even though the concept of director independence was not well understood in China at the time.

---

1. China Securities Regulatory Commission and the State Economic and Trade Commission, Code of Corporate Governance for listed companies in China, 2001.

The code also called for boards to have an audit committee, a remuneration committee, and a nomination committee, and laid out their broad duties in line with Western corporate governance codes. It also called for a board strategy committee. Then, unlike the codes in unitary board structures, the Chinese code called for listed companies to have a supervisory board responsible to the shareholders.

The code also referred to:

- the selection of management personnel
- incentives and discipline of management
- disclosure of corporate information and information on corporate governance
- details of controlling shareholders' interests

An expert who has followed the development of governance in China over many years, commented that:*

"SOE reform in China has gone through many stages as well as ups and downs. There were various initiatives in an official document published in 2015, which included:

(a) shifting from managing SOEs' running and operations, to managing SOEs' capital structure, ownership, etc.

(b) separating SOEs into business-oriented, as against social-oriented entities, and dealing with these two categories separately

(c) recognizing that the government need not own more than 50% of the shares of SOEs; thus recognizing that selling down the stake of the government in individual firms could actually help raise more funds to deal with broader SOE reform issues. The selling down of the government's stake also means that private investors (including overseas investors) are invited to come in to help SOE reform at the management level."

* Please see *Chinese government guideline enhancing SOEs reform*, retrieved on August 19, 2018 from http://www.gov.cn/zhengce/2015-09/13/content_2930440.htm.

China thus created a unique form of corporate governance structure for listed companies—a board of directors, with some independent outside directors, and a board of supervisors, with both employee and shareholder representatives—thus combining elements of both the German-style two-tier board model and the unitary board model's use of outside directors, as well as recognizing China's political concept of employees being masters of enterprises. Although some commentators suggested that China's model is more closely aligned to the Japanese model, which is essentially a unitary board system, it provides for the independent outside directors on the board to form a separate committee outside the board.

Independent directors on listed company boards of directors were drawn principally from universities, the professions, the relevant industry, and government. Hong Kong provided some independent directors, but there were few foreign nationals. Employee directors on SOEs boards often opposed corporate reform, resulting in protracted negotiations at board level.

In the earlier days of the corporate governance reforms, many boards tended to be weak and could be dominated by a powerful chairperson. Boards were often tightly knit groups built on business and personal contacts. Genuinely independent directors were often appointed to meet legal requirements but mainly played an advisory role. Over the years, however, as the effects of a public listing and the influence of professional advisers became apparent, a greater degree of professionalism could be found in some listed SOEs. Over time, those in senior board positions and their professional advisers gained experience. More executives in senior managerial positions also had training and more knowledge; some had business school MBAs.

CEOs of SOEs are transferred by the Chinese government.

The executive director of a financial institution had insight into how Chinese SOEs function. He explained that:

"CEOs have a pecking order or hierarchy within the Chinese government bureaucracies. For example, a CEO would be ranked no. 1 in the company, but he might rank 142 in some ministry's line-up of seniority."

"Every CEO is expected to finish his appointed term and, if he had performed well, he might be promoted to the next senior level. CEOs are moved or transferred as determined by the Chinese government, not by their own board of directors, even if the SOEs are listed companies. Succession planning for CEOs is not done at the SOE level."

"CEOs of listed SOEs have no incentive to drive up share value by having their company perform above market or better than expected. That's not their concern. So many SOEs are extremely risk averse: the CEOs must be in compliance and the company must not commit any crime. If they are found to be in non-compliance, and regardless how well they have performed for the company, they will be let go."

One feature of SOE governance in China is not found in other countries: the selection and appraisal of chief executives. In the unitary board model of corporate governance, the board selects, appraises, and if necessary replaces the CEO. In the dual-board model, the supervisory board, working with the executive board makes the decisions. In China's SOEs, however, chief executives are chosen by and report to government officers in SASAC, perhaps working with the institutions overseeing that industry. Consequently, chief executives of SOEs are in a powerful position in dealing with members of their own management and supervisory boards. The board of Chinese SOEs has no need to plan succession or use corporate executive search firms (head hunters) to fill a CEO vacancy.

The performance of the chief executives of SOEs is also assessed at government level. Not only are financial and other corporate performance criteria used, but CEOs are also expected to comply with government edicts and regulations. It has been suggested that this can make CEOs risk averse. CEOs throughout the SOE sector are also ranked and promoted to other SOEs by government officers. This system applies even to those SOEs that are listed on a stock exchange and have outside shareholders.

According to the company laws, the board of supervisors should play a fundamental role in corporate governance by overseeing finances, ensuring the due diligence of directors and senior management personnel, safeguarding company assets, reducing the company's risks, and protecting shareholders' interests. In practice, commentators have criticized the effectiveness of some supervisory boards, because their members had less education and professional experience than did the directors and managers they supervised. Moreover, members of companies' political party committees often took positions of chairperson and vice chairperson of their companies' boards of supervisors, introducing a political element into supervisory board deliberations.

The Communist Party Plenum in 2013 called for the market to play a decisive role in the economy, while confirming that the state sector should remain the main body of the economy despite the large number of private enterprises that now generated a significant proportion of China's GDP.

The plenum emphasized that major industries and their corporations—energy, transport, heavy industry, telecommunications, finance, for example—should remain SOEs with external investment. In many cases, as we have seen, a minority of their shares have been floated on the Hong Kong, Shenzhen, or Shanghai stock exchanges, and a handful overseas in London or New York.

Other outstanding issues that the plenum recognized included the need for land reforms, pension problems raised by an ageing population, and the challenge of the floating population of over 200 million, moving from rural areas to the towns and cities, who were denied rights because they were not registered under the *hukou* system, which is a government registration system determining where people are allowed live.

The Chinese government's attempt to reassert control over SOEs

SOEs remain central to China's economy. They include vast companies in the oil, telecom, steel, finance, and other major sectors. In many cases, as we have seen, a minority of their shares have been floated on the Hong Kong, Shenzhen, or Shanghai stock exchanges, and a handful overseas in London or New York.

The corporate governance of these enterprises has been significantly influenced by Western experience. For decades, governance has been left to companies' boards of supervisors and boards of directors, under the oversight of SASAC and the CSRC. State involvement at a higher level had tended to be distant. Some felt that the CPC had been pushed aside in the rush to economic growth and wealth, and the party's leadership undermined.

Not any longer. In October 2016, China's president, Xi Jinping, asserted that "the ultimate bosses of China's state-owned enterprises must be China's Communist Party organs."[2] The president told a high-profile conference of top officials and SOE executives that "after decades of fading into the background, Communist Party's leadership must be boosted in SOEs." The message was clear: the party must reassert its grip on the state sector.

The two-day work conference concluded that the Communist Party must increase its role, especially in ideology, oversight of personnel, and key decisions in the country's biggest industrial and financial enterprises.

"Leadership by the party was the root and soul and a unique advantage of China's state firms, and any weakening, fading, blurring or marginalization of party leadership in state firms will not be tolerated," Xi is quoted as saying. "We must unswervingly uphold the party's leadership in state-owned enterprises, and fully play the role of party organs in leadership and political affairs. We must ensure that wherever our enterprises go, party-building work will follow."

This was the first time that the country's leadership had addressed a meeting specifically on the Communist Party's leadership in state businesses; the first time, in fact, that they had shown any interest in corporate governance. Xi said that China's state firms had to remain loyal to the party's course to be "a reliable force that the party and the nation can trust" and "an important force in firm implementation of the central leadership's decisions."

Since the 18th Party Congress four years ago, the leadership has called for SOEs to be companies "with Chinese characteristics," which means ultimate leadership by the party. In the published comments, the president did not specifically mention boards of directors. He said the Communist Party's should be "embedded" in corporate governance. He also said the leaders of China's state firms should be seen as Communist cadres, serving party interests in the economic realm.

A number of reasons might be suggested why China's leadership has chosen to reassert its ultimate control over SOEs:

- to reverse a slide towards Western capitalist thinking and reassert Communist values.

---

2. *South China Morning Post* (2016, October 12).

- to reinforce the president's sweeping anti-corruption campaign. Corrupt officials in SOEs, as well as the military and the government, have already been punished, but corruption remains endemic.
- to improve performance of the SOEs and spur innovation as the country faces falling economic returns after many years of double-digit growth.
- to build party loyalty and improve control over a huge population, whose relatively affluent middle class now has aspirations to greater independent thought. The existing control over the media, the Internet, and public discussion would be reinforced if SOE management supported party ideals.

The expert on corporate governance in China, quoted earlier in this chapter, also commented that:

"In reality, SOE reform is a complicated process, and there have often been arguments as to how far things have actually improved. Major issues making China's SOE reform and governance very different from the 'Western model' are the important role they play in the national economy and the complications arising from the policy of the Communist Party to control them.

Some specific manifestations of these problems are:

(a) Senior management of SOEs are appointed and removed by the party (not the board). Senior management of SOEs and government policymakers could be shuffled around from time to time.

(b) SOEs have to serve the interest of the party and of the government, and this comes before the interests of shareholders.

(c) This means that SOEs could not be looked at as business entities alone but as part of the national economy.

The dual role of China's SOEs will continue to raise issues and arguments with other countries when they 'go global.' This will be an interesting subject to watch."

The governance of private companies in China

Much of the writing on China's approach to corporate governance focuses on the corporatization and listing of SOEs, what the Chinese call "ownership-diversification." The freeing of enterprise development in China, as it moved from a centrally controlled planned economy to a market-oriented one, has resulted in a resurgence of private business development. The governance of private enterprise firms in China is quite different from the governance of the SOEs both in their processes and the issues they face.

Many of the privately owned firms are family-based businesses that are relatively small, often with only a handful of employees and have intent to keep ownership within the family. The predecessors of many of these company founders were businesspeople in mainland China that left the country in successive waves of the diaspora.[3] Unsurprisingly, therefore, the new firms often reflect the business attitudes and governance processes of the overseas Chinese firms that we mentioned in Chapter 1, including being family-centric with close family control and dependent on a social fabric that emphasizes social harmony and discourages sibling confrontation.

The boss calls the final shot on everything

A lawyer, experienced in corporate law in China, commented that:

"For many privately owned enterprises the boss, not the Board, calls the final shot on everything. The management and governance structure in place are mostly for show, and the boss still gets the final say."

"In practice, this has meant the boss can bypass any rules or procedures. He alone is king. With the new corporate governance infrastructure in place, for example, the CEO typically doesn't want to give up his power and have a problem with imposition of new rules. I have noticed that none of the board issues which should have been discussed by the board had been tabled at all. There was [sic] simply no board meetings. There were no minutes. The company secretary is [sic] weak and incompetent generally."

"One recommendation for any foreign firm, dealing with a company in China, is to conduct a corporate governance review of the current infrastructure before any dialogue."

Researchers Zhong and Zhang[4] show how private enterprises have increased dramatically during China's transition from a planned to a market-led economy and that family business now forms the majority of such private enterprises. They illustrate the incentives for private ownership and highlight how family-based culture is vital. They suggest that trust based on close family relationships replaces trust in government institutions. Trust-sharing arrangements between family members and within the firm are vital. A system of social networks and influential relationships, called in Chinese *guanxi*, allows business relationships and dealings in the private sector to flourish.

---

3. For more information on the business methods of overseas Chinese, see Redding, 1993.
4. Zhong and Zhang, 2013.

However, some of the private company incorporations are significantly larger than are most of the family firms. They cover a diverse range of industrial sectors and cities.

Some of these large private companies have been floated on a stock exchange through an initial public offer. In such cases the sponsoring financial institution, advising on the float, is more likely to pay attention to the record and motivation of the company's founders rather than written longer-term plans. Consistency of performance is more important than is rapid growth, which might not be sustainable. Again, trust at the personal level is crucial. Mutual trust, rather than financial analysis, is the key to good long-term relations between a company's founders and potential investors in China. When trust exists, substantial funds can be made available by financial institutions and fund managers.

In a few cases, significant private companies have been listed abroad in New York or London. In these circumstances the company must meet the demands of the regulators—the US's SEC rules or the UK's corporate governance code, which is part of the London Stock Exchange's (LSE) listing requirements. Consequently, Chinese companies listed overseas typically provide a showcase for sound corporate governance. But they can still have governance issues; for example, see the case of Alibaba Group Holding Ltd, at the end of Chapter 1, which has exemplary corporate governance procedures except for shareholder relations, which raise some serious questions.

Many of the larger private companies have governance issues. A lack of transparency is a significant problem, which can be particularly challenging for foreign investors. Another challenge can be the lack of a moral compass in making business decisions. This lack of ethical standards reflects the fact that many of these companies are led by first-time entrepreneurs, with no experience of business, no moral training, and little guidance.

A few business leaders, however, do seem to be taking a professional approach to governance, particularly where some of their directors or senior executives have relevant training or experience.

For many companies corporate governance is mostly for show . . .

A Chinese banker, who has been responsible for investing in the development and success of client companies in China, provided unique insights into how Chinese businesses often function, said:

"For many companies, corporate governance is mostly for show; even for listed companies. Getting away with the least amount of effort is the game. Transparency is often low or even opaque in China and an investor needs to be aware, especially foreign buyers."

> "In China the most important thing is the integrity and behavior of the founder. Everything else is not that relevant. What I do is to visit the founder, look for 'consistency' in his behaviour. Does he deliver on his promises, for example. I track their meetings, their spending patterns, and their habits. I try to find out as much as possible on each senior executive, creating a dossier on each."
>
> "The newer companies, with young CEOs who have been to MBA programs, are more conscious of the need for stronger corporate governance."

Corporate governance researcher Leng Jing[5] considered the range of enterprises that contributed to the growth of the Chinese economy. In addition to the SOEs and the privately owned enterprises, she recognized the significance of *collectively owned enterprises*, such as urban collectives, rural township organizations, and village entities. The dawning of the market economy in China also produced joint ventures between foreign firms and their Chinese partners.

The development of corporate governance in Hong Kong

Quite unlike in mainland China, corporate governance in Hong Kong evolved under the influence of British law and corporate regulation, reflecting the British oversight of the territory up to 1997, when Hong Kong became a Special Administrative Region (SAR) of China.

In Hong Kong, corporate governance is a fascinating mélange of Anglo-American and Asian ideas. We briefly reviewed the essence in Chapter 1. The corporate governance system is an outgrowth of British company law and regulation.

When Hong Kong became an SAR of China in 1997, it kept its currency (tied to the US dollar), legal system, and institutions, including the SFC, the Institute of Certified Public Accountants, and the Law Society. On the Hong Kong stock market, most listed companies are either family firms with control kept firmly within the family, or mainland China-based corporations, plus a handful of large trading companies.

Although the Hong Kong regulatory authorities require a minimum of three independent non-executive directors, the heads of some family companies see little value in them. Their secretive, authoritarian, and family-centric approach to business does not lend itself to outside directors, who might disagree with their decisions. Furthermore, evidence of abnormal dealing prior to acquisition or merger activity has suggested insider dealing. Incidentally, most Hong Kong–listed Chinese family companies are incorporated in Bermuda or the Cayman Islands, so that, while Hong Kong's listing rules and takeover code apply, Hong Kong companies' ordinances do not (other than those applying to overseas companies).

---

5. Leng, 2009.

In 2014, after many years of deliberation, Hong Kong SAR introduced a new Companies Ordinance designed to simplify and rationalize company law. Among many other provisions, the new law extended the exposure of directors and "other responsible persons" to prosecution for failing to exercise "due care, skill, and diligence." The law also introduced a new solvency test that companies had to meet.

The Hong Kong corporate governance code is based on the "comply or explain" approach and was much influenced by the UK's Cadbury report.[6] It calls for the board of listed companies to have a majority of independent directors, audit, remuneration, and nomination committees, for director and board evaluation, and director induction and training. Compliance levels are relatively high.

Some Chinese SOEs are listed in Hong Kong

An experienced banker commented:

"The SOEs in HK are generally a different breed. They have good corporate governance. The reason they were floated in Hong Kong was to create foreign exchange (the HK$ is pegged to the US$). They also help other Chinese firms to reach overseas. The Hong Kong SOEs are drowning in cash and have been seeding bonds and commercial paper generated by other Chinese firms. Recently, one SOE was able to acquire a US$20M bond, and that SOE came to Hong Kong only a year ago. Some Hong Kong SOEs have been told to avoid foreign investment banks."

One country, two systems of corporate governance

More than two decades of dramatic economic growth that changed the face of China ultimately slowed. A substantial middle class developed with growing middle-class aspirations: property, cars, children's education, fashion, and overseas holidays. Despite controls, a more aggressive news media illuminates the political concerns of this increasingly educated, informed, and vocal population: a potential challenge to the centralist control of the state. People are more aware of the wealth and privileges enjoyed by those at the center of the party. Such concerns have generated a large number of non-governmental organizations, which, although registered, are difficult to regulate and whose governance is important.

Some deregulatory reforms had encouraged freer movement of capital, less involvement by the central bank, and wider use of second board like Hong Kong's Growth Enterprise Market (GEM), and over-the-counter stock markets. Rules on insider trading had been tightened and the crackdown on corruption continued. In Shanghai, the creation of a Free Trade Zone provided some tax incentives, the freer

---

6. The writer was a member of the committee of the Hong Kong Society of Accountants (as it was then called) that drafted the original Hong Kong code.

conversion of currencies, and allowed foreign companies to invest in industries previously out of bounds.

Commentators on corporate governance in China saw a need to improve board effectiveness noting, for example, the low attendance of independent directors at board meetings. The call was for boards to be more tough-minded business-oversight teams, rather than meetings of collaborators linked to the state national and regional authorities.

Three decades ago, corporate governance in China hardly existed. Given the dramatic and sustained economic growth since, the CSRC has done a remarkable job in developing law, rules, and regulations, and introducing appropriate corporate governance attitudes. China is also attempting to bring its accounting and auditing rules in line with international standards, while making allowances for SOEs in a transitional economy.

But challenges remain. The CSRC suffers from being both the promoter of the investment market and its regulator although this can be the case in other markets. Other problems include: the identification, training, and development of independent directors; the potential influence of members of the Communist Party, particularly when directors are also members of a company's Party Committee; and changing attitudes from the previous centralized state-directed decision-making to a market-orientated perspective.

The legal system, although it has ancient traditions, is somewhat lacking in transparency and predictability. The training of judges is still evolving. Bringing private legal action against companies is difficult although a new contract arbitration law was enacted in 2008 that set up a framework for resolving disputes. The people's courts around the country and the Supreme People's Court act primarily in what is seen as the interests of the people, in other words of the state. The recognition of contractual and corporate relationships tends to be limited, and enforcing legal judgments can be problematical.

Although corruption and rigorous penalties (including the death penalty) for wrongdoers are widely reported in the Chinese press, over all the law against commercial corruption is not well enforced.

Hong Kong's financial and corporate governance expertise has played an important role in the business evolution of China. Prior to 1997, Hong Kong experts were consulted on the creation of securities and financial regulation, on accounting and auditing issues, on the incorporation of the SOEs, and on the development of the Shanghai and Shenzhen stock markets. After 1997, when Hong Kong became an SAR of China, that interaction increased markedly. Mainland stocks were traded on the Hong Kong exchange. Interaction between the two financial markets increased. Relationships between the regulatory authorities, the accounting professions, and the business community strengthened, leading some commentators to predict a convergence of corporate governance systems.

That seems unlikely for the foreseeable future. Convergence would imply a single currency, shared company law, and an umbrella regulatory framework. Mainland China needs access to US dollars through Hong Kong's currency link. Stability and sustainability in Hong Kong's economy is vital to the Mainland. Hong Kong's company law is rooted in decades of experience of companies ordinances and case law: the Mainland's company law is emergent and subject to political pressures that reinforce the interests of the state. The regulatory institutions and the processes in each jurisdiction have different goals. For the duration of the Joint Agreement on the future of Hong Kong, "one country, two systems" seems likely to apply to corporate governance. Thereafter, the issue is more likely to be a matter of politics than of corporate governance.

References

China-United States Exchange Foundation. (2011). *US-China Economic Relations in the next ten years.* Retrieved May 1, 2018 from http://www.cusef.org.hk/wp-ontent/uploads/2016/10/Part-01_and_Part-02_Book-1.pdf.

Leng, J. (2009) *Corporate governance and financial reform in China's transition economy.* Hong Kong: Hong Kong University Press.

Lev-Ram, Michal. (2013, February 28), Huawei's Guo Ping on his company's unusual governance structure. *Fortune.* Retrieved May 1, 2018, from http://fortune.com/2013/02/28/huaweis-guo-ping-on-his-companys-unusual-governance-structure/.

Redding, S. G. (1993). *The spirit of Chinese capitalism.* Berlin: Walter de Gruyter.

Schipani, C. A., & Liu, J. (2002). Corporate governance in China: Then and now. *Columbia Business Law Review 1,* 1–69.

South China Morning Post (2016, October 12).

Tenev, S., & Zhang C. L. (2002). *Corporate governance and enterprise reform in China: Building the institutions of modern markets.* Washington, DC: The World Bank and the International Finance Corporation.

Zhang and Zhong, Q. (2013). *Governance of private enterprises in modern China*, Modern China Series. South Florida: North American Business Press.

Case study

Huawei China: Rotating CEOs and corporate culture

In his New Year message for 2017, Eric Xu, described as the company's rotating CEO, said:

> Our sales revenue (next year) is expected to reach 520 billion yuan (US$160bn), up 32% year-on-year. After years of effort, we have put in place a more streamlined delivery process, the Delivery Project is greatly improving delivery efficiency and

quality. In 2016, we at last achieved consistency of inventory accounts and goods, and made significant progress in administrative services.

Huawei is the third-biggest mobile phone manufacturer in the world, offering smartphones, tablets, and gadgets with seamless integration.

The origins of the company

Huawei was founded in 1987 by Ren Zhengfei, a veteran of the PLA. But Huawei's corporate structure remains obscure. Critics question its governance, pointing out that it did not disclose its board members until 2010 and that it continues to be secretive about its ownership. The Chinese government maintains a majority holding, and the company is suspected of still being under the influence of the Chinese military.

Apparently, to reduce the appearance of government control, many shares are held by Huawei employees, allegedly 74,200 employees out of a total of 150,000. Whether these shareholding employees have access to shareholder information, voting rights, or dividends is not known. As employees, these shareholders could be under pressure to conform to corporate instruction.

In a relatively new US government requirement, any company with 20% or more state ownership is deemed state owned, and the employees are government workers or public servants. Consequently, rigid rules apply to their behavior on anti-corruption matters such as entertainment expenses. Overseas suppliers are required to confirm that none of their own employees would collude with Huawei's employees and to report any such attempt.

Huawei has been challenged by both the US government[7] and the Australian government[8] on their business methods. Huawei was sued by US firm Cisco in 2003 for alleged infringement of intellectual rights.

On rotating CEOs

The company has an executive management team (EMT) of eight people, which is part of the full board. The full board meets monthly. A strategy of rotating the role of CEO has been adopted. Three people have been CEO since 2012, all members of the EMT. The rotation appears to have speeded up in recent years. According to Huawei's website: "three Deputy Chairmen take turns to act as the Rotating and Acting CEO for a tenure of six months. In 2015, the three rotating CEOs were:[9]

---

7. Lev-Ram, Michal. (2013, February 28)
8. Government maintains NBN ban on Chinese telco Huawei after security briefings. (2013, October 29). Retrieved May 1, 2018 from http://www.abc.net.au/news/2013-10-29/government-maintains-nbn-ban-on-chinese-telco-huawei-after-secu/5051622.
9. Rotating CEOs. (2018, January 10). Retrieved May 1, 2018 from http://www.huawei.com/en/about-huawei/corporate-governance/rotating-ceos.

- Hu Houkun: October 1, 2014–March 31, 2015
- Xu Zhijun: April 1, 2015–September 30, 2015
- Guo Ping: October 1, 2015–March 31, 2016

The rotating CEO is responsible for finance and crisis management and chairs the EMT. For other EMT matters, decision-making is consensual. On completing his term, the retiring CEO continues as a member of the EMT.

According to Guo Ping, a previous CEO, the idea of a rotating CEO came from the book *Flight of the Buffalo* (by James Belasco and Ralph Stayer), which suggests that the head buffalo in a herd or the lead bird in a V formation of flying geese would switch the lead role with others during their migration.

The CEO's New Year strategic message

Huawei CEO Eric Xu's 2017 New Year message was titled "focusing on creating value for customers, and achieving sustainable growth." He wrote:

> Fear not the drifting clouds that block your eyes: beneath shifting sands bright gold still lies. The year 2016 has seen a flock of black swans—both political and economic—sweep across the globe. Nevertheless, we have remained focused on our strategy and have patiently applied ourselves to making breakthroughs and creating real value for our customers.

Developing his thoughts on the corporate strategy, he added:

> In 2016, our carrier business continued to reinforce its position in network products and services. With cloud, video, and operations transformation as our strategic priorities, we helped grow the industry and move it forward. Throughout this process we have significantly boosted the working capital efficiency of our carrier business while maintaining robust growth.
>
> In close cooperation with our partners worldwide, our enterprise business has delivered innovative products and solutions that help our customers address the challenges of digital transformation. Together, we are building a collaborative ecosystem that promotes shared success. These efforts have translated into profitable and sustainable growth for Huawei in key industries, such as smart cities, energy, finance, transportation, and manufacturing.
>
> Our consumer business has made decisive breakthroughs in the high-end segment of the global smartphone market, taking Huawei's brand influence to the next level.
>
> An intelligent world is on the horizon as new technologies like cloud computing, the Internet of Things, video, big data, and artificial intelligence advance at blazing-fast speed. Carriers around the world are gradually shifting their network construction models from an investment-driven approach to one that is more value-driven. Moving forward, we will work to enable carriers' networks to support more connections; help them position video as a basic service and achieve business success; lead the transformation of their IT systems towards cloud architecture;

and assist them in building digital operations that deliver a real-time, on-demand, all-online, do-it-yourself, and social (ROADS) user experience. Where we stand now, Huawei must maintain a global view and adopt a wider perspective of the industry as we help carriers to transform and thrive with more revenue streams. This is a clear strategic decision for us in this new era.

We will create a joint development model wherein Huawei, our customers, and our partners grow together throughout the digital transformation journey. Our ultimate goal is to become an enabler of industry digitization and a preferred partner throughout this process.

Smart devices will take on an infinite number of forms in the intelligent world. Keeping up with rapidly evolving consumer demand for smart devices will require continuous investment in artificial intelligence, human–machine interface, big data, and other cutting-edge technologies.

In 2017, we will face even greater global political and economic uncertainties, and the information industry will continue to transform. We must identify the challenges before us. Looking ahead, we will take the following measures to address the critical issues that Huawei may encounter in business, operations, organization, and talent.

We must sustain profitable growth and maintain healthy cash flow. The key to this is to improve quality, especially the quality of our contracts and operations. Huawei has realized double-digit revenue growth over the past few years. That said, there has not been much improvement in our operating efficiency and cash flow. Our general and administrative expenses have grown faster than our revenue and sales gross margin have, and our cash-to-revenue ratio is on the decline. The future macro environment is full of risks: the ongoing transformation of the industry, mounting business pressures faced by our customers, and escalating economic uncertainties around the globe. As we aim to seize new opportunities, we must be better prepared for risks.

All business units must pursue profitable growth and healthy cash flow. To do this, they must make every effort to increase operating efficiency, reduce general and administrative expenses, manage long overdue inventories and accounts receivable, and improve cash flow.

We must avoid unnecessary formalities. We should focus on creating value and solving problems for our customers. We will emphasize the following in 2017:

- We will build capabilities around our strategy and changes in business, so as to truly help customers rise above their challenges and difficulties.
- We will firmly implement Huawei's eight principles for improving the work ethic of managers.
- Our human resource policy should help reduce entropy in our workforce, infusing the organization with life and passion.
- We will continue to comply with the law and create a favourable business environment.

Questions for discussion

1. Is a rotating CEO a good idea? Why?

2. How often should the role of CEO rotate?

3. What are your reactions to Huawei's strategic perspective offered by the CEO in his New Year message?

   The CEO's full New Year message can be read at: http://www.huawei.com/en/special-release/new-year-message-2017?ic_source=corp_box121_newyear&ic_medium=hwdc.

4

Culture and Ethics in Chinese Corporate Governance

Bob Tricker

Gregg Li

In this chapter we consider:

- ❖ what culture is and why it is relevant to corporate governance
- ❖ Modern business ethics in China
- ❖ the essence of contemporary Chinese business culture
- ❖ corporate social responsibility with a Chinese face
- ❖ the effect of culture in overseas Chinese businesses
- ❖ insights into business ethics in modern China
- ❖ the influence of religion on the development of corporate governance
- ❖ the proliferation of Buddhist, Confucian, and Daoist thoughts in modern China
- ❖ comparison of Buddhism with Confucianism and Party ethics
- ❖ Communist Party ethics
- ❖ the need for a moral compass in Chinese corporate governance

What culture is and why it is relevant to corporate governance

Culture can be thought of as the social heritage of beliefs, expectations, and values that people share. Over the years, the culture of a country is influenced by its geography; its history of social, economic, and political change; and its religion. Culture is molded by situations that affect relations between individuals, institutions, and the state. Culture influenced by experience, education, and law, is reflected in the language, and is passed on by life in families and organizations. The culture of a country influences what is thought of as acceptable, important, and right or wrong. It affects how people think and act. It is fundamental to understanding corporate governance. For companies, culture means the way things have been done around the company. Often nebulous and unclear, culture would come to reinforce or slow down any corporate governance practices introduced by a board of directors.

In the late twentieth century, when ideas about corporate governance began to be discussed, much of the thinking and practice was influenced by countries that shared Anglo-American culture: a belief in the rule of law; the importance of the rights of individuals to personal freedom and ownership of property; individual accountability, and the existence of accountable, democratic institutions, including an independent judiciary.

In the United States, corporate governance practices stemmed from the rule of company law laid down by state jurisdictions and at the federal level by regulation from the US SEC. In the UK, and subsequently in most Commonwealth countries associated with the UK (including Hong Kong), the corporate governance of companies was controlled by companies acts, and for listed companies by corporate governance codes, reinforced by stock exchange rules, which required companies to report compliance with the code or explain why they had not.

Protecting the family is highly valued in Chinese society

A qualified accountant and CFO of a listed company, who has traveled widely in China as internal auditor, commented that:

"Because of the focus on family, I believe family members are less embarrassed if a family member is exposed for corruption. This value set contrasts with those of Western or Hong Kong society, where no family would want to be associated with a family member that is corrupt. In other words, some Chinese believe taking advantage of the government can be seen as an acceptable and tolerable behavior [as everyone seems to be doing it]. The Beijing government is too distant to care. The key is to benefit the family at the expense of the government; and if there's a draw between the two, family always comes first. It is not unusual for those caught to bargain with the authority to let their family members go. They would let their kids live in Canada, or go to finishing schools while they, as the main culprit, would go to jail."

Many then thought that other countries would gradually converge with these Western corporate governance models, because they needed to raise capital, trade in securities, and do business globally. Institutions such as the World Bank and the OECD[1] have put considerable efforts into advising developing countries, including China, about modern corporate governance practices.

In China, the rules exist but enforcement is lax

A financial expert, who has lived in mainland China since the 1990s, gave some insight into the management of SOEs in China:

"There's a huge amount of manuals with instructions on everything, quite Byzantine. The laws in China are actually quite comprehensive. The Mainlanders have taken procedures and policies to such an extreme that there's hardly

---

1. The Organisation for Economic Co-operation and Development.

anything without a procedure. For example, as a director of a US firm, I had to sign declarations of 'no conflict' all the time. Unless these are signed, nothing moves.

But the Chinese generally have a lax latitude on enforcement. This is how they get things done, working around the rigid system. I could get away with delaying signing things, sometimes for over a year, while I got on with business. This is one stark contrast with how policies and procedures work in US companies. In the US, things are simply too black or white."

These arguments are seldom heard these days. Capital can be raised elsewhere than in London or New York. Securities can be traded on other stock exchanges.[2] Globalization became a dominant feature in world trade as some countries offered significantly lower cost of goods or services. Subsequent attempts by some countries to protect their own industries and labor force challenged the onrush of globalization. Controls on the flow of people, money, information and ideas also retarded globalization.

The globalization of the movement of goods, services, money, people, and information that had occurred, some thought, would inevitably lead to a convergence of intellectual insights, politics, and ideology. This notion, which might be termed "globalism," seems unlikely to survive. Instead, in the twenty-first century, discussion about corporate governance has increasingly recognized the significance of local culture to successful governance practices.

The quality of compliance in corporate governance is pretty shoddy . . .

A Hong Kong lawyer, who has extensive experience of due diligence, fraud investigation, and legal compliance in China, emphasizes that:

"The core message is that, although systems and practices do exist in China, the quality of execution and compliance is pretty shoddy."

Modern business ethics in China

Following the global financial crisis in 2008, modern business ethics has gradually become much more prominent and ubiquitous. The call for Corporate Social Responsibility (CSR), whereby corporations are expected to find ways to give back to the society beyond just taxes, or the demand of fair treatment for factory workers, or the requests for higher level of transparency on the pay levels of CEOs has now become the norm of good business ethics in China as well. Corporate sustainability

2. The stock exchanges of Singapore and Hong Kong now rank third and fourth in significance after London and New York.

means managing the entire supply chain. To many Chinese, ethics means the manner in which they would want to live their lives while they are on this earth.

The essence of contemporary Chinese business culture

The early moral influence in China was Confucianism, founded around 500 BC. This was not a religion with deities or beliefs in a life hereafter although rituals were involved. Rather, Confucius taught respect for others and a sense of continuity based on hierarchy: older people, the head of the family, the family clan, scholars, officials, and ultimately the emperor. Confucianism was about the practicalities of everyday life. Subsequently, in parts of China, Buddhism, Daoism, and other religions, including Christianity, added to the impact.

The overall effect was a civilization based more on a sense of relationships rather than on strong religious beliefs, with their associated moral values. In its origins, the Confucian social code sought harmony and filial piety through a hierarchy of proper relationships between emperor and subject, father and son, husband and wife, brother and brother, and friend and friend. These relationships are based on mutual trust and interdependence, for the mutual benefit of all parties.

In China today, in both personal and business dealings, special relationships or connections, known by the Chinese word *guanxi*, are paramount. Both Chinese and Western scholars have sought to determine the real meaning of the word.[3]

Leung and Wong[4] explain that "four dimensions are embedded within *guanxi*: opportunism, business interaction, dynamism, and protectionism." They further comment that their research has "revealed that *guanxi* practice in China is essentially ethical. But the ethical standard varies depending upon the legal framework within a specific location." All Chinese build a *guanxi* web of connections as they go through life. These relationships, which reflect trust between the parties, can be flexible over time, provide protection, favors, and other benefits but also create obligations. Therefore, Chinese would make it a practice to reach out to people whom they do not know and build at least a working relationship.

Historically, relationships that existed in the financial community, in which deals were sealed with a handshake, reflected a similar mutual trust. In today's Western culture, deals need written contracts signed under the law with the threat of subsequent litigation. In China, to deal with this *guanxi*, we have learned that some companies just assume everyone is connected and install procurement systems that automatically require two independent appraisals for large purchases.

An effect of *guanxi* networks is that they enable people to build up a sense of their own worth as seen by others. Often called "face," the fear of "loss of face", or the need to "save face," is found in many cultures and reflected in many languages,

---

3. Redding, 2013
4. Leung & Wong, 2001.

but the notion originated in China and continues to be a fundamental concept in personal and business relationships.

The writers have experience in the US, the UK, and Hong Kong with MBA students. Using case studies in discussion in class, American students, and to a lesser extent, British students, will argue their case competitively, sometimes aggressively, in front of their peers. Moreover, they defend their analysis and proposals against other students. The Chinese students, though possibly more intelligent, will not engage in a confrontational exchange for fear of losing face. Harmony is more important. Small group presentations are usually more productive to achieve the learning experience.

Decision-making is collective. No one department has overall authority.

A regional director of a professional firm, selling its services throughout Asia, has dealt with some large Chinese SOEs for nearly 30 years. He described the difficulty he sometimes had with finalizing a contract with some of these "huge bureaucracies":

"No department or manager has 'super authority.' It is consensual. An American firm would say 'my lawyer held it up because he felt this part isn't right.' He is seen to be accountable. The Chinese would say: 'someone from another department has a problem with this,' but you won't know which department. This makes it impossible to consummate a contract. I am never told why . . . Although a contract is not signed, we are often into the program and are not paid. This is an issue with other overseas firms."

Regarding the contract, the Chinese side does not have a point person to sign. No one is put in a position to be held singularly accountable. Hardly anyone has explicit authority, and no one is made to be explicitly powerful.

Corporate social responsibility with a Chinese face

In 1970, Milton Friedman argued that the purpose of business was to make a profit, to create wealth, and to increase shareholder value in the longer term. It was the role of governments, he argued, to set the rules for companies' behavior. In the Western business world, the "Friedman debate" has largely been resolved. Friedman lost.

The widely accepted view today is that companies do have a responsibility to their stakeholders—employees, suppliers, customers, and others affected by their actions—as well as to society at large. That companies do have CSR are widely accepted although there are those who still agree with Friedman.

In the UK prior to 2006, company law required directors to act in the best interests of the company, which effectively meant in the long-term interest of the shareholders. But the 2006 UK Companies Act specifically spelled out a statutory duty to recognize the effect of board decisions on a wider public. For the first time, UK company law required companies to consider employees, suppliers, customers, and other business partners, as well as the community and the environment, in their decisions. The formal duties of company directors now included:

> A director of a company must act in the way he considers, in good faith, would be most likely to promote the success of the company for the benefit of its members as a whole, and in doing so have regard to:
> (a) the likely consequences of any decision in the long term;
> (b) the interests of the company's employees;
> (c) the need to foster the company's business relations with suppliers, customers and others;
> (d) the impact of the company's operations on the community and the environment;
> (e) the desirability of the company maintaining a reputation for high standards of business conduct; and
> (f) the need to act fairly as between members of the company.

In China, the situation is different. When state agencies ran business, setting production quotas, fixing prices, establishing staffing levels, and so on, profit was not a meaningful measure of performance; and rules for social, political, and environmental requirements were set by the state. The corporatization of the SOEs and the creation of a market-driven economy changed all that, allowing China to become the second-largest economy in the world in two decades. As Irwin[5] pointed out:

> China's economy has changed during the last quarter of a century from a centrally planned system that was largely closed to international trade, to a more market-oriented economy that has a rapidly growing private sector and is a major player in the global economy. Some of the biggest companies in the world are found in China. Their names largely unknown in the West, some operating in over 50 countries, they control extraction, manufacturing, supply and distribution networks in many different industries.

Profit and return on investment has now become meaningful measures of performance. CSR was also recognized as significant. It was first introduced in response to requirements from major overseas customers who were largely American corporations. During contractual negotiations for CSR, standards had to be set and met. Subsequently, state industry bureaucrats realized that CSR measures would also be a useful means of setting standards for their SOEs while constraining excesses in their activities.

China's rapid economic transformation, urbanization with massive movement of population, and the demographics of an aging population (amplified by the 1979 one-child family policy) have led to concern over social and economic inequality. China's huge industrial growth in recent years has also caused significant environmental degradation—serious air pollution, soil erosion, and water shortages. The

---

5. Irwin, 2012.

need for business enterprises, which were at the core of these problems, emphasized the need for CSR to be taken seriously.

Irwin[6] also commented that:

> Many Western investors have found that commitment to CSR—with the public benefits it brings—can be very helpful in winning local or central government officials over to supporting a company's investment objectives. Understanding that the Government will evaluate any CSR initiative in terms of its overarching goal of a 'harmonious society' is crucial to evaluating what is achievable in China.

Reflecting the growing recognition of the importance of CSR, in 2009, the China Banking Association issued CSR Guidelines for financial institutions. These guidelines suggested that the CSR reports should cover responsibility for economic, social, and environmental issues. In 2008, the Chinese Academy of International Trade & Economic Cooperation (CAITEC) published guidelines on "Corporate Social Responsibility Compliance for Foreign Invested Enterprises," which emphasized the need for companies to consider social needs as well as profit. The guidelines encouraged companies to engage in research and development with local universities, respond when public emergencies occurred, and develop procedures to meet environmental emergencies.

The effect of culture in overseas Chinese businesses

Later in this book we will explore the effect of culture on the governance of vast SOEs and other businesses in China. But before that, there is another field of experience that is worth considering: the governance of firms run for many years by Chinese outside mainland China.

Over the years, as a result of the Chinese diaspora from the Mainland, Chinese business people, typically called the "overseas Chinese," have played a fundamental part in the business life of Southeast Asia. Many companies in the significant Asian economies—Singapore, Taiwan, Malaysia, Thailand, Indonesia, Hong Kong, and the Philippines—are owned by Chinese families.

In the governance of overseas Chinese companies, power is exercised through relationships between the key players, particularly between the dominant head of the family and other family members in key top management positions. The board of directors in these companies tends to play a legal, supportive role. Some of these companies are quite diverse groups with considerable delegation of power to the subsidiary units, but with the owner-manager, or a family-orientated small group, still holding a strategic hand on the tiller.

---

6. Ibid.

Research into the management of overseas Chinese companies, Redding[7] has suggested some distinguishing characteristics, which reflect governance practices. These studies have shown that overseas Chinese firms are:

- family-centric with close family control;
- controlled through an equity stake kept within the family;
- entrepreneurial, often with a dominant entrepreneur, so that decision-making is centralized, with close personal links emphasizing trust and control;
- paternalistic in management style, in a social fabric dependent on relationships and social harmony, avoiding confrontation and the risk of the loss of "face";
- strategically intuitive, the business seen as more of a succession of contracts or ventures, relying on intuition, superstition, and tough-minded bargaining rather than strategic plans, brand creation, and quantitative analysis.

Where such companies are listed on a stock market, the outside shareholders tend to be in a minority. Consequently, regulatory authorities emphasize the importance of disclosure and the control of related-party transactions.

Although many corporate governance codes require independent non-executive directors, the independence of outside directors is less important to the owner than their character, trustworthiness, and overall business ability are. Of course, corporate governance problems exist in Chinese and overseas Chinese companies: corruption, insider trading, unfair treatment of minority shareholders, and domination by company leaders, to name a few.

Insights into business ethics in modern China

Interviews with professional experts and businesspeople who have been intimately involved in the recent development of companies in China, though differing in detail, all have a similar orientation. Business ethics is rapidly improving, and the party seems to be providing the spiritual underpinning. Business ethics in modern China is quite unlike those in the rest of the world, as can be seen from the following insights. As generalization is difficult, a few passages from insiders should provide the reader a better glimpse of the reality:

"The standard of ethics is unbelievably low . . ."

An investment banker with a professional financial qualification from a Chinese university, who is now executive director responsible for investing in developing companies in China, commented:

---

7. Redding, 2013.

"Ethics (in the companies I work with) are nearly non-existent. Businessmen will do anything for money, fame, or love. The standard of ethics is unbelievably low, but this is to be expected, as many are first-time entrepreneurs. Many of them have not been exposed to religion and therefore have no understanding of morality.

If there are no rules, then many believe everything can be done, which is the British way. But others believe in the reverse, which is the American way: one can only do what the rules allow. Both types of individual can be found in China at the same time."

The lack of professionalism

A professional accountant, whose insights were quoted earlier in this chapter, also commented on business ethics in China:

"One reason for the lack of ethics (in Chinese companies) is the lack of professionalism in China. In Western countries, no accountant would sign off on any document unless these documents were true. A professional accountant always does and verifies any claims. Because professionalism is weak (as professionalism was only introduced a few years back), many accountants would just look the other way. Many foreign accountants would resign rather than falsify any financial records. This may not be true for many Chinese accountants, who are less committed to such ideals. For example, anyone can get false accounts verification from a banker, and a good accountant never relies on such a paper. Any professional can be bribed. One needs a good professional accountant, and that accountant has to be much smarter and more streetwise to see through veils of deceit."

Don't get caught . . .

An auditor who was responsible for preparing Chinese companies for listing in the late 1970s, and continues to be much involved, said about business ethics in China:

"The perception and standards of ethics (of many Chinese executives) is: 'Don't get caught.' Because everything is typically opaque, one has to rely on relationships to build trust and confirm reliance. Opaqueness also means you can get away with it, as long as you are not caught. Not telling people or not being explicit is one way of protecting and reinforcing this veil. This seems to be the unspoken rule of many managers of SOEs, in those days. Guanxi is so important. You have to trust those whom you know."

On business ethics in China

The managing director of a professional firm involved in China over the years said:

"Ethics is different these days in China. People are too money hungry. Today, we appear to have less time, and now we trade our values for other things. The future is getting more unpredictable, so people have a tendency to want payback now. Investing in the future is not as important for many. Even here in our firm, we are more expedient and want money now, not later. Forget about long-term people development. But such behavior is also more common with suppliers these days."

"There's always a person on the China side who will do the impossible to get things done. Both sides know who this person is. It's the Chinese way of plausible deniability. You don't want to know what or how this person does things. He just does."

Corruption has to be in millions or billions to be worthwhile

The managing director of a private equity firm in Hong Kong with extensive China experience said:

"Typically it is during procurement that corruption is exercised. But I have found that the SOEs are much cleaner and I would rather work with these guys than with the private firms. I believe that foreign firms are much better off working with the SOEs because they have gone through many types of reform. SOEs cannot and won't collude with you for a few thousand or hundreds of thousands of dollars. It is suicidal, because of the overlapping checks and balances. Someone would find out and you are barred for life, or worse end up in jail. Corruption has to be in millions or billions to be worthwhile, and that means there needs to be collusion across the company. There is a reason: people are transferred often. The executives want promotion, as that brings lots of fringe benefits. But demotion means a huge loss of face. Executives are motivated to do well because they want to be promoted. Corruption was bad 10 years ago, but after the 2007 reforms, it is no longer a real problem."

The reason for this is that the executives want promotion (as that comes with lots of fringe benefits and face). Demotion is huge face-losing. Each executive is incentivized to do well because he or she wants to be promoted.

Chinese up there forgot what ethics are . . .

A lawyer with extensive experience of due diligence, fraud investigation, and legal compliance in China, commented that:

"Before the crackdown on corruption by the Party before 2017, many Chinese had forgotten what ethics is. Breaking and getting away with things seems to be the acceptable practice now, since lots of super-rich and government bureaucrats have done the same. [They believe that] it is foolish not to do the same."

"Trust in their system is low, so people rely on the trust of friends. If they trust you, they will trust you entirely, with all their wealth. Everyone knows the system is rigged, so if you are not caught, then it must be proper. But lawyers are gaining respect; so are teachers. This is a good thing."

"For public companies, it is common for workers to abuse the system and use company goods for their families—using a company car for private outings, that sort of thing. It is expected. In China, you can buy receipts and make up your accounts."

"Then again, we shouldn't be too harsh on the Chinese. Other countries are also corrupt. In the United States we recently had the Wells Fargo case in which employees [of this bank] were asked to increase the number of account holders and cross-sell products. For example, if a customer had a bank account, he or she should be sold a credit card account as well. If a staff member was not able to expand the customer base or cross-sell, he or she would be removed."

The influence of religion on the development of corporate governance

Religious beliefs in every country affect personal values, relationships, and attitudes to authority. They influence morals, ethical standards, and acceptable business behavior. Underpinning beliefs are reflected in the way business decisions are made, corporate entities operate, and corporate governance practices develop in different countries.

The United States was founded by the Puritans seeking religious freedom. The founding fathers, the majority of whom were lawyers, placed great emphasis on their constitution, the rule of law, and democratic rights. Those same traits are reflected in the governance of American companies to this day. Legal contracts, litigation, and shareholder rights are still at the forefront of business issues.

In the United Kingdom, in contrast, the approach to corporate governance was more flexible, less rule-based and litigious, reflecting the broader traditions of Britain's religious inheritance. The Church of England, rejecting control from Rome, established freedom of expression and tolerated other non-conformist religious traditions, which became embedded in British culture. The voluntary approach to corporate governance—"conform or explain why not"—reflects this more flexible, voluntary approach.

Other countries influenced by Britain during the days of the British Empire (including Australia, Canada, South Africa, other countries in Africa and the West Indies, as well as Hong Kong and Singapore) shared these corporate governance influences.

In Germany, the teachings of Martin Luther, 500 years ago, shaped the country's language and changed its way of life. Luther influenced belief in the moral imperative to seek principle and order, to be prudent with money, and to avoid debt. Southern European nations, influenced by Roman Catholicism, take a less austere approach, a distinction that is still being played out among the nations that adopted the euro as their national currency. Northern European nations were also affected by the teaching of John Calvin, which emphasized the importance of working for the community, not just for their families and themselves. Germany's co-determination laws view companies as partnerships between labor and capital. In the two-tier board governance structure, the supervisory board contains representatives of the workers as well as the shareholders.

The influence of religion on corporate governance practices can be seen strikingly in Japan. Shinto, the national religion, and Buddhism have been the dominant religious influences. Even though relatively few Japanese now identify with either religion, belief in spirits is widespread. Shrines to spirit deities are commonplace.

Social cohesion is a dominant feature of Japanese business life, with high levels of unity throughout the organization, non-adversarial relationships, lifetime employment, enterprise unions, personnel policies emphasizing commitment, initiation into the corporate family, decision-making by consensus, cross-functional training, and promotion based on loyalty and social compatibility as well as performance.

The Japanese *keiretsu* networks connect groups of Japanese companies through cross-holdings and interlocking directorships; member companies tend to inter-trade extensively. Chairpersons and senior directors of companies in the *keiretsu* meet regularly and have close, informal relationships. Although the paternalistic relationship between company and lifetime "salaryman" is under economic pressure, boards still tend to be decision-ratifying bodies rather than Western-style decision-making forums. Boards tend to be large, made up of the higher echelons of the management hierarchy, with close informal relationships between the members. Meetings of the entire board tend to be ceremonial, and honorable titles are used on social occasions.

Of course, the cultural significance of religion does not mean that religious organizations played any part in the development of corporate governance norms. Indeed, in some countries, the UK and Japan for example, many people no longer claim any religious affiliation. But the religious inheritance influenced those who developed corporate governance processes, because culture affects beliefs about what is appropriate and acceptable. In each of the countries mentioned above, the religious culture provides the ethical context, the moral influence in creating law, running business, and developing corporate governance practices.

The proliferation of Buddhist, Confucian, and Daoist thoughts in modern China

This section begins with a quick overview of the status of Buddhism in China, which started as a barely permitted religion under the atheist Communist regime, to becoming the largest religious group anywhere in the world today. After having covered Buddhism, we will touch on the new Confucianism and Daoism as well.[8]

Buddhism with its "open" beliefs and philosophy may again be in the right position to blossom in China in the future. A key reason for this, we believe, is that the party's search, and permission, for a philosophy to help combat growing unethical business practices in the Mainland. Buddhism should fill in gaps not covered by Confucianism and party ethics. Buddhism appears to be slowly gaining support, to again become a pillar of modern Chinese thought and culture along with New Confucianism and interestingly, the Community Party, as the third pillar.

Despite the popularity of Buddhism in modern China, influential Buddhist businesspeople in China have been rare. How Buddhism has been translated into business ethics is not so evident. One would expect to be seeing more business codes of Buddhist ethics being endorsed by a company's board of directors. But this is not yet the case.

As China came out of the Cultural Revolution, and stepped into globalization, with the temptation of wanton greed in some quarters, a demand grew for more spiritual and non-material guidance against unethical business excesses. Buddhist ethical beliefs, along with Confucianism to a certain extent, have had some relevance for modern business in China and are being recruited into China's fight against the excesses of greed reflected in the Four Modernizations: a balanced drive for harmony, growth, and prosperity with control and anti-corruptive practices. Buddhism in China, post 1980s and following Deng's Four Modernizations, has become more popular and pervasive.

In fact, we believe that this growing popularity of Buddhism has been made possible also by a declining standard of ethics and morality in China. We suspect the Chinese authorities have realized this and have quietly allowed Buddhism to flourish. How deeply Buddhism can be entrenched into the ever-changing Chinese psyche in the future will depend on leadership, Buddhist as well as party leadership. Buddhism can only become stronger with more practitioners in leadership

---

8. Because China has not been too transparent about the development of Buddhist practices, we have had to rely on direct interviews. Materials for this paper have been compiled from interviews with Chinese businesspeople, from a review of the literature on business ethical standards, and corporate governance in recent press, academic journals, and from interpreting government policies for the listing of companies.

positions who can exemplify and demonstrate to investors and outsiders that Buddhist practices work in twenty-first-century China.

Comparison of Buddhism with Confucianism and Party ethics

Buddhist morality is far-reaching. Through its various teachings, Buddhism also promotes practices of generosity, equanimity (fair treatment to all, regardless of status), compassion, selflessness, non-violence, humility, chastity, purity, patience, contentment, abstinence, temperance, benevolence, liberality,[9] reverence, gratitude, tolerance and acceptance of other's points of views, impartiality and righteousness, and respect for the environment (circular economy). Buddhists have many precepts and many are embedded in sutras.

Buddhism sits well with societal ethics endorsed by the party. First, Buddhism is an individualistic religion and the aim is self-perfection.[10] Anything that helps the individual to attain enlightenment is considered good. Anything that deprives the individual of this goal is considered bad. But Buddhism is also a religion for society; what is good for an individual is also good for society. From a societal perspective Buddhism advocates benevolence, liberality, reverence, gratitude, and tolerance in particular.[11] These virtues would complement both the party's code of ethics and Confucianism.

Although the communist ideals have no room for religion in Chinese society, China has been deeply ingrained by the religions and philosophies principally of Buddhism, Confucianism, and Daoism. It is impossible to isolate the impact of any one in particular. Mao failed to remove Confucianism with his Cultural Revolution. These systems of religious and philosophical thought have laid the groundwork for the acceptance of "foreign" practices that might affect how practices of control and transparency under modern corporate governance would be adapted in China.

China has been a melting pot for things that work. Sustainability is made stronger through practice. These religions and philosophies, and the moral principles that they endorse, will continue to influence how foreign ethical standards and practices are adopted in China. In corporate governance practices, any foreign practice that works would be adopted; and anything that would not, would be immediately removed. Nothing is ever taken for granted.

Chinese are practical people. The Chinese culture is not based on monotheism and talk of metaphysics, the next life, or the afterlife. Like Confucianism, Buddhism has highly practical moral standards and avoids the metaphysical. "Buddhism is a religion of common sense, with practicability as its characteristic

---

9. Liberality is an extension of benevolence. Benevolence is a charitable feeling, while liberality is charitable actions. See Tachibana, 1994.
10. Ibid., 270.
11. Ibid., 271.

feature.[12] Pragmatism, a term later hijacked by Deng in the drive towards the Four Modernizations, probably most aptly describes the Chinese culture. This is a culture with morals and ethics that focus on humanism, on nature, on human welfare, on compromises, and on the present. The teaching of Karma from Buddhism is ingrained in the psyche of many Chinese, everyone ultimately held responsible for his or her own action and with no justification for wayward decisions or divine will.

Buddhism, Confucianism, and Daoism are ingrained in the Chinese psyche. To what extent is difficult to assess, particularly after the Cultural Revolution. The Confucian philosophy of life is confined to this life, and it teaches everyone to participate in life and contribute to society—with order, hierarchy, harmony, compassion, and respect of the family and ancestry, known as filial piety. There are six core traditional Confucian values on ethical conduct that center on human beings, very similar to Kant:[13]

1. Benevolence (*ren*),
2. Righteousness (*yi*),
3. Ritual propriety (*li*),
4. Wisdom (*zhi*),
5. Trustworthiness (*xin*), and
6. Filial piety (*xiao*).

The idea of righteousness or uprightness (*yi*) relates to living and behaving according to moral principles, rather than on material gain and excluding self-interested or egoistic behaviors. Confucianism, like Buddhism, is about self-control, self-cultivation, and the refinement of one's character. But unlike Buddhism, Confucian places greater emphasis on relationship and the unique rituals and respects between certain types of relationship.[14] Of the two philosophies, Confucianism has played a much more central role in the Chinese psyche and is often referred to as the core of being Chinese, more so than Buddhism. Unique to Confucianism is the discussion of "face" or *mianzi* or *lian* in Chinese, and giving each other sufficient "face" underpins much of Chinese business ethics.[15]

Likewise, Confucianism has become more popular in China today, we believe, because of authorities' implicit recognition that ethical conduct in business does need additional support. China was primarily an agrarian society, and the rapid ascent in economic development inevitably put business ethics and morality to the test. Moreover, the Cultural Revolution, for many, removed many fundamental religious and traditional philosophical beliefs, including what is right and what is

---

12. Ibid., 6.
13. Froese, 2013.
14. There are five types of relationship that require special and constant attention: sovereign and subject, father and son, husband and wife, elder brother and younger brother, and between friends. The relationships between mother and daughter, or between mother and son, are not emphasized, and this absence reflects the culture prominent during the Confucius period.
15. Fan, 2001.

wrong. Confucian philosophy, with its stress on harmony, order, and hierarchical relationship, would seem to be a natural belief system for the Community Party despite past misgivings the party had with Confucianism.

Today, the "New" Confucianism is being sponsored by the United Front Department, and the establishment of Confucian Institutes since 2004 have been an instrument of goodwill to foreign countries. How the world has turned![16] By 2014, China had opened 465 Confucius Institutes in 123 countries to promote the Chinese culture and language.[17] China has no qualms about endorsing Confucianism.

What about Daoism? Daoist thought and practices of sustainability, respect for nature, duality, change, and resilience have permeated Chinese society as well. But Daoism also brings superstition and does not address business ethics or Buddhism. The party has been eager to get rid of superstitious practices, which are still prevalent in villages.

Communist Party ethics

The CPC, which reportedly has 89 million members,[18] sets a specific foundation for ethical conduct. The CPC's code is even more realistic and practical than is Buddhist ethics. In early 2010, the party issued the 52 Code of Ethics, replacing the old code of 1997, and in 2015 further raised the bar.

This new code of ethics forbids party officials from receiving any sort of bribes or from indirectly benefiting their friends and relatives. Children, spouses, relatives, and in-laws are specifically forbidden as beneficiaries in certain transactions. Frugality, independence, for-profit activities, and vagrant partying were banned with a combination of other policies, particularly on a new one issued on January 1, 2016, by the Political Bureau of the CPC Central Committee.[19] The "combined" code stipulates that party officials today would no longer be allowed[20] to:

- engage in for-profit activities;
- use official vehicles for personal errands;
- establish enterprises;
- trade power for sex;
- register companies outside China;
- own stocks or bonds of non-listed companies;
- undertake overseas tours;

---

16. During the Cultural Revolution, Confucian behavior and practices were heavily condemned.
17. Ching, 2014; Peter, 2012. This article looks at the role the institute is playing outside China and encourages tighter scrutiny.
18. Zhang & Yao, 2013. The number of CPC members in China had surpassed 85 million by mid-2013, according to the latest figures from the Organization Department of the CPC Central Committee. By December 31, 2015, that number had risen to 88.758 million.
19. Huang, 2015; Zhang, 2015.
20. Chinese Communist Party issues code of ethics to ensure clean governance. (2010, February 24).

- undertake high-cost "recreational" activities from weddings to funerals;
- engage in insider trading;
- play golf (as this would be considered an immoral behavior);
- take citizenship overseas; and
- take part-time employment.

In general, party cadres are not allowed to engage in activities against social norms, professional ethics, and family virtues.[21]

The key reasons seem to be the need to tackle corruption (the 2010 code outlined 52 unacceptable practices). The party expected that the code would be more strictly enforced than would the law, especially for party officials. Since late 2012, more than 244,000 officials have been punished.[22]

The Communist Party appeared to have resorted to strengthening party ethics along lines of traditional Confucian virtues, known as *de* in Chinese, which are not exactly ethics in translation. In ancient China, virtue, which was primarily Confucian in nature, was what was considered proper and the right thing to do. Here, virtue is applied more like instruments of governance, which for the party would include, among other things, according to Brødsgaard:[23]

a) belief in the socialist and communist ideal;
b) serving the people;
c) collectivism;
d) patriotism;
e) love of science;
f) love of work;
g) revolutionary heroism;
h) revolutionary humanitarianism; and
i) new types of social public ethics, professional ethics, and family virtues.

The need for a moral compass in Chinese corporate governance

The Cultural Revolution, between 1966 and 1976, put a temporary halt to the influence of Confucianism. The Red Guard uprooted professionals and intellectuals to work in the fields; families were moved to communes; so-called bourgeois tendencies were attacked; religious practices refuted; and private property seized. Massive starvation around the country followed.

China's more recent economic history has also had a destabilizing effect. Millions have left their villages and the land and moved to urban towns and cities to work in factories. Although belief in spirits still survives, together with reverence for ancestors over the generations, the massive social distortions created first by the

21. Ibid.
22. Sha, 2017.
23. Bianzhi and cadre management in China: The case of Yangpu. In Brødsgaard & Zheng, 2006.

Cultural Revolution and then by urbanization destroyed centuries-old traditional family and village culture.

In the society that is emerging in China, ancient traditions and beliefs, though not forgotten, have faded. The Confucian ethic with its strict sense of filial piety and ancestor worship, social propriety, norms of family and community behavior, allied with a strong sense of hierarchy, has ceased to have much effect as populations have moved from family homes in villages to urban life in cities.

Social conditions and new institutional structures, including large numbers of new businesses, no longer support the old ideology. In China today, many people, particularly the young, have no religious inheritance. They lack role models and norms for ethical behavior. There are few signposts for what is acceptable in business. The only overarching ideology available is that of the Chinese Communist Party. However, central authorities have made some attempts to stabilize society by rehearsing the Confucian traditions of respect for order and obedience to the higher authority of government, as explained.

Corruption in the construction industry in China

The experience of a professional who owns a Chinese architectural firm, mentioned earlier in this chapter, is that:

"The construction and architectural industry has become very competitive. There isn't much innovation. Hong Kong is not a big enough market for us to achieve scale, so reaching into the Mainland was sensible. We have to be all things to all people. We build schools, small houses, small projects, and our competitors do the same."

"But, Chinese Mainlanders these days no longer consider Hong Kong architects special. We are seen more like Chinese professionals who don't speak fluent Putonghua. That aura of earlier years has gone, which means we can't command that level of fees. We are now only 50% more valuable than the locals. It wasn't like this 10 years ago."

He gave further insights into corruption:

"In every country, the construction industry is known for corruption. But I believe corruption in China today is much more tolerable and manageable than it was 20 years ago."

"We have a code of conduct, and we try to keep it as simple as possible. This sets a decision framework for our partners and suppliers as well. It is not very specific, and we can't be anything but clean. No code can cover all contingencies. My firm has not condoned corruption of any type."

"There are three reasons for this: Firstly, we try to take on the role as a consultant and not as the owners (developers) of the projects. Owners in China pay us to provide professional input, and then there's hardly any reason for bribes. We carry out the work as professionals and avoid being put in a position to bribe others. We have purposely chosen this role in China, and have survived there since early 2000. We always work with a local partner, who will provide any 'cushion' if needed. By taking this role, we are taken out of the loop of corruption."

"Secondly, if there is any corruption, it is of a larger amount and might involve the government or the developers. Our role is negligible compared to the total amount of the project. It may also be because my chairman is a devout Christian. For example, he refused to do any projects in the gambling industry, so we lost money when Macau was booming. But these are our firm's values. Would we maintain these values in the future, when the chairperson passes on? Maybe, maybe not. We need flexibility going forward."

"Thirdly, the Mainlanders are much richer these days, and they don't need to bribe you. Before, we had to spend long hours after dinner building guanxi. Now they don't even want to wine and dine you. Time has changed the way we practice ethics. It's perfectly fine for us."

References

Brunner, J. A., Chen, J., Sun, C., & Zhou, N. (1990). The role of guanxi in negotiations in the Pacific Basin. *Journal of Global Marketing*, 3(2), 7–24.

Buttery, E. A., & Wong, Y. (1999). The development of a guanxi framework. *Marketing Intelligence & Planning*, 17(3), 147–155. doi:10.1108/02634509910271605

Desjardins, J. (2016). All of the world's stock exchanges by size. Retrieved April 30, 2018 from http://money.visualcapitalist.com/all-of-the-worlds-stock-exchanges-by-size.

Friedman, M. (1970, September 12). The social responsibility of business is to increase its profit. *The New York Times Magazine*.

Hofstede, G., & Bond, M. H. (1988). The Confucius connection: From cultural roots to economic growth. *Organizational Dynamics*, 16(4), 5–21.

Irwin, J. (2012, July). *Doing business in China: An overview of ethical aspects* [PDF version]. Retrieved April 30, 2018 from https://www.ibe.org.uk/userfiles/chinaop.pdf.

Lee, K. H., & Lo, W. C. (1988). American business people's perceptions of marketing and negotiating in the People's Republic of China. *International Marketing Review*, 5(2), 41–51.

Leung, T., & Wong, Y. (2001). The ethics and positioning of guanxi in China. *Marketing Intelligence & Planning*, 19(1), 55–64. doi:10.1108/02634500110363826

Pye, L. (1982). *Chinese commercial negotiating styles*. Cambridge: Oelgeschlager, Gunn & Hain.

Pye, L. (1986). The China trade: Making the deal. *Harvard Business Review*, 74–80.

Redding, S. G. (1993). *The spirit of Chinese capitalism*. Berlin: Walter de Gruyter.

Spencer-Oatey, H. (2012). What is culture? A compilation of quotations. *GlobalPAD Core Concepts*. Retrieved April 30, 2018 from https://warwick.ac.uk/fac/soc/al/globalpad/openhouse/interculturalskills/global_pad_-_what_is_culture.pdf.

Tung, R. (1982a). US-China trade negotiations: Practices, procedures and outcomes. *Journal of International Business Studies, 13*(2), 25–37.

Tung, R. L. (1982b). *US-China trade negotiations*. New York: Pergamon Press.

Wong, Y. H. (1997). Relationship marketing in China: Guanxi, favouritism and quality of business development. *Management Review*, 43–57.

Wong, Y. H. (1998a). An integrated relationship (guanxi) marketing model in China. *Journal of Professional Services Marketing, 18*(1), 25–48.

Wong, Y. H. (1998b). Key to key account management: Relationship (guanxi) model. *International Marketing Review, 15*(3), 215–231.

References for the Buddhist section

Bloom. (2014). Buddhist tycoon Chen Feng built Hainan Airlines into a global empire. *South China Morning Post*. Retrieved April 30, 2018 from http://www.scmp.com/business/china-business/article/1476897/buddhist-tycoon-chen-feng-built-hainan-airlines-global.

Bodhi, B. (1995). *Nourishing the roots: Essays on Buddhist ethics*. Buddhist Publication Society. Retrieved April 30, 2018 from https://www.accesstoinsight.org/lib/authors/bodhi/wheel259.html.

Bond, M. H. (Ed.). (2008). *The psychology of the Chinese people*. Hong Kong: Chinese University Press.

Brødsgaard, K. E., & Zheng, Y. (Eds.). (2006). *The Communist Party in reform*. London: Routledge.

Buddhism in China. (n.d.). Retrieved April 9, 2018 from http://www.chinatoday.com/culture/china_religions/buddhism_china_religion.htm.

Chen, K. K. (1973). *Buddhism in China: A historical survey*. Princeton, NJ: Princeton University Press.

Chinese Communist Party issues code of ethics to ensure clean governance. (2010). *News of the Communist Party of China*. Retrieved April 9, 2018 from http://english.cpc.people.com.cn/66102/6900695.html.

Ching, F. (2014). Reconsidering the wisdom of Confucius. Retrieved April 9, 2018 from http://www.theglobeandmail.com/opinion/reconsidering-the-wisdom-of-confucius/article20863786.

Fan, Y. (2002). Guanxi's consequences: Personal gains at social cost. *Journal of Business Ethics, 38*(4), 371–380.

Froese, K. (2013). *Ethics unbound: Chinese and Western perspectives on morality*. Hong Kong: Chinese University Press.

Guang, X. (2017). Buddhist social morality. Unpublished class notes and discussions.

Harvey, P. (2000). *An introduction to Buddhist ethics: Foundations, values and issues*. Cambridge: Cambridge University Press.

Hernandez, J. (2016). China's tech-savvy, burned-out and spiritually adrift turn to Buddhism. Retrieved April 9, 2018 from https://www.nytimes.com/2016/09/08/world/asia/china-longquan-monastery-buddhism-technology.html?_r=0.

Hodus, L. (2003). Buddhism and Buddhists in China. *Authorama*. Retrieved April 30, 2018 from http://www.authorama.com/buddhism-and-buddhists-in-china-10.html.

Huang, Y. (2014). The 2008 milk scandal revisited. *Forbes*. Retrieved April 9, 2018 from https://www.forbes.com/sites/yanzhonghuang/2014/07/16/the-2008-milk-scandal-revisited/.

Huang, Z. P. (2015, October 23). China's Communist Party has banned its members from meeting alone or criticizing the party. *Quartz*. Retrieved April 9, 2018 from https://qz.com/530534/chinas-communist-party-has-banned-its-members-from-meeting-alone-or-criticizing-the-party/.

Irwin, J. (2012). Doing business in China: An overview of ethical aspects. Institute of Business Ethics. Occasional Paper 6. Retrieved April 9, 2018 from https://www.ibe.org.uk/userfiles/chinaop.pdf.

Kiely, J. (2016). *Recovering Buddhism in modern China*. New York: Columbia University Press.

Kieschnick, J. (2003). *The impact of Buddhism on Chinese material culture*. Princeton, NJ: University Presses of California, Columbia, and Princeton.

Magistad, M. (2011). Finding balance: Buddhism and modern life in China. Retrieved April 9, 2018 from https://www.pri.org/stories/2011-12-01/finding-balance-buddhism-and-modern-life-china.

Mattis, P. (2012). Reexamining the Confucian Institutes. Retrieved April 30, 2018 from https://thediplomat.com/2012/08/reexamining-the-confucian-institutes/.

Moxley, M. (2010). Religion-China: Buddhism enjoys a revival. Inter Press Service. Retrieved April 9, 2018 from http://www.ipsnews.net/2010/11/religion-china-buddhism-enjoys-a-revival/.

Peter, M. (2012, August 2). Reexamining the Confucian Institutes. Retrieved April 30 2018, from http://thediplomat.com/2012/08/reexamining-the-confucian-institutes.

Pham, S. (2016). Alibaba points to politics after US puts it back on fake good blacklist. Retrieved January 31, 2017 from http://money.cnn.com/2016/12/22/technology/alibaba-notorious-markets-fake-goods-us-trade.

Powers, J. (1995). *Introduction to Tibetan Buddhism*. Ithaca, NY: Snow Lion Publications.

Redding, G (2013). *The spirit of Chinese capitalism* (Vol. 22). Walter de Gruyer.

Resnick, D. (2015). What is ethics in research and why is it important? National Institute of Environmental Health Sciences. Retrieved April 30, 2018 from https://www.niehs.nih.gov/research/resources/bioethics/whatis.

Saddhatissa, H. (1997). *Buddhist ethics*. Boston: Wisdom Publication.

Samdhong, R. (2009). Fifty years of persecution have strengthened our resolve, says Tibetan prime minister in exile. *AsiaNews*. Retrieved April, 30, 2018 from http://www.asianews.it/news-en/Fifty-years-of-persecution-have-strengthened-our-resolve,-says-Tibetan-prime-minister-in-exile-14688.html.

Sha, L. (2017, August 29). 中纪委披露查出违反八项规定新数据 24万人中有哪些"大老虎" [Central Commission for Discipline Inspection disclose new data on violation of Eight-Point Regulation of CPC]. Retrieved April 30, 2018 from https://www.sohu.com/a/168108837_114988.

Tachibana, S. (1994). *Ethics of Buddhism*. Richmond, Surrey: Curzon Press.

Tricker, R. I., & Tricker, G. (2014). *Business ethics: A stakeholder, governance and risk approach*. London: Routledge/Taylor & Francis Group.

Yang, S. (2016). Life in purgatory: Buddhism is growing in China, but remains in legal limbo. *Time*. Retrieved April 30, 2018 from http://time.com/4260593/china-buddhism-religion-religious-freedom/.

Zhang, X. Y. (2010). Buddhism in China. *China Today*. Retrieved April 30, 2018 from http://www.chinatoday.com.cn/ctenglish/se/txt/2009-06/19/content_203310.htm.

Zhang, Y. (2015). Revised party rules against misbehavior. *China Daily*. Retrieved April 30, 2018 from http://www.chinadaily.com.cn/china/2015-10/13/content_22167809.htm.

Zhang, Q., & Yao, C. (2013, July 1). China's Communist Party membership exceeds 85 million. Retrieved April 30, 2018 from http://english.cpc.people.com.cn/206972/206974/8305636.html.

Case study

Foxconn and Apple Computers

When Steve Jobs, the billionaire head of Apple computers, was shown around the facilities of their supplier Foxconn in Shenzhen, China, he was impressed by the movie theaters, swimming pools, and other facilities that he saw in this booming city of 17 million people. When subsequently Jobs learned that workers at the huge Foxconn factory were attempting suicide, he said that he found the situation "troubling" but that he was "all over it."

Foxconn International Holdings Ltd., which is part of the Hon Hai group, is one of China's largest exporters and has around 800,000 employees, half of them in Shenzhen, just across the border from Hong Kong. Many Apple i-products have Foxconn components.

The Hon Hai Precision Industry Company Ltd. was founded by Taiwanese Terry Gou in 1974. A strict disciplinarian and an apparent workaholic, Gou's mantra was "time is money and efficiency is life."

Foxconn's Longhua plant was built as a factory town in the countryside north of Shenzhen when land in China's Pearl River delta was cheap. It attracted tens of thousands of young people (mostly in their late teens or early twenties) leaving the poverty of the provinces and expecting that a factory job would offer them a "city life" with friends and plenty of money. Instead, some felt that had become cheerless human machines who were too exhausted to enjoy what little free time they had. They were hired to work eight-hour shifts, but the majority increased their earnings with substantial overtime.

At the start of each shift, thousands of workers in identical uniforms sang the company song. The public address system broadcast music and propaganda. Posters urged the workers to: "let the company get stronger and stronger," and "achieve goals unless the sun no longer rises." They worked standing in one place under constant camera supervision. Pay was docked under a discipline scheme, which handed out points for being late, yawning, talking, or having long fingernails. Although the plant had modern dormitories, workers slept in three-tier bunks with no air-conditioning in summer, when temperatures could reach 30 degrees Celsius. Eating facilities were considered good, but the quasi-military atmosphere was dispiriting.

Following a spate of suicides of employees jumping off roofs, the company took action. Wire fences were put on roofs, and nets were erected below buildings. Social workers were recruited. A suicide prevention hotline was installed and averaged two calls a day. Spotter teams were created to detect employees with possible problems. The Shenzhen Mental Health Centre offered support, and monks were brought in to ward off evil spirits.

Basic pay was also increased significantly, and excessive overtime was restricted. But this meant that some employees were no better off financially.

Under Shenzhen law, employers are required to pay compensation for death at work. As a good employer, Foxconn paid significantly more than the legal require-ment. Foxconn management now feared that some employees might have killed themselves to get this generous compensation for their families. Consequently, all employees were required to sign a declaration that their dependents would not expect compensation if they killed themselves.

Although the suicide rate was alarming, a visiting psychology professor from Tsinghua University pointed out that it was actually lower than the average for young people in the rest of China.

Foxconn had been lauded by the Chinese press for creating jobs in modern surroundings. Now the firm became an object of criticism and undercover investigations.

Labor in Shenzhen today is no longer cheap. Manufacturing has moved inland and, in some cases, to other cheaper countries. Foxconn has invested in automated production lines to maintain its competitive edge.

Questions for discussion

1. Who should take the blame for the suicides at Foxconn: Terry Gou the owner, the company's top management, its board of directors, major customers like Apple, or the employees who jumped off the roofs?

2. Had you been invited to advise Terry Gou at the time, what would you have said?

5

The Ecosystem and Regulatory Framework of Corporate Governance in China since 1978

Gregg Li

In this chapter we consider:

- ❖ the general ecosystem and the various participants since 1978
- ❖ the roles and interlinkages among these participants
- ❖ other forces that are shaping the governance of companies
- ❖ the first Code of Corporate Governance of 2002
- ❖ the 2006 Company Law and Securities Law[1]
- ❖ other relevant legislation

Corporate governance has been completely rewritten since the reintroduction of the Four Modernizations in 1978 in China.[2] Over time, new institutions have been set up to regulate commerce and corporate governance.

China is still changing rapidly indeed, and its perception of good practices is being molded every day by local conditions, foreign ideas, and government policies but also by the Chinese government and the party. Many foreign investors have questioned the sanity and existence of corporate governance in China. Does it exist at all? The unequivocal answer is yes but unlike the way most from the West would understand it. Corporate governance has taken on a Socialist and a Chinese characteristic.

But corporate governance practices are quite different between that of an SOE and a non-SOE. Conversely, between a family-run private firm and one that is recently listed. As China evolves, we believe eventually there will be many different forms of corporate governance to reflect the many different types of institutions. The current Chinese institutions in place have helped to draw and attract organizations to acceptable norms and practices. Correspondingly, there isn't one best practice in corporate governance in China today but many, and eventually over time, each type of organization will find its own niche in its myriad forms.

---

1. Zhengquan Fa (证券法), 2007.
2. The Four Modernizations was introduced in government policy by Zhou Enlai in 1964 and reemphasized by Deng Xiaoping in 1978, stating that the top priority was to realize Four Modernizations.

Background of the current ecosystem

The Chinese government has realized that there needs to be a fundamental change in how firms are set up, governed, managed, and owned, sold, and are able to acquire foreign firms and be acquired themselves, particularly as the Chinese government has decided to strengthen its dualistic market-oriented economy, albeit with a socialist orientation.

With a population at 1.3 billon—and growing—China has no choice but to continue to find ways to streamline its SOEs, which have been heavily subsidized by the banks over the years; to grow its entrepreneurial SMEs; and attract more foreign-controlled entities into China. Efforts to get some of its companies listed on the HKSE, the NYSE, LSE, and NASDAQ have helped introduce China to international corporate governance standards. Although such actions have helped to put higher standards into the ecosystem, these actions are still not enough. Foreign best practices are useful as references, but given the context and the immature legal system, China needed to introduce different elements of corporate governance at its own pace.

The current corporate governance ecosystem has been established through four major periods. A major period is the third between 1993 and 2003, which saw a tremendous number of changes to the old.[3] The fifth period has already started.

- The first period, the **Pre-Reform Stage**, was from 1978 to 1984, starting with the Four Modernizations.
- The second period, the **Economic Reform Stage**, lasted from 1984 to 1992, and this paralleled the meteoric rise of the Chinese economy.
- The third period, the **Transitional Stage**, from 1993, lasted until 2003, and saw the greatest changes and installation of new corporate governance practices and regulations, and the recognition of the modern enterprises with separation of management and ownership.
- The fourth period, **Convergence Stage**, from 2004 to probably 2017, China attempted to harmonize its corporate governance systems and laws mainly with those of the UK and the US. As the world became even more chaotic and unpredictable, as Donald Trump became the US president with policies less favorable to free trade, and as China's dynamo began to slow down, we should expect to see a new strategy from China on how to deal with globalization. We believe the issue should be about less control but more about when and how to shape a company's governance structure so it can remain resilient, strong, flexible, and relevant. Instead, the party wanted more control and less corruption.
- The **Emergence Stage**, from 2017 onwards, as China began to acquire companies abroad and as its companies move westward through the Belt and

---

3. For discussions before 2015, see Hu & Hu, 2004. See also Chen, 2015.

Road Initiative, we should expect to see a period of emergence of new forms of corporate governance. We are seeing China's mixed ownership model, whereby the party plays a strategic part in both private and SOEs.

The old centrally planned economy had had difficulty catching up with market demand and vast amounts of funds had been needed from abroad to develop the economy and the infrastructure at the turn of the century. (Today, China is relatively richer and has sent its companies to acquire strategic assets abroad.) Twenty years ago, money was slowly moving into China, but without a proper and well-tested corporate governance structure, good capital would not remain unless proper governance was endemic. Investors abroad and domestically all wanted a reasonable return to their investment, but how China has journeyed into this challenge is reflective more of China's own context than what foreigners would want to see.

One of the boldest moves by the central planners to kick-start this process in delegating control, was to slowly release control over the SOEs and turn these massive companies into listed companies, or in the spirit of "corporatization," pushed ownership to other shareholders. Listing these SOEs in New York, London, Singapore, and Hong Kong effectively released control from the state over to the market or allowing these firms to enter into the arena of international corporate governance. A very smart move and in fact this was one of the policy contributors which provided a subsequent knock-on effect on the rest of the economy, and provided the fuel for hyper-growth in China during the early years of this century. China's economic development was intricately linked to the development of corporate governance.

The Chinese understood very well that the first sector that must bear higher standards in corporate governance was the banking sector. A healthy financial intermediary was fundamental to a healthy economy, and the Chinese banks were in deep trouble, reportedly with some holding close to 40% non-performing loans. Believing the German-Dutch model of a two-tier board, which would allow a more collective approach in control, the Chinese began to study and learn corporate governance practices from abroad. The government would take some portions from overseas and discard others. According to James Stent, a seasoned banker in China, the Chinese were very good at identifying their problems although they were still learning how to solve them. Although the Chinese were excellent students, they were foremost realists and practitioners. They would experiment. They sent delegations abroad and invited experts to forums, and piloted different arrangements. This was possible because all along, they knew the party was in full control and could step in with administrative control. "[I]n corporate governance of Chinese banks we find the framework of global standards of corporate governance adapted in practice to Chinese culture, guided by the presence of the Party."[4]

---

4. Stent, 2017, p. 104.

Replacing the state as shareholder

China began to move from a state-controlled economy to a market-led economy in the late 1980s. Until 1978, most enterprises were state owned and governance was mostly "administrative." After the 1980s, China kept administrative control as the last resort and used it to rein in wayward firms (see the Vanke case at the end of this chapter), where the government had to resort to market takeover mechanisms and administrative measures.

During the earlier periods of corporate governance reform in China, the state kept a good proportion of the listed shares and maintained the last line of control. A key reason for this was to be able to handle uncertainties, just in case the market or the firm would face challenges that no one had predicted and through intervention at the ownership level some leverage could be used to rein the control back into place. Another reason was that such shares could always be disposed of later, preferably at a higher stock price, or be injected into some mutual funds to represent the health and welfare insurance portion for the firm's employees. The Chinese did signal to the public that it was the intent that all shares would eventually be held by the public or by independent third parties. Some shares would be later moved to asset management firms where they would be disposed of through market mechanisms.

In the early period of the Chinese stock markets, shares were held by three parties: government, legal persons, and public individual investors. The state shares and legal person shares were neither transferable nor tradable (except with domestic institutional investors upon approval by the CSRC). They accounted for about 37% and 28% of total shares respectively in 2002; public investor shares (A and B shares), which are the only tradable shares, accounted for about 35%.[5]

The performance of the SOEs was difficult to measure due to their need to serve multiple masters. Monitoring was thought to be difficult. The involvement of the state raised the issue of unfair treatment by one class of shareholders. In fact, the authors believed that in using its control for purposes other than value maximization, the state was in a position to exploit minority shareholders who have limited recourse. The state was indeed walking a fine line. In practice, it appeared the state knew exactly what it had wanted to do all along, to leverage the market for capital and push the institutions into a higher level of efficiency with the help of outsiders. Improving shareholders' rights and controls would be introduced much later.

As China became more open and its market institutions became more established, the arguments for having non-tradable shares and tradable shares began to give way. Other problems stemming from such share arrangements included these issues:

---

5.   Zhou & Cheung, 2003, p. 197.

- Potential return between tradable and non-tradable shareholders, whereby non-tradable shareholders could only receive stock dividends as a reward for holding the stock and not upside gain from selling the stock;
- Relative ease in manipulating price for listed shares, as only one third of the total shares were traded in the market; and
- Non-tradable shares tending to be severely undervalued, constraining the financing function of the stock market.[6]

After several failed attempts in converting the non-tradable shares, the CSRC in mid-2005 launched the **Non-tradable Share Issue Reform**. As of end of 2006, over 90% of listed companies completed the converting process and this unprecedented exercise was considered a success. Many considered this to be a factor in the rise of Chinese stock market in 2006.[7]

However, according to Mr. Shang Fulin, chairman of the CSRC at that time, making the shares tradable did not mean they would be released in the market, especially for shares of the SOEs owned by the state. That would be too dangerous and chaotic. The Chinese government preferred stability and control. State-owned assets authorities would consider the overall strategic layout of the state-owned sectors.[8]

Transition into modern corporate governance

Three key initiatives sparked the change to modernization following Deng's Modernization Drive in 1978. The first was finding a novel way to sell off state assets and restructure SOE companies; the second, to open the door to limited foreign competition so that local companies could learn to play by market rules; and the third, how changes to how incentives would be awarded. Let's begin with the last initiative.

Deng implemented the contract responsibility system whereby farmers and factories could keep any excess beyond an agreed quota. The excesses could be sold in the market, and the proceeds would be kept by the responsible party. Apparently this brilliant idea had come about because some farmers had secretly sold their excesses on the market despite heavy controls. Deng just accepted the inevitable.

Also, during this period, SOEs were being corporatized. One of the more successful of the Chinese government's initiatives was the effort to corporatize 900 SOEs in its transition into structuring these firms for a greater level of self-control. China's experiment with new forms of governance paralleled the development of the securities and futures markets in the late 1970s, during the time of their liberalization of

---

6. Cai et al., 2007.
7. Ibid.
8. State share reform not "'selling out all shares'" (2005, June 27).

the economy.[9] Some of the restructuring solutions began at that time included ways for exchanging a portion of government ownership for convertible bonds that could be sold to private investors. For the first time, state-owned organizations could be listed on stock exchanges. Another initiative that would enhance the level of corporate governance was the opening up of the Chinese market to international competition with China joining the WTO. This encouraged local exporters to play by, and be governed by, international rules that ranged from international intellectual properties, to branding, to price setting. To compete effectively, state firms had to drastically improve their efficiency.

During the periods leading up to the Transition Period (1993–2003), which saw the newest changes in corporate governance systems, China began to quickly establish a series of laws and regulations to reinforce the infrastructure. The enterprise law was changed and the Company Law was first set up in 1994.[10] The rights, duties, and power of directors and shareholders were laid out and how the party would be linked to the companies were also clarified. IAS replaced the socialist Enterprise Accounting Standards, and the IAS slowly became the norm.

In fact, according to Nick Tan, a China audit partner at Deloitte,[11] by 2017 the accounting standards and practices at many SOEs had reached international levels. IAS is very close to International Financial Reporting Standards (IFRS) and US Generally Accepted Accounting Principles (GAAP), and although the auditing procedures and definitions are slightly different, the resultant calculations are very close. For practical reasons, he doesn't see much difference anymore. The key difference lies in how the accountants account for financial instruments and intangibles.

By 2001 the CSRC had adopted guidelines for establishing independent boards of directors in listed companies. The rules required at least one third of the board to consist of independent directors. This was more onerous than those of listed companies in Hong Kong whose level of corporate governance was the same as those in the UK, the US, and Singapore. By January 2002, China's Code of Corporate Governance for listed companies was formulated, and companies were given a grace period to move from having at least two independent directors to one third, by June 2003. China was learning. Its government leaders would study the best from overseas, adapting and piloting leading practices that might work in China.

Labeled as an emerging market in 2007, the best way to describe China's governance system today is with a view of diversity, whereby all types of governance systems at the corporate level existed at one time or another. China has been a vibrant ground for experimentation. In settling on some types or forms of well-recognized standards, China's own corporate governance system can be described as in infancy. It was only in December 1990 that the Shanghai Stock Exchange (SSE) and the Shenzhen Stock Exchange (SZSE) began their operations. Only Chinese

---

9.   China's securities and futures markets (2007, February).

10.   Company Law was announced on December 29, 1993 and enforced in July 1, 1994.

11.   A private interview with Nicholas Tan, October 25, 2017.

citizens living in the Mainland could purchase A-shares, (or retail shares), until 2007/08. In December 2016, Shenzhen and Hong Kong instituted a new stock trade link that allowed retailer consumers from one end to purchase shares at the other, effectively opening up the market further.[12]

According to the CSRC, as of June 2007, there were 1,477 listed companies in China with over an aggregate market capitalization of RMB 16,623 billion.[13] By the end of 2015, the number had nearly doubled, to 2,800 companies with a market capitalization of RMB 3 trillion.[14] We are reminded that the first joint stock company, the Beijing Tianqiao Department Store, was founded in August 1984, nearly 35 years ago.[15] **In other words, the mechanisms allowing you and me, who live outside China, to own stocks in Chinese companies did not exist a few decades ago, just long enough ago for most readers to remember that this is still within our lifetime.** In contrast, the stock markets in New York, London, and even Hong Kong existed long before many of us were born.

But we have to remember that corporate governance in China is even younger than this. Corporate governance really didn't take off until the 1990s around the world, and China quickly jumped on the bandwagon. This timing has been key. The parallel and timing is striking. Within a span of a few years, China has made some tremendous strides on the corporate governance front, as expected, but at the same time created lots of new corporate governance challenges. In 2006, with the listing of Industrial and Commercial Bank of China (ICBC), China's version of HSBC, and at that time, the largest IPO in the world, pushed Hong Kong's position in fundraising to the second highest in the world, after London. This was possible as ICBC needed to comply with the governance requirements of multiple international exchanges . . . and it did so with flying colors. Its market capitalization is bigger than that of HSBC, which by asset was still much larger.

Although corporate governance had been still relatively new, the Chinese authorities over the last decade continued to push and revise a number of initiatives into the market and rode the wave like a good surfer would. These included new corporate and securities laws, Code of Corporate Governance, better systems and approaches to securing shareholder rights, new Enterprise Risk Management (ERM) and new ESG directives, and stronger accounting standards that were more in line with international standards.

The development of private rights in China

The idea of private ownership had been a thorn on the side of the Communist Party, still the only ruling political party. Central to the argument are property rights. The

---

12. A stock trading link between Hong Kong and Shenzhen will go live next week (2016, November 27).
13. Statistics of June 2007 (2007, July 10).
14. Grace & Jian (2017, June 19).
15. Ibid.

National People's Congress (NPC) in March 2007 addressed this issue through a discussion of property rights and made some critical decisions. The new NPC law gave individuals the same legal protection for their property as the state. This is an important development, as it strengthened the rule of law and moved the country away from the concept of joint ownership as understood under the philosophy of "communism." This latest law, however, did not bring full property rights and does not give peasants marketable ownership rights to sell their land. Nonetheless, to move from shared ownership of land to semi-private ownership is a historical moment.

Many types of shares in China

All shares in effect carry a vote of one, but this only works if one is allowed to exercise that authority. There are many classes and types of shares in China, which is not the case in other countries. Institutional investors have tended to downgrade such development as it goes against the grain of international best practices in governance. One share, one vote has been the holy grail of corporate governance in many jurisdictions around the world although weighted voting shares have existed alongside.

In China, some shares in effect have no voting power because the system does not allow the holder to vote. These are called non-outstanding shares. The mechanisms are not yet fully developed; proxy doesn't exist in some companies. Market failures, such as not allowing owners to buy or sell through a lack of brokerages, effectively limit that principle. But this is changing.

By 2013, China even experimented with preference shares and the so-called N Board (for innovative companies) for the SSE. There are numerous types of shares issued in China, and chances are there will be more hybrids to come as China begins to experiment with mixed forms of shareholding.

Table 5.1 shows the different types of shares allowed in the local exchanges and the shares that are structured for overseas markets in the current maturity of the Chinese shareholding arrangement.

Table 5.1: Types of shares and their definition*

Types of Shares listed in China	Definition
A-share	Held by the Chinese public, it is denominated and payable in renminbi and freely traded by the local population only. With QFII (Qualified Foreign Institutional Investor), foreigners may participate into the market and buy up to 10% of a company's shares. These are listed on the Shanghai and Shenzhen Stock exchanges. (As of December 2016, through the Hong Kong–Shenzhen and Shanghai links, investors in Hong Kong could buy these A- shares as well.)

Table 5.1 (continued)

Types of Shares listed in China	Definition
A-restricted share	Held by the Chinese government and not tradable until the Chinese authorities decided that they can be. Restricted in a general sense. As of 2007, about 63% of most listed companies' shares that are SOEs are restricted. The split share reform, or non-tradable share reform, is to eliminate non-tradable shares.[†]
B-share	Denominated in renminbi, it is payable in USD or HKD, listed in China, but designated for foreign investors. It is not as liquid as A-shares. In the past, only foreigners were allowed to trade B-shares. Starting from March 2001, Mainlanders could trade B-shares as well if they were buying shares for foreigners, mainly overseas Chinese. However, they must trade with legal foreign currency accounts. These shares were created in the mid-1990s. Generally, due to lower demand, B-shares were priced lower than were A-shares despite having the same voting and dividend rights. Foreigners who purchased B-shares might have gained control over a target company, as in the case of Isuzu and Itochu of Japan buying into the Beijing Light Bus Company in 1995.[‡]
H-share	These are shares of SOEs that are floated and listed on overseas exchanges, particularly those in Hong Kong, New York, London, and Singapore. In Hong Kong, the highest-rated H-shares are known as red chips.** ** **Red chips** There are two types: (1) mainland Chinese companies with Hong Kong subsidiaries (2) Hong Kong listed Chinese companies that do the bulk of their business with mainland China.
J-share	Chinese shares listed on the Tokyo Exchange
L-share	Chinese shares listed on the LSE, mostly at the AIM Market there
ST-share	A subset of A-share, referring to those companies reporting loss in the previous year. "ST" refers to "Special Treatment." ST-share companies reporting loss in the second year will become ST-share companies and continued loss will mean delisting from the exchange.
S-share	Shares sold on the Singapore Exchange. Reportedly about 14% of listed companies at the Singaporean Exchange were Chinese companies in 2006. S-shares are denominated in Singapore dollars and all shares are tradable.
T-share	Shares tradable on the Tokyo Stock Exchange
N-share	These used to be Chinese shares listed in New York, such as PetroChina. This category is now included in H-shares.

Table 5.1 (continued)

Types of Shares listed in China	Definition
P-share	This type of share is owned by companies controlled by PRC nationals, founded in the PRC but are trading outside PRC and incorporated outside the PRC (Cayman Islands, British Virgin Islands, etc.), its assets or revenue derived from the PRC. Traded in Hong Kong.

* Rogers, J. (2007). *A bull in China: Investing profitably in the world's greatest market.* New York: Random House (pp. 24–29).
† According to Shang Fulin, chairman of CSRC, the shares are tradable but this does not mean the government will sell them. See more at FTSE Russell, Guide to Chinese share classes. (2017, April). Retrieved May 1, 2018 from http://www.ftse.com/products/downloads/Guide_to_Chinese_Share_Classes.pdf
‡ Gu, M. K. (2017) *Understanding Chinese company law* (3rd ed). Hong Kong: Hong Kong University Press.

Due to the recent A-share market revival, many companies listed overseas grabbed the opportunity to enjoy higher valuation by returning to the home market. As of June 2007, a few dozen companies were listed on both the A-share market and H-share market.[16] As the different classes of shares operate under different supply and demand conditions, they receive different valuations. However, other than the price difference, all shares carry the same voting power and dividend entitlements.

Merging the different types of shares has started to occur, but slowly. New rules in the future for A- and B-shares to be merged into the one share will give foreign investors less restrictions when buying and trading. In fact, such share split has created a mistrust of the market and has played even more of a role in keeping investors (especially institutional investors) out of the market. Limiting the type of shares and giving all shares the same voting power, dividend entitlement, and access will go a long way in bringing in foreign investors and allow Chinese firms to raise international funds.

Getting ready to pounce

By 2006, the Chinese stock markets were experiencing bull runs, and there was an overflow of capital into companies with domestic investors eagerly looking for investment opportunities. Many firms were overvalued, and many people believed the bubbles would eventually burst.

Again, the call for better corporate governance surfaced during that period. Investors advocated that those firms with proper and well-tested corporate governance should, in the long run, receive the proper recognition from the investors and

---

16. Statistics\of June 2007 (2007, July 10).

that all firms should strive to achieve better governance. The problem, however, for many investors, was understanding what indeed was proper corporate governance for the various types of firms in China, given the history and context of China. The definition and scope of corporate governance further evolved. Today, the discussion of environment and the circular economy, issues of sustainability and innovation, risk management, and CEO compensations (higher and not lowering the compensation that has dominated the discussion in the US) have now become the norm at most boardrooms in China. In fact, of the 50 most innovative companies in 2017 that are changing the world for good, four are in China.[17]

Such demands for good governance came not only from domestic investors but also from international institutional investors. Attracted by the prospect of strong growth, a stable political system, increasingly favorable climate for foreign investors, and potentially limited downside risks, international investors naturally began to invest more and more into China. China was the darling of investment, alongside Korea, India, and Vietnam. Even Warren Buffet invested in PetroChina during the early periods. The Carlye Group, a large private equity holding, went shopping for good companies in China; and this was followed by Blackrock, another huge private equity, and many smaller funds.

These international and more sophisticated investors demanded higher levels of protection for their investment in state-owned firms and private investments, and these included demanding companies install working elements of good corporate governance practices such as higher levels of disclosure, independence of the board, transparency, risk management, and a clear separation of ownership from management. These governance practices needed to be at international standards in order to attract and to retain more funds, and China for one, had been keen to raise its level of governance as fast as it could.

The key participants in the ecosystem

The primary drivers for corporate governance reform in China have involved the interplay among a number of parties. Together they form the institutional framework for companies and the major players in this ecosystem include:

- The State Council;
- The Chinese Communist Party, which through the two-tier structure has a power link into the boardrooms of SOEs;
- The CSRC, or China's equivalent of the SEC in the US[18] and the SFC in Hong Kong;

---

17. Fortune (2017, October 27).
18. The CSRC is authorized to conduct supervision and regulation of all the securities and futures markets. Other organizations engaged in securities transaction are under centralized supervision of CSRC as well. The CSRC has the dualistic roles of monitoring the market and consummating the regulations. It has the authority to approve IPO and delist non-performing companies as well, a direction that is considered more appropriate by some. In Hong Kong, this dual role is separated, and the SFC provides the overall supervision.

- The China Banking Regulatory Commission (CBRC);
- The China Insurance Regulatory Commission (CIRC);
- The Ministry of Foreign Trade and Economic Cooperation (MOFERT);
- The NDRC which is the state's long-term planning czar;
- The State Asset Management Bureau (SAMB);
- The Ministry of Finance (MoF);
- China Accounting Standards Committee (CASC);
- SASAC, which reports directly to the State Council;
- The State Economics and Trade Commission (SETC);
- The State Administration of Foreign Exchange (SAFE);
- People's Bank of China (the de facto Central Bank);
- The Securities Trading Automated Quotation System (STAQ) or China's version of NASDAQ;[19]
- The Hong Kong Stock Exchange and Clearing (HKSE);
- The SSE; and
- The SZSE.

Of the many parties identified above, the State Council is one of the few institutions to watch closely, as it has final and overriding authority over all regulatory bodies, such as the various ministries. We are reminded here that in China, the Communist Party and the national policies have a direct and fundamental impact on and relevance to the rate and maturity of the evolving corporate governance infrastructure. Readers are best reminded to bear this in mind. The state has a direct interest and administrative control over all enterprises, unlike in the US or the UK.

The important issue to note about this ecosystem is that many of these participants were undergoing rapid changes as well during the turn of the century. To understand China, one has to understand uncertainty and change. Many of these institutions were new and had new powers presented to them by the State Council. Some, like the MoF, were draconian, and the change at that time was more to devolve their authority over time to other institutions. This was the time of turbulence and chaos, of power struggle and compromises.

The Chinese government abhors chaos and has installed layers of governance control on organizations as added precaution. The performance of the chairperson and CEOs of SOEs is evaluated by the Communist Party through the Party Committee. "Personnel-related requirements of corporate governance are uncomfortably grafted onto a Chinese system in which the Party is heavily involved in making the key appointments," according to James Stent, once an INED in two Chinese banks.[20]

---

19. Walter & Howie, 2006, pp. 35–38. According to the authors, this platform is now defunct, and it closed on September 9, 1999. Trading has moved to a Third Board.
20. Stent, 2017, p. 108.

The establishment of SASAC was an important event and helped to cement a strong foundation for corporate governance. The government has to set up an institution to manage the transfer of valuable assets from the State to the market . . . and SASAC was the solution. According to Chen Qintai at the 2004 OECD Forum in Shanghai,[21] the 16th Party Congress in 2002 presented guiding principles for state-owned asset management system reform, and in 2003, the new government established a special entity to oversee state-owned asset management and issued regulations for state-owned asset supervision and management. This effectively moved the control from administrative to the control of capital. SASAC would control and allocate based on capital and the state would no longer manage the SOEs. This was a historical development indeed.

China's corporate governance information infrastructure was still relatively weak compared with international standards at that time although the relevant regulators, including the MoF and the CASC, have been making significant progress in setting a variety of accounting standards and licensing systems that are linked closer to IAS. But the importance the government has placed on corporate governance information has been changing as well, and interested parties are advised to watch closely at this development.

For example, an important milestone by SASAC in 2007 was their issuance of a new directive in ERM that would guide state-owned organizations in the adoption and execution of such a viable information system in managing risks. The directive reaches into the information of risk:

> Enterprises should establish a risk management information system that covers all basic processes of risk management and internal control, including collection of information, storage, analysis, testing, distribution, reporting, disclosure, etc.[22]

The State-Owned Assets Supervision and Administration Commission (SASAC)

SASAC was established in 2003 as a new way to deal with the transfer of SOEs and state assets. The Chinese government continued to introduce new ways and means to improve governance and management and the establishment of SASAC was a milestone. The entity is entrusted by the government to perform:

> the responsibility as the investor, guides and pushes forward the reform and restructuring of state-owned enterprises; supervises the preservation and increment of the value of state-owned assets for enterprises under its supervision, and enhances the management of state-owned assets; advances the establishment

---

21. Chen (2004, February 26).
22. The central enterprise comprehensive risk management guidelines (2006, June 6).

of modern enterprise system in SOEs, and perfects corporate governance; and propels the strategic adjustment of the structure and layout of the state economy.[23]

With such a heavy responsibility, SASAC, however, was too new and was not part of the government administrations already in place and faced certain limitations at the outset. According to Barry Naughton, a renowned expert on China's political economy, SASAC "has no legal warrant" and "the most important regulations coming out of SASAC are issued out of the Director's Office, but co-signed by the Minister of Finance." Part of it is that the government "has been struggling to pass a law on State Assets for over a decade, so far without result."[24]

In addition, SASAC was only responsible for looking after enterprises under the supervision of the Central Government, excluding financial enterprises. SASAC reported directly to the State Council. The number amounted to 155 as of September 2007, but this number will go down further as SASAC continues to restructure and combine the central enterprises.[25] All other SOEs were under supervision of the local governments, and they fell under the care of local State-Owned Assets Management Authorities.

The important distinction is that SASAC was tasked to manage the key SOEs. These SOEs are known as "Central SOEs" or "PSOEs" since they had a direct link to the central authorities, and given they are "strategic" and "national" assets, the attention on structuring a new form of corporate governance has a special significance. They need to be studied and considered apart from other SOEs. We should expect the Chinese authorities to have uniquely new governance practices that are not endorsed or sanctioned for other SOEs.

The role of SASAC should evolve over time. As more and more shares are sold to the market, shouldn't SASAC have less to manage? Eventually as these SOEs shares are sold, what would happen to SASAC? What and how should SASAC evolve? These are fascinating questions to be explored in future chapters and books on corporate governance. One proponent, Barry Naughton,[26] believed that SASAC should strive to follow the Temasek model of Singapore. Reality or illusion? Readers should keep a close watch on the development of SASAC in the next few years.

According to a top executive of a Central SOE in early 2017,* there were now 122 SOEs left under SASAC's overview.† "The most recent one released into the market was Postal Bank of China. SASAC has been using Hong Kong as a platform to help clean up and professionalize many of these SOEs."

---

23. See http://en.sasac.gov.cn/n1408028/n1408521/index.html.
24. Naughton (2004, January 14–15).
25. List of Central SOEs (2018).
26. Naughton, 2006 and SASAC, 2005.

Culture has played a major part in how much and how well these SOEs can transform themselves, even with an IPO. According to this executive, three elements are still being resolved as new corporate governance practices are being put in place:

- **Transparency**, or the attempt by SOEs to whitewash SASAC with too much information or none at all. Deciding the right amount of transparency is an ongoing learning experience for SASAC.

- **Balancing Party Member's Influence**, or the political clout that these individuals would have on the board, with the need and expectations of the market. These members would toe the party line, and the recent one is absolute compliance with anti-corruption procedures.

- **Weak management of the Board of Directors.** Boards are poorly managed given the lower quality of directors, but SASAC has been working hard to cover this shortfall. Few directors understand their roles or are knowledgeable of their obligations. Few have clues as to their roles and responsibilities. How to make corporate governance work in practice is a challenge. The board does not have true authority in CEO succession, investment decisions, and M&A decisions; and salary increases are mandated along some guidelines from SASAC. Many boards have been set up initially for show, but they are mindful of their obligations to the market. Some never have any intention to give authority to outside investors. Boards are not given the authority to change their business model. That has been set in stone by the powers above.

---

* Private interview with this top executive in 2017.

† According to the list at http://www.sasac.gov.cn/n2588035/n2641579/n2641645/index.html, by late 2017 only 98 were left.

The China Securities Regulatory Commission (CSRC)

Another important institution, the CSRC, supervises the securities and futures markets. Similar to the SEC in the US or the SFC in Hong Kong, the CSRC aims to:[27]

- promote and develop the market infrastructure,
- perfect the operations of the infrastructure,
- develop the corporate bond market, and
- tighten market supervisions.

The State Council established the CSRC in 1992, and today, the CSRC reports directly to the State Council. It has one chairperson, four vice chairpersons, and one

---

27. China Securities Regulatory Commission, 2007, p. 6.

secretary of Disciplinary Inspection Commission (on the vice-ministerial level). As of 2007, it employed more than 2,000 staff and had expanded into 36 securities regulatory bureaus and two commissioner offices in Shanghai and Shenzhen.

Two important articles in the Securities Law (2005) are relevant for our discussion. The Securities Law was first promulgated on December 29, 1998 and took effect on July 1, 1999. It was later amended and that became effective on January 1, 2006.

According to Article 179 of the Securities Law the CSRC is mandated to perform the following supervisory functions and duties:

- Formulate the relevant rules and regulations on the supervision and administration of the securities market and exercise the power of examination or verification;
- Carry out the supervision and administration of the issuance, listing, trading, registration, custody and settlement of securities;
- Carry out supervision and administration of the securities activities of the securities issuers, listed companies, stock exchanges, securities companies, securities regulation and clearing houses, securities investment fund management companies, and securities trading service providers;
- Formulate the standards of securities practice qualification and code of conduct and carry out supervision and implementation;
- Carry out supervision and examination of information disclosure regarding the issuance, listing, and trading of securities;
- Offer guidance for and supervising the activities of the securities industry associations;
- Investigate and punish any violation of any law or administrative regulation on the supervision and administration of the securities market; and
- Perform any other functions and duties as prescribed by any law or administrative regulation.

According to Article 180 of the Securities Law, where CSRC performs its duties and functions, it has the power to take the following measures:

- Carry out an on-the-spot examination to a securities issuer, listed company, securities company, securities investment fund management company, securities trading service provider, stock exchange or securities registration and clearing institution;
- Make an investigation and collect evidence in a place where any suspected irregularity has happened;
- Consult the parties concerned or any entity or individual relating to a case under investigation;
- Refer to and photocopy such materials as the registration of property right and the communication records relating to the case under investigation;
- Refer to and photocopy the securities trading records, transfer registration records, financial statements as well as any other relevant documents and materials of any entity or individual relating to a case under investigation; seal up any document or material that may be transferred, concealed, or damaged;

- Consult the capital account, securities account, or bank account of any relevant party concerned in or any entity or individual relating to a case under investigation; in the case of any evidence certify that any property as involved in a case, such as illegal proceeds or securities, has been or may be transferred or concealed; or where any important evidence has been or may be concealed, forged or damaged, freezing, or seal up the foregoing properties or evidence upon the approval of the principal of the securities regulatory authority under the State Council;
- When investigating any major securities irregularity such as market manipulation or insider trading, upon the approval of the principal of the securities regulatory authority under the State Council, restrict the securities trading of the parties concerned in a case under investigation, whereby the restriction term shall not exceed 15 trading days; under any complicated circumstance, the restriction term may be extended for another 15 trading days.

The 2002 Code of Corporate Governance

In January 2002, the CSRC released its first Code of Corporate Governance for Listed Companies in China. The code laid down the legal relationships between shareholders and directors, executives and management, and the trustees. The roles, responsibilities, and requirements for directors and supervisors as well as stakeholders' rights and related items were presented. The code also set additional disclosure requirements. **Let's look at this code in more detail, as this is relevant in 2018.**

The 2002 Code of Corporate Governance required listed companies to set up incentive and control systems, and by 2007, leading companies have included risk management as a more sophisticated form of control system. Some listed companies established a risk review and internal control system for directors, supervisors, and management, and set up a performance-linked remuneration mechanism. These firms continued to push the boundaries of good governance. It was expected that by 2008, leading firms would consider even annual board review, which was made a best practice in 2007 in the UK. China was rapidly catching up.

Related to this, in 2001, the CSRC published a set of guidelines for listed companies on independent directors and required independent directors to:

- approve major related party transactions,
- propose appointment or removal of auditors,
- call meetings of board or shareholders,
- appoint an external auditor or consulting organization, and
- agree proxies before a shareholders' meeting.

The 2002 Code called for information on:

- membership and structure of boards of directors and supervisors;
- the performance and evaluation of the board of directors and supervisors;

- the performance and evaluation of independent directors;
- the state of corporate governance, any gap with the codes, and reasons for the gap; and
- plans to improve corporate governance.

The mandate to improve corporate governance in 2002 was a top priority for all sectors, and this force was permeating government bodies, regulators, intermediaries, corporations, investors, and joint ventures, for locals and foreigners alike operating in China. Other than having an immature legal system which was relatively weak, with a judiciary that was not independent of the state, there were still a number of issues that needed to be resolved. For example, the separation of ownership and management of a company was still a revolving concept in China.

By May 2017, the State Council wanted to push through more reform and expected key initiatives to be completed by the end of 2017. The State Council issued a circular on May 3 to improve the legal personal management structure and modern corporate system of SOEs. The State Council felt confident it could begin to release some of its tight controls. It strengthened the role of articles of associations, demanded that majority of external directors be established in wholly owned SOEs, and expected SOEs to manage their own risks, discipline, and gains and losses.[28]

According to audit partners whom we interviewed, the internal control systems generally were effective. The key, however, was on improving managerial controls and not on operational controls, as the latter were watertight. Besides, major losses would come from the lack of managerial controls. Ensuring these managerial controls are in place and that managers are not permitted to override controls would be two particular audit areas that they would pay special attention to.

China joining WTO and NASDAQ

China's determination to enter the WTO at the beginning of the twenty-first century did raise great concerns about such impact on the governance front in China, on issues of harmonization, and difference in expectations. Before putting its foot onto the battlefield of the world's markets and letting efficient competitors enter China with minimal restrictions, China must first deal with the existing problems in its own market, especially problems like bureaucracy, corporate governance, counterfeit, and corruption, and not only in SOEs but in hundreds of thousands of civilian enterprises.[29] Naturally, by opening up the market, China would be able to deal with these problems by letting the firms themselves worry about these issues and find ways to deal with them at their own level and speed. And experiment with this idea they did.

---

28. Xu (2017, September 20).
29. Kan, 2001.

One of the ways of joining the world and forcing the required improvement in corporate governance was asking Chinese firms to list themselves on NASDAQ and other international exchanges, and compete head-on with some of the world's best. By August 9, 2007, 11 Chinese firms were listed on NASDAQ.[30] Some medium-sized firms in China even experimented with the adoption of the Sarbanes-Oxley requirements despite it not being a local requirement or a requirement for eventual listing in Hong Kong or the local exchanges that were the preferred exchanges in 2007.

By the end of 2006, there were almost 80 million investors.[31] In 2005 the CSRC introduced the split-share structure reform and began converting non-tradable shares of the 1000+ listed SOEs into tradable shares, the process of which was approaching an end in 2007. With the introduction of Qualified Foreign Institutional Investors (QFII) scheme in 2002 and Qualified Domestic Institutional Investors (QDII) scheme in 2007, China began to allow capital to get in and out of the country via institutional investors and to loosen its strict control over the operations of security houses and brokerages.

By 2008, an agreement was made between the CBRC and the US SEC that would allow Chinese individuals to purchase shares in the US stock markets.

The 2006 Company Law and Securities Law

As in most countries, the need to update the set of company laws is a continual process. This is no different for the PRC, where the old Company Law and Securities Law of 1999 was replaced by the Company Law and the Securities Law of the PRC in 2005 at the 18th Session of the Standing Committee of the Tenth National People's Congress on October 27, 2005. These two sets of laws became effective on January 1, 2006.[32] A new set of company law and securities law was born.

According to King and Wood, one of the largest and youngest law firms in China, in their monthly bulletins,[33] the new laws made crucial modifications which included:

- reducing requirements and simplifying procedures for establishing companies;
- increasing the liabilities of directors, supervisors, and senior managers;
- improving the management structure of listed companies; and
- imposing additional responsibilities on brokers.

The directors' legal risks have dramatically increased as a result of the New Company Law and the New Securities Law.

30. See http://www.salon.com/wire/ap/archive.html?wire=D8QTFPO81.html.
31. CSRC, 2007, p. 3.
32. Guo & Li, 2006.
33. Ibid.

Relevant to this discussion are detailed changes to the following, according to the King and Wood's bulletin.

Duties of loyalty and diligence to the company

The duty of loyalty requires that a board member subordinate his or her personal interest in the event of a conflict of interest between the company and the board member. The duty of diligence requires that a board member exercises reasonable care in the management of the company and fulfills his or her duties in accordance with all relevant laws and the company's charter.

Liabilities of board members

Board members are liable when they breach statutory duties and contractual obligations. The New Company Law further defines the liabilities of board members. Shareholders can sue the directors and the law protects the shareholder's right to sue directly by filing a lawsuit in the People's Court, if any director or senior manager injures shareholders' interests by violating any laws, administrative regulations, or any provisions of the articles of incorporation.

As a result of these new regulations, the risk and liability attributed to board members has increased dramatically. Any board member who exercises his or her powers illegally will be subject to court action and liable for damages towards the company or the shareholders.

Board members are specifically liable for:

- providing loans or guaranties to a third party (when a board member decides to provide loans or guaranties which violate the law or the company's charter, and such violations incur damages to the company; the board member who abused his or her powers risks being sued by the shareholders and is liable to compensate the company's losses);
- engaging in competing activities;
- abusing the directors' power;
- injuring the company interests via affiliated party transactions (interested directors and non-interested directors of a listed company are subject to statutory duties to abstain from voting on the affiliated party transaction);
- engaging in stock price manipulation (Whenever directors, supervisors, senior managers or any shareholders holding more than 5% of the outstanding shares of a listed company engage in short-swing transactions, the company or its shareholders can sue the liable parties and demand that they disgorge the profits from the short-swing transactions to the company. A "short-swing transaction" refers to the purchase and sale of stock of the company within 6 months by a director, supervisor, senior manager or any

shareholder holding more than 5% of the outstanding shares of a listed company).

Potential criminal liabilities of directors

The New Company Law expands the breadth of the directors' duties, increasing directors' legal liabilities, both civil and criminal . . . In addition, it is now codified that directors may not accept any bribes or other illegal income, or misappropriate company funds or property . . . In fact, directors who violate the duties set forth in the New Company Law will be criminally liable.

Accordingly, these violations now correspond to and result in such crimes as (1) the manipulation or looting of a listed company; (2) failure to disclose required company information; (3) obtaining loans or credit from financial institutions by fraudulent activities; (4) fraudulent bankruptcy; (5) manipulation of the securities or futures markets; and (6) embezzlement of trusted property.

Insurance for director's liabilities and the company's operating risk

The law also referenced the coverage possible under director's and officer's liability insurance (D&O) and is consistent with international practices. It is expected that the company will purchase D&O insurance for the directors that protects the directors' property and assets against litigation, and shields civil liability for the directors. It is observed internationally that the coverage does not cover compensation arising from criminal activities of the director. According to King and Wood, most of the lawsuits are brought by injured third parties as a result of a director's intentional violation of laws or the company's charter which are excluded from the insurance coverage, rather than the damages incurred due to the director's negligent commercial judgment.

Other important legislation

By mid-2016, many of the relevant legislations were already in place, but the primary legislation was still the official Company Law. Listed companies by now had to install articles of association, similar to those in many jurisdictions around the world. This set of documents called The Guideline of Articles of Association of Listed Companies added a few tricks to the 2002 Corporate Governance Code. The articles must include procedures on how to conduct meetings for shareholders, boards, and the supervisory board.

For further information, this is the relevant legislation:[34]

---

34. Grace & Jian, 2017.

- 2001: The Guidance Opinions Regarding Formulating Rules Concerning Independent Directors of Listed Companies
- 2002: Code of Corporate Governance (CSRC)
- 2003: Directive on quarterly reporting (CSRC)
- 2005: Bank governance guidelines (China Banking Regulatory Commission)
- 2007: Convergence of accounting and auditing standards with IFRS and ISA. Not complete adoption, however.
- 2007: CSRC launched three-year campaign to strengthen listed company governance: use of funds, operation of board, internal controls
- 2007: The Administrative Measures on Information Disclosure by Listed Companies
- 2008: SSE launched its Corporate Governance Index.
- 2013: CBRC new Corporate Governance Guidelines for commercial banks
- 2013: The Guidance on Launch of Preference Share Pilot Programme (November 2013) (This is an interesting piece of legislation that introduces another new form of shares.)
- 2014: China Association for Public Companies (CAPCO) issues guidelines for Independent Directors in discharging their duties.
- 2014: The Rules on Shareholders' Meetings of Listed Companies (2014 version)
- 2014 version: The Administrative Measures on Takeover of Listed Companies (the "**Takeover Code**")

According to the OECD, in addition to these securities-related legislations, the addition of the following further strengthened the corporate governance foundation for China:[35]

- A new Corporate Bankruptcy Law was enacted in 2007 which applied to SOEs, foreign investment enterprises, and domestic companies.
- The Criminal Law (2006) was designed to match the amended Securities Law and Company Law, to give a more complete definition of legal liabilities in the securities field, improve the laws governing the securities market, and promote its healthy development.
- The Law on the State-Owned Assets of Enterprises (2009) was promulgated to safeguard the protection of state-owned assets, allow the state-owned sector to play a dominant role in the national economy, and promote the development of a socialist market economy.
- The Accounting Law (2000) laid out requirements on accounting practices, special provisions on companies' accounting practices, accounting supervision, accounting offices, accounting personnel, and legal liability.

---

35. OECD, 2011.

Current situation

The development of corporate governance in China has been remarkable. The CSRC and the newer SASAC have done a remarkable job of introducing the basics of sound corporate governance practices into China. Of course there are inevitable problems, including the identification and training of suitable directors, the changing of old attitudes developed in the SOEs, ensuring compliance with the regulations and codes, plus corruption and the nature of the legal system and potential political influence on the judiciary. Issues of individual accountability, roles, and quality of independent non-executive directors, transparency, and other issues have continued to plague corporate governance in China.

Nevertheless, in a decade CSRC, SASAC, and the State Council of the PRC have laid down a corporate governance system that took the US and the UK over a century to create.

No doubt the corporate governance framework in China will continue to evolve. Inevitably there will be corporate collapses and catastrophes, as elsewhere in the world, that will lead to new laws, regulations, and procedures. The massive and continuing economic growth in the PRC is already making big demands on the corporate governance framework. But the balance of influence is shifting. Overseas investors are keen to make inward investment riding on this success. China is generating massive financial reserves and is buying companies overseas, and adapting to corporate governance standards of other jurisdictions. At this stage Chinese companies have begun to dictate the corporate governance nuances that they require from companies abroad if they are to invest in them.

References

A stock trading link between Hong Kong and Shenzhen will go live next week. (2016, November 27). *Fortune*. Retrieved May 1, 2018 from http://fortune.com/2016/11/27/china-hong-kong-shenzhen-trade/.

Cai, J., et al. (2007). What will privatization bring: The non-tradable share issue reform in China. *SSRN Electronic Journal*. Retrieved May 1, 2018 from http://ssrn.com/abstract=981682.

Chen, J. J. H. (2015). *A primer on corporate governance in China*. New York: Business Expert Press.

Chen, Q. T. (2004, February 26). State shareholders should become an active force in promoting and establishing effective corporate governance. Retrieved May 1, 2018 from http://www.oecd.org/corporate/ca/corporategovernanceofstate-ownedenterprises/31452400.pdf.

China's securities and futures markets (2007, February). Retrieved May 1, 2018 from http://www.csrc.gov.cn/pub/csrc_en/about/annual/200812/P020090225529643752895.pdf.

China Securities Regulatory Commission. (2002). *Code of corporate governance for listing companies in China*.

China Securities Regulatory Commission. (2007). *China's securities and futures markets.*
China Securities Law. (2005). Adopted at the 6th Meeting of the Standing Committee of the 9th National People's Congress on December 29, 1998, revised at the 18th Meeting of the Standing Committee of the Tenth National People's Congress of the People's Republic of China on October 27, 2005. Effective January 1, 2006.
Clarke, D. C. (2014). Corporate governance in China: An overview. University of Washington School of Law: December 5, 2014.
Fortune (2017, October 27). Mapping the World Changers. *Fortune.* Retrieved May 1, 2018 from http://fortune.com/change-the-world/visualizations/?iid=recirc_ctwlanding-zone1.
Ge, C. (2017, June 9). Shenzhen Metro to become biggest China Vanke shareholder as Evergrande cashes out. *South China Morning Post.* Retrieved May 1, 2018 from http://www.scmp.com/business/companies/article/2097697/shenzhen-metro-become-biggest-china-vanke-shareholder-evergrande.
Grace, Y. & Jian, F. (2017, June 19). *International comparative legal guide.* Retrieved May 1, 2018 from http://www.iclg.co.uk/practice-areas/corporate-governance/corporate-governance-2016/china.
Gregory, N., & Tenev, S. (2001). China's home-grown entrepreneurs. *The China Business Review*, Jan.–Feb.
Group Overview: CHINA VANKE CO., LTD. (2017, October 27). Retrieved May 1, 2018 from http://www.vanke.com/en/about.aspx.
Guo, J., & Li, Y. M. (2006). Directors' liabilities and risks management: A new era under the amended company law and the amended securities law. *King and Wood Special Bulletin.*
Ho, S. S. M. (2003). *Corporate governance in China: Key problems and prospects.* Center for Accounting Disclosure and Corporate Governance, The Chinese University of Hong Kong.
Hu, A. G. & Hu, G. (2004). Corporate governance in China in the transitional era. Working Paper. Center of Chinese Studies, Tsinghua University.
International Finance Corporation. (2005). Step by step: Corporate governance models in China—The experience of the international finance corporation.
Institute of International Finance. (2006). *Corporate governance in China: An investor's perspective.* Institute of International Finance. March 2006.
Kan, W. (2001). Is China ready for the WTO? *Company Secretary*, *11*(2), 39–41.
Management Team: WANG Shi, Chairman of Board of Directors. (2017, October 27). Retrieved May 1, 2018 from http://www.vanke.com/en/about.aspx?type=5.
Naughton, B. (2004, January 14–15). Market economy, hierarchy, and single party rule: How does the transition path in China shape the emerging market economy? Paper presented at the International Economic Association, Hong Kong.
Naughton, B. (2006) Claiming profit for the state: SASAC and the capital management budget. *China Leadership Monitor*, Spring, no. 18. Retrieved from May 1, 2018 from http://media.hoover.org/documents/clm18_bn.pdf.
List of Central SOEs (2018). [央企名录]. Retrieved on August 1, 2018 from http://www.sasac.gov.cn/n2588035/n2641579/n2641645/index.html.
OECD (2011), Corporate Governance of Listed Companies in China: Self-Assessment by the China Securities Regulatory Commission, OECD. http://dx.doi.org/10.1787/9789264119208-en.
Peverelli, P. J. (2006). *Chinese corporate identity.* Abingdon, Oxon: Routledge.

SASAC Rising. (2005). *China Leadership Monitor*, Spring, no. 14. Retrieved May 1, 2018, from http://media.hoover.org/documents/clm14_bn.pdf.

State share reform not "'selling out all shares'" (2005, June 27). Retrieved May 1, 2018 from http://www.china-embassy.org/eng/gyzg/t201442.htm.

Statistics of June 2007. (2007, July 10). [2007年6月统计数据] *CSRC*. Retrieved May 1, 2018 from http://www.csrc.gov.cn/pub/zjhpublic/G00306204/zqscyb/200808/t20080818_108687.htm.

Stent, J. (2017). *China's banking transformation*. New York: Oxford University Press.

Summer Zhen. (2017, June 21). Vanke founder Wang Shi to step down as chairman. *South China Morning Post*. Retrieved May 1, 2018 from http://www.scmp.com/business/article/2099291/vankes-founder-wang-shi-step-down-chairman.

The central enterprise comprehensive risk management guidelines (2006, June 6). [中央企业全面风险管理指引]. Retrieved May 1, 2018, from http://www.tarivon.com/UpLoadFile/UploadFiles/2012112717554441.pdf. Chapter 8.

Vanke company overview. (2017, October 27). [公司资料]. Retrieved May 1, 2018 from http://www.aastocks.com/tc/stocks/analysis/company-fundamental/company-information?symbol=02202.

Vanke company News (2017, March 27): Vanke's net profit rises 16% to RMB 21.02 billion, sales amount in 14 cities exceed RMB 10 billion, actively explores new businesses. Retrieved May 1, 2018, from http://www.vanke.com/en/news.aspx?type=8&id=4328.

Walter, C. E., & Howie, F. J. T. (2006). *Privatizing China: Inside China's stock markets*. Singapore: John Wiley & Sons, Asia.

Wang, G. C. (2005). *Case studies of corporate governance*. Beijing: Economy and Management Publishing House.

Wang, S. (2017). *The Vanke way: Lessons on driving turbulent change from a global real estate giant*. New York: McGraw-Hill Education.

Xu, Jasper. (2017, September 20). Roundtable event with ACGA ("Asia Corporate Governance Association") about the China corporate governance. Retrieved May 1, 2018 from https://www.linkedin.com/pulse/roundtable-event-acga-asia-corporate-governance-association-jasper-xu.

Yueh, L. (2013). *Enterprising China: Business, economics, & legal development since 1979*. Oxford: Oxford University Press.

Zhen, S. (2016, December 23). What's next for Baoneng and Evergrande after the tussle for Vanke? *South China Morning Post*. Retrieved May 1, 2018 from http://www.scmp.com/business/article/2056888/whats-next-baoneng-and-evergrande-after-tussle-vanke.

Zhengquan Fa (证券法) (2007) [Securities Law of the People's Republic of China]. Retrieved December 11, 2007 from http://www.npc.gov.cn/englishnpc/Law/2007-12/11/content_1383569.htm.

Zhou, W. Q., & Cheung, Y. L. (2003). Some issues of corporate governance in China stock market. *Capital Journal* Issue 197.

Case study

Vanke: A Chinese conglomerate

History and overview

Vanke (Code: 2202.HK; 000002.SZ), founded in 1984, is one of the largest modern Chinese real-estate development companies in the PRC. It develops housing properties, as well as other retail and industrial properties related to the urban auxiliary services. As of July 2016, Vanke was listed on Fortune Global 500 as the 356th company by revenue.

The company experienced one of the most contentious corporate raids in recent years. The tussle eventually ended after 18 months with the stepping down of Wang Shi, its flamboyant founder, in June 2017, and redefined the rules for raiding and aggressive takeover in China. The Chinese government eventually stepped in and put the clamp back onto the company. Apparently this tussle even changed the insurance industry in China.[36]

The root of Vanke started outside properties. It began as the Vanke-Shenzhen Modern Scientific Education Instruments Exhibition & Sales Centre, established in 1984. Its main business was importing and selling office automation equipment, professional film, and TV equipment. At that time, it was reportedly the largest supplier of professional photography equipment in Shenzhen. Then in 1988, cooperating with Xin'an County of the Bao'an District in Shenzhen, it invested in its first land development project called the Gushu Village Hunggangling Vanke Industrial Park.[37] Its foray into properties continued, and by August 1990, the first housing project, called the Vanke-Shenzhen Sky View Garden, was completed.

The company succeeded in its IPO dream in 1989. With the revised name of Shenzhen Vanke Co., Ltd., it became the second company listed in SZSE later in 1991. The company originally wanted to keep its instruments and other businesses, and established its "integrated business" development model by dividing its business into 10 segments: import & export, retail chain, real estate development, finance & securities investments, culture, film and TV production, advertisement design and releasing, production and sales of beverage, printing and plate making, machining, and electrical engineering. By 1993, however, the board decided to give up the "integrated business" model. Instead, Vanke decided that its major business would be to develop residential housing for the public. To rebrand and reposition itself, Vanke was listed on the HKSE after converting its B-shares to H-shares in June 2014.

---

36. Summer Zhen (2017, June 21).
37. Group Overview: China Vanke Co., Ltd. (2017, October 27).

Business overview

The brand continues to reposition. Today, Vanke is known as an "integrated urban service provider" and has again started to venture into new businesses, such as commercial property, logistic property, long-term rental apartments, skiing business, pension, and has even dabbed in education. In 2016, Vanke acquired SCPG, another real estate company with strong capabilities in commercial development and operations management, and decided to use SCPG as the vehicle for realizing Vanke's commercial property platform.

Vanke divides its domestic markets into four sectors—Guangshen Region, Shanghai Region, Beijing Region, and Central & Western Region—covering 65 cities in China. In 2016, according to its annual report, Vanke's sales exceeded RMB 10 billion in each of the 14 cities. Of the 40 cities where it had business, it stood as one of the top three providers.

In 2016, Vanke achieved revenue of RMB 228.92 billion, representing a 24.2% increase compared to revenue of 2015. Profit attributable to shareholders amounted to RMB 21.02 billion, representing an increase of 16.0% compared to that of the previous year.[38]

Vanke's founder: The saga of Wang Shi

Wang Shi, the founding chairman of Vanke, was born in 1951 in Guangxi. He's known to be an avid mountaineer, a marathon runner, and a philanthropist. In 2003, Wang Shi reached the top of Mount Everest, becoming apparently the first entrepreneur in China who achieved this goal. Wang Shi is a colorful character, and his flamboyant personality has made this story even more interesting. (For a personal account of his life and his view of the takeover bid, please refer to his self-authored book.)

He has had a military background. He joined the PRC Military in 1968, and was discharged in 1973, where his last posting was with the Water and Electricity Supply Department of Zhengzhou Railway. His experience apparently helped him to gain various positions with the Guangzhou Railway Bureau, Foreign Trade and Economic Cooperation Committee of Guangdong Province, and Shenzhen Special Region Development Company[39] and eventually helped him to establish the Shenzhen Exhibition Centre for Modern Science and Education Equipment in 1984. When Vanke was officially established, Wang Shi became the chairman of Vanke and remained as the general manager for just another year.

He has been a spokesperson for many other enterprises, like Motorola, China Mobile, Ping An Insurance, and Volkswagen. Through these activities, he has gained

---

38. Company News (2017, March 27): Vanke's net profit rises 16% to RMB 21.02 billion, sales amount in 14 cities exceed RMB 10 billion, actively explores new businesses.
39. Management Team: Wang Shi, Chairman of Board of Directors (2017, October 27).

Figure 5.1

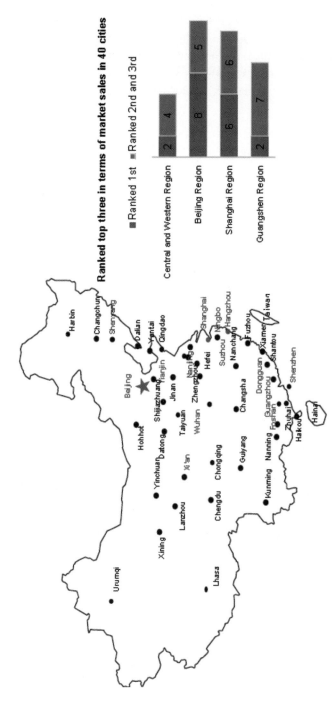

Source: *China Vanke Co., Ltd. 2016 Annual Results.*

wide public support and made a name for himself. However, critics complained that as a chairman of a listed company, Wang Shi should not be spending too much time doing things which are not relevant to Vanke's operation. By 1998, Wang Shi became so popular that he was included in the list of "20 Persons in the Past 20 Years of Reform and Opening-up." By 2000, he was selected as CCTV's Economic Figure of the Year 2000.[40]

Vanke's vision, mission, and values

- Vanke's vision[41]

  To maintain an industry leader in China's property sector and to be an outstanding green enterprise

- Vanke's values: Create a healthy enriched life

  Customers are always our partners; Talent is Vanke's asset; Transparent corporate governance; Provide sustained growth and leadership.

- Vanke's mission

  Celebrate life and build cities

- To achieve its mission,

  Vanke is committed, through its standardized, transparent corporate culture and reliable, focused development model, to becoming a respectable enterprise that is most popular with customers, investors, and employees.

Vanke: Business partners mechanism

Wang had believed in looking at his executives as business partners. In April 2014, Vanke came up with a means to help management gain ownership through the Business Partners Mechanism, which is composed of three parts:

1. Business Partnership Shareholding Scheme,
2. Project Co-Investment System, and
3. Event Partners Management.

1. Business Partnership Shareholding Scheme means employees may use their bonus to purchase Vanke's stocks.

2. Project Co-investment System allowed executive team members to invest in their own projects on a voluntary basis. He borrowed this idea from private equities.

---

40. Wang, 2017.
41. Group Overview: CHINA VANKE CO., LTD., 2017.

3. Event Partners Management allowed employees to participate in projects outside their immediate work areas.

In November 2015, for its innovation in corporate institutions, Vanke Business Partners Mechanism was awarded the "Shenzhen Jinpeng Revolution and Innovation Prize."[42] In their 2016 Annual Results Presentation, Vanke has the following description about the effect of its Business Partners Mechanism:

> As of the end of February 2017, the Group had 308 co-investment projects, of which 3.4% equity interest were being held by its business partners. The average duration in obtaining the co-invested projects to the first phase construction commencement and launch of the first phase of the project, as well as cash flow recovery had significantly shortened.

Vanke: Takeover battle with Baoneng

Jun Wan, as the initial attacker, began to acquire a little over 10% of Vanke's shares through the open market. The leader was a person called Zhang Guoqing, who was the GM of Junan Securities and who had the financial support of Hainan Securities. The attack was suspended when Wang Shi successfully got a suspension order of Vanke stock from the SZSE. Wang Shi's connection apparently had helped him to secure the temporary suspension. But the saga was enough to raise the attention of other aggressors.

Baoneng Group is a Shenzhen-based conglomerate in insurance and properties, the main businesses in insurance, covering real estate, logistics, and trade. It had a very low profile before this takeover battle that attracted widespread public attention. Baoneng was the aggressor. At one time it became Vanke's largest shareholder in December 2015, after increasing its stake in Vanke to 24.26%.

China Resources Vanguard (CRV) is an SOE and was the largest anchor shareholder of Vanke from 2000 to 2015. It had been known that CRV was supportive of Vanke's strategy and is a strategic partner. CRV was introduced by Wang Shi in 2000, as a white knight when Wang and his management team were being pushed out by several shareholders at that time. Wang Shi won, and CRV has remained an anchor ever since. It was Vanke's largest shareholder before Baoneng replaced it in 2015. In January 2017, CRV agreed to sell its entire stake (15.3%) in Vanke to Shenzhen Metro.

Shenzhen Metro Group is a subway operator controlled by the Shenzhen government. During the takeover battle, Wang Shi wanted to introduce Shenzhen Metro as a white knight. But apparently that negotiation did not end well for Wang Shi. SMG announced that it would terminate negotiation just three days before buying shares

---

42. Ibid.

from China Resources. After buying out Vanke's stake in China Resources, SMG ultimately became the largest shareholder of Vanke and Vanke regarded Shenzhen Metro as "Cornerstone Shareholder." Some believed this later development was a direct outcome of government intervention and not something that Wang Shi had wanted.

The corporate raid

This tussle began in 2015. Baoneng and another raider and competitor of Baoneng, China Evergrande Group, wanted to buy into Vanke. Both started a leveraged buyout of Vanke by redirecting its funds from their insurance units. By the end of 2015, Baoneng had acquired a substantive share and became Vanke's largest shareholder. When Baoneng's attempt picked up speed, China Evergrande also stepped up its purchase of Vanke shares from the market.

The motivation for Baoneng apparently was due to a regulatory change in the insurance industry. In 2015, China's stock market was disastrous, and the China Insurance Regulatory Commission had lifted the upper limit of permitted holdings for insurance companies from 30% to 40%, as a means to lift the market. Burdened with high liability costs, insurance companies took the initiative to raise their share of long-term equity investment, and some attributed to the need to hedge changes to fair-value basis in the accounting principle that was being adopted. Many private insurance companies were increasing their holding of equities, and Baoneng wanted to take advantage of this. And Vanke was in play.

But Wang Shi wasn't without his connections. He was able to garner support from the public and the government. Wang Shi aggressively and openly lambasted these raiders.

But it was Wang Shi who had made an error in judgment that had allowed his company to be taken over. In 1988, Vanke had its first shareholding restructuring, the state owning 60% and employees owning the remaining 40%. Wang Shi was no longer the owner of the firm, and he wanted to be seen as a professional manager, fully capable of running this business with his team. In 1991, Vanke went public and the state and employee's portion was diluted by 68%.

Eventually, both Baoneng and China Evergrande got into trouble for this game. The insurance regulator, the China Insurance Regulatory Commission, later penalized both for their aggressive actions. But this initial lack of oversight by the insurance regulator had already raised another set of suspicions in the market.

The first was that with excessive regulations to come, insurance companies in the future would have their capacity or avenue limited in delivering their promised payouts to policyholders or to investors. They would no longer be allowed to invest in such actions as a means to raise returns. The second was that a mechanism of corporate governance, ridding of ineffective management through acquisition of shares from the market, was being deterred by administrative government control.

Baoneng's war chest was funded primarily by insurance premium, 80% of which came from one of its subsidiaries and one product, Foresea. Foresea's universal life insurance product was the company's top product.[43] (This product was subsequently banned by the insurance regulator following its investigation into Baoneng.) This action literally took the steam out of Baoneng's corporate raid.[44]

Evergrande, in contrast, fared worse. It had funded the raid by taking on more debt, and pushed its debt-to-equity ratio to 400%. After the failed raid, it agreed with the regulator to transfer all its shares to Shenzhen Metro, even at a loss.[45] According to its spokesperson, the disposal would result in a loss of RMB7.07 billion for Evergrande. According to the *South China Morning Post*,[46]

> Evergrande already made 4.7 billion yuan in paper loss, as Vanke's share price declined after its initial purchase. After spending 36 billion yuan amassing Vanke shares, Evergrande's own share price hadn't fared any better, falling 12.65 per cent from the time it declared its hand on August 15, to December 16 when it conceded it had no intention to control Vanke. That's wiped out almost HK$10 billion in its market value.

During the tussle, Vanke had reached out to the Shenzhen Metro as its white knight, and eventually the state-backed subway operator became the largest shareholder, holding 29.38%.

Event timeline

2015

July: Baoneng Group began to raise its stake in China Vanke.

December 4: Baoneng becomes Vanke's largest shareholder after increasing its stake four times to 20% and apparently with the intent to oust the current management team.

December 18: Trading in Vanke's shares was suspended (again). Chairman Wang Shi said Vanke did not welcome the involvement of Baoneng, which by then had a 24.26% stake. Vanke announced it was planning to issue new shares to be used for major asset restructuring and acquisition. Another company called Jushenghua, which was controlled by Baoneng, was able to acquire up to 22.45% through the secondary market.

---

43. Universal insurance has been a controversial insurance product. This product, without proper safeguards and oversights by regulators, can be used by the policyholder to move substantial sums out of China. It is a type of cash value life insurance product that provides a savings elements. It works like this. The buyer pays a huge initial sum, say US$5 million premium all at once, for a life insurance policy that returns an annuity over the life of the insurer. The combined principal and interests would give back a sufficient amount, usually much more than a monthly stipend, to the insurer, who by that time, could be living overseas.
44. Zhen (2016, December 23).
45. Ge (2017, June 9).
46. Zhen (2016, December 23).

2016

January 6: Trading in Vanke shares resumed in Hong Kong, but its Shenzhen-traded shares remained suspended, pending an asset-restructuring plan.

March 13: Vanke sought state-backed Shenzhen Metro Group to come in as the white knight to fend off Baoneng's potential hostile takeover. Initially, Wang had sought out CRV to raise their share, but CRV was not interested. The move to bring in Shenzhen Metro as a last resort angered CRV.

June 17: Baoneng and CRV, Vanke's two largest shareholders, rejected the property developer's proposal to introduce Shenzhen Metro, during a board meeting. CRV bought more shares and became the largest shareholder again.

June 26: Baoneng filed a proposal for removing all of Vanke's board members and asked Vanke's board to convene general meeting of shareholders to vote.

July 1: Baoneng's proposal for convening general meeting of shareholders to vote for removing Vanke's board members was vetoed by Vanke's board.

July 19: Baoneng further increased its stake to 25.4%. Vanke issued a report that Baoneng had committed illegal control of its asset. Evergrande joined the battle and increased its stake to 14.07%.

December 3: The authorities stepped in and began to clamp down on leveraged buyouts in the stock market and sent inspection teams to the insurance units of Baoneng-Foresea Life Insurance to check if there were any non-compliance activities.

December 5: The China Insurance Regulatory Commission suspended Baoneng's unit Foresea Life Insurance from selling "universal life" products.

December 9: The commission banned Evergrande Life, the insurance arm of Evergrande, from trading in stocks.

2017

January 12: China Resources agreed to sell its entire stake (15.3%) in Vanke to Shenzhen Metro. Wang Shi to step down as chairman.

March 12: Vanke and Shenzhen Metro signed a strategic cooperation agreement to reach close cooperation and common development by relying on the "metro + property" mode. Vanke's board of 11 was up for re-election. CRV had three seats. Neither Baoneng nor Evergrande had any seat at this time.

June 30: Wang Shi indicated he would be stepping down as the chairman of Vanke.[47]

---

47. Ibid.

Vanke: Corporate governance architecture

The governance architecture of Vanke is shown in Figure 5.2:

Figure 5.2

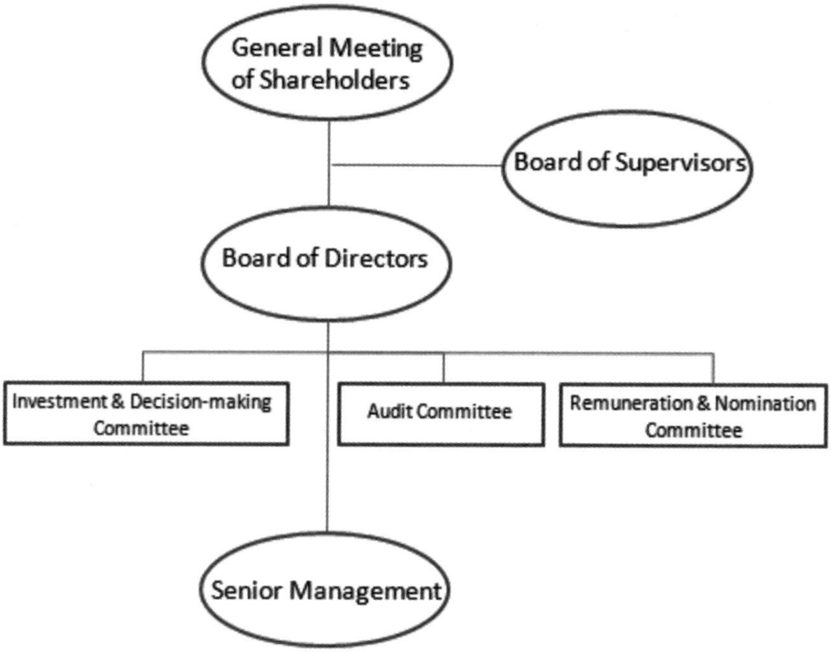

Source: *Vanke 2016 Annual Report.*

Since the tenure of the board of directors is only three years, scheduled to expire on March 27, 2017, the fight for the control of the company would continue on to July 2017. We should expect a continual shift in membership.

In early 2016, the board of directors had 11 members:[48]

Three executive directors:

- WANG Shi, chairman of the board
- YU Liang, director and president (who later became chairman, president, CEO, and an executive director after ousting Wang Shi)
- WANG Wenjin, executive director and vice president

---

48. See http://www.vanke.com/en/investors.aspx?type=15&id=4132.

Four non-executive directors:

- QIAO Shibo, director and deputy chairman
- SUN Jianyi, director
- WEI Bin, director
- CHEN Ying, director

Four independent non-executive directors:

- ZHANG Liping
- HUA Sheng
- LAW Elizabeth
- HAI Wen

The board has three specialized committees:

- Audit Committee
- Remuneration and Nomination Committee
- Investment and Decision-making Committee

The Supervisory Committee currently has three members:

- XIE Dong
- LIVASIRI Ankana
- ZHOU Qingping

The Current Board, as of June 2017, changed to:[49]

- YU Liang (chairman & president & CEO & executive director)
- LIN Maode (vice chairman & non-executive director) from Shenzhen Metro
- WANG Wenjin (executive vice president & executive director)
- ZHANG Xu (executive vice president & executive director)
- XIAO Min (non-executive director) from Shenzhen Metro
- CHEN Xianjun (non-executive director) from Shenzhen Metro
- SUN Shengdian (non-executive director)
- KANG Dian (independent non-executive director)
- LIU Shuwei (independent non-executive director)
- NG Kar Ling, J. (independent non-executive director)
- LI Qiang (independent non-executive director)

The new seats from Shenzhen Metro came from the SOE that had agreed to buy a 14.07% stake in Vanke from rival developer Evergrande. This made Shenzhen Metro the largest owner, at 29.38%. Shenzhen Metro is now the white knight, and the Chinese government appears to be in firm control.

---

49. Vanke Company overview (2017, October 27).

Questions for discussion

1. What corporate governance issues can you identify from this takeover battle between Vanke and Baoneng? What sort of role should government authorities have played during such battles?

2. What can Vanke do to prevent takeover threats like this in the future? What has been done outside China?

3. Should a chair be a spokesperson of another company's product or endorse another company's positioning?

4. Should employees be allowed to invest directly into the project taken by their company? What are the benefits and the risks?

5. What are the advantages in combining the role of nomination and the role of remuneration into one committee? Ping An kept them separate. Why?

6

The Regulatory Framework of Corporate Governance in Hong Kong

Bob Tricker

In this chapter we consider:

- ❖ the evolution of corporate governance in Hong Kong
- ❖ corporate governance institutions
- ❖ the Independent Commission Against Corruption (ICAC)
- ❖ relevant professions
- ❖ nominated advisors (NOMADS)
- ❖ some classic corporate governance cases
- ❖ the Hong Kong Companies Ordinances
- ❖ Hong Kong Corporate Governance Code
- ❖ Hong Kong Stock Exchange Listing Rules
- ❖ Hong Kong Financial Reporting Council (FRC)
- ❖ core competencies for an effective director (HKIoD)
- ❖ influences for the future

The evolution of corporate governance in Hong Kong

We briefly mentioned Hong Kong's history in Chapter 3. That history proved to be fundamental to the development of corporate governance. Following their defeat in the First Opium War in 1842, China's Qing dynasty government was forced to cede Hong Kong Island to Britain. In those days Hong Kong was a barren place, known for its fishing and its pirates. The establishment of trading companies, known as the "hongs," led to the development of trade. Subsequently, China granted a further lease to the peninsula north of Hong Kong Island (Kowloon) and then further land (the New Territories) up to the border with China. At the time Britain was ruled by Queen Victoria, and Hong Kong became part of the British Empire.

Consequently, as Hong Kong developed, it came under the influence of British law, British commercial and banking practices, and British traditions. It had its own government bodies, its own law courts, and its own currency. By the later part of the twentieth century, after its liberation following the World War II, Hong Kong had created the institutions necessary for a major international financial and commercial center in Asia Pacific. It had a thriving banking sector, a significant stock market, the relevant accounting, auditing, and legal firms and their related professional institutions. It also created the regulatory bodies necessary for sound corporate governance.

Corporate governance institutions

Regulators

The Companies Registry

Companies operating in Hong Kong must follow Hong Kong company law, currently the 2014 Companies Ordinance. The registry supervises the incorporation of companies in Hong Kong although many Hong Kong–based companies were incorporated in offshore tax havens, such as the Cayman Islands, to avoid the filing of company information and to avoid tax.

The registry records the details of both local and overseas companies operating in Hong Kong. It keeps the statutory returns that companies are required to make. These are open to public inspection, and the registry provides facilities for inspecting and obtaining copies of the information. The registry's website at http://www.cr.gov.hk/en/home/ describes its major services and provides information on the Companies Ordinance.

Securities and Futures Commission (SFC)

Until the mid-1970s, stock and commodities markets in Hong Kong were largely unregulated. After a stock market crash in 1973–1974, the government intervened, and the core legislation governing the securities and futures industry was enacted. The legislation was administered by two part-time commissions—one for securities and the other for commodities trading—and their executive arm (the Office of the Commissioner for Securities and Commodities Trading), which were established as part of the government. This structure remained largely unchanged for over a decade, during which time there was rapid change in the securities and futures markets, both internationally and in Hong Kong.

In April 1986, the existing four stock exchanges in Hong Kong were combined to create the Stock Exchange of Hong Kong (SEHK) (and later become HKSE after a restructuring). However, financial markets worldwide were expanding and changing, and the SEHK executive staff sometimes lacked relevant experience and knowledge. Governance of the exchange was in the hands of an insider group who dominated executive decisions and tended to treat the exchange as a private club rather than a financial utility.

The global financial crisis in October 1987 hit stock markets around the world on what became known as "Black Monday." Hong Kong was not immune, and the Hong Kong market was closed to avoid its collapse. As a result, the Hong Kong government formed a committee to investigate the practices in the SEHK that had led to its closure. A report was commissioned from Ian Hat Davison, the senior partner of the London office of Arthur Anderson, one of the "Big Five" accountancy firms. The Anderson firm subsequently collapsed following a calamitous relationship by its New York office with Enron, resulting in the "Big Five" becoming the "Big Four."

In Hong Kong, Ronald Li, previously chairman of the HKSE, was arrested by the ICAC on corruption charges relating to his time as chairman, charged, and found guilty. Control of the HKSE was then vested in a 14-member management committee.

The Davison Committee reported in May 1988, concluding that the Office of the Commissioner for Securities and Commodities Trading had insufficient resources to regulate the rapidly growing and changing Hong Kong market properly. The committee found that too much effort had been spent on ineffective routine vetting, instead of the active monitoring of markets and intermediaries. The two commissions were not regulating effectively because they lacked strong direction and had become passive and reactive, instead of being active and proactive. The committee recommended the creation of a single statutory body outside the civil service, headed and staffed by full-time professional regulators and funded primarily by the market. In their view, such a body should have broad investigative and disciplinary powers to enable it to perform its regulatory functions effectively. The SFC was created in 1988, in line with the Davison Committee recommendations, as an independent non-governmental statutory body outside the civil service, responsible for regulating the securities and futures markets in Hong Kong.

The SFC has considerable investigative and disciplinary statutory powers, and responsibility for:

- setting and enforcing market regulations, including investigating breaches of rules and market misconduct;
- licensing and supervising intermediaries that conduct activities under the SFC's regulatory responsibility;
- supervising market operators, including exchanges, clearing houses, share registrars and alternative trading platforms, and helping to enhance market infrastructure;
- authorizing investment products and offering documents prior to their distribution to retail investors;
- overseeing regulations governing takeovers and mergers of public companies;
- overseeing regulations governing The Stock Exchange of Hong Kong Limited's regulation of listing matters;

- cooperating with and providing assistance to local and overseas regulatory authorities; and
- helping investors understand market operations, the risks of investing and their rights and responsibilities.

For more information, see http://www.sfc.hk/web/EN/about-the-sfc/our-role/.

The powers of the SFC were strengthened in 1997, following the Asian financial crisis, and the powers of the SFC were consolidated in the 2003 Securities and Futures Ordinance. The global financial crisis, which began in 2007, led to further strengthening of corporate regulation. As a member of IOSCO (the International Organization of Securities Commissions), the SFC played an important role in fostering cross-border cooperation on corporate governance matters throughout Asia-Pacific and around the world.

Most recently, the SFC has strengthened its ongoing collaboration with the authorities in mainland China on enforcement issues and other regulatory matters. The SFC was also instrumental in the creation of the Hong Kong–Shanghai Stock Connect system, which facilitates trades between the two stock exchanges and brings growing interaction between Hong Kong and Shanghai financial markets.

Hong Kong Stock Exchange (HKSE)

HKSE can trace its roots to 1891. Since then various amalgamations and mergers led to the unified stock exchange that exists today. According to the World Federation of Exchanges, in 2017, exchanges in the United States (NYSE and NASDAQ) were the two largest followed by the exchanges in China, (Hong Kong, Shanghai, and Shenzhen). London, including Europe, came third, followed by Japan, fourth, and Singapore, fifth. Hong Kong's market capitalization is approximately HK$30 trillion, (US$38 billion), with just over 2,000 stocks listed on its Main Board, around half being companies in mainland China. The rest are companies based in Hong Kong, around 5% based elsewhere in the world. Five of the top ten stocks by value listed on the HKSE board are mainland China-based companies. In recent years, HKSE has led the world's exchanges in the number and value of companies listed through IPOs, almost all of them companies from mainland China.

However, HKSE enjoys a unique status, being both a publicly listed company and the stock exchange regulator in Hong Kong, working closely with the SFC. This inherent conflict between HKSE's responsibilities to its shareholders and its public interest function has been widely recognized. Below is the rating organization Standard & Poor's comment in their corporate governance analysis of HKSE:

> While there is a strong correlation between the long-term public interest of HKEx maintaining its leadership role in Asian financial markets and the consequent financial benefits to its shareholders, it is important to be alert to situations where the public's interests may conflict with those of shareholders, particularly given a

board structure that suggests a primary accountability to the former. It is important to note that Standard & Poor's see no evidence of any major conflicts around HKEx's dual accountability to both shareholders and the public at large, nor does Standard & Poor's believe that the HKEx has ever misused its regulatory influence to benefit its own financial performance . . . the ongoing public debate over the appropriateness of HKEx's regulatory role vis-à-vis listed companies, while being itself a listed company, may eventually lead to changes to both HKEx's regulatory role as well as its overall governance structure.

The governance of HKSE is in the hands of its board of directors with 13 members: 6 are elected by the shareholders to represent investors' interests and 6 are appointed by the Hong Kong government, through the Financial Secretary, to represent the public interest. The board appoints the CEO, the thirteenth, who is the only executive member of the board. All of the shareholder-elected and public interest-appointed directors are non-executive and independent of the company and its management.

The company has adopted a staggered board system in which only two directors are up for election at a time. This acts as some defense against any attempt by a predator to take over the company. The board chairperson is elected by the directors from among them. The directors select the CEO.

In response to the charge that HKSE effectively regulates itself, the company states that conflicts of interest between the regulatory and commercial functions of HKSE are avoided by an organizational firewall which separates the two activities. Nevertheless, this can raise issues at board level, where the two functions come together, as can be seen in the case study at the end of this chapter.

The actual shares of HKSE are widely held. No single shareholder owns more than 5% of the shares; indeed, there is a 5% limitation, imposed by the government. HKSE also routinely provides details of major share ownership. Around half the shareholders are from outside Hong Kong. Concern has been expressed that shareholding brokers could act in concert to affect decisions to their own benefit, but there is no evidence of this having happened in recent years. In the early days of the company, broker members of the exchange held all the shares, but the aggregate number of shares held by brokers has fallen substantially.

The company recently adopted quarterly financial reporting, which sets a new standard for listed companies in Hong Kong. The board has three board committees—audit, nomination, and remuneration—all composed of non-executive directors.

HKSE introduced a second board in 1988—the Growth Enterprise Market (GEM)—to raise capital for smaller, and often riskier, developing companies. But in recent years market and regulatory concerns have been raised about the quality and performance of companies listed on GEM. These include concerns about price volatility of GEM securities after their IPO, whether there was an open market for all GEM listings and the possible exploitation of GEM as a means of achieving a

Main Board listing without a commensurate due diligence process. HKSE proposed changes to the GEM listing rules to address these concerns.

The CEO and the directors recognize that, strategically, HKSE needs to stay abreast of developments in the region and around the world. They are aware that market conditions change. Hong Kong's preeminence in listing major mainland China companies could not be maintained indefinitely: some China companies have already listed in New York or Singapore, rather than Hong Kong. There was also a need to broaden capital markets access in Hong Kong by opening up to a more diverse range of potential listed companies to strengthen Hong Kong's listing regime, and to improve the quality of the exchange's markets, while enhancing Hong Kong's competitiveness as a global financial center.

So a new trading board was proposed, which would be designed to attract companies that could not otherwise list in Hong Kong, such as those that had not yet reached profitability, companies with non-standard corporate governance features, and mainland China companies that wanted to have a secondary listing in Hong Kong.

For more information, see www.HKEx.com.hk.

The Independent Commission Against Corruption (ICAC)

After the end of World War II, bribery and corruption became endemic in Hong Kong. Civil servants, firefighters, and police, whose pay was relatively low, usurped their power. To get any sort of government license, a place in a government hospital, or to call out the fire brigade or avoid a police summons, officials expected a gratuity, called by the Cantonese "tea money," which was actually a bribe or "kickback." Much larger sums could be involved in government contracts, customs assessments, and building works, involving those in higher authority.

In 1974, the Hong Kong's British Governor, Sir Murray MacLehose, faced up to the situation and created the ICAC, an organization independent of the civil service and the police, reporting directly to the governor. This line of accountability was perpetuated after the 1997 handover by Britain to China. The Commissioner, the head of the ICAC, is appointed by the State Council of the PRC in Beijing, on the recommendation of the Chinese-nominated Hong Kong Chief Executive.

In the early years many of the ICAC officers were drafted from police forces in Britain. Some years of turmoil followed, and many police officers and customs officials being prosecuted, including some senior officers. But eventually, ICAC prevailed. Attitudes towards bribery and corruption began to change for the better. Hong Kong is now recognized as one of the least corrupt places in the world, ranking second in Asia after Singapore.

Over the years, ICAC has widened the focus of its operations beyond government, public bodies, and the customs and police, to include businesses, the financial services sector, the media, and society at large. Its span now covers official bribery, commercial bribery, and conspiracy. A recent development has been on cyber-crime, which is crucial given Hong Kong's dependence on commerce and financial services.

ICAC is organized into three divisions: operations, corruption prevention, and community relations. Investigations are typically triggered by corruption reports filed through a whistle-blower hotline, at ICAC district offices, or from the police.

In the Bribery and Corruption Report 2017, Global Legal Insights comment that:

> Hong Kong continues to have a reputation for strong anti-corruption laws and an effective enforcement regime. Coming in at rank 18 of the 2015 Transparency International Corruption Perception Index (CPI), Hong Kong is currently ranked a shared second in Asia (together with Japan). Recent years have seen a number of high-profile enforcement actions which clearly demonstrate the ICAC's determination to continue fighting corruption at the highest echelons of Hong Kong's government as well as the business community. The ICAC's success in these high-profile enforcement actions will likely be the key to Hong Kong climbing up the CPI ranking once again and reinstating its strong anti-corruption reputation.

When the sovereignty of Hong Kong switched from Britain to China in 1997, the Basic Law establishing the change of jurisdiction provided for a "Commission Against Corruption." This was the phrase used in the Chinese version of the law, which took preference, so the ICAC was recognized by the incoming authorities. However, in recent years, some questions have been asked about the independence of the ICAC, alleging examples of undue influence from officials with close ties to the Chinese authorities in Beijing.

As a signatory to the United Nations Convention Against Corruption (UNCAC), China is required to provide mutual assistance to other jurisdictions on corruption issues. As an SAR of China, Hong Kong has similar responsibilities.

The ICAC's website is at http://www.icac.org.hk/en/home/index.html.

Relevant professions

The Judiciary

Hong Kong Bar Association

The Law Society of Hong Kong

Company law is a cornerstone of sound corporate governance. A judicial system that makes the law, reliable courts that uphold the law, and a legal profession to advise on and to practice the law are essential components. Hong Kong has them all.

After the handover in 1997, the principle of "One Country, Two Systems" was implemented in Hong Kong, leaving Hong Kong's common law legal system intact. The judicial system continues to operate independently.

The Judiciary

The Judiciary in Hong Kong exists "to maintain an independent and effective judicial system which upholds the rule of law, safeguards the rights and freedoms of the individual, and commands confidence within and outside Hong Kong." The legal system in Hong Kong is based on the English system of common law, a hierarchy of courts, jury trials, and judges' decisions becoming precedents for future cases.

In the court system of the HKSAR, the supreme court is the Court of Final Appeal. It plays an important part in the development of the common law in Hong Kong. The court was established on July 1, 1997, on the transfer of sovereignty to China, replacing the previous right of appeal to the Judicial Committee of the Privy Council in London.

The Court of Final Appeal hears appeals involving important questions of law, including particular points of public and constitutional importance. The court can invite judges from other common law jurisdictions to sit on the court, and some distinguished judges from Australia, New Zealand, and the UK have served as members of the court.

The independence of the courts is an important feature of the Basic Law enacted on the transfer of oversight to China. An issue arose in 2014, when the PRC published a paper on Hong Kong's autonomy, which suggested that patriotism to China was a prerequisite for judges in Hong Kong. Lawyers protested and the president of the Law Society, who appeared to support the idea, received a motion of no confidence.

The Judiciary's web site is at http://www.judiciary.hk/en/index.

The Hong Kong Bar Association (HKBA)

The Hong Kong Bar Association is the professional organization of barristers, who are self-employed independent legal practitioners and advocates providing legal services, usually on instructions from solicitors. The HKBA was founded in 1949 and now has around 1,300 practicing members.

HKBA endeavors to promote friendly relations with the legal profession in the region, creating a Standing Committee on Greater China Affairs in 2000, to communicate with law-related professional institutions and judicial officials in mainland China, Taiwan, and Macau.

The HKBA website is at www.hkna.org.

The Law Society of Hong Kong

The origins of the Law Society of Hong Kong stem from 1907. The society is the professional certification body for solicitors to practice law in Hong Kong. It maintains the standards of practice and ethics in the profession and represents the interests of its members. It represents around 10,000 practicing solicitors, (these lawyers or attorneys are called "solicitors," reflecting the British practice), around 80% of whom are ethnic Chinese although there are around 80 foreign law firms registered in the territory.

For more information, see http://www.hklawsoc.org.hk/pub_e/default.asp.

Hong Kong Institute of Certified Public Accountants (HKICPA)

HKICPA evolved from the Hong Kong Society of Accountants, which was established in 1973. The institute operates under the Professional Accountants Ordinance and regulates entry into the accounting profession through its postgraduate CPA examinations. The HKICPA issues practicing certificates and is responsible for maintaining the professional conduct and standards of its members. The institute sets the accounting, financial reporting, and auditing standards and ethical codes applicable in Hong Kong.

Some members of the institute work as sole practitioners. Others are in accountancy firms working on accountancy, audit, and taxation matters. Yet others work in management consultancy, accountancy, and finance in companies, or in other occupations. HKICPA has around 36,000 members and 18,000 registered students.

The Hong Kong Society of Accountants, the predecessor of the HKICPA, wrote and published the first Hong Kong Corporate Governance Code, which reflected the UK's Cadbury Code amended for the unique circumstances of Hong Kong companies. Subsequently, the code was incorporated into the HKSEs' listing rules, as we will discuss subsequently.

For more on HKICPA see http://www.hkicpa.org.hk/en/.

Hong Kong Institute of Chartered Secretaries (HKICS)

Under the Hong Kong Companies Act, all companies are required to have a company secretary. The UK Companies Act has a similar requirement although in the US the function is typically known as the corporate secretary or counsel.

HKICS is the professional body responsible for qualifying, registering, disciplining, and representing the interests of company secretaries in Hong Kong. Its members work for listed companies (38%), private companies (28%), secretarial services firms (23%), and government or other public bodies (11%). The institute has around 6,000 members and 2,500 students. The majority of the members and students are located in Hong Kong. However, HKICS also acts as the China Division of the UK-based Institute of Chartered Secretaries and Administrators (ICSA) and the Mainland's interest in the company secretarial function is growing.

Significantly, HKICS has branded itself as the professional body dedicated to promoting good corporate governance in Hong Kong and mainland China. Its research and publications emphasize aspects of corporate governance. The HKICS official website is at https://www.hkics.org.hk.

Hong Kong Institute of Directors (HKIoD)

The HKIoD represents directors in Hong Kong through advocacy and encouraging sound corporate governance. Though not an examining or regulating body, the institute's code of conduct calls for honesty, legality, diligence, accountability, and integrity, to foster the long-term success of companies. Continuing professional development is a key component of its activities.

The institute began as the Hong Kong branch of the London-based Institute of Directors. On the handover of sovereignty to China on 1 July 1997, Hong Kong members became members of the HKIoD, a company limited by guarantee that had been incorporated the previous year.

HKIoD has developed a set of core competencies for directors, which we will follow later in this chapter. Further information of the work of the HKIoD is at http://www.hkiod.com.

Nominated advisors (NOMADS)

In recent years, HKSE has added more companies to its board through initial public offerings than have other exchanges around the world. The reason is simple: the listing of China-based companies and additions to the GEM board. To be listed, HKSE rules require companies to apply through a nominated adviser (NOMAD), that is an experienced corporate financial adviser, with appropriate knowledge, skills, and experience, approved by HKSE. The NOMAD plays a vital role in promoting the company's listing and subsequently maintaining it. Consequently, a NOMAD needs a sound understanding of the company, its key players, and its strategy.

Typically, in guiding a company through admission to the market, the NOMAD will undertake a thorough due diligence study of the company and its finances, advise its management on its role in running a public company, prepare the admission documentation, and ensure that the company meets, and continues to meet, HKSE Listing Rules.

Some classic corporate governance cases

During the 1970s, Hong Kong business was rooted in a few British trading houses and companies run by a handful of Chinese entrepreneurs, whose families had fled from Shanghai to Hong Kong in the 1920s.

Among the trading houses were Swire, Hutchison, Hong Kong Land, and Jardine Matheson. Hutchison had run into financial problems and the Hong

Kong Shanghai Bank bailed them out, appointing W. R. A. (Bill) Wyllie to run the company. He merged it with his own company, the Whampoa Dock Company, forming Hutchison Whampoa, which was eventually acquired by Cheung Kong Holdings, the flagship of Li Ka-Shing.

Among the more predominant Chinese entrepreneurs were Li Ka-Shing, Sir Y. K. Pao, and Stanley Ho Hung Sun. Their businesses were typically conglomerates operating in diverse sectors although Ho's principal interests were in gambling in Macau. But all had significant investments in property, riding on the rising (and sometimes falling) switchback of Hong Kong's property prices.

The Hong Kong Chinese enterprises were typically run with the Chinese family-orientated low-key approach, quietly seizing opportunities when the time seemed propitious, rather than aiming for a long-term business strategy. Local investors invested in these companies to share in the entrepreneurs' good fortune, seeing themselves as an outer ring of the family circle.

In the late 1970s and early 1980s, however, some corporate governance issues arose. The government appointed inspectors to examine stock market price manipulation. Limitations in securities and company law were highlighted by difficulty in prosecuting James Coe and alleged dealings in the Sun King Cheung Hing Yip Company. Another discovery was that some companies had used their wholly owned subsidiary companies to buy shares in the parent company, thus limiting the possibility of a predator takeover.

There were also some takeover battles. In 1978, Sir Y. K. Pao acquired a stake in Wharf Holdings, a public company in the Jardine Group, which entitled him to a seat on the board. Over the next two years he built his stake up to 30% but said he intended to go no further. While he was away on a business trip to Mexico, Hong Kong Land made a bid for Wharf. Pao came back to Hong Kong secretly and checked into a hotel. Working with his financial advisers, Wardley, he decided the Hong Kong Land bid was insufficient and made a counter-offer which succeeded.

Then along came George Tan Soon Gin. Nobody in Hong Kong seemed to know where he came from or where he acquired his money. In 1979, Tan bought an inconsequential listed property company, Mai Hon Enterprises, and changed its name to Carrian Investments Ltd. Tan was flamboyant and ostentatious. At the Royal Hong Kong Jockey Club he was seen in the box with the chairman of Hong Kong Bank. Retail investors liked him and liked the company's name which in Chinese could imply "the best." Carrian shares soared in value.

Tan's first major property deal came in 1980: the purchase of Gammon House in Central. It was sold shortly afterwards for a substantial profit and eventually renamed Bank of America Tower. In 1981, Tan joined a consortium with a Malaysian entrepreneur to buy Hong Kong's General Bottling Company. The same year, Carrian joined a consortium to acquire the site of the old Miramar Hotel, and another to build tower blocks of luxury apartments. It was reported that Carrian had also invested in property developments in Australia, California, and China.

Carrian next launched a travel-related division, acquiring Kent Travel, Hong Kong's largest fleet of taxis, the Carrian bus fleet, and a firm providing ground handling facilities at Hong Kong's Kai Tak Airport. There were rumors that Tan was negotiating a takeover of Britain's Laker Airways. Tan did effect a merger with the respected Grand Marine, a shipping company, and ordered three new ships.

In mid-1981, Tan entered the financial services sector, acquired 10% of the Union Bank of Hong Kong, and 46% of China Underwriters. Both were listed companies. Under the takeover rules, acquiring 46% should have triggered a general offer to all shareholders, but Tan negotiated an exception to the rule.

To finance all these activities, Carrian became very heavily geared, owing large sums to banks in Hong Kong and around the world. Surprisingly, these banks seemed prepared to rely on the security of the transactions and Tan's reputation. During 1982, Carrian's shares tripled in price, leading some analysts to suggest they were overvalued. But investors, particularly the small retail investors, continued to have faith in Tan. Other critics wondered how Tan could manage his portfolio of such diverse businesses. But he had recruited a team of experienced managers, many of them expats.

In October 1982, Carrian indicated that it had liquidity problems. Creditor banks rescheduled their loans. An interim dividend was cancelled. An issue of further shares was planned, to be largely underwritten by Hong Kong and Shanghai Bank.

Faced with this downturn in Carrian's fortunes, the Hong Kong rumor mill began to spin. Suggestions of bribery surfaced. Questions were asked about the adequacy of the creditor banks' due diligence inquiries. These were reinforced when it emerged that Tan had been declared bankrupt in 1974 in Singapore.

Trading in Carrian shares was suspended in January 1983. But Tan struggled on until the summer, with many attempts to salvage Carrian. Then in September 1983, the police and the ICAC raided the Carrian offices and took away a vast number of papers and the company's computers. Tan could no longer operate.

Eventually, Tan, his CEO, Bentley Ho, and four other people were brought to trial on charges of conspiracy to defraud investors and creditors. Their trial, which started in March 1984, was the most costly in Hong Kong history. After 18 months, to the surprise of many and the consternation of the prosecution, the judge, Mr. Justice Barker, decided that on the evidence presented there was no case to answer. The saga of Carrian was over. Although, at least one analyst believed, on the basis of the evidence produced in the trial, that had his business information not been seized, Tan might have been able to negotiate Carrian's survival. Nothing like that has happened since in Hong Kong.

The ICAC continued to bring prosecutions alleging bribery or wrongful conduct in public office against officers in the public sector. It also pursued cases in the private sector. Recent seminal cases included a well-known TV host of Hong Kong–based Television Broadcasts Limited being charged with conspiracy to accept an advantage, when he was paid an appearance fee for filming in a shopping mall, without informing his employer. Other recent cases in the financial services industry have been brought against a bank manager for paying bribes for account referrals, and against a manager of an international bank for accepting benefits from a customer for giving preferential treatment.

The Hong Kong Companies Ordinances

The Companies Ordinance (Chapter 622 of the Laws of Hong Kong) and its subsidiary legislation came into effect on March 3, 2014, after many years of deliberation. The new Companies Ordinance provided a modernized legal framework for the incorporation, operation, and regulation of companies in Hong Kong and was designed to simplify and rationalize company law. Among many other provisions, the new law extended the exposure of directors and "other responsible persons" to prosecution for failing to exercise "due care, skill, and diligence." The law also introduced a new solvency test that companies needed to meet.

In developing company law and corporate governance regulation today, the HKSAR liaises with the CSRC in Beijing but is also influenced by developments in governance practices in other countries, including the US and Commonwealth countries such as Australia, Canada, Singapore, and the UK.

The full text of the Companies Ordinance can be read on: https://www.elegislation.gov.hk/hk/cap622?p0=1&p1=1.

Hong Kong Corporate Governance Code

The early 1990s saw some noteworthy corporate collapses in the US, the UK, Australia, Japan, and some other countries, often the result of fraud, ineffective boards of directors, or over-dominant company leaders. An interest developed in the way that corporate entities were governed as distinct from the way they were managed. The phrase "corporate governance" began to be used to describe the work of boards of directors, relations between companies and their shareholders, and the way that power was exercised over companies. The first book to use "corporate governance" in the title had been published in 1984. The academic research-based journal *Corporate Governance—An international review*, which has today become the leading international corporate governance research journal, was launched in 1993, and for the next eight years was edited from the University of Hong Kong Business School. Corporate governance codes of principles and good practices were published in some countries. The first was the UK's seminal Cadbury Report, *The Financial Aspects of Corporate Governance*, published in 1992.

Hong Kong's first reaction to the growing interest in corporate governance was an amendment to SEHK Listing Rules. The UK Cadbury Report had emphasized the importance of independent directors in balancing the interests of the executive directors and to serve on boards' audit, remuneration and nomination committees, which the report had advocated. In April 1993, SEHK introduced a significant change to demonstrate Hong Kong's commitment to sound board-level practices and to maintain its growing reputation as an international market. All companies listed in Hong Kong were required to appoint two independent non-executive directors to their boards. The initial reaction of commentators in Hong Kong was not enthusiastic: some questioned whether there were people with the relevant experience to undertake the role; some argued that the business world in Hong Kong was closely connected and few people could genuinely be considered independent; while others felt that the idea of independent directors was alien to the way the dominant owner-managers of many Hong Kong family businesses ran their companies.

Then in December 1995, the Hong Kong Society of Accountants (HKSA) published *Report of the Working Group on Corporate Governance*. The HKSA report recommended, among other things, that listed companies should:

- form an audit committee of the board;
- have three independent non-executive directors
  (SEHK Listing Rules already called for two);
- include in their annual report:
  - a general statement of corporate governance practices,
  - confirmation that the company was a going concern, and
  - a statement of internal control by the directors.

On audit committees, the report commented, "we are in support of audit committees as a useful and formal channel to facilitate communications between the board, external auditors, senior managers and the internal audit function." The report also proposed:

- improvements to SEHK Listing Rules;
- refinements of the SEHK Code of Best Practice;
- auditors reviewing non-financial information given in annual reports and reporting any inconsistencies with the audited financial statements; and
- a change to SEHK's Code of Best Practice, increasing the call for at least two board meetings a year to four, good practice being six.

However, the report rejected the separation of chairperson and CEO roles recommended in the Cadbury Report, commenting that "many Hong Kong companies are dominated by a combined Chairman/Chief Executive Officer (CEO). Therefore we do not believe separation of function is practical in many cases; although we see the argument for separation in the longer term particularly with institutional investor pressure."

In the mid-1990s, the typical company listed on SEHK was a Chinese family business with a minority of the voting shares in the hands of the investing public.

In 1996, almost 90% of companies listed in Hong Kong had a major shareholder who by himself or with family members owned 25% or more of the share capital. Of course, in recent years the percentage of Hong Kong–based family companies has dropped as more China-based companies, with significant state holdings, have been listed in Hong Kong.

In January 1997, the HKSA Corporate Governance Working Group published the *Second Report of the Corporate Governance Working Group*, which surveyed the experience of Hong Kong-listed companies on the adoption of audit committees, the information published on directors and substantial shareholders, and whether annual reports disclosed a finance director or CFO. Though the results were patchy, the idea that sound corporate governance was desirable had taken root. Later that year, HKSA's Corporate Governance Working Group published *A Guide for the Formation of an Audit Committee*. In 1998, the HKSA Corporate Governance Committee published *A Guide for Directors' Business Review in the Annual Report*. Recognizing Hong Kong's "unique business environment," but observing the growing international call for increased transparency and disclosure, the HKSA report aimed to provide directors with a summary of best practices regarding their duties for a management discussion and analysis in their company's annual report.

In 1998, the SEHK Code of Best Practice was updated to include a reference to audit committees: "The board should establish an audit committee with written terms of reference which deal clearly with its authority and duties. Amongst the committee's principal duties should be the review and supervision of the (company's) financial reporting process and internal controls."

An important step in Hong Kong's securities and futures regulation was taken with the approval in 2002 of the Securities and Futures Ordinance, which came into operation on April 1, 2003. The ordinance widened the regulatory powers of the SFC. The then SFC chairman, Andrew Sheng, said that "the Ordinance sets Hong Kong firmly on the path to reinforce its position as an international financial center, but success depends on the co-operation of all market participants—intermediaries, professional services providers, issuers, investors and other interested parties. The SFC is ready for the challenges that the responsibilities and powers under the Ordinance to implement and enforce the law, improve the quality of the market, and protect investors."

In 2006, the HKSE Listing Committee set out the corporate governance requirements for companies listed in Hong Kong. Appendix 14 of the Listing Rules, the Code on Corporate Governance Practices, replaced the previous code. It set out the principles of good corporate governance with two levels of requirement: (a) code provisions and (b) recommended best practice. Listed companies are expected to comply with the code provisions: they must state whether they have complied with the code provisions for the relevant accounting period in their interim and annual reports, or if not to explain why they have not. The recommended best practices are for guidance only. Listed companies are encouraged, but not required, to state whether they have complied with these recommended best practices. The Hong Kong Code was supplemented by Appendix 16, which concerns financial and other reports, and Appendix 23, Corporate Governance Report, which discusses the information to be provided in companies' regular corporate governance reports.

In the early years of the twenty-first century, it was widely assumed that corporate governance principles and practices would gradually converge with those of the US model. But that view faced a major setback in 2001, with the failure of the vast American company Enron, followed by the worldwide collapse of its auditor, Arthur Andersen. The US authorities responded quickly in 2002, with the Sarbanes-Oxley Act, which laid down new laws for director-level disclosure and auditor behavior. Now company directors in the US faced severe penalties, including jail, if they failed to obey the law. But this legal approach to corporate governance ("obey the law or face the consequences") stood in stark contrast to the classical discretionary underpinning of corporate governance ("comply with the code or explain why you have not") applied in Hong Kong, the UK, and most other common law jurisdictions. The dilemma of whether corporate governance is better determined by the mandatory rule of law or by the discretionary application of principles remains unresolved.

The Hong Kong SFC reinforced its regulatory activities, bringing successful actions against insider trading and market manipulation. It has also banned or suspended directors for irregularities, and investigated alleged regulatory failures. For example, in 2008, the SFC investigated the selling of Lehman Brothers' "minibonds" and negotiated a repurchase agreement with two banks. Successful enforcement actions in 2009 sent four people to jail for conspiring to manipulate the share price of Asia Standard Hotel Group. This was the largest market manipulation case to date in Hong Kong and the first indictable prosecution for this kind of offence under the Securities and Futures Ordinance. In 2010, the SFC fined two Merrill Lynch corporate entities HK$3.5 million for the failure of their financial control systems.

The Hong Kong Code on Corporate Governance Practices, which forms Appendix 14 of the HKSE Listing Rules, sets out the principles of good corporate governance and two levels of recommendations: (a) code provisions; and (b) recommended best practice, which were desirable but not mandatory. Companies are required to report that they have followed the provisions or explain why they have not.

In essence the Hong Kong Corporate Governance Code calls for:

- The company to be headed by an effective board

Provisions

  ❖ The board to meet regularly, at least four times a year
  ❖ All directors to be able to add matters to the agenda
  ❖ At least 14 days' notice to be given for board meetings
  ❖ All directors to have access to the advice of the company secretary

❖ Minutes of board and board committee meetings to be kept to record "in sufficient detail matters considered by the board and decisions reached"
❖ Directors to be able to seek independent professional advice
❖ Potential conflicts of interest to be considered by the board, not by circulation.

Recommended Best Practice

❖ Company to arrange insurance cover for directors against legal action
❖ Board committees should also adopt the provisions in this section
❖ A clear division of responsibilities between management of the board and the management of the business

Provisions

❖ The roles of chairman and CEO to be separate
❖ The chairman ensures that directors are properly briefed on board issues
❖ The chairman to be responsible for ensuring directors receive vital information

Recommended Best Practice

❖ The chairman should provide board leadership
❖ The chairman should ensure good corporate governance practices
❖ The chairman should encourage all directors to contribute fully
❖ The chairman should meet with the non-executive directors without the executive directors at least once a year
❖ The chairman should ensure effective communication with shareholders
❖ The chairman should facilitate effective contributions from non-executive directors and ensure constructive relations between all directors

• The board structure to be balanced between executive and non-executive directors and have an appropriate balance of skills and experiences

Provisions

❖ Independent directors to be expressly identified

Recommended Best Practice

❖ The independent directors should represent at least one-third of the board (the HKSE Listing Rules also require a minimum of three independent non-executive directors)
❖ The company's website should list all directors, identifying the independents

• The appointment of directors to be formal and transparent with policies for re-election and succession plans. Reasons for resignation or removal of a director to be given.

Provisions

❖ Non-executive directors to be appointed for a specific term

❖ Directors appointed to fill a casual vacancy to be re-elected at the next AGM

Recommended Best Practice

❖ An independent director should be considered not independent after nine years

❖ A nomination committee should be established with published terms

❖ Prior to election, information about independent directors should be circulated with the reasons for the nomination and details of their independence

- Every director to keep abreast of the work of the company and his/her responsibilities as a director. Non-executive directors have the same responsibilities as executive directors.

Provisions

❖ Newly appointed directors to receive a formal induction

❖ Non-executive directors must contribute to strategy, policy, performance, accountability, resources, key appointments and standards of conduct

❖ Every director must ensure they have sufficient time for the office

❖ Directors must comply with the Model Code on securities transactions in Appendix 10 to the Listing Rules

Recommended Best Practice

❖ All directors should participate in continuous professional development

❖ Each director should disclose other public company offices and time involved

❖ Non-executive directors should attend meetings of the board and its committees, providing relevant skills and experience, and meetings of shareholders to understand their views

❖ Non-executives should contribute to strategy and policy

- Directors to have timely and appropriate information

Provisions

❖ An agenda with relevant papers must be sent to all directors at least three days before the meeting

❖ Management has an obligation to give the board relevant information

❖ All directors are entitled to all board information and to have their queries answered

- The board to present a balanced, clear and comprehensive assessment of company performance, position and prospects

Provisions

❖ Management must provide the board with relevant information
❖ Directors must acknowledge in the corporate governance report their responsibility for financial accounting, with sufficient information for investors to understand the company's situation
❖ The board is responsible for presenting clear and understandable accounts

Recommended Best Practice

❖ Companies should announce and publish results within 45 days
❖ Reasons should be given if companies do not publish quarterly accounts

- The board to ensure sound and effective internal controls

Provisions

❖ The directors, at least, annually review the effectiveness of internal control systems and so report in the corporate governance report

Recommended Best Practice

❖ The board's annual review should consider changes since the last review, the extent of risks and the company's ability to respond; the scope and quality of risk management; board information; management control weaknesses; the effectiveness of reporting and compliance
❖ The corporate governance report should explain how the code provisions have been met
❖ Companies should ensure that disclosures are meaningful and not misleading
❖ Companies without an internal audit function should review the need annually

- The board to ensure suitable arrangements for the work of the audit committee (which is required under the provisions of the Listing Rules)

Provisions

❖ Full minutes of audit committee meetings to be kept
❖ A former partner of the audit firm cannot be a member of the audit committee within a year after ceasing to have an interest in the firm
❖ The terms of reference of the audit committee to cover relationships with the company's auditor, the review of the company's financial information, the oversight of the company's financial reporting system and internal control procedures
❖ The audit committee must publish its terms of reference

❖ If the board disagrees with the audit committee's relations with the auditor the matter should be reported in the corporate governance report

❖ The audit committee must have sufficient resources

Recommended Best Practice

❖ The terms of reference of the audit committee must include the company's arrangements to facilitate and protect employees reporting improprieties (whistle-blowing)

The code has further sections on directors' remuneration, delegation by the board to management, and communication with shareholders.

The Hong Kong Code on Corporate Governance Practices, which forms Appendix 14 of the SEHK Listing Rules, can be downloaded at: www.hkex.com.hk/eng/rulesreg/listrules/mbrules/documents/appendix_14.pdf.

For more on auditors' reports under the Hong Kong Companies Ordinance, see http://app1.hkicpa.org.hk/ebook/HKSA_Members_Handbook_Master.pdf.

KPMG "Five Guiding Principles for Audit Committees"

www.kpmg.com/aci/docs/~ACI_5%20Guiding%20Principles-WebFINAL.pdf

Hong Kong Stock Exchange Listing Rules

Further information of the Listing Rules of the HKSE, with explanatory notes, can be accessed at:www.hkex.com.hk/eng/listing/listing.htm and at http://en-rules.hkex.com.hk/en/display/display_main.html?r.

For more information, see:

Chapter 13 Hong Kong Stock Exchange Listing Rules: www.hkex.com.hk/eng/rulesreg/listrules/mbrules/documents/chapter_13.pdf

Chapter 14 Hong Kong Stock Exchange Listing Rules: www.hkex.com.hk/eng/rulesreg/listrules/mbrules/documents/chapter_14.pdf

Chapter 23 Hong Kong Stock Exchange Listing Rules: www.hkex.com.hk/eng/rulesreg/listrules/mbrules/documents/chapter_23.pdf

Hong Kong Financial Reporting Council (FRC)

Hong Kong's Financial Reporting Council (FRC) became operational in 2007, as an independent statutory body under the Financial Reporting Council Ordinance 2006. Its role is to:

- conduct independent investigations into possible auditing and reporting irregularities in relation to listed entities,
- enquire into possible non-compliance with financial reporting requirements by listed entities, and
- require listed entities to remedy any non-compliance identified.

The FRC can initiate investigations and respond to issues raised by anyone with information suggesting an auditing or reporting irregularity by a listed company, or non-compliance with reporting requirements. But the FRC does not itself have disciplinary or prosecution powers. Auditing or reporting irregularities identified by the FRC are referred to the HKICPA for follow-up action and non-compliance with reporting requirements to the SFC or the SEHK.

Core competencies for an effective director (HKIoD)

The HKIoD, following a series of workshops initiated by their training committee, identified five groups of skills, knowledge, and qualities necessary to serve as an effective director:

Group 1: Corporate Business functions, at a strategic, rather than operational, level

- Strategic planning
    - Change management: vision of change and aligning the company accordingly, downsizing or right-sizing, merger and acquisition, corporate restructuring, IPO, policy development
    - Monitoring and follow-through from strategic planning to implementation
    - Managing performance: installing performance appraisals and instilling confidence
    - Evaluation of results
    - Contingency planning, risk management and crisis management

- Finance
    - Interpretation of financial statements
    - Evaluation and monitoring of the financial health of a business and identifying warning signals
    - Determining the level of details and frequency of reporting for effective direction
    - Financing alternatives
    - Business/project planning and appraisals

- Marketing
    Concepts of marketing strategy
    Processes in developing marketing strategy
    Evaluating marketing strategy

- Production and product/service delivery
    Customer needs and market demands
    Processes in production or service development
    Customer care and after-sale support

- Organization and human resources
  - Organization development, culture, and structure
  - Directing and motivating senior management
  - Compensation tools
  - Continued training and education
  - Succession planning
  - Evaluation of organization effectiveness and HR strategy

- Information technology
  - IT as a tool in business development
  - IT as a tool in management
  - Strategy of investment in IT
  - Evaluation of IT strategy

- Compliance and legal knowledge for business

Group 2: Power, responsibility, and liability of the board and the individual director

- Significance of corporate governance
- Duties to stakeholders—shareholders, employees, creditors, regulators, and community
- Fiduciary duties
- Responsibilities in directing management, disclosure, accountability, and avoiding conflict of interest
- Relevant knowledge in Companies Ordinance, Articles of Association, Directors' service contracts, compensation, termination, resignation
- Risks, Directors & Officers liability insurance
- Winding-up

Group 3: Board development and boardroom practice

- Board structure, culture, and decision-making processes
- Board proceedings, running board meetings, and calling of general meetings
- Roles and relationships—Chairman, Managing Director/CEO, NEDs, INEDs etc.
- Working with committees
- The Audit Committee
- Working with external professionals, lawyers, auditors, advisers
- Board audit/assessment
- Continuing development and training of directors
- Update on law, rules, and regulations (listing and funding sources).

Group 4: Individual attributes and qualities

- Communication skills including language proficiency
- Vision and creativity

- Team-building and team-playing skills
- Analytical and synthesizing skills
- Judgment and decisiveness
- Coaching and facilitation skills
- Initiative and taking action
- Networks and skills to influence
- Health—mental and physical
- Emotional stability
- All qualities associated with IQ (intelligence quotient), EQ (emotional quotient), AQ (adversity quotient), CQ (creativity quotient), VQ (virtue quotient).

Group 5: Business Ethics

- Corporate sustainability
- Social responsibilities and the justification of a corporation
- Stakeholders' relations
- Anti-corruption practices, checks, and balances
- Equal opportunities
- Data protection (privacy)
- Environmental protection
- Ethical investment
- Transparency
- Corporate citizenship
- Contribution to professional or industry development

Influences for the future

Impacts on corporate governance principles, policies, and practices could come from three different directions: from within Hong Kong itself, from abroad, or from China's central authorities in Beijing. Let us consider each one, recognizing that these are possibilities, not predictions. Any catastrophic event—natural, political, economic, social, and cultural—could affect world trade, economic well-being, and, hence, the governance of companies. Almost all significant developments in governance in recent years have been in response to catastrophic events and corporate collapses.

Influence on the development of corporate governance from within Hong Kong

Corporate governance procedures and practices in Hong Kong have always stemmed from perceived needs, albeit sometimes rather slowly. The Davison Report that led to the creation of the SFC was a response to company collapses and the perceived excesses of some founder-directors and in a few board rooms. The 2014 Companies Ordinance was the outcome of years of deliberation, reports, working parties, and proposals. Given the interests of the government and the professional bodies already mentioned, there seems every reason to expect this evolution will continue.

Influence on the development of corporate governance from abroad

Hong Kong's companies ordinances and corporate governance codes drew heavily on British experience. Subsequent developments of corporate governance practice took account of developments elsewhere in the world. Ongoing international trends emphasize the significance of corporate social responsibility, sustainability, and the environment. There is a continuing trend to emphasize the interests of a range of stakeholders, as well as the rights of shareholders. A shift towards corporate governance by regulation and law, away from following voluntary codes, can also be detected. There is no reason to believe that Hong Kong will be immune from such influences.

Influence on the development of corporate governance from mainland China

Over 20 years have passed since China signed a joint agreement with Britain to assume responsibility for Hong Kong. It was agreed that Hong Kong's way of life would not be changed for 50 years.

However, on the twentieth anniversary of the signing of the joint agreement, Xi Jinping, visiting Hong Kong for the first time as the president made it clear that Beijing would no longer honor the treaty. This statement, subsequently confirmed by a government spokesperson, was seemingly an attempt to deter calls for multi-party democracy, universal suffrage, and greater autonomy, which had been demanded by young people in Hong Kong.

However, if China no longer recognized the joint agreement, other aspects of the treaty could be ignored in the future. From a corporate governance perspective, this could mean future calls for *representation* (the appointment of one or more party members to the boards of significant Hong Kong companies), *participation* (the requirement for a board subcommittee to ensure that the expectations of the party were being followed and the interests of the people being met), or ultimately *harmonization* (requiring companies to create supervisory boards with employee and party representatives, as in China's Companies Act).

Clearly, it would not be in Beijing's or Hong Kong's interest to call for changes that could damage international business confidence, produce economic decline, or lead to an exodus of jobs, companies, or people. But over the next 20 or 30 years, the continuing integration of Hong Kong's interests with those of the rest of China could lead to such proposals. After all, over half of the companies on the Hong Kong stock market boards are already mainland China companies.

Of the three influences—internal to Hong Kong, from abroad, and from China—the most significant is likely to be the continuing impact of China on corporate governance in Hong Kong. In the long run, given the massive importance of China on the world stage, this will be in Hong Kong's long-term interest. In the process, China will benefit from Hong Kong's experience, influence, and reputation around the world as new ways are found to govern the Chinese state and its companies.

References

Barrie, R., & Tricker, G. (1991). *Shares in Hong Kong: The centennial history of the Hong Kong Stock Exchange*. Hong Kong: The Stock Exchange of Hong Kong.

Hong Kong Exchange and Clearing Ltd. (2011). *Corporate governance codes and principles: Hong Kong* [PDF version]. Retrieved May 1, 2018 from www.ecgi.org/codes/code. php?code_id=356.

Hong Kong Stock Exchange Listing Rules, Appendix 14. (2016, July 22) *Corporate governance code and corporate governance report*. Retrieved May 1, 2018 from www.hkex.com. hk/eng/rulesreg/listrules/mbrules/documents/appendix_14.pdf.

Yu, B. Rudge, L., & Slaughter and May. (Eds.). (2014). *Hong Kong corporate governance: A practical guide* [PDF version]. Retrieved May 1, 2018 from http://www.hkcg2014.com/ pdf/hong-kong-corporate-governance-a-practical-guide.pdf.

The study reports and practice guidance on corporate governance published by the Hong Kong Institute of Certified Public Accountants: http://www.hkicpa.org.hk/en/membership-and-benefits/professional-representation/corporate-governance/publications/ gov-publications/.

Case study

Hong Kong Stock Exchange: A director's right to know

After graduating in mathematics from Exeter College, Oxford, David Webb gained experience as a merchant banker in London before moving to Hong Kong in 1991, to continue his investment banking career. Subsequently, he became a corporate governance activist, lobbying for greater transparency and accountability of boards of Hong Kong listed companies. His website (www.webb-site.com) is a constant source of revelations, insights, and commentary on listed company practices. Having purchased shares in all of the companies in the Hang Seng index, he regularly demands polls on resolutions he feels are not in the interests of minority shareholders.

Webb was elected as an independent non-executive director of the company that owns the HKSE in 2003. Subsequently, he criticized the Hong Kong government, which held over 5% of the shares listed on HKSE, for voting those shares to influence the appointment of directors, who might share their political orientation, to the boards of influential Hong Kong companies, thus "interfering in business in a way governments should not." Webb resigned his directorship before its expiry, complaining that the management of HKSE was withholding information from him. This was denied by management.

Commenting on the issue, John Brewer, a Hong Kong barrister, noted the international case law that emphasized directors' personal liability to acquire sufficient knowledge and understanding of the company's business to be able to discharge their duties as directors. He cited case law from Australia in which the presiding judge had stated:

> It would be difficult for the court to over-emphasize the importance of the directors' statutory rights of access to corporate information. They are the foundation of the system of corporate governance . . . Directors cannot be expected to carry out any of their substantial responsibilities, including their fiduciary duties and to attend to the solvency of the company and its general management, unless they can be sure of having full and unfettered access to the documents of the company.

Webb is a significant investor in smaller Hong Kong companies and is a member of the Hong Kong Securities and Futures Commission's Takeover and Mergers Panel.

Question for discussion

What information might the management of the stock exchange not want to provide to David Webb?

7

Corporate Governance of Chinese Family Businesses

Gregg Li

In this chapter, we consider:

- ❖ the governance of family businesses in China
  - ➢ number of family businesses
- ❖ key challenges
- ❖ growth and succession
  - ➢ the mindset and psyche of the early founders of modern China
  - ➢ limited gene pool
  - ➢ government partnership or administrative control
  - ➢ succession: transferring power to the next generation
- ❖ characteristics of Chinese family businesses and family values
  - ➢ paternalistic governance
  - ➢ characteristics of enduring family businesses
- ❖ the East Asian experience: ownership, control, and dilution
  - ➢ the return of the sojourners outside China
  - ➢ successful multigenerational Chinese family businesses

The governance of family businesses in China

Family businesses have been a core contributor to the economic dynamo of China and bring a special challenge to the governance of these entities. As in other parts of the world, family businesses and entrepreneurs with family backing play a critical part in strengthening and stabilizing an economic ecosystem. Family provides the first source of finance and labor. But family businesses in China also bring different challenges, including potential nepotism, sibling rivalry, acrimonious fighting for inheritance, the need for family legacy and control, or the forced sale of businesses due to the death of the founder. These days it is very much about succession, as nearly 80% of the next generation has indicated their unwillingness to join, according to a Jiaotong University study. How power is distributed, shared, groomed, and controlled at the core takes on a perspective on its own due to the history, people, context, and culture in China.

The family businesses in mainland China are about the first and second generations, and we will focus on this aspect. But to really appreciate the challenges and diversity of family businesses in a broader context, one has to consider the confluence and origins of these family businesses from outside China as well. We will supplement the domestic discussion with overseas Chinese, particularly as a lever to kick-start this economic dynamo during the early days of the Four Modernizations.

The sea of Chinese family businesses is being fed by several streams. The first stream is those family businesses that have arisen recently in mainland China, mostly first and second generation, due to the youth of privately-owned enterprises in China. There are millions of these family firms. The second subtle stream is the Chinese family businesses that have been created outside China, mostly in East Asia, and mostly beyond the second generation, but are actively doing and seeding new businesses in the Mainland. The third subtle stream is the return of the wealthy families, from Hong Kong primarily, who collectively have sparked many new businesses during the early days, including Xintiandi, the affluent shopping, eating, and entertainment district by Vincent Lo. Many foreigners in and travelers to Shanghai have visited Xintiandi, but few have heard of visionaries like Vincent Lo.[1] Size, quality, and impact symbolize the third stream. Three streams, each bringing its own set of nutrients and runoffs, have contributed to the richness and diversity of family businesses in China and the surrounding areas.

Number of family businesses

As far as we can gather, there is no official data on the number of family businesses available for public consumption. A dated piece, from the National Bureau of Statistics of the PRC[2] which compared China's family businesses with counterparts in the US, indicated that in late 2003, the majority of the 2 million private enterprises were actually family owned and run. Average annual revenue was RMB 5.8 million (roughly US$707,000), with 60 employees, compared with US$4.8 million, with 50 employees for the US. Many of the family businesses were first registered during the period from 1993 to 2000, whereas most of those in the US were registered after WWII. (Because many of the family businesses were first registered in late 1990s, succession for these first batches is currently a major point of review.) For China, most of the registered family businesses at that time were in manufacturing (38.3%),

---

1. Vincent Lo, a business tycoon, is currently the chairman of the Trade Development Council in Hong Kong and the chairman of the Hong Kong–based Shui On Group, which is a building material, construction, and property development company. Lo in 1984 worked with the Shanghainese Communist Youth League to develop the Xintiandi area.

2. National Bureau of Statistics of People's Republic of China 2003. 中美私营家族企业比较 [Comparison between Chinese and American private family business].

restaurants, and dining (21.4%), construction (5.9%), and agriculture (5.6%). The makeup of these families was mainly the founders and their blood relatives. The average age of the founders in 2003 was 42.9 years old, which means by 2017, many would be in their 60s. Children, siblings of the founder, and close relatives of the spouse are the typical types. Father and son, and husband and wife are the two dominant types.

As private business took off after the turn of the century, family businesses also grew rapidly. Recent estimates put the number of family businesses in China at 6 million as of 2015, or roughly 80% of the total number of private enterprises, which sat at 7 to 8 million at that time.[3] This does not include the 34 million individual micro family businesses.[4] Since the state sector only accounts for about a third of the GDP, the rest would have to come from the private enterprises, the majority of which would be family businesses or former TVEs (town and village enterprises which were formerly communes and brigades). Furthermore, according to these and other sources, more than one-third of China's listed companies today reportedly are family controlled. Another China expert even suggested that as nearly 90% of Chinese private enterprises are family run, China could have as many as 3 million entrepreneurs facing the issue of succession.[5] Regardless which recent figures are more accurate, the sheer volume of family businesses is significant. Because family business is a major force of business in China, how well they can be governed, particularly as they move from one generation to the next, is worthy of attention today.

Key challenges

Governing a family-run business is difficult. Ownership concentration and family management are two key characteristics unique to family businesses. Unquestioned control by the founder and patriarch is crucial. Likewise, family members are actively participating[6] and are paid. These two characteristics are sufficient to create new methods in governing such entities.

The founder relied on family members, not the best managers he could hire. But in return, he got loyalty. Most family businesses reward loyalty more than they reward competence. But businesses are run best by competent individuals and are not a democracy, which sometimes large multigenerational family businesses can become, and where fairness means everyone gets employment, competent or otherwise. To the patriarch, effective governance in family business can be fundamentally about institutionalizing decision-making, and the Chinese patriarch has purposely

3. According to a report by the research organs of the All-China Federation of Industry and Commerce in 2012, around 85.4% of China's private enterprises belong to family businesses, in which individuals or families own a controlling stake of more than 50%. China's rich reluctant to take over family firms: Report (2012, March 17).
4. Steen & Baldwin, 2017; Cai, 2015.
5. Chong (2016, December 18).
6. Chu, 2016.

worked with and promoted a process of decision-making that puts him squarely at the center, for as long as he's alive.

With the expansion of the family business, the relationship among the owners, managers, employees, and suppliers would become more complex. Just for the family alone, mixing generations can be an added challenge, but governing becomes even more difficult due to differences in value. In family businesses that have several generations working in the same company, and where majority of the younger generations have been educated abroad gaining liberal ideas, the notion of having a similar set of values is no longer a given. Whereas the earlier generation believes in shared decision-making, possibly egalitarian compensation, and business authority based on family rank, the younger generation tends to believe in holding an individual accountable, meritocracy, and business authority based on ability and not blood. The basis of value is one fundamental challenge to the fabric of governance for family businesses for large family conglomerates. This, however, is not the current issue for domestic family businesses but definitely for overseas Chinese family businesses building new businesses in the Mainland.

In our experience, family-run businesses, as compared with non-family ones, often face other sets of special challenges in governance and would require different means to handle such challenges. As a preview, incompetent family members are rarely removed; perhaps sidelined but still influential. Those family businesses that have survived three generations appear to have quite a different set of challenges than do younger family businesses. These challenges, for example, run the gamut from how decision-making is delegated to how much they would trust outsiders. These scenarios below should better explain these challenges:

1. **Letting go:** The founder (or patriarch, which is a better term), despite his increasing age, typically does not want to leave the business. He comes to work in a suit every morning and still signs every paycheck. Procrastination in the transfer of power compounds the problem. The patriarch often believes the decision and method of letting go is his decision, his way, at his time.

2. **Succession:** Who will take charge after the departure of the patriarch? Succession usually follows a well-defined pecking order, based on birth order and gender. The firstborn is often the next successor, and as a result of the one-child policy, both sexes are now welcome. Lawsuits outside China are often the last recourse if succession is not properly managed or exercised.

3. **Culture clash:** Often the founder of the first generation is an entrepreneur, with minimum university education. The second and the third are typically Western educated, with university degrees. One estimate is that in mainland China, 88% of the children of founders have university degrees and 52% of them have studied overseas, at schools such as Harvard, Wharton,

and the London School of Economics.[7] Western management style clashes with Chinese management style head on. The children want to modernize their business with long-term investment, while the parents claim such expenses are inappropriate and not in sync with reality in China.

4. **Perception of unfair expropriation:** The general perception from investors is that the family will exploit the business for self-gain. Insider dealing, or excessive compensation for family members, would be examples. We remain to be convinced that this is universal although a few families have used their listed vehicles to subsidize their private businesses. Minor abuses are likely but nothing detrimental, in our opinion, as family members do check and balance the power with other family members. We have seen examples where the annual pay scale is determined by seniority in the family and not by function or by scope. The lack of independent audit does not help. For private firms, most families would forgo the need for an independent audit or auditor and just rely on the financial controller and supervisory oversight for control.

5. **Diversity in management style:** Each member of the family comes with history and personality. They attend a different school or have a different communication style, social network, or management competency set. In the past, the parents had to deal and build a relationship with government bureaucrats, something that the younger generations do not want. Making political compromise is less likely. Old ties are difficult to maintain once the patriarch steps down. Handshakes to seal a deal and verbal promises are the forgotten practices of the past.

6. **Entrenchment of members . . . can't fire incompetent ones:** The family hardly removes family members who are below expectations. Often these incompetent members are kept on, and their presence can be problematic for outside professionals who would nominally carry the load of these family members but not their titles. These members still receive their salary entitlement.

7. **In-group and glass ceilings:** Many family members are instinctively unwilling to trust non-family members or friends brought in by other family members. Some professionals in the business have a perception that they will never be able to get to the top, that limited space belongs automatically to family members. This has meant that the family has difficulty keeping good professionals in the company.

8. **Dispersed shareholdings:** These can become an issue over time and increasingly difficult to command a majority for change, especially with too many cousins holding smaller proportion of the shares. Mainland Chinese families have yet to encounter this problem. As the family moves into third

and fourth generations, family members start to demand an equal voice in the business. Slowly business decisions become a democracy, and to be seen to be fair, everyone gets a vote. Over time, as the shares would be diluted, the core and controlling branch may no longer hold a majority. Getting consensus becomes more difficult, especially when the patriarch is no longer around. Slow decision-making can quickly destroy any strong business.

9. **Limited career development:** Over time, younger generations may come to expect certain things from the family business, expectations that the family is an ATM, for withdrawing whenever money is needed. Some expect the family will take care of their career if they join the family business. Once they join, departing for greener pastures becomes a new issue as incumbents slowly lose their edge. Once a family member joins the business, it is nearly impossible for that family member to leave and join a competing business. Being headhunted into a related business is one luxury that family members do not have. A person's career, once having entered the family business, automatically closes behind him or her.

10. **Loss of interest by the next generation:** This happens when the younger generation has no interest in working for uncles or in a traditional or seemingly sunset business. They see their young values have changed and are irreconcilable with traditional ones. The patriarch typically won't want to sell the business he founded, and not at fire-sale prices. The first generation was hardcore, and many were in manufacturing operations. The younger generation prefers industries like finance and e-commerce, 3D printing, organic farming, and branded fashion. According to the Jiaotong University survey conducted in 2012 on 182 Chinese family firms, over 82% of the next succeeding generation in the Mainland did not want to continue in the parents' business.[8] Compared with the 2003 survey by the National Bureau of Statistics cited earlier, about 40% of the family members would join the family business 15 years ago.[9]

Designing a new governance architecture that can cater to these challenges, while at the same time being mindful of practices and changes in best practices in corporate governance both locally and globally, is the real challenge the Chinese family will need to face. Unless there is a new and acceptable system that can flex with these changes and allow debates to turn into dialogues, the family business will break apart. The bamboo network now needs modern "bamboo scaffolding."

As in most parts of the world, family businesses often started with family capital, mainly to create income for the immediate family. As the business began to expand, it needed more outside capital. Uncles, aunts, and friends were brought

---

8. China's rich reluctant to take over family firms: Report (2012, March 17).
9. National Bureau of Statistics of People's Republic of China, 2003.

into the ownership but often as employees, sometimes with a minority stake. As more outsiders came into the picture, share ownership of the family could become diluted. Typically however, the family will aim to retain 51% or more of the shares—never giving up control. In corporate governance, boards generally have a longer horizon in planning than do most executives. Similarly, like having the long-term aims of a board, a family's goal would tend be long term. Family businesses generally prefer steady and upward growth over short-term profit for themselves or other shareholders or hyper-growth for the sake of growth. The more sophisticated famiies would add a second pillar, the family council, that would run parallel to their business council.

During succession, the typical family avoids placing some of its share with outsiders such as with banks or suppliers. Control within the family and the avoidance of the dilution of control is still the spirit of family ownership. To do this, apart from ensuring that the proportion of shares sold by family members to outsiders would remain relatively insignificant, families try to restrict the approval of share transfers by company article or bylaws to non-family members. Increasingly, for sophisticated and rich families, founder's shares are being placed into trusts where the next generation and those after that would come to enjoy the fruit of the founder's labour. Another way to control the number of shares, especially when there is a need to acquire a large number of shares for publicly listed companies, was to prioritize the voting power of the shares. Instead of having A-shares, which are freely transferable, they would issue B-shares that carry a larger number of votes.[10]

The case of Swire Pacific in Hong Kong is a good example but cases of A and B shares are less popular, giving potentially to weighted voting shares where the family shares have more weights. Family shareholders outside China often would deploy various measures to enhance their control of a family firm, including dual-class stock, blockholding, cross-holding and pyramidal ownership structure. These are not yet well developed in China. The transfer of shareholding and power from one generation to the next has been a major area of study in the field of family business governance.

In fact, this issue of succession could be the tip of an iceberg, and some authors even suggested how well this transition is being handled has a direct implication on the health of the Chinese economy today.[11] The majority of the first registered family businesses are now in their 30s and ready to introduce new successors. Many of the young successors were born in the 1970s and 1980s, heavily influenced by the Internet, and are not interested in joining the old-tradition businesses.

Even if succession of one generation is effective, the chance of another is slim. We have to put this in perspective: fewer than 30% of family businesses around the world can survive by the third generation, according to a 2010 McKinsey

---

10. Lawton & Tyler, 2001.
11. Cai, 2015.

Study.[12] This is consistent with a Chinese proverb: "wealth does not go beyond three generations."[13]

PriceWaterhouseCoopers (PwC), a management consultancy, conducted a global survey on family businesses in 2014 and 2016. In 2014, the survey covered 40 countries and 2,378 families, and of the respondents from China, 80% expected further growth in the next five years. The 2014 survey further elaborated that 53% of family-owned businesses in China had plans to float their business or sell their business, while only 28% had planned to pass ownership to the next generation; but by 2016, that intent had risen just slightly.[14]

Presently, Chinese family businesses in the Mainland are mostly young, in their first few generations that is, compared with those in Japan and Europe that can be hundreds and sometimes over a thousand years old and into many generations. Nearly six decades of war, famine, political turmoil, and family breakups since the end of the eighteenth century have effectively wiped out any legacy of family businesses in China. The one-child policy in China has also meant a patriarch has very limited choices in succession. The governance of family businesses in China requires a special review because of the context and the resultant challenges.

Furthermore, family businesses at the core in mainland China today are mostly older first and younger second generation, private entities; the Chinese family businesses in surrounding areas such as Hong Kong, Singapore, Taiwan, Indonesia, Malaysia, or the Philippines are much older, in the third or fourth generations. The more recent ones in China today grew out of the TVEs or collectives as the run-up to 1978, the beginning of the Four Modernizations. It is only recently that China has introduced aspects of capitalism with private ownership, venture capital, and private equity, and other sophisticated financial instruments and regulations, including inheritance and trust regulations and practices. Young businesses face different challenges in governance, and the involvement of families bring added dimensions. Also, many Chinese family businesses that grew outside the Mainland since the Communists took over in 1949 have since returned and played their part in springboarding the economy. We will explore this outside factor later in this chapter.

In mainland China, the list of billionaires has continued to grow, and prominent founders in their first generation (mostly individuals) such as Ma Huateng, the founder of Tencent, are now living in Hong Kong. Over a few decades, we may

---

12. Caspar, Dias, & Elstrodt, 2010.
13. It's also a British saying: "rags to riches and back to rags in three generations." Governing and running a family business empire is probably one of the most difficult but most rewarding challenges for entrepreneurs. To do this well takes immense fortitude, foresight, and latitude on the part of the entrepreneur, the family, as well as from professionals whom they employ. Great family businesses last multiple generations, many with the benefits and wisdom of professional advisors. Marginal family businesses can hardly last one generation, never mind from rags to t-shirts in three.
14. PwC, 2016.

expect to see a few relatives joining their businesses. Other prominent individuals and their family business include:[15]

- DING Lei: company is called NetEase, an Internet company.
- LI, Robin: company is called Baidu.
- MA, Jack: companies are Alibaba and Ant Financial.
- PANG Shiyi and Zhang Xin: company is called Soho China.
- WANG Jianlin and his son, Wang Sicong: company is called Wanda; in real estate and entertainment (We will cover this case.)
- WANG Wei: company is called SF Express, a logistics company.
- WANG Zhongjun and Wang Zhonglei: company is called Huayi Group, in chemicals and advanced materials.
- YAO Zhenhua: company is called Baoneng, in Investment and real estate
- ZONG Qinghua and his family: company is called Wahaha, in beverages

Growth and succession

For family businesses that started inside China, with the benefits of a larger family, the ownership of some family businesses can be diversified or concentrated, as in a village clan under the same surname where an entire village of a thousand would own workers or be working for one company. At other times, a family could own a business on a collective undivided basis, and shares have yet to be strictly divided by the founding brothers. Here, everyone is expected to pool his or her non-disposable income back to the patriarch or to a family pool, and no one has any designated amount of share. Trust in the relationship superseded trust in law.

The mindset and psyche of the early founders of modern China

The early pioneers in modern China had a unique mindset, and many cited that these founders came from a special tough breed. Some of them were probably caught in the Cultural Revolution during their youth. Not trusting in authorities and harboring a high sense of insecurity are traits expected of these founders. In the early days of modernization when the government apparatus was immature, policies were often short-lived, supply chain was unreliable, and tax was arbitrary. Unlike today where one must leverage on and ride on Chinese government policies, these founders could only trust certain government officials whom they knew. Corruption was pervasive, and the only few one could trust were family members and a select few business partners.

To require someone else to govern a business and using Western governance practices such as setting up a board of directors was inconceivable.[16] Instead, the

---

15. Lu (2017, March 14).
16. National Bureau of Statistics of People's Republic of China, 2003. In the same research cited by the National

patriarch would stretch himself and through diligent and hard work impose tight internal management and fiscal control and rely heavily on a team of loyal employees and family members. He knew the costs of everything, of every nut and bolt, and he prided himself knowing these accounting figures. Trust within a closed circle was the formula, and tight connection with mutual support was sacrosanct. Outsiders, particularly independent ones who had no connection or understanding of the current business, were not invited.

But founders who wanted a long-term and sustainable business for their family were not the only entrepreneurs. Those who wanted a quick buck, the opportunists and operators who would throw family names around for credit, were also rampant. Early days of entrepreneurism has often been caricatured by the Zhejiang or Wenzhou entrepreneurs. These were arrogant rich peasants on the prowl for opportunities and quick wins. They were tight-knit, focused, and ruthless in business.[17] Unlike their brethren, the Shanxi entrepreneurs, whose family values were legends in the Ming to the Qing dynasties, the Zhejiang and Wenzhou entrepreneurs were hard-line capitalists with few ethical qualms. The Shanxi entrepreneurs were known to build courtyards and renovate homes for their families. A few Shanxi entrepreneurs even created China's first generation of the modern bank. The new modern-day family entrepreneurs in China urgently needed to create a new reputation, a new hero, and a new genre of bourgeois.

It was not until 1987 that there was some certainty that what a founder would earn, he could keep. Long-term and potentially sustainable family businesses finally had a chance. Before 1987, high-level government corruption was rampant, and market socialism had just begun.

Limited gene pool

Because of the one-child policy in China, which came into force in 1979, founders typically had a limited selection when it came to succession. If they were to have children, only one was allowed, and funding his or her education abroad would require creative movement of funds out of China, since foreign exchange was heavily regulated and easily restricted. Increasingly, children of successful family businesses in the Mainland who were able to benefit from an education abroad were reluctant to return home and assume a leadership role in their own family business. There are many reasons. Some of the well-educated children do not return to their parents' businesses in mainland China because:

    i.   the parents do not think their children can or should cope with the challenging or chaotic business and political environment in China;

Bureau of Statistics in 2003, only 15.8% had some sort of board of directors in 1995, but that number had risen to 47.5% by 2002.

17. Fishman, 2005.

ii. the children do not believe they would be given a reasonable amount of freedom to run/upgrade their businesses;

iii. each side carries a working mindset that is different; father is all work and son is all play (as seen by the father);

iv. the children remain overseas and act as an insurance plan for the parents;

v. the children perceive their family businesses as generally backward, and they would like to work for a big or foreign organizations even when in mainland China; or

vi. the children are simply not interested (as in the case of Wanda's Wang Jianlin, later in the chapter).

Passing things to others, like the founder's siblings or cousins, is less preferred, albeit sometimes necessary. In the mainland culture, the patriarch always passes his business to a son or a daughter, as the case may be, as often there is only one child. (Outside China for a Chinese family business, the preference is often to the eldest son.)

Handing things over to a daughter does happen. Recent handovers have included handing the reins from Zhou Chengjian, founder of Metersbonwe, one of China's largest fashion chains, to his daughter, Hu Jiajia. She became the chairwoman and the chief executive. Liu Yonghao handed over the reins of the agribusiness called New Hope Liuhe, to his daughter, Liu Chang, in 2013. We have touched on the case of Wahaha, where the father handed his business over to his daughter, Kelly.[18]

But there are always exceptions, and China is the land of experimentation when it comes to governance. Ruan Shuilong, the founder of Longsheng Group, originally groomed his eldest son, Ruan Weixing, as his successor in the business but passed it instead to the younger, more capable son. Ruan Weixiang, the second son, came later into the family business on his father's request after graduating from Fudan University. Using his technical knowledge, the second son introduced new products, raised profit earnings, and even changed its business model. The group further invited outside professionals onto the board.[19]

Government partnership or administrative control

In the Mainland, the government can sometimes play a pivotal role in business affairs, and in this case, succession. When Li Haicang, the founder of Haixin Group, was shot dead in the office in 2003, the family business was on the verge of collapse. The secretary of the County Committee and other local government officials rushed

---

18. Ibid.
19. Zhejiang Longsheng Group Co. Ltd. 2018. This company was founded in 1970. It primarily operates in the dyestuff industry and engages in real estate, auto parts, and financial investment. Currently the group owns 18 factories in 12 countries, has established agencies in 50 countries and regions, and occupies nearly 21% of the global market shares in their areas of trade. It owns nearly 100 subsidiaries with 9,000 employees in total.

to the funeral and sent the message that development strategy of the company would remain unchanged. Li Chun-yuan, the founder's father, acted as the authority of the family and announced a plan to pass the business to Li Zhaohui, Li Haicang's son. The father managed to moderate potential conflicts from other brothers and avoided a power struggle. Within one month, the succession was completed.[20]

Succession: Transferring power to the next generation

As in most businesses, Chinese family businesses prefer to retain ownership and management control with the passing of the founder. As the founder departs from the business, typically near the last day of his life, the business is passed to another family member, usually a son.

A minority of family businesses is wise enough to engage professionals to run their firm. The smartest ones install transitional governance architecture to shift power gradually to the next generation. Often, however, the shift of power is sudden and tumultuous, and the resultant new empire under the new management is often hostile to those remaining. An apt Chinese proverb proclaims: "Each son of heaven brings along his own entourage." Power struggle is hardly ever genteel.

According to Jean Lee, the co-director of the Center for Family Heritage at CEIBS in Shanghai, more than half of mainland China's family businesses face a succession dilemma.[21] In the Mainland, the movement from the first to the second is more the issue, as 15 to 20 years have now passed since the founding of those businesses.

Because this is only the beginning of the succession issue for the Mainland, the jury is still out on whether in general the transition has been successful or not. But this transition from first generation to second generation in mainland China, and the resultant impact on the economy, according to Peter Cai, can be a tipping point for China.[22]

The current movement is not only the shifting of power from one generation to the next but a complete change in the traditional business model as the owners move into the digital economy. Many old guards don't even like to use email and have their secretary print out the email. Today, the younger generations are using WeChat apps on their smartphones to make payments from bus fares to online purchases. The concept of a business has changed considerably in the age of digitalization.

---

20. Shanxi Haixin Iron and Steel Group Co., Ltd. (山西海鑫钢铁集团有限公司), 2018. This company was the second-largest steel company and the largest private company in Shanxi Province. It was considered one of the pillars of the local business, with over RMB 4 billion in assets. The group operates a steel mill and produces iron and steel products. Haixin Group was placed 184th in the Top 500 Enterprises in China. In 2014, the group stopped all national production for eight months due to heavy debt. In 2015, the group was acquired and regrouped into Jianlong Iron and Steel Co., Ltd.
21. Flannery, 2016.
22. Cai, 2015.

The Juneyao Group in Shanghai, the first private flight enterprise in China, was founded in 1991 by three siblings, Wang Junyao, Wang Junjin and Wang Junhao. In 2004, however, Wang Junyao, chairman of the board, suddenly died of cancer. The siblings, Wang Junjin and Wang Junhao, immediately took up the role of chairman and vice chairman respectively. In 2005, the siblings brought in even more professionals. Four years before Wang Junyao's death, the board had made a plan of dividing the shares into three parts equally: 1/3 owned by family, 1/3 owned by the management team, and 1/3 by the public. Under this ownership design, Juneyao Group was able to bring in more professional managers. This sort of share transfer and ratio split, however, is rare in China.*

* The Shanghai Juneyao (Group) Co. Ltd. was founded in 1991. It operates private charter flights and engages in the business of aviation transport, commercial retail, financial services, information technology, and the production of milk. At present, the company owns three listed subsidiaries and has over 15,000 employees. In 2017, the company ranked 242nd in the Top 500 Private Enterprises in China. For more information, please see 均瑤新掌門滬上亮相. Retrieved on June 6, 2018 from http://www.juneyao.com/mtgz/900.jhtml; Group Introduction retrieved on June 6, 2018 from http://www.en.juneyao.com/GroupIntroduction.jhtml; 社會評價, retrieved on June 6, 2018 from http://www.juneyao.com/shpj2/index.jhtml; 范博宏 (2012)《關鍵世代：走出華人家族企業傳承之困》(北京：東方出版社)，頁45。

Characteristics of Chinese family businesses and family values

A family business is basically a business that is predominantly owned and controlled by family members.[23] The family has significant influence on how the business is to be run, and run in the interest of the family. We have seen cases where a Chinese family will purposely maintain a losing business for a close relative so that individuals would have employment. Making profit was not the aim of this business; keeping the family working and working together was.

Roger King, director of the Tanoto Centre for Asian Family Business and Entrepreneurial Studies at the Hong Kong University of Science and Technology, often encouraged his students to think on this question: "Which is more important, the family or the business of the family?" Deciding what is good for the family and what is good for business may not be in alignment and definitely not a simple answer. This difference in perspective has posed a fascinating challenge to governance but also adds a fuller picture to governance. What indeed is the ultimate aim of governance? Is it to enhance shareholders' value, or the value of the participating family members? Our discovery has been that most traditional families would choose the latter. A family that believes in birthright and not meritocracy would tend to seek a more egalitarian form of compensation, titles, promotion, and authority for those working in the business. In a few large family businesses that we have advised, we

23. Academics would define this more precisely whereby it is a business that is owned by one or more family members who together control at least 20% of the total votes outstanding See La Porta et al., 1999.

have found that the compensation for their family members in business in the early days was nearly the same, regardless of their role or function. The only significant difference was due to their seniority in the family.

A challenge to family rule is that not everyone in the family has grown up or believes in the same value system. For a Chinese family, having four or five generations present in the same room is considered a family blessing, and a strong dose of Chinese traditional culture has kept many wayward ideas, usually from young members of the family, at bay. But that stability is increasingly under attack as more and more in the younger generations are educated abroad and often return with a different set of value systems. They are now running the subsidiaries and are contributing to the family's profit. Questioning authority, rejecting harmony, and asking for recognition for themselves, and for higher pay have been some of the pressing demands from the young generation, noted the patriarchs.

The case of Wahaha, China's top beverage company, makes an interesting example. Wahaha literally means "laughing baby" and started from a joint venture with Danone in 1996 (another interesting case of ineffective joint-venture corporate governance). The Hanzhou company is now run by Kelly Zong, the daughter of the founder, Zong Qinghou. Kelly, dubbed "Fu'erdai" or the "rich spoilt second generation" by her detractors, was educated abroad and graduated from Pepperdine University in California. Exposed to foreign business models and unwilling to make political compromises, she has made known her distaste for working with the Chinese government.* But Zong Qinghou, her father, who started his career during Mao's Cultural Revolution and in those days formed his view of the world, has no desire to completely let go. He has been involved in shifting his business into retail and mall operations.† Sharing power and shifting power base take on special dynamics.

* Heng Shao (2014, June 2).
† Dong, Emma (2013, April 21).

Chinese generally respect their elders, and this Confucian tradition has been reinforced through rituals, everyday greetings, in the language itself, and in everyday habits. In many family homes, everyone waits for a turn to partake of the family meal until the head of the family has ceremonially picked his choice of dishes with his chopsticks. This respect for the elders and tradition, known as filial piety, underpins the relationship between patriarch and his linage, and the founder and those who came after. As with the Inuit who have a name for different types of snow, the Chinese have a family title for every member of the family within a family tree. Everyone has a role and a place. This family pecking order is respected, reinforced through generations of Confucian culture. Wedding invitations, seating arrangement, announcement of arrivals, addressing of a person, and even the required Chinese characters in a person's name are all heavily influenced and reinforced by this tradition.

Paternalistic governance

The way many Chinese family enterprises are governed today, with top-down authoritarian governance, reflects the culture of paternalism in China since time immemorial and shows the influence of Confucianism. Paternalism has been rooted in the Chinese family structure for many generations. That is, the father or patriarch of the family sees himself as having the role and justification to care for family members. Father knows best. Father's authority cannot be challenged.

In certain cases, despite a clear plan for succession, the patriarch would step back in, sometimes out of the need to bring back credibility or to reconnect the needed relations. The Guangsha Holding Group[24] is such an example, whereby a change in macro policy brought back the patriarch. Lou Zhongfu, the founder of the group, had planned and instigated the succession as far back as 1994. However, suspension of subway construction in Hangzhou and new policies issued by the State Council in 2002 significantly affected the cost and sales of its main business, real estate. Moreover, the group didn't receive a promising return in its previous diversified investment. As a result, Lou Zhongfu returned and took charge in 2006, due to the heavy debt that the successor had incurred.

According to many researchers,[25] this form of paternalistic leadership is mostly prevalent in overseas Chinese family businesses, and three components tended to stand out: authoritarianism, benevolence, and moral leadership. One patriarch explained to us that this means to rule with an iron fist, be stern, and only be compassionate when that's the only course that has remained. We suspect that the further away a family has moved away from the ancestral home in mainland China, the higher the tendency to hold onto traditional values ingrained in the patriarch's mind at the time of his departure.

This is in fact the case we have seen with many of the successful Chinese family businesses operating outside mainland China. Father is the chairman and has veto rights to all and any major decisions. He does not have a swing vote but a decisive vote. His rule is absolute. If there are ten different businesses, father will be the chair

---

24. Guangsha Holding Group Co., Ltd. (广厦控股集团有限公司), 2018. This company is located in Dongyang, Zhejiang and engages in business of construction, real estate, energy, finance, health care etc. Zhejiang Guangsha Co., Ltd., one subsidiary of Guangsha Holding Group, is the first listed company in the construction industry in China. At present, the company owns over 100 subsidiaries and over 120,000 employees, with total assets of RMB 30 billion. In 2015, the group realized annual revenue of RMB 89 billion. In 2017, the company ranked 37th in the Top 500 Private Enterprises in China, 187th in the Top 500 Enterprises in China. Company overview of Guangsha Holding Group Co., Ltd.
    See Fan, 2012, 25–40.
25. See research work by Gordon Redding, 1993.

of all ten businesses, never mind that he would never find the time to chair the requisite four board meetings per business. Formal title and recognition is necessary. To the youth, these are manifestations that are unnecessary and pretentious. For those educated abroad with Western values who are taught to question authority, this is the one spark that has fueled many heated debates between the generations. A few researchers even see this visible challenge to power as "the most important continuity dilemma of contemporary Chinese family business."[26]

Many authors, notably Redding[27] and Suehiro,[28] tended to suggest the overseas Chinese family was unique and that its structure and affiliation network had a rationality of its own. This uniqueness created an organizational form that had existed until today. According to Redding, there would be three principal heritages of the Chinese (or rather overseas Chinese): paternalism, interpersonal trust and relations, and a sense of insecurity. And these heritages had had these effects on the corporate world such that:

- ownership and control are not separated;
- control is personal, decision-making is centralized and from the top;
- professional management is rare; and
- distinguishing between personal assets and company assets is difficult, as ownership and management are one and the same.

Characteristics of enduring family businesses

For our initial research and based on the clients we have worked with outside the Mainland, Chinese family businesses that have endured multiple generations seem to have certain common characteristics. The most obvious one is having a continual base of customers across the generations, be those in food production, automobiles, or clothing. Family brand gets stronger over generations. Business and taste may change, but family business will endure if the family is able to keep up with the changing adaption to the markets and are able to provide quality products with a strong brand. Lee Kum Kee has been making oyster sauce for generations, as Cadbury[29] has been making chocolates.

We have noticed that great enduring Chinese family businesses share some of these common practices:

1. **Knowing how to preserve the family's unique assets and values.** Family and employees alike can recite the family story that reflects values unique to the business. There are deep reasons for existence and staying together. Many Chinese families have family codes and value statements posted on

---

26. Lansberg & Gersick, 2009, p. 4.
27. Redding, 1993.
28. Suehiro, 1993.
29. Cadbury is now owned by US Kraft after a bitter takeover battle with the family.

family websites. The successful ones purposely make these explicit and embed them in operational policies.

2. **Believing in and encouraging open communications.** Like all families, Chinese families get into hasty arguments that could lead to irreconcilable differences. We have seen that in successful family businesses family members will openly challenge one another but stop short of personal attacks. The use of independent outside directors on the board can help to resolve problems. International experts on the governance of family companies often recommend the creation of a family council to protect the interests of family shareholders. The family council does not take part in the management of the governance of the company but liaises with the board to ensure that the needs of family shareholders are met. A family council can be particularly useful when shares are inherited by the second or subsequent generations, some of whom are involved in management while others are not. For example, in a Hong Kong family company, one branch of the second generation is now running the business, while the other branch of the family lives in Canada. Family members in management want high salaries and opinions, with reinvestment for the future; the Canada-based shareholders, in contrast, want to see profits, dividends, and cash flow. The board is not in a position to resolve such family shareholder matters. But the family council, which includes members of both sets of shareholders, meets to discuss and resolve disagreements before bringing their conclusions to the board.

3. **Purposely setting up fiefdoms.** Chinese family businesses are usually horizontally and vertically integrated, and many related businesses are created out of opportunities. Suppliers are sometimes connected at the shareholding level. Despite shared ownership, smart families will avoid overlapping management roles and have each child look after one separate business. One son looks after division A, another division B. Divisions A and B have a few things in common. There is hardly any reason to assume or be put in a position to work congenially.

4. **Paying attention to developing and rapidly grooming the next generation.** Some families would appoint an "uncle" to specifically look after the development of new hires from the next generation. As the business grows, it will need new talents, and some of these talents will be from future generations of the family as well as those from loyal employees. Both sets of potentials are treated equally.

5. **Being mindful of the family contribution to society.** Business and practices change but values remain consistent. Strong family businesses focus on markets and relationship and are mindful of the contribution the family has played and needs to play in a society. Strong families donate and participate in NGOs and contribute a proportion to philanthropy. Many train their family members to be leaders for the NGO sector as well. (Here we see an

inclination to stewardship, whereby they are aspiring to a higher purpose at their jobs, motivated by the higher-level needs of the family.)

6. **Focusing on a family business.** Strong families would identify an industry that can represent the core of the family. They tend to niche themselves, ideally trying to establish an enduring business that would continue to be in demand years hence. Once they have identified the business, they would prefer to own the complete supply chain, such as Esquel, in textile manufacturing and apparel; and Lee Kum Kee, makers of oyster sauces.

7. **Focusing family control to a few is key.** Eventually, other family members and even outsiders will be invited to participate in governance but hardly in ownership. Strong family businesses have outside directors and family members on their boards but are able to maintain control by a select few in the family.

8. **Removing the glass ceiling.** Successful family businesses are those that can readily employ outside professionals and be able to merge corporatization with family values. Eventually, the family will come to realize and begin to engage outside professionals, as a family gene pool is still limited. Sir Li Ka-Shing was credited for having invited outside professionals onto his management team and is known to run his meetings in English, which is not his first language.

The East Asian experience: Ownership, control, and dilution

To appreciate the broader context of family businesses in China, one has to look outside China and consider the tumultuous periods of China which pushed many entrepreneurs into neighboring countries. This bamboo network outside China has its roots in China. In fact, in Asia today, family-run firms account for more than 60% of all listed companies in Southeast Asia, and the majority of those have their roots in Chinese or Indian ancestry.[30]

The old Maritime Silk Road, the collapse of the Nationalist Government in 1949, the Taiping Rebellion, and even the hardship of the Cultural Revolution from 1966 to 1976 are some of the major events that pushed many young men living in coastal cities to neighboring enclaves surrounding China. They were sojourners and dreamed of returning home. Many left with few possessions except the dream of a better tomorrow. Few were millionaires like Sir Y. K. Pao, who took his fleet from Shanghai and Ningbo, and made Hong Kong his home, thus building his Wharf empire and Wheelock Marden as the Communists took ownership of China in 1949. Along the many coastal ports, many families set sail from Quanzhou (a city next to the Taiwan Strait in Fujian Province) or from Zhongshan (a small city near the mouth of the Pearl River Estuary) and built businesses along the Maritime

---

30. The Economist Intelligence Unit, 2014.

Silk Road. Those businesses that have extended outside China, moving along the Maritime Silk Road into Malaysia, Singapore, and the Philippines, have fared well and sometimes survived into their fifth and even sixth generations.

Li Shek-Pang, the founder of the Li family banking empire in Hong Kong that created the Bank of East Asia, started by buying second-hand cargo vessels moving goods between Hong Kong and Saigon.[31] Most estimates suggest that Chinese families control as much as 80% of the midsize enterprises throughout the region. This was the period that fueled the "bamboo network."[32]

For those entrepreneurs that could survive the gauntlet of the early years, success ensued and expansion into neighboring enclaves and hometown was important. Such a move was a testament to a venture that had started decades before. The successful patriarchs were well tested, battle-hardened, and had managed to survive revolutions, typhoons, unfriendly neighborhoods, workers' rebellions, and government interventions. Many had relied on their clans back home for liquidity. Nearly all kept a very low profile and did not want any limelight that would attract unwanted attention from hostile neighbors and jealous clan members. Ownership belonged solely to them. Transparency was not the norm.

Lang and Young[33] studied the pervasiveness of the governance of Chinese family companies in Singapore, Taiwan, Malaysia, Japan, Hong Kong, Thailand, Philippines, and Indonesia. Using publicly available information, they investigated 3,000 East Asian companies and found that family-controlled businesses in Indonesia accounted for a proportion of 60%–70%; Philippines approximately 50%, and Thailand approximately 61.6 %. Others included Singapore (30%), Taiwan (48.2%), South Korea (48.8%), Hong Kong (66%), and Malaysia (67.2%). Japan was at the bottom of the list with 9.7%.

At the earlier stages of a typical Chinese family business, there would be no clear separation between owners, directors, and top management. The majority of Chinese family businesses outside China actually started out this way. The founder and his immediate family would play all the managerial and operational roles at the same time. They would have to govern their organization, plus run the company on their own.

When it comes to succession, the transfer of power can be disastrous for some, particularly if the Chinese family business is outside China. In 2014, Joseph Fan at Chinese University found that the transfer from one generation to another leads to a drop in value. His research indicated that Asian firms in general should expect to lose 60% of the value in the first transfer of power. This is probably the single deepest drop next to bankruptcy. His team used a research base that covered 217 Chinese-run publicly listed companies across Hong Kong, Singapore, and Taiwan.

---

31. Ching, 1999.
32. Weidenbaum & Hughes, 1996.
33. Lang & Young, 1996.

One conclusion he was able to draw was that the reason is most often the incompetence of the successors.[34]

The return of the sojourners outside China

Going home and receiving a hero's welcome has been a dream for many wayward patriarchs. Many do eventually return home, and in so doing would establish a branch of business in mainland China, so that relatives may partake in the business and share the success of the patriarch. At the patriarch's ancestral home, one would find town halls and city centers donated by the patriarch. Patriarchs who are not able to make the trip themselves would rely on their children to do so on their behalf. Many families eventually returned and reinvested in the local economy due to favorable government policies. In fact, relying on returning rich families to help ignite economic growth was an effective means for the Chinese government during the early period of the Four Modernizations.

Some of the families that have returned and played a pivotal role in modernization have included many families that had been residing outside the Mainland before the 1980s. The Wharf Group, which was founded by Sir Y. K. Pao, has returned and invested in business from Shanghai to Wuhan, as Sir Li Ka-Shing's empire has reinvested in properties from Beijing to Shanghai.[35] Vincent Lo's Xintiandi and similar Xintiandi developments from Hangzhou to Chongqing have started many new property developments in China.

The New World Development Group, a conglomerate with interests in property, hotels, infrastructure, and department stores, and notably the thousands of retail jewelry stores called Chow Tai Fook that are dotted throughout China, is now under the helm of the 3Gs (third generation): Adrian Cheng, Brian Cheng, and Sonia Cheng. They are the children of Henry Cheng, the son of Cheng Yu-Tung, who is the founder patriarch and founded New World in 1970. Cheng Yu-Tung started his venture into jewelry in Guangzhou, China but made his millions in Hong Kong. His family is now back and well established in the Mainland. In fact, these 3Gs were one of the first to introduce Western management practices, having lived and studied abroad.[36]

---

34. Fan, 2014.
35. Li was one of the first to jump into the bandwagon when China invited family businesses to return or to join. Recently, however, Li has begun to sell off his controlling stakes in both mainland China and Hong Kong, investing in Israel and other locations instead.
36. SCMP (2015, March 20). New World Development has a market capitalization of HK$81 billion, of which 43% is owned by the Cheng family.

Successful multigenerational Chinese family businesses

Surprisingly in profitability, family businesses (particularly those that have been listed) often do better than non-family business in the long run. According to a landmark study by Anderson and Reeb,[37] firm performance in the S&P 500 was comparatively higher for family-founded businesses. Family-owned firms performed better than did non-family firms. Further, when the CEO was a member of the family, performance was better. Apparently four critical choices in governance arrangement can help family firms do better, according to another paper by Miller and Breton-Miller.[38] The choices of governance arrangement are the level of family ownership, family leadership, the broader involvement of multiple family members, and the planned or actual participation of later generations. The combination of these choices does affect the firm's performance, they argued. In other words, how extensive and tightly knit is the overall family in running their business has a direct correlation with business performance.

The longevity of a business is a sign of success. Most of the long-lasting patriarchs and their families have the added advantage of residing in Hong Kong where inheritance tax is non-existent.

- The CHENG Family. Properties, jewelry, and hotels. Established 1970. New World Development. Current Patriarch: Henry Cheng
- The CHENG Family. Properties, hotels. Established 1991. Wing Tai Development.
- The KWOK Family, looking after Sun Hung Kai Properties. Market capitalization of over US$49 billion. Established 1963. Matriarch: Siu-Hing Kwong.
- The LEE Family. Henderson Development. Established 1976. Patriarch: Lee Shau Kee
- The LEE Family. Lee Kum Kee. Established in 1888. Current Patriarch: Lee Man Tat.
- The LO Family. Shui On Construction. Current Patriarch: Vincent Lo.
- The LI Family. Looking after CK Hutchison Holdings and with a market capitalization of over US$36 billion. Other companies include Cheung Kong. The family empire employs over 310,000 people in more than 50 nations.[39] Patriarch is Sir Li Ka-Shing.
- The LI Family, looking after the Bank of East Asia. Patriarch: Mr. David Li.
- The YANG Family. Looking after Esquel Group, global scale textile and apparels manufacturer. Established 1978, Patriarch: Yang Yuan Loong (deceased). Marjorie and Teresa Yang currently in charge.

---

37. Anderson & Reeb, 2003.
38. Miller & Breton-Miller, 2006.
39. Forbes, 2018.

Other less prominent ones, dotted throughout Asia:

- KHOO Family. Maybank in Singapore.
- KWEK Family. Hong Leong Group in Singapore and Malaysia.
- LAW Family. Bossini in Hong Kong.
- LO Family. Vincent Lo's Shui On Group. His family ran the Great Eagle empire.
- LU Family. Ronald Lu & Partners. In architecture.
- PAO Family. BW Group in Hong Kong.
- SY Family. SM Investment Corporation in the Philippines
- TAN Family. Luen Thai Group of Companies.
- TSAI Family. Cathay Financial.
- TSAI Family. Want Want China, based in Taiwan.
- WEE Family. United Overseas Bank in Singapore.

Conclusion

Corporate governance is about the exercise of power. For many Chinese domestic families, at the time of transition and emergence of new family members into the business, corporate governance becomes a critical concern as power now needs to be shared. The next generation faces challenges in restructuring how decisions are made and shared. They want to exercise their power by changing the governance structure, governance process, authority, veto power, roles and responsibilities, succession, and other governance issues related to the remaining family businesses but doing so with respect to culture and custom.

Sharing power with those family members remaining, introducing new ways to work together and to make decisions together, underpins this period of chaotic power struggle for Chinese family businesses. In our experience, if this transition and the installation of the new team are done carefully and with consideration, we should expect to see a continuation of the family business by the next generation . . . but only until the next period of succession.

Interestingly, because some Chinese founders typically do not like to give up their authority until they are no longer able to work, by the time they officially retire, their sons and daughters will be near retirement age as well. The transition then is not just about transferring power to the next generation but also to the ones after. This is another phenomenon that we have noted. Finding viable and fair options to award retirement plans to the family members who are retiring within five years becomes an added complication. As power shifts, in our experience, the following concerns would arise for the owners remaining. Finding solutions to these new challenges will be needed:

1. **Divide or Exit:** Should family members continue to work together as a family, now that the conglomerate may be much bigger? Should members

divide up the empire? How should family members be allowed to exit the business? What should be the proper discount, and how would that affect the business working capital? Finally, how should they best reallocate ownership of the current business?

2. **Concerns for Family Stakeholders:** How much power or influence should the family allocate to those who are not in the same business? How do they engage family stakeholders? How should they develop and groom the sons and daughters of the family's loyal workers?

3. **Managing Risky Investments:** As the family's wealth grows, how to handle excess wealth becomes relevant. Should the family set up a private equity or venture fund to finance highly risky businesses introduced by other members of the family? How do they take advantage of other potential businesses in the portfolio as they become mature? Should they give responsibility to another family member? Or, is the timing right for floating the company through an IPO?

4. **Management and Leadership Development:** How should talents in the family be grown so they can be ready and inserted when a company is ready for IPO?

5. **Governance of Subsidiaries:** As the business empire expands, there will be many layers of boards. What are the information channels, frequencies, and levels for each level of the board? How should they set up an oversight committee or a form of risk and audit committee, if this is needed?

As the businesses of the family expand and power is passed to the next generation, uncertainty sets in. Inevitably, these are just some of the concerns for those new to power.

Obviously, these issues need not be unique to Chinese family businesses. But Chinese family businesses are in transition. It is the combination of unique circumstances as we have explained in this chapter that has made the Chinese family businesses worth further investigation. The context, which includes the opportunities with the opening of the domestic and international markets (Wanda buying companies abroad for example), coupled with the limited gene pool due to the previous one-child policy, meshed with the coming together of divergent cultures of the returning students and the family is uniquely Chinese.

Assuming 80% of private companies are family businesses, and many are now in their period of transition from one generation to the next since the Four Modernizations of 1978, we should expect to see the issues covered in this chapter become more prevalent and topical.

References

All-China Federation of Industry and Commerce (2012, March 17), Retrieved April 30, 2018 from http://en.sjtu.edu.cn/news/xinhuanetchinas-rich-reluctant-to-take-over-family-firms-report/.

Amit, R., Ding, Y., Villalonga, B., & Zhang, H. (2015). The role of institutional development in the prevalence and value of family firms. *Journal of Corporate Finance, 31*, 284–305.

Anderson, A., & Gupta, P. P. (2009). A cross-country comparison of corporate governance and firm performance: Do financial structure and the legal system matter? *Journal of Contemporary Accounting & Economics, 5*(2), 61–79. doi:10.1016/j.jcae.2009.06.002.

Anderson, R., & Reeb, D. (2003). Founding-family ownership and firm performance: Evidence from the S&P 500. *The Journal of Finance, 58*(3), 1301–1328.

Bartholomeusz, S., & Tanewski, G. A. (2006). The relationship between family firms and corporate governance. *Journal of Small Business Management, 44*(2), 245–267.

Cai, P. (2015). China's new economic crisis: Keeping the family business. [PDF version]. The AsiaLink Essays 2015. Retrieved August 19, 2017 from http://asialink.unimelb.edu.au/__data/assets/pdf_file/0020/2034137/Chinas-New-Economic-Crisis.pdf.

Caspar, C., Dias, A. K., & Elstrodt, H. (2010). The five attributes of enduring family businesses. McKinsey & Company. Retrieved March 29, 2018 from https://www.mckinsey.com/business-functions/organization/our-insights/the-five-attributes-of-enduring-family-businesses.

China's rich reluctant to take over family firms: Report. (2012, March 17). Retrieved April 30, 2018 from http://en.sjtu.edu.cn/news/xinhuanetchinas-rich-reluctant-to-take-over-family-firms-report/.

Ching, F. (1999). *The Li dynasty: Hong Kong aristocrats*. Hong Kong: Oxford University Press.

Chong, K. P. (2016, December 18). China's second generation shuns family business. *Strait Times*. Retrieved April 30, 2018 from http://www.straitstimes.com/world/chinas-second-generation-shuns-family-business.

Chu, H. H. (2016). Legal origin and corporate governance for Chinese family business: Evidence in Hong Kong, Taiwan and mainland China. *SSRN Electronic Journal*. doi:10.2139/ssrn.2890184

Claessens, S., Djankov, S. D., Fan, J. P., & Lang, L. H. (2000). On expropriation of minority shareholders: Evidence from East Asia. *SSRN Electronic Journal*. doi:10.2139/ssrn.202390.

Charitable Donation. (2018). Retrieved April 30, 2018 from https://www.wanda-group.com/csr/charitable_donation/.

Dong, Emma (2013, April 21). "Zong Qinghou: Work, tea, and cigarettes." *Financial Times*. Retrieved on June 6, 2018 from https://www.ft.com/content/222e3198-9c97-11e2-9a4b-00144feabdc0.

Family Business Governance Handbook—IFC. [PDF Version]. (n.d.). Retrieved March 28, 2018 from http://www.ifc.org/wps/wcm/connect/159c9c0048582f6883f9ebfc046daa89/FB_English_final_2008.pdf?MOD=AJPERES.

Family Enterprise Statistics from around the World. (n.d.). Retrieved August 22, 2017 from http://www.ffi.org/page/globaldatapoints

Fan, J. (2012). *The critical generations: Out of the succession struggle of Chinese family businesses*. [關鍵世代：走出華人家族企業傳承之困]. Beijing: Eastern Publications.

Fan, J. (2014). Do Asian family businesses destroy themselves? Chinese University of Hong Kong. Retrieved August 2, 2017 from http://www.cuhk.edu.hk/english/features/professor-joseph-fan.html.

Fishman, T. C. (2005). *China Inc.: The relentless rise of the next great superpower*. London: Simon & Schuster.

Flannery, R. (2016). More than half of China's family businesses face succession dilemma. *Forbes*. Retrieved August 19, 2017 from https://www.forbes.com/sites/russell flannery/2016/07/24/more-than-half-of-chinas-family-businesses-face-succession-dilemma/.

Forbes (2018). *K. S. Li*. Retrieved April 30, 2018 from https://www.forbes.com/profile/li-ka-shing/.

Guangsha Holding Group Co., Ltd. (广厦控股集团有限公司) (2018). Retrieved April 30, 2018 from https://www.bloomberg.com/research/stocks/private/snapshot.asp?privcapId=22533918. Please see Company Profile. Retrieved April 30, 2018, from http://guangsha.com/en/web/index.php/about.

Heng Shao (2014, June 2). "The vexation of China's second generation rich." *Forbes Asia*. Retrieved on June 6, 2018 from https://www.forbes.com/sites/hengshao/2014/06/02/the-vexation-of-chinas-second-generation-rich/#502c9ef037f0.

Lang, L., & Young, L. (2000). Minority interest, majority concern. *Company Secretary*, *10*(11): 38–42.

Lansberg, I., & Gersick, K. (2009). *Tradition & adaptation in Chinese family enterprises: Facing the challenge of continuity*. 2nd ed. HSBC Private Bank.

La Porta, R., Lopez-de-Silanes, F., & Shleifer, A. (1999). Corporate ownership around the world. *The Journal of Finance*, *54*(2), 471–517.

Lawton, P., & Tyler, E. (2001). *Division of duties and responsibilities between the company secretary and directors in Hong Kong*. Hong Kong: The Hong Kong Institute of Company Secretaries.

Lu, N. (2017, March 14). Top 10 Chinese people in China in 2017. Retrieved April 30, 2018 from http://www.china.org.cn/top10/2017-03/14/content_40455443.htm.

Miller, D., & Breton-Miller, I. L. (2006). Family governance and firm performance: Agency, stewardship, and capabilities. *Family Business Review*, *19*(1), 73–87. doi:10.1111/j.1741-6248.2006.00063.x.

National Bureau of Statistics of People's Republic of China (2003) 中美私营家族企业比较 [Comparison between Chinese and American private family business]. Retrieved April 30, 2018 from http://www.stats.gov.cn/tjzs/tjsj/tjcb/zggqgl/200309/t20030911_37419.html.

PwC. (2016). Family business in China and Hong Kong: Evolving with the times while navigating a competitive environment. [PDF Version]. Retrieved April 30, 2018 from https://www.pwchk.com/en/migration/pdf/gfbs-cnhk-nov2016-hk.pdf.

Redding, S. G. (1993). *The spirit of Chinese capitalism*. Berlin: Walter de Gruyter.

SCMP (2015, March 20). *Third generation moving up at New World Development* Retrieved April 30, 2018 from http://www.scmp.com/business/companies/article/1742561/third-generation-moving-new-world-development.

Shanxi Haixin Iron and Steel Group Co., Ltd. (山西海鑫钢铁集团有限公司) (2018). For more information, see 从阿斗变李总 [From a child to CEO]. Retrieved April 30, 2018 from http://finance.ifeng.com/leadership/jdrw/20080118/1278891.shtml.

Steen, A., & Baldwin, K. (2017, April 5). Family business in China: Is there a succession crisis? Retrieved August 19, 2017 from https://www.familyownedbusinessadvisors. com/2015/10/family-business-in-china/.

Suehiro, A. (1993). Family business reassessed: Corporate structure and late-starting industrialization in Thailand. *The Developing Economies, 31*(4), 378–407. doi:10.1111/ j.1746-1049.1993.tb00032.x.

The Economist Intelligence Unit. (2014). *Building legacies: Family business succession in South-east Asia* [PDF version]. Retrieved April 30, 2018 from https://www.labuanibfc. com/clients/Labuan_IBFC_78C2FF81-703A-4CAA-8926-A348A3C91057/contentms/ img/resource_centre/publication/download/Building-Legacies-Family-Business-Succession-in-Southeast-Asia.pdf?1519689600.

Tong, C. K. (2014). Rethinking Chinese business networks: Trust and distrust in Chinese business. *Chinese Business*, 97–117. doi:10.1007/978-981-4451-85-7_6.

Wanda Group. (2018). Retrieved April 30, 2018 from https://www.wanda-group.com/.

Wanda and IBM sign agreement to bring IBM cloud to China through new Wanda Cloud Company. (2017, March 19). Retrieved April 30, 2018 from https://www-03.ibm.com/ press/us/en/pressrelease/51838.wss.

Ward, J. L. (2011). *Keeping the family business healthy: How to plan for continuing growth, profitability, and family leadership*. Basingstoke: Palgrave Macmillan.

Weidenbaum, M. L., & Hughes, S. (1996). *The bamboo network: How expatriate Chinese entrepreneurs are creating a new economic superpower in Asia*. New York: Free Press.

Zhejiang Longsheng Group Co. Ltd. (2018). See *About Us*. Retrieved April 30, 2018 from http://www.longsheng.com/en/index.php/aboutus.

Zheng, Y. P. (2017, August 28). *SCMP*. Wanda rebuffs rumours its chairman Wang Jianlin had been barred from leaving China. Retrieved April 30, 2018 from http://www. scmp.com/business/china-business/article/2108550/wanda-rebuffs-rumours-its-chairman-wang-jianlin-barred.

Case study

Corporate governance at the Wanda Group

Wanda Group: Overview

The Wanda Group was established in Dalian in 1988 and became one of the largest conglomerates in China. By 2015, it had developed four main business lines: commercial properties, culture, Internet, and finance. It ranked 385th on the Fortune Global 500 List in 2015. In 2016, its assets amounted to RMB 796.2 billion with operating revenue of RMB 255 billion. It is in fact the world's largest movie theater operator since its market is the world's most populous nation. Given the youth of this private family business, the founder, Wang Jianlin, was still very much in charge. Wang has two sons and one daughter, and they are mostly not in the business. The second generation, his daughter, potentially is the heir apparent, and this rumour has been rapidly gaining credibility.

According to its 2016 Annual Report, Chairman Wang Jianlin said Wanda will continue expansion in the cultural industry, accelerate transformation of Dalian Wanda commercial properties, adhere to internationalization, and build the Wanda brand globally. Wang did not believe in having other family members run the business and thought the business should best be run by outside professionals. Since the firm's Chinese name literally means "everything can be done," we will have to wait and see if he can easily go against tradition.

Wang was on a shopping spree around the world a few years back. The group has continued to expand abroad due to China's dull properties market, buying AMC theaters in the US in 2012, yachtmaker Sunseeker in the UK in 2013. Wang wanted to build hotels next to the Thames River in Vauxhall, but this plan was dropped in 2015. He bought a building in Sydney from the Blackstone Group and even bought into a Spanish football club called Atletico Madrid.

Unfortunately by late 2017, the company needed more liquidity and sold 77 of its hotels and 13 theme parks to Chinese developers, apparently when the Chinese government started to scrutinize its books and tightened bank lending to the company.[40]

Commercial properties

Wanda Commercial Properties is reportedly the world's largest commercial properties enterprise, based on its land bank. It has opened and operated 187 Wanda Plaza projects in Chinese cities from Beijing, Shanghai, Chengdu to Kunming, and has plans to open 50 more in China in 2017. The company became a listed company through the HKSE in January of 2015 (03699.HK) with a market capitalization over HK$220 billion. However, in less than 21 months, in September 2016, it was privatized and delisted from HKSE.

Cultural Industry Group

Wanda Cultural Industry Group is China's largest cultural enterprise as well, with annual revenue of RMB 64.1 billion in 2016. Under the Cultural Industry Group, Wanda has Wanda Cinemas, Wanda Theme Parks, and Wanda Sports. It operates one of the largest movie chains in China and owns a substantive portion of the AMC theaters overseas. In 2017, unfortunately, the board made a wrong bet and invested millions more in purchasing entertainment companies in the US, just when the Chinese government was against such a policy.

---

40. Zheng (2017, August 28).

Internet Technology Group

Wanda Internet Technology Group is known for its "Ffan" pay technology. Other subsidiaries under the group include a credit rating company, an online credit company, and even big data analytics companies. This group uses artificial intelligence, big data, cloud computing, scene application, and other technologies to realize digital upgrades of industrial entities and to provide new services for Wanda's clients. In 2017, it signed an agreement with IBM to operate IBM Cloud in China.[41]

Financial Group

Wanda Financial Group already has operations in investment, and asset management, insurance, and plans to become a full-licensed financial group in the future.

Wanda Group: Mission, vision, and values

Mission

"Charitable Wealth, Common Prosperity."

Over the past 29 years, Wanda Group has donated a total of RMB 5.45 billion in cash to numerous charitable causes, making it one of the largest private donors in China.[42]

Vision

Wanda Group's vision is "International Wanda, Centennial Business." The term "international" is an implication of the company's global ambition and size, management, and global reach. Moreover, "Centennial enterprise" stands for the company's pursuit of long-term and sustainable growth. By 2020, it was their intention to have become a world-class multinational corporation with assets of $200 billion, market capitalization of $200 billion, revenue of $100 billion, and net profits of $10 billion.

Values

"Integrity, Innovation, Self-discipline, Harmony."

Social value is their most important value.

---

41. Wanda and IBM sign agreement to bring IBM cloud to China through new Wanda Cloud Company (2017, March 19).
42. Charitable Donation, 2018.

Main characteristics[43]

1. Dare to Innovate
2. Commit to Integrity
3. Take the Lead in Sustainable Development
4. Value Employees
5. Keen Focus on Philanthropy
6. Commit to Excellence
7. Have Strong Execution
8. Keep Tradition Alive

Wang Jianlin and his family business

Wang Jianlin was born in 1954 in Sichuan. He started his career with the PLA, and that gave him his foundation from 1970 to 1986. He was discharged as a regiment commander. His opportunity came when he joined the Xigang District in Dalian and quickly rose to become the general manager of the Xigang Residential Development Company.

How he had come to own and founded Dalian Wanda Group has not been too transparent, however. The predecessor of Wanda was a state-owned residential property developer (most likely it was the Xigang Residential Development Company). During the shareholding system reform of SOEs in 1991, the company became the Wanda Group, state-owned capital still being the largest shareholder and employees holding 20% stake. In 2002, Wang Jianlin started the privatization of Wanda. By 2004, state-owned capital had exited Wanda completely, and one year later, employees' stake disappeared gradually from the ownership structure of Wanda. Wang Jianlin held nearly 100% stake of Wanda by 2008.

Cross-holdings

As we can see from the diagram of Wanda ownership (Figure 7.1), 0.24% stake of Wanda Group was owned by Wang Jianlin, and 99.76% was held by Dalian Hexing, which is controlled by Wang Jianlin and his son, Wang Sicong, holding 98% and 2% stake of Dalian Hexing respectively. Wanda Group also held 51.07% of Wanda Commercial Properties and Wang Jianlin held 7.93%.

---

43. Wanda Group, 2018.

Figure 7.1

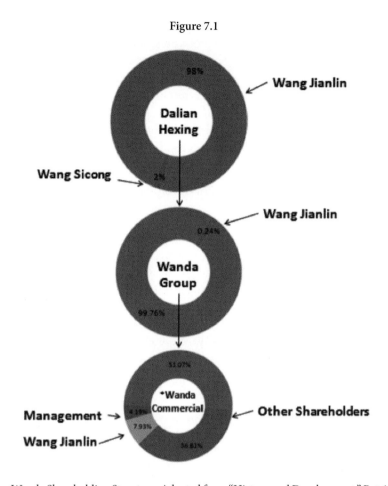

Source: Wanda Shareholding Structure. Adapted from "History and Development." Retrieved May 28, 2018 from http://www.hkexnews.hk/listedco/listconews/SEHK/2014/1223/a3778/EDWCP-20140910-15.PDF. ©2014 by HKEX News.

Wang Jianlin isolated his family members from Wanda Group business; none of Wang's relatives work at Wanda. He said, "It is really difficult to do this because I am an emotional person. Sometimes, I just send money to relatives and suggest them to do other business, but it cannot have business connections with Wanda." As for his son, Wang Sicong, also a director of Wanda, he said, "it is just a nominal position." He once gave Wang Sicong RMB 0.5 billion to establish a private equity company, and by now, Wang Sicong has already invested in several successful projects in the PC gaming industry like Forgame, iDreamSky, and Hero Entertainment. Additionally, Wang Jianlin professionalized the management team. At Wanda, Wang Jianlin is only the chairman. There is a professional management team, Ding Benxi being the CEO.

Although Wanda Group is absolutely controlled by the Wang family, Wang Jianlin wanted to promote and instill a professional managers' system into his organization. Unlike Chinese parents who instinctively want their children to succeed their family business, Wang did not believe in succession by family members. He would have no part in nepotism and promoting his children. Wang Jianlin once said in 2005 that his son Wang Sicong was not necessarily his successor. He stressed that there is no ceiling for the development of professional managers in Wanda and professional manager could also be his successor if he is capable.

Wanda Cinemas: Marching to the international stage

The vision of Wanda Group is "International Wanda, Centennial Business." One of the best examples to demonstrate "international Wanda" is the international outreach of Wanda's movie theaters. Wanda Cinemas was established in 2005 and went IPO successfully in 2015. In recent years, Wanda Cinemas aggressively merged and acquired several companies inside and outside the film industry. Currently, Wanda Cinemas has become the largest Chinese movie theater operator, with about 2,700 screens in 311 theaters across China, Australia, and New Zealand. In April 2017, Wanda Cinemas changed its name to Wanda Film. Wanda even partially owns the AMC entertainment chain in the US, which has 2,200 screens in 244 theaters across the US.

Wanda: The slump of bonds and shares

On June 22, 2017, shares of Wanda Film dropped as much as 9.9% in the morning. Share trading was suspended in the afternoon. At the same time, many bonds issued by Dalian Wanda Group reported a substantial decrease in prices. For example, 16 Wanda 01 Bond listed on the SSE also plunged, falling from RMB 96.90 to RMB 94.25, by around 2.8%. The trend of price of 16 Wanda 01 Bond is shown in Figure 7.2.

According to the *South China Morning Post*, several Chinese large overseas asset companies including Wanda, Fosun, and HNA were being placed under scrutiny by local banks, under a directive by the CBRC that was aimed at cracking down on money laundering and reducing financial risks ahead of the 19th Party Congress. The party controlled the tune. In mid-June, the Banking Regulator had required banks to check their credit exposure to these selected companies and related banks to prepare a risk analysis. Several banks thus took a risk-off position and began to sell bonds of these companies, which could have triggered the panic selling of shares on June 22.

However, by the end of the next day, prices returned to reasonable levels. Wanda Commercial Properties issued a statement saying that the company was in a very healthy financial condition with abundant cash and had no default risks.

Figure 7.2

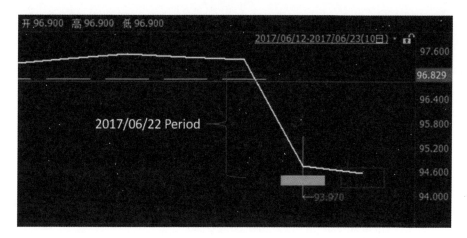

Source: Screenshot from Wind Financial Terminal.

"The company has normal daily operations and there is no other information that is necessary to be brought to the attention of the public."

Questions for discussion

1. Although Vanke and Wanda Group both have businesses in real estate, Vanke is listed at the group level. What are the different influences on corporate governance on Vanke and Wanda? Which company is more transparent?

2. What do you suppose are the reasons behind the delisting of Wanda Commercial Properties from the HKSE?

3. Basically, we can say Wanda Group is 100% owned by the Wang Jianlin family. It does not have any outside anchor shareholder. Vanke introduced Shenzhen Metro (an SOE) as its largest and cornerstone shareholder, whereas Wanda Group is 100% private. What do you think may be the reasons?

4. What do you think could be the potential reasons for the unsuccessful acquisition of DCP overseas? Nowadays, many Chinese companies are carrying out their own globalization strategy. What corporate governance issues do you think would emerge during this process?

5. Do you think political risk is sometimes much more important than are financial and operational risk for business, especially in emerging markets like China?

8

The Functions and Practices of the Board of Directors in China

Gregg Li

In this chapter we consider:

- ❖ what boards do: performance and conformance
- ❖ strategy formulation in Chinese companies
- ❖ policymaking in Chinese companies
- ❖ supervising executive activities in Chinese companies
- ❖ ensuring accountability in Chinese companies
- ❖ succession planning in China

What boards do: Performance and conformance

In Chapter 1, we saw that corporate governance involves overseeing management, ensuring that the enterprise is meeting its objectives, and running in the right strategic direction. In fact, governance has two basic complementary elements: overseeing performance and ensuring conformance. These two wax and wane based on the changing nature of the firm's business model.

The performance role involves working with senior management to formulate corporate strategy and develop corporate policy. The conformance role supervises management activities and ensures compliance with corporate governance norms, providing accountability to legitimate stakeholders.

In a unitary board, which has both executive directors and independent outside directors, the board is responsible for both performance and conformance activities. In the two-tier board system, the executive board is responsible for mostly management performance, while the supervisory board ensures mostly conformance. The degree of intensity and separation of functions between the executive board and the supervisory board has depended more on the maturity of the firm and the speed of change in the industry that provides the ecosystem.

In the system of governance designed for Chinese SOEs (described in Chapter 3), the responsibilities of the board of directors and the board of supervisors can be ambiguous and fluid. The main board, which has both executive directors and at least a third of independent directors, has both performance and conformance responsibilities. The supervisory board, which includes employee representatives, has more a conformance role, monitoring management proposals and actions, while ensuring that the interests of the workers and the state are met. In China, the supervisory board has less power of oversight and typically does not have authority to remove any director on the main board.

Taking on Chinese characteristics

Partly because of the speed of change in the understanding and practices of corporate governance and partly because of an onslaught of new regulations from the authorities, Chinese boards in recent years have been struggling to keep up. Managing uncertainties and keeping things ambiguous slowly became a Chinese characteristic. For many directors, learning about modern "corporate governance" practices along with modern "management" practices have been simultaneous. Even today, improvement in the quality of directorship can vastly improve the quality of corporate governance in Chinese enterprises. The legal system in China fundamentally affected and gave China its own unique characteristics.[1] Since 1993, the impact and quantity of new legislation has sent shockwaves to the directors. Company law became reality only in 1994, and during this transition into modernization, organizations were forced to be efficient and millions of workers were laid off. Governing at those stages had meant having to swallow tough and bitter medicine but without the benefits of certainty that the medicine would work. Downsizing, layoffs, restructuring into non-SOEs,[2] and massive changes—practices that boards typically do not enjoy—were commonplace. Based mostly on the OECD Code, China's Code of Corporate Governance, which would provide practice guidelines for directors, was formulated only in 2002 (which was retracted and has yet to be republished by 2017).

According to independent directors who have sat on Chinese listed companies, the single most important impediment to the proper growth of corporate governance is the lack of quality directors. "Directors who can assist in streamlining board procedures, install independent vetting of connected transactions, or understand the implications of new technology are a rare breed in China," said Moses Cheng, who is one of the first INEDs in China. To illustrate the types, scope, and range of legislations new directors must comprehend and master, the shortlist below shows the new practices and understanding many directors would have to master since the year 2000:

---

1. Denis & McConnell, 2003.
2. According to Cai, Park, & Zhao, 2008, the number of state-sector workers fell from a peak of 113 million in 1995 to 88 million in 1998 and further, into 64 million in 2004.

- The Accounting Law (2000) which lays out requirements on accounting practices, special provisions on companies' accounting practices, accounting supervision, accounting offices, accounting personnel, and legal liability.
- The Guidelines on Independent Directors (2001, CSRC).
- The Code of Corporate Governance for Listed Companies (2002, CSRC) governs shareholders and shareholders' meetings, listed companies and controlling shareholders, directors and board of directors, supervisors and the supervisory board, performance assessment and incentive and disciplinary systems, stakeholders, and information disclosure and transparency.
- Directive on Quarterly Reporting (2003, CSRC).
- The Provisions on Strengthening the Protection of the Rights and Interests of Public Shareholders (2004).
- The Regulations on the Administration of Company Registration (2005).
- The Guidance on Listed Companies' Articles of Association (2006).
- The Rules on Listed Companies' Shareholders' Meetings (2006).
- In 2006, a fundamental review of Chinese Company Law was enacted, creating two types of limited company—the limited liability company (LLC private companies) and the joint-stock company (JSC public companies)—bringing the legal context much in line with the company law of other countries. The responsibilities of company (board) secretaries were established. Securities Law was enacted in the same year. In 2007, CSRC launched a three-year campaign to strengthen listed company governance: use of funds, operation of board, and internal controls.
- The Criminal Law Amendment (6) (2006), which gave a more complete definition on legal liabilities on disclosure, insider's information, and market manipulations.
- The Regulations on the Takeover of Listed Companies (2006).
- Convergence of accounting and auditing standards with IFRS and ISA (2007). Not a complete adoption, however.
- The Administrative Measures on Information Disclosure by Listed Companies (2007).
- The Regulations on Major Asset Reorganization of Listed Companies (2008).
- The Basic Standards for Enterprise Internal Control (2008).
- The Law on the State-Owned Enterprises (2009).

Professionalization of directors is one of the biggest challenges faced by China today, and improvement in this area should provide the single largest improvement to the quality of corporate governance. To work around the current limitations, many directors have learned to be purposely ambiguous and nebulous with their roles, because this was probably the only form of protection they could control and adopt. As long as they knew where they could protect themselves, and as long as visible internal control, command, and communication were clear, other issues could be negotiated or sidestepped or even compromised. The key is not to be overly explicit and be assured from being held singularly for non-compliance: plausible deniability in another form. Although we could explicitly list the half a dozen functions that directors should be practicing as in the West, we have found that the Chinese counterparts have tended to put more emphasis on the interrelationship among these functions. As long as proper governance can be installed and exercised through others or with other means, directors preferred to be invisible. This "relationship" is often difficult to notice, like the dark energy in space, which everyone claims is there but has yet to be identified.

According to Alec Tsui, former CEO of SEHK and one of the first professional independent directors in China,

> Understanding real power in the boardroom requires finesse and patience . . . All shareholders, from aboard or domestically, want the same thing, that is, a reasonable return to their investment in Chinese companies. As an INED, our role is to ensure this is understood and that proper compliance is being enforced. As long as CSRC, in working closely with INEDs, pushes hard on enforcement to improve the protection of investors, then the system of INED can work in China and China's corporate governance is as good as everyone else. Chinese boards are very long-term and focus much more on sustainability and growth, than their Western counterparts, who are more generally governed by each quarter.

Corporate governance in China is more long-term and subtle than obvious. A director from Luen Thai, a listed company in apparels, told us:

> I totally agree that all boards should supervise their management team, hold them accountable, decide on the policies, formulate strategy, ensure succession and other good practices . . . but to us in China, because we don't have too many qualified directors readily available, we have to improvise. Depending on which directors we can find to sit on our boards, we will make some adjustments. We just have to ensure that most of these functions are played out at different levels and can be shared with management. These are subtle differences in governance for Chinese firms, and being able to manage the directors as we grow in sophistication and understanding in governance, is the real game for us.

Moses Cheng further added,

> To operate successfully in China, one has to assume independence is a luxury. At our boards we just assume everyone is somehow connected and we install tougher checks and balances on nearly all possible connected transactions. For example, a board member can easily request for two extra independent assessments when we are buying supplies from a connected third party. In fact, we often asked for this. Management now instinctively know what to do. In China, *guanxi* is the norm and everyone tries to be connected. A good director helps management to understand the extra safeguards and systems they must put in place. To the foreign investors, the proper question they should be asking is: "How much more are they willing to formalize connected transactions?" You see, it is all a matter of costs.

The authorities have also reinforced this character of subtlety. As new legislation was put into place, the authorities were just beginning to test their power of enforcement and exercised considerable restraints since many directors were not aware of many of the new regulations or implications on their roles. According to our interviews with Chinese and foreign lawyers operating in China, few negligent directors have been prosecuted even up to 2017. Jean Chen,[3] describing one extreme, noted that the weaknesses of the current corporate governance system could be attributed to the incompleteness and weakness of the legal enforcement system. Like Alec Tsui, she also believed that improvement in enforcement would be hugely important in improving corporate governance in China. Although lax enforcement may have been true in the recent past, we believe that the authorities are becoming increasingly more explicit on enforcement and interpretation, despite the subtlety that many directors have practiced in their art of governance.

A senior partner of a law firm in China argued that the lack of enforcement and not corruption is the single most damaging issue of corporate governance in China today. He further elaborated that a client of his was caught red-handed, but the authorities only handed down a warning. This same crime would have closed a company in Hong Kong, he said.

"There are both good and terrible companies, on both sides of the fence. Good private firms have strong and effective management; but for the mainland firms, the values of the good firms are not being reflected in their stock price, if they are listed in the Mainland. The markets are quite volatile in the Mainland but growth is not. Retail investors don't trust the institutions or government enough, and consequently don't trust the shares of these listed vehicles sufficiently. In other words, by strengthening the market's trust of these regulatory institutions, the Chinese government can really push the economy upward. In China, and generally speaking, the understanding of directors in view of their duties or their role in CG is relatively much weaker. That is changing, however. Hong Kong was like that years back."

The practice of governance in China has varied considerably over the years, and we are beginning to sense it has begun to settle in pockets of possibilities that often reflected many Chinese characteristics and style of management. Due to the rapid changes in China, any form of generalization is a dangerous undertaking. The only possible commonality is the variety and intensity these practices have being undertaken. The quality of corporate governance is as varied and as complex as China itself. No generalization is possible or fair. Individual accountability, transparency,

---

3. Chen, 2015.

governance code, with regulatory institutions ready to cite non-compliance, which are taken for granted, are not the current norms in China. The culture in China is one of collective and shared accountability. Opaqueness has been the working norm for many SOEs, but this too is changing.

To begin with the proper understanding of governance practices in China, one has to separate first the types of boards into those that are state-owned and those that are not. The state-owned ones, or SOEs, have a good deal in common but are largely commercial instruments of the Communist Party, which might exercise its influence through the Party Committee that would decide which individual sits on which level of the board. The larger and more strategic the SOEs, as in the case of Central SOE or CSOE, the higher the level of subtle oversight by their respective Party Committee and the stronger the expectations of their adherence to new legislation and administrative regulations in their industry.

Strategy formulation in Chinese companies

Corporate strategy sets the direction of the company. It determines the business, or businesses, that the enterprise is in; it recognizes the company's competitive market environment; and it determines the level of risk that the company is prepared to take and the range of resources that would come to be employed. Some companies attempt to define their corporate purpose in a mission statement.

In formulating strategy, the board must come to a shared view of the company's purpose and future direction. Behind every sound corporate strategy is an idea or vision of what those leading the company want it to be and to be seen to be. In formulating corporate strategy, the principal purpose of the organization is identified, its core values established, its risk profile determined, and its longer-term direction set. Hence, a role of the board is to ensure the "agreed" vision can be realized in the long run, and at the very least for most companies, that the company's mission can be delivered in, say, three to five years.

The extent that the directors get involved in strategy formulation varies considerably. Management is to deliver on the results based on the agreed strategy. Directors are to help tease out the strategy, and once set, to step aside and let management perform. When the executive directors (directors who have executive power or who are now a part of management) wield the power on a board, strategic thinking tends to be done by the senior management group and then, as necessary, the board questions their thinking and ratifies strategic decisions.

One style is "emergent," that is, various strands slowly come together to form a norm. These strands are not purposely "created" by management but are more "being recognized" by management. In many private boards or those dominated by founders, their style seems to be "emergent." There are a dozen strategies all moving at the same time, and any one may end up as the dominant strategy. The market and executive prowess would ground that strategy. That is, a combination of factors provides the context for more an emergent type of strategy formulation in many private firms.

These may include:

- the volatility that many firms have experienced in their own market;
- the dearth of sound market data in China with which to make business judgment;
- the lack of good management team;
- the lack of enforcement on governance by the authorities, as cited;
- past behaviors that lend themselves for quick decision-making; and
- the exercise of power through strategic formulation in private firms often concentrating on the founder.

This is the case in many of the relatively new private companies in China. Given the dynamic socioeconomic situation, particularly in the Pearl River Delta area[4] and the development of smart cities where technology is dominant, boards have to understand their strategic situation, identify business opportunities, recognize their financial implications, consider competitors and technological change, recognize associated risks, and decide among strategic alternatives. In China, they will also have to be cognizant of the government policies that are being promoted by the government and the Communist Party, as any strategy going against administrative ruling will be unsuccessful. Not understanding or not being in line with the current government policies and political wind has often been cited as a top risk in China for foreign firms. This too, is a Chinese characteristic.

Styles are generally very different for SOEs. Domination by incumbent executive directors was seen in many SOEs during the early days of the market-orientated reforms, when SOEs were being corporatized. Although outside directors were required on SOE boards, many of them lacked experience, while the executive directors knew the business, its business contacts, and its politics. They also had relationship links with the authorities in government agencies and oversight bodies. Questions were asked whether independent directors really knew enough about the business and its industry to make a realistic contribution. Others wondered whether some outside directors had the time to make a worthwhile input. Those questions are still asked in some SOEs. An assumption exists that these lay outside directors are there to provide "conformance" with the government requirements. It would be an added advantage that these directors would be knowledgeable with internal control, risk management, and other professional demands.

---

4. TDC, 2018. Shenzhen, Hong Kong, Guangzhou, Dongguan, Huizhou, Zhaoqing, Foshan, Jiangmen, and Zhuhai. According to the Hong Kong Trade Development Council, the PRD area is located at the Pearl River estuary where the river enters the South China Sea. In 2015, it was one of the most vibrant zones in China, with a real GDP growth of 8.6% and only 4.3% of China's population. Today however, the Greater Bay Area is the new focus and PRD has been subsumed into this geographic strategy.

Boards dominated by executive directors obviously benefit from their inside knowledge and experience. The challenge is whether they take a sufficiently critical perspective. In the words of one commentator: "executive directors wear two hats, being both managers and directors. When serving on the board they are marking their own examination papers." Well-informed, knowledgeable, and independent outside directors can play a vital role in strategy formulation by offering alternative insights, raising important questions, for example about risks involved, and by challenging conclusions.

Fortunately, there is a growing professionalism at SOE board level, particularly in SOEs that are listed on UK or US stock exchanges. SOE directors now have more experience and some younger ones have business training and MBAs. Getting an Executive MBA (for those who usually don't have a first degree) is still a rewarding undertaking and bonus reward for many senior people.

To meet their board-level responsibilities, all directors need the ability to think strategically. What does that mean? Sun Tzu, a great strategist during the Zhou dynasty, emphasized the need to "*think with the mind of the enemy.*" What are the potential threats and where might they come from? Are there unrecognized opportunities? Some directors, who used to receive instructions from central authorities, found such attitudes hard to develop. But directors of SOEs had to learn, particularly if their shares were floated on a stock exchange. The ways in which strategy was formulated in SOEs were mostly administrative in the past. Moving towards a market economy had meant the central authorities have given more freedom to each board to find its own path. An explanation from a seasoned banker should shed some light on how strategy in the past has been handed down.

A senior banker with over 30 years of experience in China with the likes of Citibank and others explained to us how power is handed down and how strategy is formulated at many SOEs.

"For the SOE, there are two lines of power. One is the visible line, which is the chairman/CEO organization chart line. The other is the Political Commissars or Party Secretaries. This person has kept dossiers on all senior staff and determines the succession and development of senior managers in the SOEs. He does not report to the CEO. This person also recommends the right individuals to sit on the Supervisory Committee. The typical title of the person is Head of Human Resources. The party directives are passed to the Political Commissar, who will order the CEO to do what is required by the party. Increasingly, not every CEO is a party member, so the push will be from the chairman and the board. The chair is usually a party member. As Jiang Zemin said, 'to change China, one must start with the party.' The party's goals and aspirations are the end game; CG is only a means. Don't get this confused."

He further added,

"The party issues directives and this sets the tone in the form of 'policies' that all companies must follow. Hence, in China, the tone of the national policy has major implications on decisions to be made by the board of any company. National policies come first. To enforce control and report variances, Chinese management doesn't like to document things as this will set them up whereby they would have to provide evidence. The preferred means is through dialogue, and that's why senior people always prefer discussion and not emails or documents. Manage-by-walking-around is highly respected and a must for any good Chinese manager."

The executive board

As cited, SOE boards are increasingly expected to deliver on the results. That responsibility increasingly falls flatly on the executive board or management board. The role of the executive board in formulating a strategy and executing that agreed strategy now happens more for the same party. It is increasingly similar to what happens in a unitary board outside China. In this case and contrary to Western boards, however, the SOEs have an immediate audience (the supervisory board). For this system to have any chance of establishment and regularity, each management board naturally would need stronger outside independent directors who also understand the industry and are able to keep management in check, have stronger independent audit, more professional assessment of operational risks, and strong board procedures at the minimum. In fact, these and other mechanisms were the types of tools that CSRC and other authorities have endorsed and encouraged SOEs to undertake.

Policymaking in Chinese companies

Strategies remain nothing more than statements of intent, no more than dreams, unless they are turned into action. "A strategy is a coherent mix of policy and action designed to surmount a high-stakes problem," according to Professor Rumelt of UCLA, and "it is a not a dream." To make strategies operational, companies need policies, procedures, plans, and, in some cases, one-off projects. Policies (sometimes called standard operating procedures or SOP in China), operational procedures, and plans provide management with criteria against which the board can subsequently monitor their performance and fulfill their duty of management supervision.

Corporate policies can be thought of as the rules, systems, and procedures provided by the board to guide and constrain executive management. Obviously, the details of corporate policies depend on the scale, diversity, and type of operation.

Top management may play a large part in the development of such policies as well as in their implementation. In other cases, the board may delegate a lot of policymaking to the CEO and top executive team. Such policies, for example, might cover customer relations and marketing, product pricing, technology, innovation and research, employees and labor relations, suppliers and purchasing, downstream distribution and sales, capital expenditure and control, accounting and financial controls, risk assessment, and how corporate values and ethics are exercised and endorsed.

Every board has a duty to ensure that appropriate policies are in place, that they are functioning effectively, and are regularly reviewed in the light of changing circumstances. Some boards identify specific issues that are so important that they should never be delegated to management and always referred to the board; for example, decisions on top management appointments, acquisition proposals, or capital expenditure over a given amount. In such cases, the directors create a policy reserving such decisions to the board.

Risk management policies are of particular importance at board level. The global financial crisis showed that many boards, not only of financial institutions, had failed to appreciate fully their companies' exposure to risks. Corporate governance codes now expressly recognize directors' responsibility to ensure that risk management policies are in place and that risks are adequately assessed.

In SOEs, some policies are determined by Central Government authorities—the office responsible for that industry or the central financing authority, for example. As SOE boards became increasingly responsible for the formulation of their own strategies, those boards had to create supporting policies to enable management to make plans.

In the private sector and in enterprises owned by municipal and village entities, governing bodies have to ensure that suitable policies are in place to support their corporate strategies.

Policies need to flow from corporate strategy. Boards have a responsibility to ensure that appropriate policies exist, either by setting them themselves or by approving those proposed by management. Then the board needs to ensure that appropriate management systems are in place to confirm that policies are working and updated when necessary.

From the SOEs we move to how the varieties take on added dimensions for private firms, where from one extreme we have predominantly the founder's strategy forming the core strategy and policy setting, and on the other, the management team working on formulating and delivering on the strategy as a team. In China, the founder's strategy is the mainstream for private firms, and this is similar to many companies in other countries where the founders are often the largest shareholders and are the CEO. In China, entrepreneurs were given a new lease on life post 1978, and with added protection through legislation, many firms grew quickly from mere start-ups. The founder's culture predominated. These firms were often young and given new markets in green pastures, to run as fast as possible and to adapt as quickly as possible. If rules did not exist in a market, then the mentality in the early period was acceptable and viable. The projects in setting up policies for management consulting firms and accounting firms proliferated as many were tasked to design and install standard policies and procedures, which by that time had been well refined outside China. Getting professionals installed and then tasking management to follow policy control and operating procedures has been a beneficial method for both operators and consultants.

In fact, for many enterprises pursuing an IPO, this practice of getting professionals to install quickly a system of policies and systems of governance proved to be expedient but could also be superficial. The key is having these practices become everyday norms and habits. But such resolve requires huge trade-offs in time and mandated resources that many companies and founders may not be willing to make or set aside.

There needs to be frequent and constant reminders, education and training on governance practices, ethical leadership that can showcase and demonstrate a new culture of governance and transparency, strong and visible compliance, a reward system that favors fair play, sound audit and independent auditors, while at the same time, those following these new order of things can see the benefits. Leadership must be able to demonstrate clearly there exists a direct link of good corporate governance to company performance and stronger societal acceptance.

We spoke to a senior partner of a regional accounting practice who heads up their China Practice, on this issue. He emphasized that the results in transforming private firms to well-governed listed entities that can be owned and shared by others have been challenging thus far. "Often successful founders are egoistical, eccentric, and not likely to change their behaviors," he said. "Many still harbored the belief that they own their company (after IPO) and somehow they quickly return to their old behaviors and put the whole company at risk." He further elaborated,

"Because power is typically centralized, introducing checks and balances and a culture that fosters that has been extremely difficult. The Hong Kong SFC is aware of this, and not too happy.

A company's ethics is based on the founder, and usually, it is pretty shoddy. If that person isn't educated, we can forget about ethics or believing in ethics. They are witty, but not ethical. Some, having earned their first bucket of gold, often in criminal or unscrupulous ways, are looking at ways to transform and legitimize themselves. As long as these founders are earnest and show a pattern of consistent clean behaviors, however, we would help them. But one has to be mindful that the Chinese culture has fostered founders who can be emperors. They are uncontrollable, and often such streaks of wanton behaviors have gotten them into trouble with the SFC."

The pattern goes as follows. Private enterprises usually have a cash flow problem. They borrow to the extreme, and gearing is extremely high. There is never enough to cover all the debts; hence, interest payment is a huge issue. Often we see 80% gearing. The issue of going concern is questioned. Finance cost is high. Return to shareholders is thus very low. This means we see enterprises pulling in huge amounts, but net profit is small. The key reason is the high interest expense.

"Next, the founder, who is used to his own authority, would invest some of his listed stocks and use them as collateral in other dealings, in the hope of getting some return to pay off his interest. He does not tell his board, however. Unfortunately, these outside dealings, often highly risky, would go belly up, and their banks would call the loan. News eventually gets out and the listed company's asset drops in quality and value . . . next, the stock price of the listco plummets."

The mindset of checks and balances was never there. Founders still believe it is their own private company and would put money where they want.   ·

The above story may seem extreme. The switch in mindset has been difficult for many, albeit not unexpected. China is a fast-evolving market with deep history and tradition. Rules are young. Nonetheless, for the astute and careful shopper, gems are rare but still available. Buyers beware.[5]

Strategy formulation and policymaking together form the board's performance role. We now come to the conformance roles: supervising executive activities and providing accountability.

Supervising executive activities in Chinese companies

All governing bodies have the primary responsibility to monitor management performance and to take action, if necessary, to improve it.

In China, the private sector is relatively new and, consequently, practices are evolving and experience being gained. A typical board is likely to be dominated by the founder directors supported by senior executives, some of whom may also be directors. Depending on the nature and financing of the business, others may be involved as non-executive outside directors, including family relations, close

---

5. Readers may want to investigate these large Hong Kong–listed companies in the recent news. Some have been delisted due to filing misleading and erroneous information, fund misallocation, and other anomalies. Some are still alive but struggling and have been suspended as of July 2017: Huishan Diary, Hanergy, LeEco, China Metal Recycling, Real Gold Mining, Sino Forest, and Hontex International.

business contacts in a *guanxi* network, or providers of finance. In this section we explore some of the ways the Chinese have approached this challenge.

In the state sector, monitoring management performance and taking necessary action had a longer tradition. Reporting to government authorities on the achievement of goals on production, employment, finance, and other political demands were well established before the SOEs were corporatized. After corporatization, however, additional control methods were needed to satisfy the requirements of SOEs' new governing bodies: the supervisory board and the main board, with its independent outside directors.

As its name implies, the primary role of the supervisory board is the supervision of management activity. Like its counterpart in the two-tier German system of corporate governance, a vital part of the supervisory role is to protect employee interests. Management decisions that could affect employment levels or conditions, health and safety at work, or the rights of workers would be legitimate concerns of the supervisory board, as would developments that might affect the long-term viability of operations, such as plant closures, automation, or financial matters that could affect the continuation of the company as a going concern. But unlike the German model, the supervisory board also has a specific duty to represent the interest of the party and, hence, Central Government, ensuring that political mandates and guidelines are being followed.

The role of the main board, with its independent, outside directors, is not unlike that of a Western-style unitary board, except that, at least initially, few of the independent directors had experience or a real appreciation of the role and powers of outside directors.

Basic information to meet the needs of both supervisory and main boards is typically provided by financial accounting systems, supplemented by budgetary and management control systems, also mainly in financial terms. Such systems are widely used by companies in Hong Kong and other cities in the Pearl River Delta area, as well as private firms and the subsidiaries of other companies elsewhere in China.

Some SOEs have many production units and subsidiary companies. In such cases profit centers may be established for reporting by each unit. The classical problem of transfer prices for goods and services traded between units can then arise. Suboptimization can also occur, that is where a profit-responsible unit improves its own results by taking action that is detrimental to the enterprise as a whole.

But management reporting and control systems rooted in financial data have limitations: they do not reflect non-financial performance criteria. Consequently, some companies use non-financial criteria to be monitored and reported by management to their boards. Frequently called KPIs, they are widely used in Hong Kong and increasingly elsewhere in China.

In an SOE manufacturing products, for example, KPIs might be developed to monitor:

- productivity
- output and quality levels
- employee level and conditions
- employee health and safety
- worker and management training
- environmental protection (particularly important given China's pollution problems)
- consumer satisfaction
- political performance such as party membership
- overseas investment including acquisitions abroad
- development of automation information systems
- anti-corruption performance
- research and development expenditure and success
- social responsibility (in the old days, many large SOEs were effectively townships, responsible for community services, including workers' housing, schooling, and health services).

According to some Chinese investment bankers, many SOEs have rolling KPIs. There are annual targets but executives are pushed to deliver higher targets and expected to do better, on a rolling basis. If the executives don't do well, they are demoted rather than fired. But they would get the message. These SOEs' officers are tougher on targets than are their American counterparts. Often, these targets come from the top down. For some American multinationals, these are known as "Stretched Targets" where targets have a tendency to creep upwards during the year.

"But in China since decision-making is collectively based, everybody else would take the heat too. Usually everybody gets some contribution for delivering the 'bad and good' results. In SOEs, it is common to have another team doing the same things but competing with the first team."

The bankers have found this unique setup to be consistent. There's another department doing something similar, and they compete directly with the first team. This brings competition and clarity. This "internal competition" is how some SOEs monitor and encourage performance at the working level.

Chinese are not very open to outsiders with such KPIs. For example, China Evergrande Group (HKG:3333), whose value was up and down for the last five years, at one stage was rumored to be bankrupt. This company now has RMB 300 billion net worth. "One should not just look at superficial indicators with such SOEs," confided one banker.

Determining the non-financial performance measures necessary to satisfy a supervisory board can be difficult, and identifying measures that can be quantified to monitor such criteria can present a real challenge.

The interrelationship between supervision and execution in China's SOEs can sometimes be seen through the relationship between the chairperson and the CEO. The chairperson, in reality, formulates the strategy with the CEO; then the CEO is tasked with putting the necessary mix of policy and action designed to surmount that strategy. Subsequently, the chairperson would supervise the quality in the delivery of the plan. How power is shared, exercised, and checked by one another is a dance that should be studied separately. The chairperson and the CEO are dependent on one another, and accountability is mutually linked.

The senior banker further explained how this dance is actually done in many Chinese boardrooms.

"[T]he company is structured in ways that the chairperson can exercise his power. The chairperson typically never has an argument with his CEO openly because difficult discussions and decisions are first taken outside the boardroom. The CEO cannot disagree with the chairperson openly. This is taboo.

In Chinese companies, disagreements are allowed but only outside the board meeting. In board meetings, there is no dissent, and as a committee they would stamp the decision collectively. Board meetings are not used for 'discussion.' They are for formal 'approval.' Decisions are mostly agreed before they are taken at the board level.

The chairperson will dictate the goals usually and unlike American types of goals, the CEO is given a line not to be crossed. If business performance drops below this line, the CEO is removed or demoted. The CEO can ask the chairperson for help (but since the chairperson was also given a target), but there's hardly any help possible. The chairperson, however, can offer other types of resources (from other companies).

Consensus in strategy and policy is usually required before any key decision is made. This ensures continuity and support in the long run. The key is having the right individuals in central power who would come to make such decisions.

It is a silly idea of breaking the role of the CEO and the chairperson. 'This misses the argument,' he further argued. When there is a separation, the chairperson is always much more powerful. He's not just a chairperson of the meeting but the strategist and commander (not the CEO). When there is no separation and there's only one person doing both roles, this person will never have a chair on top of him. It's a face issue."

> He further elaborated:
>
> "A typical and smart CEO will also defer key decision to the chairperson. The chairperson would usually let the CEO make it, however, but only after the CEO has asked for such permission. This is the Chinese way. The CEO is held accountable to the chairperson for 'delivering' the results although the decision to go ahead may not be his alone. Often the CEO is told what targets to make and it is not subject to negotiation. But in reality, most chairpersons hardly want to be rigid and just let the CEO run with their goals."
>
> To check the power of the CEO, the chairperson sometimes would engage the visual or statutory control measures used in corporate governance but would also put his own people as the CEO's deputy. Often the deputy or the CFO belongs to the chairperson. This is how the chairperson would exercise his form of supervision.

Sometimes the roles of the CEO and that of the chairperson can be purposely adversarial, for the sake of supervision. We have to remember this is a land of experimentation when it comes to corporate governance. In this particular case, the Communist Party wanted a competent CEO to run an SOE in the energy sector, but the party wasn't able to find this individual in China. A search netted an individual from Hong Kong.[6] A compromise was struck such that the CEO would report to the board, not to the chairperson. On the day-to-day running of the business, the CEO could not get his or her team to execute certain actions without the implicit approval of the chairperson, however. The CEO is held responsible to deliver the KPIs, but his senior team would report to and be evaluated by the chairperson. If the chairperson is a party member, then he or she doubles as the political commissar or implicitly as the head of human resources.

China is a country that is extremely populous, and over the years this density has fostered a culture that is more encompassing, inclusive, and less individualistic. It is difficult to live by yourself with so many people. Harmony is considered a virtue and open challenge is not. Chinese Zen Buddhism (or Chan Buddhism) is about being aware of your surroundings, of others, as much as it is about compassion. Confucianism is about accepting and working within order and hierarchy. Everyone has a role and a relationship. Daoism is about living harmoniously and with nature. Finally, Communism is about the sharing of wealth and assets. Chinese historically have had low trust in institutions and relied on relationships that they can touch and interact with; family, friends, and immediate co-workers are those worth caring for and should be consulted on important decisions. In corporate governance terms, this would mean that decisions are often collectively made when

---

6. Market expectations of professionals from Hong Kong tend to view them as competent, cross-cultural, with strong ethics but fiercely independent.

leadership is not explicit, and interestingly, can be hierarchical when leadership has been explicitly identified (President Xi, for example, whose decision is final). This range of decision-making culture is also being played out in Chinese companies and affects how many decisions are actually made.

For private firms that are controlled by the living founder, the norm of decision-making is often hierarchical, whereby the "Lao Ban"[7] or "Taipan" is expected to be "equal above all." He alone can change a policy. He alone can set exceptions. A factory owner once told us that he could set a policy that no one can smoke in this factory, except him. And he would not be challenged. In China, rule by the owner is often the norm for many companies. How this may play out in reality is best described with a comment from Chinese investment bankers operating in China.

According to several Chinese investment bankers who have been helping SOEs and private firms list themselves in Hong Kong, the power between the chairperson and the CEO carries a special subtlety. Although power is generally shared and consensual decision-making is often the norm, how power is actually exercised takes on a slightly different twist. The chairperson often has the veto vote, not a swing vote. It is called the "**One Ticket Vote**." To understand this is important, one banker asserted:

"Let's say you have a key decision to make and the chairperson would let the board debate the various issues. At the end, there seems to be a consensus around the room on what decision the board would then take. The chairperson then steps in and makes a decision. He doesn't have to follow consensus, but usually he does. The side that has lost the debate has lost face [and that comes back to you eventually]. The chairperson doesn't have a swing vote but the definitive vote.

If the final decision somehow was wrong, and although the chairperson has made that wrong decision, the executives who have failed to argue the case and weren't cognitive-sufficient to build a winning case would receive some of the blame. In reality this means the executives must be able to lobby the chairperson beforehand."

Interestingly, for a CEO whose power base is often nebulous, the style of decision-making is often consensual. No department really has a final say on anything, except perhaps the CEO or the chairperson. For someone who does not understand the subtlety in culture, misunderstanding often occurs. An American for example, in a negotiation, may say that his lawyer has an issue with this clause

---

7. Literally translated as the owner, the boss, or the old man.

and won't approve it.[8] Your Chinese counterpart in a negotiation may in turn, say that a department has an issue with this clause and he won't mention any names.[9] In Chinese negotiation tactics a blunt "no" would not be given. A delay is often a preferred way for them to say "no."

But this misunderstanding can cut both ways. In 2008, when an earthquake struck Sichuan, many had expected that Vanke, China's largest listed property developer, would quickly reach out and donate financial support. But Vanke, which is a listed company and wanted to comply with proper governance rules, needed board approval. Consequently, the final decision came slowly. Its founder, Wang Shi, saw the delay and quickly stepped up to the plate but gave the wrong signal. He announced that Vanke would donate RMB2 million and told his employees not to donate more than RMB10 each. Because of his action, he was reportedly lambasted by netizens, ("citizens of the net"—people actively involved in online communities, or the Internet in general), for his superficial donation and insensitivity to having his own employees contributing their shares. Granted, it wasn't his money to spend and proper protocol should have been followed. Some pundits thought the Chinese society needed to understand the new protocol in spending other people's money.[10]

In China, the phrase "We need to touch the bottoms of wine glasses" is a polite way of inviting the other parties for an informal gathering, to check understanding and to harmonize decision-making, without losing face. Controversial discussions are often taken out of the main boardroom.

Ensuring accountability in Chinese companies

The board's responsibility is to be accountable to those parties who have a legitimate claim to know how the company, and therefore its board, is performing. Accountability is often clarified and reinforced with rules, policies, instructions, job descriptions, and structures; and to ensure everyone understands where accountability lies, organizations would set up apparatus to inform, document, and train their employees so everyone knows where he or she stands. In China, however, accountability is very much shared, collectively.

In SOEs, which are still wholly owned by the state, this means reporting regularly and on time to those state authorities who have a right to be informed. These are Central Government departments that are responsible for that particular industry or industries, such as the CSRC, SASAC, the financial authorities, and the tax authorities at the central and possibly the municipal levels. SOEs incorporated as companies under the China Companies Act also need to meet the reporting requirements of the act. Additionally, the banks and financial institutions have a

---

8. The lawyer's accountability and professionalism is thus implied.
9. By not citing names, that individual is thus protected. He won't lose face should he be confronted and no one would need to know.
10. Eventually, Vanke's board approved an RMB 100M package to help rebuild homes. Diao, Y. (2008, June 6).

role to play. How much funding they would provide to an SOE or how quickly is in fact a form of mutual reporting.

SOEs that have also floated some of their shares on a stock market, in Shanghai, Shenzhen, Hong Kong, or abroad must also meet the reporting requirements of that stock exchange. The listing rules of each exchange specify what information must be provided to the exchange and what information must be made available to the company's shareholders. The China Companies Act and the stock exchange listing rules also lay down requirements for reports to be audited.

In the case of a private company, incorporated under the China Companies Act, the directors must provide members (that is, the shareholders) with regular financial accounts including specified detailed information. The CSRC and the listing committees of a stock exchange on which a company is listed also require specific information to be filed, as do the tax authorities.

Companies may decide to provide more than the legal requirement. Increasingly, listed companies are recognizing a need and an opportunity to engage with their shareholders and the market for potential investors, by providing more detailed information about the company, often through websites devoted to shareholder interests.[11]

Moreover, in recent years, some companies have recognized a wider responsibility to provide relevant information about their activities to a range of connected stakeholders, such as employees, suppliers, and customers. Other companies go further and accept a responsibility to be accountable to society at large. In fact, some INEDs (Independent Executive Directors), are arguing that SOEs have seriously and earnestly introduced meaningful CSR projects, which are overseen by the Party Secretary.

However, a few companies still take the strictly legal view, arguing that, provided that they obey the law and the minimum demands of the stock exchange, they owe no wider duty of disclosure or accountability to stakeholder groups. They argue that if a society expects wider accountability, it is up to the legislature to enact laws accordingly.

Financial reporting

The China Companies Act lays down the criteria for accounting and financial records and for financial disclosure and audit. For details, see http://www.npc.gov. cn/englishnpc/Law/2007-12/12/content_1383787.htm.

---

11. For example, see Tricker, 2016.

Entertainment expenses

At the operational control level, a unique characteristic of many SOEs is their flexibility on expense control, particularly on entertainment expenses. The Chinese have probably used this mechanism to ameliorate the hard reality of expense control and accountability that come with international accounting practices, and balance this with the need to maintain relationships through discussion and dialogue. Since eating is a favorite pastime, meetings are often conducted over meals where pleasantries, war stories, and business discussions are often intermixed.

Foreign executives are often at a loss to understand why their Chinese counterparts seem to have huge expense and entertainment budgets. According to professionals working with Chinese leaders, the system works well given the reality of the situation. That is, the system of compensation and reward is quite different for state workers. Typically, they would be provided with housing and have the authority to host business meals as needed. Senior employees are paid poorly but are provided with a good deal of access, privileges, and credit. One banker whom we interviewed even asserted that senior executives have huge discretionary authority when it comes to expenses. The higher up they are, the more flexibility they have in how to apply those expenses, to the extent that, if unchecked, some may even purchase items for their relatives.[12]

Succession planning in China

Increasingly, succession planning or the development of future leaders has become a dominant role of the board of directors.

In China, succession planning for large SOEs is the role of SASAC.[13] Often these state authorities would move the CEOs without notice and put them into competing firms. This could create havoc and misunderstanding with many international institutional investors, some of whom had invested in specific SOEs because of the leadership under a certain individual. A key reason for such seemingly drastic measures is that this has often been a standard procedure for control and accountability within the Communist apparatus, whereby a CEO and a new team of financial experts would be tasked to identify any abnormality put in place by the old team. Frequent and unexpected transfer is a powerful means to keep corruption at bay.

For private firms, succession is now a challenge. In China, the more notable firms are often founder-based and first generation, and given the youth of many large private enterprises, succession has not been a topic of discussion. But time is

---

12. These days when corruption attack has been rampant across China, state executives have been less willing to wine and dine. Golfing is completely forbidden. The irony these days is that many state executives have preferred not to be hosted by Americans, because American executives have entertainment budgets.
13. And to a lesser extent, to the supervisory board of the SOE.

changing quickly. With the stepping down of many titans such as the founders of Vanke, the market will begin to take notice.

Raising the functions and practices of corporate governance

The Chinese have been quite earnest in their pursuit of raising the quality of corporate governance in SOEs and in private firms alike. Since each type of firm differs considerably in governance understanding, practice, and maturity, solutions in raising the quality of corporate governance have many forms as a result.

As an example of changes in board governance, we highlighted a few areas that seem to have resonated with many chairpersons and shareholder groups. In our experience, Figure 8.1 presents the various mechanisms that companies, SOEs, and private firms have attempted to install as means to raise corporate governance to an institutional-wide framework.

Figure 8.1

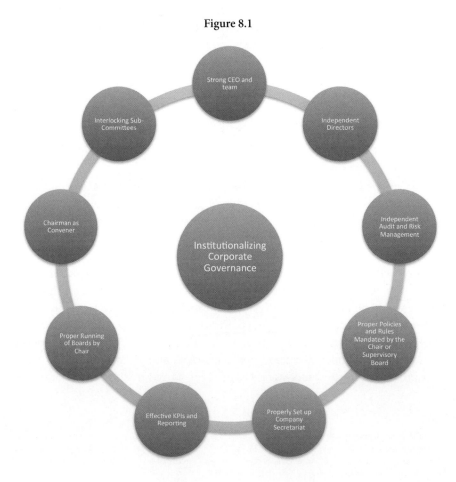

The notable and popular emphasis in raising quality has tended to revolve around these elements in recent years (starting from twelve o'clock):

- **CEO and team:** Putting in place a professional team, with focus on the CEOs and the support team. A strong and effective CEO, with the right CEO office, can extend his or her leadership and impact.
- **Independent non-executive directors:** Searching, placing, and developing quality independent directors. Currently having a third of INEDs on the board is the preferred practice, even if the firm is a private firm.
- **Independent audit and risk management:** Other than the audit committee and its independence, increasingly many firms are being exposed and are accepting new risk management oversights. Although a discussion of a chief risk officer is premature for many, the establishment of a separate risk management committee or a joint audit and risk management committee is becoming popular.
- **Proper policies:** Setting in and auditing against the policies is becoming a normal practice. For private firms, albeit internal audit is a rarity, it is now becoming more popular because boards understand it is a habit and behavior that needs to be nurtured over time. For a few firms, instituting clear job descriptions with clear accountability, which is mostly a Western practice, has been tried.
- **Properly set up company secretariat:** Probably one of the weakest and potentially offering the most value in remedy, is the setting up of a company secretariat team. In China, many firms have followed the practices and high standards of company secretaries from Hong Kong and have come to recognize the importance of proper minutes and board meetings.
- **Installing and fine-tuning KPIs or key performance indicators:** Installing KPIs or metrics that can reflect the level of performance and conformance is now encouraged and expected. Naturally, the next challenge is to tighten the standards behind each KPI and ensure variances are reported and discussed by the CEOs in their reports to the board. Some organizations have even introduced KRIs or key risk indicators and risk appetite statements.
- **Proper running of the board by chairperson:** Given the history and culture, the chairperson is often placed above all other directors. He or she does more than just chair meetings, and often other directors would defer key decisions to the chairperson. The dynamics of the chairperson and the CEO have been described in this chapter. Simply separating the chairperson and the CEO, as done in the UK and not done mostly in the US, is insufficient as a statement without the proper understanding of the cultural context.
- **Chairperson as convener:** Often founders or majority owners would have a title of "chair," and given the face value and power this post would convey, the title of chair carries tremendous clout and prestige for the individual.

Many chairpersons may not show up for board meetings unfortunately, but board meetings need to have their agenda set and meetings run properly. Without this, governance is not properly exercised. An absentee chair, however honorary, does not work. Honorary chair or emeritus chair should have been the proper title for these individuals and where attendance is not mandatory. An alternative is to ask each board meeting to have a convener be present.

- **Interlocking subcommittees:** Subcommittees are venues where the directors and management executives would jointly work towards exercising governance. This is where practice of governance can be extended below that of the CEO. To raise effectiveness and impact further, boards have interlocking subcommittees where there are overlapping members between subcommittees.

Conclusion

In this chapter we have reviewed the many ways boards in China function in practice. Although there are many apparent similarities with the issues faced by the boards of Western companies, the cultural differences in Chinese responses are striking. This is true whether the Chinese company is an SOE, (listed or not), a private company, (listed or not), or one still dominated by its founder. These differences will require different means to which governance can be exercised properly. Additional safeguards to mitigate such risks will need to be introduced.

We studied the performance and conformance aspects of the board's responsibilities. We saw how strategy formulation, policymaking, executive supervision, and accountability had all acquired Chinese characteristics in practice.

Anyone dealing with Chinese companies, whether as a negotiator, investor, or partner, needs to be very sensitive to these cultural nuances and not to assume that because business situations seem similar in East and West, the approach to them will be similar. The differences may be subtle, but they are very real.

References

Cai, F., Park, A., & Zhao, Y. (2008). The Chinese labour market in the reform era. In L. Brandt & T. Rawski (Eds.), *China's great economic transformation* (pp. 167–214). Cambridge: Cambridge University Press.

Chen, J. J. (2015). *A primer on corporate governance: China.* New York: Business Expert Press.

Denis, D. K., & McConnell, J. J. (2003). International corporate governance. *Journal of Financial and Quantitative Analysis, 38*(1), 1–36.

Diao, Y. (2008, June 6). Vanke says sorry with 100M yuan. *China Daily.* Retrieved November 30, 2017 from http://www.chinadaily.com.cn/china/2008-06/06/content_6741301.htm.

Rumelt, R. P. (2017). *Good strategy, bad strategy: The difference and why it matters.* London: Profile Books.

Saich, T. (2015). *Governance and politics of China.* Basingstoke, Hants: Palgrave Macmillan.

So, A. Y., & Chu, Y. (2016). *The global rise of China.* Cambridge: Polity.

Stent, J. (2017). *China's banking transformation: The untold story.* New York: Oxford University Press.

TDC, 2018. The Pearl River Delta area. Retrieved April 30, 2018 from http://china-trade-research.hktdc.com/business-news/article/Facts-and-Figures/PRD-Economic-Profile/ff/en/1/1X000000/1X06BW84.htm.

Tricker, B. (2016). *Shareholder communications for listed issuers: Five imperatives to break the monologue.* [PDF version]. Retrieved from https://www.hkics.org.hk/media/publication/attachment/PUBLICATION_A_2385_HKICS_Shareholder_Communications_for_Listed_Issuers_(Eng).pdf.

Yueh, L. Y. (2011). *Enterprising China: Business, economic, and legal developments since 1979.* Oxford: Oxford University Press.

Case study

Corporate governance at Ping An, China

Ping An: Overview

Ping An Insurance Group of China, Ltd. (**Code: 2318.HK, 601318.SH**) is a leading Chinese financial group with insurance as its core business. It has now expanded into integrating securities, trust, bank, asset management, and other diversified financial services. Up to the end of 2016, the business coverage of Ping An is shown as in Figure 8.2:

Figure 8.2

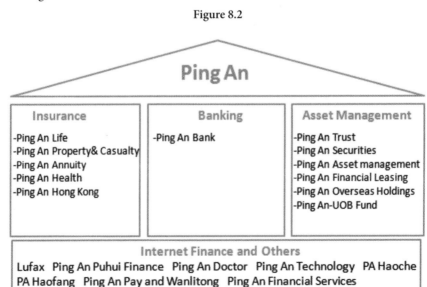

Source: *Ping An 2016 Annual Report.*

Ping An: The history of diversified ownership structure

In 1988, "Ping An Insurance Company" was established in Shenzhen as the first shareholding insurance company in China. At the time when Ping An was founded, it only had two shareholders—Industrial and Commercial Bank of China and China Merchants Group—holding 49% and 51% shares respectively. In 1992, Ping An introduced an employee stock ownership plan, resulting in employees holding 10% of Ping An shares through Employee Stock Fund.

After several years of domestic expansion, Ping An introduced Morgan Stanley and Goldman Sachs as shareholders in 1994, each holding 5.56% shares, and Ping An became the first Chinese financial institution to introduce foreign investors and shareholders. In 2002, HSBC Group spent US$0.6 billion to acquire 10% of the stocks in Ping An, in turn becoming the largest single shareholder of Ping An. A year later, in 2003, when Ping An Insurance (Group) Company of China Ltd. was formally established, Ping An already had business across different financial segments, including Ping An Securities Company, Ping An Trust Investment Company, and Fujian Asia Bank.

In 2004, Ping An Group was listed in HKSE as the largest IPO in that year. HSBC then spent HK$1.2 billion more acquiring Ping An's shares. In 2005, HSBC bought all 9.91% Ping An shares that Morgan Stanley and Goldman Sachs had held, increasing its shareholding ratio to 19.9%. In 2007, when Ping An Group was listed on the SSE, it was the world's largest IPO of an insurance company at that time.

In 2012, after 10 years of marriage with Ping An, HSBC split and sold all the Ping An shares it had held, strangely to Charoen Pokphand Group, a company from Thailand. In this transaction, HSBC received a capital gain of over US$2.3 billion.

Up to the end of 2016, the ownership structure of Ping An Group is shown in Figure 8.3.

Figure 8.3

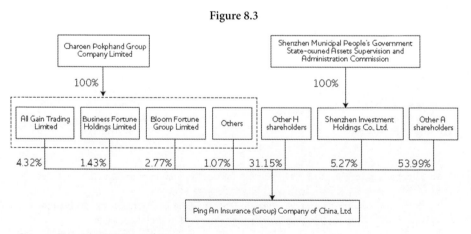

Source: *Ping An 2016 Annual Report.*

Today, the ownership structure of Ping An is relatively scattered, having no controlling shareholders or de facto controller. Only two shareholders own more than 5% of the equity interest of Ping An: CP Group Ltd., which indirectly held 1,752,331,636 H-shares of the company in total, representing 9.59% of the total issued shares of the company; and Shenzhen Investment Holdings Co. Ltd., which held 962,719,102 A-shares of the company in total, representing 5.27% of the total issued shares of the company.

Over the past 30 years, Ping An kept optimizing and diversifying its ownership structure by introducing foreign investors, employee stockholding, and so on. Ping An's final share structure is not common in the Chinese financial services industries.

Ping An: Mission, vision, and values

Today, Ping An has formed a corporate culture that integrates traditional Chinese culture with advanced Western managerial practices.

Ping An's Mission[14]

"For investors, Ping An's goal is to produce stable returns and boost asset values. For customers, the Company aims to provide the best services with integrity. For employees, Ping An's commitment centers on being a responsible employer and provides for the lives and careers of its employees. For the Society, Ping An's commitment is based on the Company's desire to give back to society and contribute to the development of the country."

Ping An's vision

"To become one of the world's top ranking financial services and insurance groups and leaders in the financial services industry. We believe that our ability to innovate has helped us maintain our leading position in the market and capitalize on the growing demand for insurance services in the PRC."

Ping An's values

"Corporate: Ping An constantly seeks to achieve excellence in all aspects of its business, building on a strong foundation of Chinese culture and traditions.

Team: Our business is based on unity, energy, learning, and innovation.

Individual: Our employees focus on integrity and trust and are continually striving for the highest achievement."

---

14. See Ping An's website: http://about.pingan.com/en/qiyewenhua.shtml.

Ping An: Corporate governance structure

The governance structure of Ping An is shown in Figure 8.4.

Figure 8.4

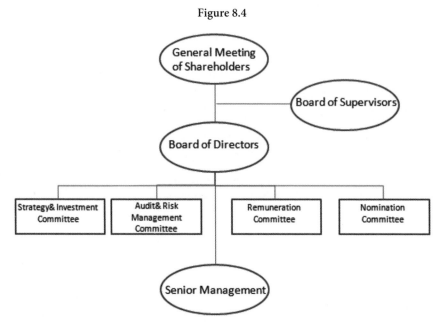

Source: *Ping An 2016 Annual Report.*

General Meeting of Shareholders has the highest authority and reportedly can vote for, elect, or remove supervisors and directors and approve the plans proposed by supervisors and directors. (Has this happened ever??)

Board of Supervisors is responsible to the general meeting of shareholders, and its duty is to examine and verify company reports made by the board of directors, to inspect the financial condition of the company and to supervise the behavior of directors and management. Ping An's board of supervisors consists of five members who have three different roles: as external supervisors, supervisors representing shareholders, and supervisors representing employees.

Board of Directors is responsible to the general meeting of shareholders, and its duty is to make significant decisions for corporate operation, to execute the resolution made by shareholders, to appoint or remove management. Up to 2016, in the board of directors of Ping An, there are seventeen members in total:

Six of them are executive directors:

- MA Mingzhe, chairman and CEO
- SUN Jianyi, vice chairman and executive vice president

- REN Huichuan, executive director and president
- YAO Jason Bo, executive director, executive vice president, CFO and chief actuary
- LEE Yuansiong, executive director, executive vice president and chief insurance business officer
- CAI Fangfang, executive director, chief human resources officer

Five of them are non-executive directors:

- LIN Lijun, non-executive director
- Soopakij CHEARAVANONT, non-executive director
- YANG Xiaoping, non-executive director
- XIONG Peijin, non-executive director
- LIU Chong, non-executive director

Six or nearly a third are independent non-executive directors:

- WOO Ka Biu Jackson, independent non-executive director
- Stephen Thomas MELDRUM, independent non-executive director
- YIP Dicky Peter, independent non-executive director
- WONG Oscar Sai Hung, independent non-executive director
- SUN Dongdong, independent non-executive director
- GE Ming, independent non-executive director

Additionally, there are four standing committees under the board of directors of Ping An. Each committee plays its roles respectively according to the assigned functions.

- Strategy & Investment Committee
- Audit & Risk Management Committee
- Remuneration Committee
- Nomination Committee

Senior Management consists of 12 members; 5 of them, including CEO, CFO, chief actuary, chief insurance business officer, are also on the board of directors as executive directors.

PING AN: Recent year performance

In recent years, Ping An is known increasingly for its rapid revenue and profit growths, which have brought remarkable return for its shareholders.

Figure 8.5

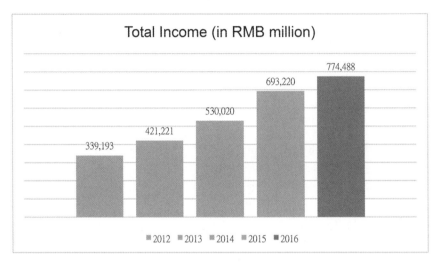

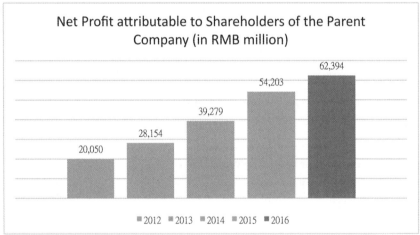

Source: *Ping An 2016 Annual Report.*

The corporate governance practice of Ping An has received recognition internationally. From 2013 to 2015, PING AN has been awarded many honors in the Corporate Governance field, including Best Investor Relations Companies by *Institutional Investor* (US), Corporate Governance Asia Recognition Awards by *Corporate Governance Asia* (HK), 3A Greater China Awards-Platinum Awards by *The Asset* (HK), and Best Corporate Governance Award in China by *Asiamoney*.

Questions for discussion

1. What do you think are the benefits of introducing diversified investors; for example, introducing foreign investors into the ownership structure of Ping An?

2. What factors should be considered when conducting this strategy for Chinese financial services institutions? Defend your argument from both investors' and investees' perspectives.

3. Are there any potential problems that may arise from a diversified ownership structure?

4. When a supervisor has been removed or not approved by the general meeting of shareholders, how does the supervisory board supervise the behavior of its directors? Does the Audit Committee report to the supervisory board? If not, how is this role exercised in your opinion?

5. Are these independent directors really independent?

9

The Governance of Chinese Companies Abroad

Bob Tricker

In this chapter we consider:

- ❖ the development of Chinese business abroad
- ❖ some classic cases of China's investment abroad
- ❖ China's experience of acquisition and merger
- ❖ China's investment in developing countries
- ❖ China's Belt and Road Strategy
- ❖ keeping governance control
- ❖ the governance of corporate groups
- ❖ board-level information for diverse groups
- ❖ transfer pricing, cost allocation, and tax planning
- ❖ balancing the needs of companies and the state

The development of Chinese business abroad

When China began its market-orientated reforms in the 1980s, no Mainland-owned companies were incorporated abroad. SOEs responded to demands from the state. Private companies were not allowed in mainland China.

In Hong Kong things were different. Many of the companies listed on the HKSE were incorporated in overseas tax havens. The major trading houses, such as Jardines, Swire, and Hong Kong Land, had interests abroad, as did other local companies. These subsidiaries offered products or services in the same line as their parent company, or were entrepreneurial attempts to make money, often in property. Two of the tallest skyscrapers in London,[1] for instance, are owned by Hong Kong companies.

Many of these subsidiaries operated in Singapore, Australia, or the UK, where English is spoken and company law was similar to Hong Kong's British-influenced law; many others were in countries in East Asia. None of them had a global brand, nor could they really be classified as multinational.

---

1. Nicknamed the "Cheese grater" and the "Walky Talky."

The reforms in mainland China meant that SOEs could now trade abroad, creating or acquiring subsidiary companies as they thought fit. Independent companies could also incorporate companies overseas and acquire assets abroad.

In the early days the Chinese paid a premium, and deals were quickly done. In their search to secure strategic assets in 2002, China's three largest oil companies brought assets in Sudan, Iraq, and Kazakhstan. CNOOC (China National Offshore Oil Corporation)[2] secured long-term oil supplies from Australia.[3] In 2005, CNOOC also attempted to acquire Unocal, a large US company, but was refused permission by the US government, which felt that China was acquiring a strategic US asset. The US Congress and the US president intervened and blocked the deal based on national security grounds. The Chinese were in shock and in denial. As Kynge pointed out in his commentary on this battle:[4]

> But whatever the lessons of CNOOC's failure, one thing was clear. The influence of the Party—so critical in the creation of China's manufacturing prowess—had been an unambiguous impediment when it came to the cause of acquiring key American corporate asset.

Slowly at first but gathering momentum, investment abroad by Chinese companies grew dramatically. Other notable deals include the Rio Tinto deal by Chinalco in 2008, and the US$15.1 billion purchase of Canada's Nexen by CNOOC in 2013. Hanergy has bought a string of distressed solar energy firms like Miasole and Alta Devices. In 2016, over US$25 billion was invested outside China. Private companies were getting involved but with smaller deals. Mindray Medical, a large medical equipment manufacturer based in Shenzhen, began its expansion by purchasing Datascope in New Jersey for US$209 million.[5] Generally these acquisitions have been in areas where the Chinese companies wanted to build expertise. Sany brought Germany's Putzmeister and as a result became a serious global player in high-tech concrete pumps. However, the government subsequently imposed controls both on the outflow of funds and the unsustainable gearing that some companies had incurred with overseas loans and bonds.

Some classic cases of China's investment abroad

The Chinese have been buying abroad, and with a few exceptions, most have been dominated by large SOEs. Most do so to meet government priorities and objectives. Some SOEs found themselves with surplus cash in their Hong Kong operations, as mentioned in Chapter 6, which enabled them to acquire companies or properties in

2. CNOOC has a listed subsidiary, called CNOOC Limited, and that is China's largest producer of offshore crude oil and natural gas. It is listed in both Hong Kong (SEHK: 0883) and New York (NYSE: CEO).
3. Kynge, 2009, pp. 132–133.
4. Ibid., p. 136.
5. Tse, 2016.

Hong Kong or abroad. Independent private companies also made significant over-seas investments. An indication of the scale and sophistication of some Chinese business acquisitions abroad can be seen in the following examples.

The Lenovo Group

Lenovo is probably best known for the acquisition of IBM's ThinkPad division in 2005. Subsequently, its acquisitions in US included Google's Motorola Mobility and IBM's x86 enterprise server division. The group has headquarters in Beijing and in Morrisville, North Carolina, in the US.

Originally listed on the HKSE, Lenovo was a constituent of Hang Seng Index China-affiliated Corporations Index known as the "Red Chips" index.

Under the leadership of Mary Ma, who was CFO from 1990 to 2007 and is now head of investor relations, Lenovo integrated Western-style accountability into its corporate culture. Lenovo's emphasis on transparency earned it the reputation for the best corporate governance among Chinese mainland firms. The company adopted quarterly reporting of financial performance, reflecting Western practice, ahead of the requirement by the HKSE.

Fosun International Limited

Fosun International was founded in 1992 by Guo Guangchang with headquarters in Shanghai. The company was incorporated in Hong Kong in 2004. It began by doing market research, then extended into real estate, health care, and insurance.

By 2011, Fosun was benefitting from industrial profits, investment profits, and asset management profits rising rapidly, moving it towards its stated goal of being "a premium investment group with a focus on China's growth momentum."

From that point, Fosun spent billions buying foreign firms in tourism, health care, fashion, and banking in the US and Europe: France's Club Med vacation business, Britain's Thomas Cook tour and travel group, Canada's Cirque du Soleil, St. John (an American clothing label), and the Greek jeweler Folli Follie. Fosun brought Portugal's largest insurance group, Caixa Seguros, for reportedly US$1.25 billion. The purchase of the Australian oil company, Roc Oil, was its first venture in the oil business. Fosun also acquired the US Meadowbrook group, a major insurer, for around $433 million, making it the first complete take-over of a US insurer by a Chinese company.

On December 11, 2015, the chairman of Fosun, billionaire Guo Guangchang, disappeared. There was speculation that he was being questioned by government officials stemming from Party General Secretary Xi Jinping's anti-corruption efforts. Trading in Fosun International shares was suspended. Liang Xinjun, CEO of Fosun, said that Chairman Guo was "assisting the judicial authorities with an investigation, but it is not because the company has problems."

On December 14, 2015, Guo reemerged in public to address the Fosun internal annual conference. He made no mention of the investigation. This sparked a sustained round of applause, which surprised representatives of the conglomerate's companies in its European portfolio. When trading in the shares resumed, the price fell by around 10%. It has been suggested that Guo has followed Warren Buffet's model for business growth using insurance assets to generate investment capital.

Wanda

The Wanda Group is a Chinese multinational conglomerate. It ranks as the world's largest private developer and owner of properties, and the world's biggest cinema chain operator, owning Wanda Cinemas, the Hoyts Group, and a majority share of AMC theaters. Its purchase of Wanda for US$2.6 billion made Wanda the largest owner of movie theatres in the world.

Wanda was founded in Dalian in 1988 as a residential real estate company, by Wang Jianlin. It was incorporated in 1992, one of the first shareholding companies in the PRC after the economic reform.

For more detailed information about the governance of Wanda, see the case at the end of Chapter 7.

Huawei

Huawei was founded in 1987 by Ren Zhengfei, a former electronics engineer in the PLA. The group's headquarters is in Shenzhen, in the Pearl River economic zone adjacent to Hong Kong. During the 1980s and 1990s, the Chinese government saw the need to modernize telecommunications. A core component of the network was telephone exchange equipment, which needed modernizing. Joint ventures (JVs) were used by some companies to secure the technology from foreign companies, but they were often reluctant. Ren took a different approach, focusing on local research and development to produce the equipment, by reverse-engineering foreign products.

Huawei contracted to build a telecommunication system for the PLA, a relatively small project in its overall business but large in key relationships. In 1994, Ren met Jiang Zemin, telling him that "switching equipment technology was related to national security, and that a nation that did not have its own switching equipment was like one that lacked its own military." Jiang reportedly agreed. In 1996, the government in Beijing adopted a policy of supporting domestic telecommunications manufacturers and restricting access to foreign investors.

The Huawei Group thrived and became a leading force in China's creation of smart cities and is now the largest manufacturer of telecommunications equipment in the world, having overtaken the US-based Ericsson in 2012.

But Huawei was also expanding outside mainland China. In 1997, it signed a contract with Hong Kong's Hutchinson Whampoa to provide a fixed-line network. In 1999, it opened an R&D center in Bangalore, India, and in 2001 opened four R&D centers in the US. By 2005, Huawei's international contracts exceeded domestic sales.

Huawei classifies itself as a "collective" and does not refer to itself as a private company. This distinction may have been related to the company's state support. Officially, Huawei is an employee-owned company, a fact that the company emphasizes to distance itself from allegations of government control. However, what "employee-owned" means in practice is unclear. The Chinese media company Caixin claimed that "even long-time employees admit the employee shareholding system is nearly impossible to understand."

The Wanxiang Group Corporation

The group is China's largest manufacturer of automotive components, headquartered in Hangzhou, Zhejiang Province. Founded in 1969 as an independent private company, it now has more than 10,000 employees. The founder was Lu Guanqiu (chairman), Weiding Lu (CEO), and Pin Ni (president).

In 2012, Wanxiang won an auction against a US-based lithium-ion battery maker, for US$256.6 million. Then the United States' Foreign Investment Committee (CFIUS) approved Wanxiang Group's Chicago-based subsidiary, Wanxiang America, to purchase the assets of Fisker Automotive, a manufacturer of hybrid (electric and gasoline) sports cars for US$150 million.

Lu Guanqui has declared that his goal is to develop the world's most successful electric car, challenging US Tesla Motors' global electric-vehicle market position. Using the imagery of a famous Chinese proverb, he said that in building electric cars: "The road is still very long. We want to concentrate for now on manufacturing in the US. If I don't succeed, my son will continue with it. If he doesn't make it, my grandson will." Lu said: "I'll put every cent that Wanxiang earns into making electric vehicles."

Wanxiang has both car and battery technology, and the financial resources. It supplies both General Motors and Ford and generates profits of over US$1 billion. The company also has approval to make electric trucks and buses in China, ensuring that the country's transportation future is in Chinese hands. Overseas car manufacturers could only build cars in China in a JV with a Chinese company. Analysts assume that Lu will start with luxury models. If so, he would have to compete with Tesla, BMW, and possibly Denza, in a JV between Daimler and BYD Auto. But Lu could surprise analysts and enter the market at the cheaper end, competing against BYD, which has underperformed expectations.

Alibaba Group Holding Limited

Alibaba is a Chinese e-commerce company, providing consumer-to-consumer, business-to-consumer, and business-to-business sales services through web portals. The Alibaba Group also provides electronic payment services, a shopping search engine, and data-centric cloud computing services. One of its main sites—Taobao—offers goods from more than 7 million suppliers.

The group began in 1999, when Jack Ma, a former English teacher, created a website, Alibaba.com, a portal to connect Chinese manufacturers with potential overseas buyers. Suppliers from other countries are supported (with more stringent checks than those for Chinese companies), but the company operates primarily in China.

In September 2007, Alibaba.com listed on the HKSE. But five years later, in September 2013, the HKSE refused to allow the company to introduce dual-class shares, which would have enabled the founder shareholders to maintain control even though they held a minority of the equity capital. Hong Kong listing rules prohibit multi-class shares giving preferential voting rights to some classes. Alibaba then listed its shares in New York, where there were no such limitations. Trading in the shares (BABA) began in September 2014.

Alibaba is now the world's largest retailer, surpassing US Walmart in 2016, with operations in over 200 countries. Its online sales and profits have surpassed all US retailers (including Walmart, Amazon, and eBay) combined since 2015. It is also one of the largest Internet companies. In 2017, Alibaba became the first Asian company to be valued by the US stock market at more than US$400 billion.

In 2015, Jack Ma bought the Hong Kong–based media group that owned the century-old, English-speaking newspaper, the *South China Morning Post*. Although Alibaba promised editorial independence, Vice chairman Joseph Tsai said that Alibaba believes that "the world needs a plurality of views when it comes to China coverage," which raised eyebrows, given China' one-party state.

Other issues between Alibaba and the Chinese government included claims of bribery and the toleration of counterfeit goods on its websites. A probe by the US SEC underlined concerns over what one analyst called Alibaba's "unusual" accounting practices. In 2017, Alibaba's revenue from outside China was just over 10%: Ma has set a goal of half the company's revenue.[6]

Other aspects of the governance of the Alibaba Group are in the Alibaba case study at the end of Chapter 1.

---

6. Chen, 2017.

Tencent Holdings Ltd.

Tencent Holdings was created by Ma Huateng, known in English as Pony Ma (*ma* is Chinese for horse). He is reputedly the richest man in China. The other attribute recognized by the public is that he is a "computer geek." Tencent is a leading provider of Internet value-added services in China and is headquartered in Shenzhen. The company's shares are listed on the HKSE. It is the second-most valuable Internet company in Asia after Alibaba. Tencent is also the world's largest gaming company. In 2015, it launched WeBank (China), the country's first online-only bank.

As a Chinese Internet company, Tencent has some advantages: Facebook is banned in China and Google has retreated from it. But Tencent recognized the importance of mobile phones early and built a platform used by 335 million people, which offers, in a single app. services that are available on Facebook, Twitter, WhatsApp, and Zynga. Moreover, the company keeps adding new functions such a taxi finder that was used 20 million times in its first few weeks.

Tencent has expanded beyond China with notable success throughout Southeast Asia and India. It has also funded some small American start-ups and acquired or taken stakes in other gaming companies around the world.

For more information on the corporate governance of Tencent Holdings go to the case at the end of this chapter.

Anbang Insurance Group

Wu Xiaohui was chairman and general manager of Anbang, an independent company, founded in 2004 with an unclear ownership structure. Its headquarters is in Beijing. The Anbang group has subsidiary companies dealing with insurance, banking, and other financial services.

The company was a little-known Chinese insurer until it launched a massive asset shopping spree, including the purchase in 2014 of the Waldorf Astoria Hotel in New York for US$1.95 billion. It also acquired stakes in several Chinese banks, including the China Minsheng Bank and the China Merchants Bank.

On the downside, Anbang backed out of a high profile US$14 billion deal with Starwood Hotels and Resorts Worldwide. It also ended talks to invest billions to renovate an office tower at 666 Fifth Avenue, New York—a building owned by the family of Jared Kushner, US President Trump's son-in-law. US regulatory approval was withheld in an attempt by Anbang to acquire US-based Fidelity & Guaranty Life Insurance.

Wu became a household name in China through his marriage to former leader Deng Xiaoping's granddaughter [reportedly they divorced in July 2017]. The marriage gave Wu powerful connections with government officials and the second generation of China's former leaders. It might also account for his legendary ability to raise huge sums of money quickly.

In August 2017, it was reported that Wu Xiahui had stepped down as chairman and was taken away by authorities. An Anbang spokesperson said that Wu could not perform his role "for personal reasons." Another source confirmed that there had "been an investigation into alleged irregularities at the company and Wu had not returned to his office or his home. "His alleged detention came after an investigation involving loans worth billions of yuan that were suspected to have come from illegal means.

Earlier in the month, Xiang Junbo, chairman of the China Insurance Regulatory Commission, was investigated and dismissed for violating anti-corruption regulations.

The cases cited above concern relatively large and high-profile companies with overseas investments. At the same time there were thousands of other smaller independent Chinese companies attempting to invest in companies abroad.

Ninebot acquires US Segway

The US company making the Segway, the famous self-balancing personal electric scooter, was acquired by Beijing-based Ninebot, which made a similar device based on the Segway model. The acquisition in 2015 was for an undisclosed amount, but around US$80 million was rumored. The purchase allowed Ninebot to acquire the technology outright. At the time, Segway was struggling in the US market. Moreover, the US International Trade Commission had agreed to investigate Segway's claim that Chinese companies, Ninebot included, were infringing on US patents.

Evergrande shopping spree overseas

Evergrande, formerly known as the Hengda Group, is China's second-largest property developers by sales. Its founder, Xu Jiayin, is a Standing Committee member of the 12th CPPCC National Committee and has been called China's Donald Trump while at the same time being honored as China's "National Model Worker." His company has been valued at US$47 billion but reportedly is carrying a debt of US$100 billion, reflecting the boom in the Chinese property market. He founded the company in 1996 and listed it in Hong Kong in 2009, raising HK$6 billion (US$769 million) in the process. In 2016, Evergrande bought properties from Hong Kong's New World Group, as well as Premier League and American Major League soccer clubs, reportedly spending over US$15 billion.

China's experience of acquisition and merger

Investment in businesses in the economically advanced world, by both Chinese state and independent companies, has often been through the acquisition of or merger with existing businesses. Unfortunately, this has led to some disappointment. Other projects by Chinese companies to invest abroad have been through partnerships or the creation of joint-venture companies with overseas companies. Bain & Company's analysis of China's outbound merger and acquisition (M&A) activity had been rising by over 20% annually since 2009. Independent companies represented a growing share of this activity although the largest deals still involved SOEs.

In the early days, the primary objective of overseas investment was to access raw materials. Now the reason is more likely to be the acquisition of technical know-how, the development and training of staff, and the generation of profit to provide a cash flow to support further overseas activities.

The failure of some Chinese M&A activities, commentators suggest, was due to overenthusiasm and lack of experience in M&A projects. A primary reason was a failure to understand the vital importance of a due diligence survey of the other company's business model and financial position, lack of understanding of local markets, and overreliance on information from banks. As a result, the Chinese partner might not have appreciated undisclosed risks, such as the effect of currency fluctuations, undisclosed financial commitments, or swings in commodity prices.

Other problems could arise with the integration of management, the establishment of management controls and reporting systems, and inadequate governance oversight. An acquiring Chinese company sometimes left the incumbent company's management team and control systems intact. That might have worked when the overseas company was mining a natural resource but failed when the complexity of the business and the need for management interaction led to misunderstandings rooted in differences in language, culture, and basic expectations.

It has become apparent that successful M&A activity needs to be part of a company's overall global strategy. One-off deals, done because they seem to offer a good profit, are seldom successful, except possibly in property although in the past some Hong Kong entrepreneurs did make money that way. More recently, some companies have made frequent and large-scale acquisitions. Sometimes called "mountain climbers," they include: China Gas, Yanzhou Coal Mining Co., and Yunan Municipal Construction Investment.

In 2013, Shuanghui International Holdings (now WH Group) acquired US-based Smithfield Foods, the world's largest pork producer. The deal was heralded as a strategic triumph, enabling the companies to benefit from concrete synergies: an integrated supply chain, premium branding opportunities, and experience sharing. But the acquirer had done insufficient due diligence, failing to test assumptions about the market in China and the volatility in hog prices between the US and China.

By contrast, China's Geely Company's US$1.5 billion acquisition of Volvo Cars in 2010 enabled Geely to outperform competitors and helped Volvo to reverse declining sales. The chairperson of Geely repeatedly emphasized that Volvo would be allowed "to run its own show." Geely improved its technological capabilities and brand image, and gained management expertise from Volvo. Volvo enhanced its relationship with the Chinese government, rebooting growth in China's market.

Most effective integrations employ a decision management office: integration leaders focus the steering group and task forces on critical decisions that deliver most value. They lay out a decision roadmap and manage the organization to a "decision drumbeat" to ensure each decision is made by the right people at the right time with the best available information. The leader of the integration task force should pay back financial and nonfinancial results for which he or she is accountable as well as the time frame.

Wang Jianlin, chairman of China's Dalian Wanda Group, told business students at Said Business School in Oxford that: "Any time is good for M&A . . . But the US, although a huge market, does have regulatory hurdles, as well as a government that at times seems highly protectionist . . . for example, a move by GSP Ventures to acquire 80% of the Dutch company, Philips, fell through after US Committee for Foreign Investment blocked the move on security grounds: Philips has several US government contracts. The US claims to be a free country, but for investing there are many complicated approval processes The United Kingdom and the US are equally important countries (for M&A projects) but Britain is the freest market in the world."

Danae Kyriakopoulou, senior economist at the Centre for Economics and Business Research in London, commented that: "Chinese companies need to acquire the know-how of the new growth sectors in order to support the economy's rebalancing away from being the world's hub for basic manufacturing and heavy industry and toward high-end economic activities. M&A with companies of those more-developed economies in those sectors is a way to do that. The pitfalls are chiefly to do with understanding of different regulatory systems and the clash of corporate cultures."

China's investment in developing countries

China has made significant investments in some developing regions of the world. Though the business rationale was typically to gain an economic advantage or secure access to natural resources, the Chinese government may also have been promoting its political, and in some cases, military strategies.

Africa

China has invested heavily in Africa. For example, in 2004, a program of road investments was agreed with Angola in exchange for a share of Angola's minerals and oil reserves. The investment funded transport links to ship raw materials vital to China's manufacturing sector from mine to harbor. Such investments also enhanced

China's soft power in Africa, promoting the Chinese model of central, state-driven political policies to counter Western claims that prosperity and freedom need liberal democratic capitalism.

Nevertheless, most of China's investment in Africa has been economic. In past decades, Chinese loans and contractors have reshaped much of Africa's infrastructure, building new ports, roads, and railroads, such as a railroad line linking Mombasa's port with Nairobi in Kenya. Investments have also been made in mines, manufacturing plants, and shopping centers. The extent of China's business interests around Africa is clearly visible. For example, all signage in a new hotel in Rwanda is in Chinese, from elevators to shampoo dispensers.

Some commentators claim that China is becoming Africa's most important economic partner. Others are more skeptical, pointing out that China's investment and funding in Africa are overestimated because they are based on pledges, not actual cash flows.[7]

But in addition to China's state-led investment in Africa, many smaller private Chinese firms have initiated projects in Africa. McKinsey, the consultants, have estimated that there are as many as 10,000 Chinese companies operating in Africa, 90% of them privately owned.

Although these smaller companies can make a quick profit, some doubt that investments Chinese state-owned firms made in infrastructure projects will ever produce the expected economic gain or show a return, particularly in poorly governed places like Angola or the Democratic Republic of Congo.

Latin America

China has been a major lender to Venezuela and Argentina, two of the most troubled countries of the region. Though seen by the leasers of Latin American countries as saviors of their economies (and their own personal position), in reality the terms of such loans have been harsh, while Chinese companies benefitted from the natural resources of these countries.

Asia

China has invested heavily in Pakistan and Bangladesh, outstripping loans these countries receive from the IMF and other Western countries. Investment in the Middle East has been directed mainly towards energy projects although in the UAE the real estate sector has also been a target. Indonesia has received significant investment in mineral resources, transportation, and the energy sector.

---

7. China goes to Africa (2017, July 5).

China's Belt and Road Strategy

The Belt and Road Initiative refers to the Silk Road Economic Belt and 21st Century Maritime Silk Road and has become a significant development strategy launched by the Chinese government in 2015, with the intention of promoting economic cooperation among countries along the proposed Belt and Road routes.[8] China will continue to invest in countries west of China, through the Belt and Road Strategy, and the government expects both SOEs and private sectors to be engaged and committed in this grand vision. Reportedly over 60 countries are to the west of China, and tens of thousands of enterprises will be involved.

Chinese companies are expected to invest heavily, beginning with outbound infrastructural projects like rails and power plants. These massive infrastructural projects typically will involve multiple stakeholders, including possibly the setup of joint-venture partnerships, and the coming together of investors and professionals from around the world. New partnerships are expected to be set up: ESPs (engineering service projects), JVs, and Project Finance; and massive financing will be needed.

But these new projects will involve an array of new risks. The diversity and immaturity of the national governance systems along the routes, the language, culture, ethical standards, corporate governance systems, accounting standards, and judiciary system of these jurisdictions vary. Governance structure to manage such risks will be needed and tested. Appendix II, "The Case of the MMMP Saudi Rail Project: Building Railroads along the Belt and Road," describes the management of the MMMP Saudi rail project and discusses some of the governance implications involved.

Keeping governance control

The classical concept of the joint-stock company, dating to the nineteenth century, is that ownership is the basis of power over a company, and each share carries one vote in shareholders' meetings to exercise that power. Unsurprisingly, founders of successful companies, whether they are tycoons of Silicon Valley or the creators of independent companies in modern China, want to maintain governance control over the enterprises they have created for as long as possible. Dual-class and multiple-class shares were designed to meet that need.

---

8. See http://china-trade-research.hktdc.com/business-news/article/The-Belt-and-Road-Initiative/The-Belt-and-Road-Initiative/obor/en/1/1X000000/1X0A36B7.htm.

Duel-class and multiple-class shares

When a company is successful, it often grows at such a rate that plowing back accumulated profit is insufficient to meet all the further opportunities for investment. Taking on loans or issuing bonds, which do not carry voting rights, the process of leveraging or gearing-up the shareholders' equity, the company, provides a temporary solution. But leveraging exposes the company to risk if profits fall, because loans and bonds demand regular interest payments. Floating more equity shares to the public is then an obvious solution. But that would dilute the founder's voting rights and risk the loss of governance control. Dual-vote or multiple-vote shares offer a solution.

Instead of adopting the one-share one-vote principle, more than one class of share is created, under the company's articles of association, giving greater voting rights to the privileged class of shares than to the ordinary shares available to the public. For example, in a dual-class scheme, the ordinary A-class shares traded on the market carry one vote each, while the B-class shares, available to the founder and other chosen people have 100 or more votes each.

However, not all stock markets allow multiple-class shares under their listing rules. The HKSE, for example, has resisted calls for the listing of companies with multiple-voting shares, supported by corporate governance commentators and some institutional investors who prefer the classical one-share one-vote principle. The hugely successful Chinese company Alibaba (for more detailed information see the Alibaba Group case at the end of Chapter 1) initially planned to list in Hong Kong but switched to New York in the largest floatation to date. Starting in 2018, the HKSE switched positions and officially allowed weighted voting shares to be used but under very restrictive measures.

Another situation in which keeping governance control can occur is in joint-venture projects.

The governance of JVs

When a Chinese company wants to operate abroad, it faces a number of governance options. It can, subject to local regulations, trade through an agent, open a branch, or enter into a local partnership. But none of these options provides the protection of limited liability and company law enjoyed by a company, nor in some jurisdictions benefits from corporate tax benefits.

To operate abroad through a company, further options are available: acquire an existing company, enter into an arrangement to merge with another company, or incorporate a new company overseas. Mergers and acquisitions by Chinese companies abroad have not been particularly successful, sometimes because of lack of experience or different cultural expectations. A popular alternative is a JV, in which the Chinese company makes a JV agreement with a local partner to incorporate a JV company. The JV agreement will stipulate the objectives of the project, the contributions required from each partner, the respective shareholdings, and the appointment of the directors. The board will normally include representatives from each partner and may also include independent non-executive directors. The chief executive of the JV company is often seconded from a JV partner. Whether that CEO should be a board member is open to question because of a potential conflict of interest. The Teletronic Riches case, at the end of this chapter, addresses the issue.

Today, however, when foreign companies want to establish themselves in China, JVs are not the preferred route. Wholly foreign-owned enterprises (WFOE) are now the preferred structure in China.

More information on some of the practical issues involved in merger and acquisition activity, based on personal experience, can be found in Appendix I: Acquiring and Partnering with Local Entities, by Richard Leung and Gregg Li. The Teletronic Riches case, at the end of this chapter, studies aspects of the governance of a JV.

The governance of corporate groups

The governance of subsidiary companies abroad raises some interesting issues for parent companies everywhere; Chinese holding companies are no exception. Essentially, a holding company must determine the governance policies and practices for the companies within its group. Broadly, there are two different philosophies for governing and managing a group of companies: subsidiary company self-governance or group-wide governance from the parent company.

Subsidiary company self-governance allows each company in the group to govern itself and to manage its own affairs, subject to overall group-wide policies on matters such as staffing, financial controls, and reporting, and on investment appraisal and resource allocation procedures. Central control is maintained by posting senior executives from the head office or elsewhere in the group to director-level and other top management positions in subsidiary companies. Profitability, return on investment, and cash flow are likely to be key measures of performance for each subsidiary. Under this system the decision-making autonomy of the board of each subsidiary company is emphasized, subject to group-wide strategies and policies. This structure was often adopted in both mainland Chinese and Hong Kong groups, particularly where communication with the subsidiary might be difficult, as in parts of Africa, or where subsidiary companies run diverse businesses, as in a conglomerate.

In subsidiary company self-governance, decision-making power is delegated to the group's subsidiary company boards, requiring each subsidiary in the group to act as an autonomous company, subject to strategic and policy demands and resource allocations determined by its parent company. In other words, the directors of each subsidiary company are expected to run their company as an autonomous entity, within group-wide strategies and policies, to meet the performance criteria required by the group head office.

In subsidiary company self-governance, the structure and membership of the subsidiary company boards becomes important. The holding company, as shareholder in the subsidiary, has the option of drawing the directors of subsidiary companies from:

- the staff of the group holding company, who might or might not be on the main board;
- the management of the subsidiary company;
- the management in other group companies; or
- independent outside directors. (In some jurisdictions outside China a proportion of the board might be required to include independent non-executive directors).

The benefits of drawing subsidiary company directors from other companies in the group include the opportunity for cross-group coordination, the sharing of expertise, training, and development of future main board directors; management development; and the building of group norms and culture. In the overseas subsidiaries of Chinese SOEs, another reason imposed by SASAC is to ensure frequent rotation of staff in key roles to provide motivation and reduced the possibility of corruption.

Group-wide governance treats all group companies as divisions or departments of the holding company, with control exercised through the group's management control system. In other words, management is exercised through the group organization structure and management control systems, not governed through the boards of each subsidiary.

In group-wide governance, the group holding company imposes management control systems and organization structures on the entire group operations, which transcend the operations of the individual subsidiary companies.

The control system divides the group into appropriate operating units, which may or may not map onto the subsidiary company structure. Group resources are allocated to these performance units through the management control system, performance criteria are laid down for management of each unit, and outputs are monitored. The power to make decisions throughout the group is delegated along the lines of the management control system, not the legal structure of the subsidiaries.

In group-wide governance, the members of subsidiary company boards are typically drawn from the management of group head office and the subsidiary company, because power lies in the management organization structure throughout the group, not in the boardrooms of the subsidiary companies.

Managers have their responsibilities delegated down through the levels of management in the organization structure and are accountable back up that structure. Managers owe their primary allegiance to their line manager, not to the directors of the subsidiary company of which their business unit may be part.

You might ask why, as holding companies control through the group management system, they have subsidiary companies at all. The reasons could be legal (the ability to contract under the laws of the country in which the subsidiary is incorporated and operates), taxation (the opportunity to reduce taxation in high-tax regimes), strategic positioning (to protect a brand name or other strategic benefit), or risk reduction (to obtain the benefit of limited liability). Because such subsidiaries are legal entities, they must, of course, fulfill their legal reporting and taxation requirements in the country in which they operate. But power lies in the management organization structure throughout the group, not in the boardrooms of the subsidiary companies.

Board-level information for diverse groups

Being sufficiently well informed about the state of the company is a challenge to every non-executive director. Typically, this can be met by sophisticated board-level information systems, supported by meetings and occasional visits to the company. But for a director of an overseas company, who is based in China, the challenge can be severe. There may be visa problems, difficulties of communication with local staff, and cross-cultural issues; overseas travel is also expensive and time-consuming.

Consequently, the provision of board-level information to directors that is accurate, comprehensive, and timely is vital. Like most corporate groups operating around the world, major Chinese companies with overseas subsidiaries have developed such systems, communicating electronically, by video link, and in written form, supported by face-to-face briefings to keep all directors, particularly the independent outside directors, informed. Electronic communication is usually straightforward between China and countries in the developed world, provided Chinese controls on cross-border data flows and data storage are met. But in the underdeveloped world, in some countries in Africa for example, electronic communication may be elementary or nonexistent.

Board-level reports are likely to include information of operations, markets, and personnel, together with reports on ongoing projects and research developments, where relevant. Financial information reflects the ongoing performance and current state of the company and is likely to include profit/loss and cash flow reports, sales revenues, and performance against expense budgets.

Reports may also be produced to ensure that group-wide corporate policies are being followed. For example, a vital role of a holding company board is to establish the group's risk profile and set risk assessment polices for companies in the group. The main board directors might limit the authority of subsidiary company boards to make decisions on capital expenditure, acquisitions, or senior appointments, reserving such decisions to themselves. Reports might also be required to show performance against other corporate policies on environment, sustainability, and governance (ESG) criteria.

For the overseas subsidiaries of SOEs, further data might be needed to meet SASAC or CSRC demands on the corporate group. The central government in Beijing, for example, was concerned at the extent and the economic effect of cross-border capital flows and monitored companies' accounts accordingly.[9]

Cyber security is crucial in the electronic communication of board-level information. The value of corporate information to potential competitors, stock market manipulators, and hostile governments can be inestimable. Hackers can also hold companies to ransom by blocking access to their own data. Cross-border data flows can be particularly vulnerable. Risk policies also need to recognize the vulnerability of the group to system breakdowns if its business model relies on international data networks.

Transfer pricing, cost allocation, and tax planning

In every corporate group, in which member companies are held profit responsible, a mechanism is needed to determine the price at which goods and services are transferred between them. In cross-border trade, most countries seek to impose an arms-length market price for goods and services transferred, to calculate import and export levies, and establish fair profit calculations for tax purposes.

Companies can shift profits to low tax regimes by manipulating transfer prices for goods and services, or allocating heavy group charges, for example, for head office costs, interest on capital, or the rights to use brands, patents, or intellectual property.

Manipulating transfer prices and allocating costs between group companies to reduce duty and tax has long been a source of international concern and negotiation. China came relatively late to this party, but Chinese companies have been accused by the European Union (EU) of under-declaring the value of imports into EU member states. An entire tax-planning industry of accounting firms, consultants, and lawyers has developed to advise firms on tax avoidance (that is, managing corporate affairs within the law of the states involved) and avoiding tax evasion (that is, breaking those laws).

Balancing the needs of companies and the state

In the Western world, governments accept responsibility for the economy, setting and regulating the boundaries within which companies can operate, but then leave firms free to pursue their own business strategies. Few countries attempt to impose a nationwide business strategy: China is one of them. By exerting control over the SOEs, the government can attempt to regulate finance, taxation, innovation, industry importance, and senior staff location and movement. The independent

---

9. See https://www.imf.org/external/np/seminars/eng/2013/sta/forum/pdf/SessionVI/Wang_Xiaoyi.pdf.

companies in China have, so far, enjoyed wider degrees of freedom. But, unlike countries in the Western world, that see corporate governance as a means of regulating companies, China sees corporate governance as a way to pursue economic growth and social change, as we will discuss in Chapter 10.

References

Chen, J. (2005). *Corporate governance in China (Routledge Studies on the Chinese Economy)*. New York: Routledge Curzon.

Chen, Y. L. (2017, August 22). Alibaba and Tencent looking riskier and placing bigger bets. *Bloomberg*. Retrieved April 30, 2018 from https://www.bloombergquint.com/markets/2017/08/13/alibaba-and-tencent-looking-riskier-and-placing-bigger-bets.

China goes to Africa (2017, July 5). *Economist*. Retrieved November 30, 2017 from https://www.economist.com/news/middle-east-and-africa/21725288-big-ways-and-small-china-making-its-presence-felt-across.

Clarke, T. (2007). *International corporate governance: A comparative approach*. New York and Abingdon, UK: Routledge.

Gul, F., & Tsui, J. (Eds.). (2005). *The governance of East Asian corporations: Post Asian financial crisis*. London: Palgrave Macmillan.

Kynge, J. (2009). *China shakes the world: The rise of a hungry nation*. London: Phoenix.

Morris, I. (2011). *Why the West rules—for now: The patterns of history, and what they reveal about the future*. London: Profile.

Norton, J. J., Rickford, J., & Kleineman, J. (2006). *Corporate governance post-Enron: Comparative and international perspectives*. London: British Institute of International and Comparative Law.

Tse, E. (2016). *China's disruptors: How Alibaba, Xiaomi, Tencent and other companies are changing the rules of business*. London: Portfolio Penguin.

Case study I

Tencent Holdings Ltd.

Tencent Holdings is a highly successful provider of Internet value-added services in China, as described earlier in this chapter. These services include access to films, books, entertainment, smartphone gaming, advertising, financial services, Internet cloud services, and many other features. Founded in 1998, Tencent has maintained steady growth. In 2004, Tencent Holdings was listed on the Main Board of the HKSE Board (SEHK .700).

Discussing recent results, Chairman and CEO of Tencent, Ma Huateng, said:

[W]e delivered strong revenue growth from multiple businesses, which enabled us to reinvest in innovations and new technologies in an increasingly competitive industry. While our games business continued to grow, we have stepped up our effort to ensure users play games in a healthy manner. Successful licensed drama serials and self-commissioned variety shows boosted user engagement and advertising revenue for our video platform.

Our payment business continued to make everyday life easier for Internet users, with increased adoption of Weixin Payment for offline transactions. We have also been increasing our investment in cloud services and AI (Artificial Intelligence) technologies, which will enable us to serve our users and business partners even better into the future. Underlying the forward-looking statements is a large number of risks and uncertainties. Further information regarding these risks and uncertainties is included in our other public disclosure documents on our corporate website.

Tencent has published a statement of its vision and values, as well as other corporate governance information.

The company's vision and values

Tencent states that its mission is "to become the most respected Internet enterprise."[10] Further, we have a "steadfast commitment to corporate citizenship, our public charity programs, and the promotion of respectful Internet communities on our user platforms."[11]

Corporate governance

Corporate governance can be defined as a set of processes, customs, policies, laws, and institutions affecting the way a company is directed, administered or controlled. Corporate governance also includes the relationships among the many stakeholders involved and the goals for which the corporation is governed. The principal stakeholders are the shareholders, the board of directors, executives, employees, customers, creditors, suppliers, and the community at large.[12]

The "governance documents" section of the company's investor relations website provides access to the Corporate Governance Statement and Corporate Governance Charter.

The board of directors

Tencent has a unitary board, consistent with the Hong Kong Corporate Governance Code and the listing rules of the HKSE. Currently, the members of the board are:

---

10. See https://www.tencent.com/en-us/investor.html.
11. See https://www.tencent.com/en-us/index.html.
12. See http://investors.telenet.be/phoenix.zhtml?c=241896&p=irol-irhome.

Ma Huateng (45)
Chairman of the board and CEO

Mr. Ma has overall responsibilities for the strategic planning and positioning and management of the group. Mr. Ma is one of the co-founders and has been employed by the group since 1999. Prior to his current employment, Mr. Ma was in charge of research and development for Internet paging system development at China Motion Telecom Development Limited, a supplier of telecommunications services and products in China. Mr. Ma is a deputy to the 12th National People's Congress. He has a Bachelor of Science degree specializing in computer and its application, obtained in 1993 from Shenzhen University, and more than 23 years of experience in the telecommunications and Internet industries. He is a director of Advance Data Services Limited, which has an interest in the shares of the company, connected to Tencent, which would have to be disclosed under the provisions of the Hong Kong Securities and Futures Ordinance. Mr. Ma also serves as a director of some subsidiaries of the company.

Lau Chi Ping Martin (44)
Executive director and president of the company

Mr. Lau joined the company in 2005, as the chief strategy and investment officer and was responsible for corporate strategies, investments, merger and acquisitions, and investor relations. In 2006, Mr. Lau was promoted to president of the company to manage the day-to-day operation of the company. In 2007, he was appointed an executive director of the company. Prior to joining the company, Mr. Lau was an executive director at Goldman Sachs (Asia) L.L.C.'s investment banking division and the chief operating officer of its Telecom, Media and Technology Group. Prior to that, he worked at McKinsey & Company, Inc. as a management consultant. Mr. Lau received a Bachelor of Science degree in electrical engineering from the University of Michigan, a Master of Science degree in electrical engineering from Stanford University, and an MBA degree from Kellogg Graduate School of Management, Northwestern University. In 2011, Mr. Lau was appointed a non-executive director of Kingsoft Corporation Limited, an Internet-based software developer, distributor, and software service provider listed in Hong Kong. In 2014, Mr. Lau was appointed a director of JD.com, Inc., an online direct sales company in China, which has been listed on NASDAQ since May 2014. In 2014, Mr. Lau was appointed a director of Leju Holdings Limited, an online-to-offline real estate services provider in China, which has been listed on NYSE since April 2014. Mr. Lau also serves as a director/ corporate representative of certain subsidiaries of the company.

Jacobus Petrus (Koos) Bekker (64)
Non-executive director

Mr. Koos led the founding team of the M-Net/MultiChoice pay-television business in 1985. He was also a founder director of MTN in cellular telephony. He headed the MIH group in its international and Internet expansions until 1997, when he became chief executive of Naspers. He serves on the boards of other companies within the group and associates, as well as on public boards. Academic qualifications include BA (Hons) and honorary doctorate in commerce (Stellenbosch University), LLB (University of the Witwatersrand), and MBA (Columbia University, New York).

Charles St Leger Searle (53)
Non-executive director

Mr. Searle is currently the CEO of Naspers Internet Listed Assets. He serves on the board of a number of companies associated with the Naspers Group, including Mail.ru Group Limited that is listed on the LSE and MakeMyTrip Limited that is listed on NASDAQ. Prior to joining the Naspers Group, he held positions at Cable & Wireless plc and at Deloitte & Touche in London and Sydney. Mr. Searle is a graduate of the University of Cape Town and a member of the Institute of Chartered Accountants in Australia and New Zealand. Mr. Searle has more than 23 years of international experience in the telecommunications and Internet industries.

Li Dong Sheng (59)
Independent non-executive director

Mr. Li is the chairman and CEO of TCL Corporation and the chairman of the Hong Kong–listed TCL Multimedia Technology Holdings Limited, both of which produce consumer electronic products. Mr. Li is a non-executive director of Fantasia Holdings Group Co., Limited, a leading property developer and property-related service provider in China that is listed on The Stock Exchange of Hong Kong Limited. Mr. Li is also an independent director of Legrand, the global specialist in electrical and digital building infrastructures, shares of which are listed on New York Stock Exchange Euronext. Mr. Li graduated from South China University of Technology in 1982, with a bachelor's degree in radio technology and has more than 22 years of experience in the information technology field. Mr. Li is the chairman of TCL Communication Technology Holdings Limited, which was delisted for privatization from The Stock Exchange of Hong Kong Limited on September 30, 2016.

Iain Ferguson Bruce (76)
Independent non-executive director

Mr. Bruce joined KPMG in Hong Kong in 1964 and was elected to its partnership in 1971. He was the senior partner of KPMG from 1991 until his retirement in 1996 and served as chairman of KPMG Asia Pacific from 1993 to 1997. Since 1964, Mr. Bruce has been a member of the Institute of Chartered Accountants of Scotland, and is a fellow of the Hong Kong Institute of Certified Public Accountants. He is also a fellow of The Hong Kong Institute of Directors and the Hong Kong Securities and Investment Institute. Mr. Bruce is an independent non-executive director of Citibank (Hong Kong) Limited and MSIG Insurance (Hong Kong) Limited. He is currently an independent non-executive director of Goodbaby International Holdings Limited, a manufacturer of durable juvenile products; The 13 Holdings Limited (formerly known as Louis XIII Holdings Limited), a construction, engineering services, and hotel development company; and Wing On Company International Limited, a department store operating as a property investment company. All of these companies are publicly listed on the HKSE. Mr. Bruce is also an independent non-executive director of Noble Group Limited, a commodity trading company that is publicly listed on The Singapore Exchange Securities Trading Limited and an independent non-executive director of Yingli Green Energy Holding Company Limited, a China-based vertically integrated photovoltaic product manufacturer that is listed on the NYSE. Mr. Bruce was an independent non-executive director of Vitasoy International Holdings Limited, a beverage manufacturing company, and of Sands China Ltd., an operator of integrated resorts and casinos. Both of these companies are publicly listed on The Stock Exchange of Hong Kong Limited.

Ian Charles Stone (66)
Independent non-executive director

Mr. Stone is currently an independent advisor on Technology, Media and Telecoms after retiring from PCCW in Hong Kong in 2011. His career in the last 27 years has been primarily in leading mobile telecoms businesses and new wireless and Internet technology, during which time he held senior roles in PCCW, SmarTone, First Pacific, Hong Kong Telecom, and CSL, as chief executive or at director level, primarily in Hong Kong, and in London and Manila. Since 2011, Mr. Stone has provided telecoms advisory services to telecom companies and investors in Hong Kong, China, Southeast Asia, and the Middle East. Mr. Stone has more than 46 years of experience in the telecom and mobile industries. He is a fellow member of The Hong Kong Institute of Directors. Mr. Stone also serves as an independent non-executive director of a subsidiary of Tencent Holdings.

Yang Siu Shun (61)
Independent non-executive director

Mr. Yang is currently serving as a member of the 12th National Committee of the Chinese People's Political Consultative Conference, a Justice of the Peace in Hong Kong, a member of the Exchange Fund Advisory Committee of the Hong Kong Monetary Authority, a steward of the Hong Kong Jockey Club, the deputy chairman of the Council of the Open University of Hong Kong, a board member and the Audit Committee chairman of the Hang Seng Management College, and an independent non-executive director of Industrial and Commercial Bank of China Limited, which is publicly listed on the HKSE and SSE. Mr. Yang retired from PwC on June 30, 2015. Before his retirement, he served as the chairman and senior partner of PwC Hong Kong, the executive chairman and senior partner of PwC China and Hong Kong, one of the five members of the Global Network Leadership Team of PwC, and the PwC Asia Pacific chairman. Mr. Yang graduated from the London School of Economics and Political Science in 1978. Mr. Yang is a fellow member of the Institute of Chartered Accountants in England and Wales, the Hong Kong Institute of Certified Public Accountants, and the Chartered Institute of Management Accountants.

The board has established the following subcommittees:

- audit committee
- corporate governance committee
- investment committee
- nomination committee
- remuneration committee

Each committee acts within agreed terms of reference, which are available on the company's website.

A Tencent acquisition

In 2016, a 50-50 merger of equals was signed between China Music, a music-streaming business in mainland China, and a far smaller rival, QQ Music, which had less than half the revenues and active users as did China Music.

The founder of China Music, Xie Guomin, explained his strategy. For a decade he had been acquiring licenses for thousands of songs, eventually building a giant library that gave his music app a dominant position in the China market. Xie discussed the situation with his private equity partner, Shan Weijian, who ran Hong Kong–based investment company PAG. They realized there was little option other than merging with the smaller and less successful rival, because QQ Music was a subsidiary of Tencent Holdings. Xie knew that when the rights to China Music's library came up for renewal, Tencent had the resources to outbid him, destroying the underlying value of his business. Explaining the rationale behind the merger deal, Xi explained that although his business was more successful than his rival's, Tencent "doesn't care about the money. They can pay ten times more than we can for content and that would quickly change their market share."

CSRC rules frustrated Hong Kong investors

The regulator of the securities market in China, the CRSC, established a rule that restricts institutional investors to holding 10% in any single stock. The 10% rule was part of a code of conduct to encourage fund managers to adopt "scientific and reasonable" strategies and risk when investing in equities.

However, the rapid rise in the value of Chinese technology stocks, such as Tencent and Alibaba, means that these companies now form a significant part of China share indexes, such as the MSCI China index.[13] With Tencent Holding's MSCI China weighting at16.3%, it is hard for investment managers to outperform the index, given the 10% limit on investment in any one share. As Hong Kong–based Take Shi Bin, a portfolio manager with UBS Asset Management told Bloomberg: "It would be a real headache for us if Tencent shares continue to surge, as it'll be difficult to find better bets."

Questions for discussion

1. What is your opinion of the structure and membership of the Tencent Board? Does it meet contemporary Western opinions on board diversity? Is that good or bad?

2. Is it a sound idea to combine the roles of chairman of the board and CEO?

3. How many non-executive directorships can one person sensibly hold?

4. Does the merger with China Music raise any strategic issues for Tencent or for the Chinese economy?

5. Is the CSRC 10% rule necessary? Should it be changed?

Case study II

Teletronic Riches Ltd.: Governance of a joint venture[14]

Teletronic Riches Limited was a JV company set up between Lichfield Teletronics Limited [Lichfield], a UK company, and Great Riches Limited [Riches], a company based in Hong Kong although incorporated in Bermuda. Riches was quoted on the HKSE although 66% of the voting stock was owned by Albert Li Cheuk Yan and his family. Lichfield was the wholly owned subsidiary of a US-based public company, listed on the NASDAQ stock exchange.

---

13. The MSCI China Index captures large and mid-cap representation across China H-shares, B-shares, Red Chips, P Chips and foreign listings (e.g., ADRs). With 150 constituents, the index covers about 85% of this China equity universe.

14. The names and some details of in this case have been disguised to keep anonymity.

The JV had been set up to manufacture the Teletronic range of integrated iPhone and recording machines in Shenzhen, China. In the JV agreement, Lichfield would provide technological know-how, specialist manufacturing equipment, and the top management; Riches would provide the manufacturing site, labor, and local management. Both sides put up an equal amount of working capital and would share equally in profits. The entire output was to be supplied to Lichfield for distribution through its worldwide marketing organization, except for sales to the market in China, for which Riches were given the rights.

Lichfield and Riches had equal shareholdings and voting rights, and each appointed three members to the board. Teletronic's managing director, Bill Torrington, was also made a member of the board. He had run a very successful division of Lichfield in the UK, and in 1997 was seconded to Teletronic on a five-year contract. He expected, when the JV was successful, to become a director of the Lichfield Main Board on his return to England.

Initially, all went well, but after three years tensions emerged. Relations between the two sets of directors on the Teletronic board were frosty. The Riches-nominated directors complained that the venture was not being given the latest products or technology. The Lichfield directors claimed that their company's products, made in Shenzhen, were being sold throughout Asia, in contravention of the JV agreement.

Bill Torrington found himself in an impossible position. He wanted what was good for Teletronic, but his Lichfield colleagues expected him to side with them. His career prospects were on the line.

Question for discussion

What should Bill Torrington do?

Case study III

Bright Food (Group) Co. Ltd.

Based in Shanghai, Bright Food is one of China's largest companies and is wholly owned by the Shanghai Municipal government. As its name suggests, it is in the food business: agriculture, food and beverage production and distribution, and supermarkets. Bright Food has partnered with some well-known overseas companies through JV companies such as Nestlé Shanghai Ltd., Coca-Cola (China) Beverages Ltd., and Pepsi (Shanghai) Ltd.

- Bright Food has four subsidiary companies, each listed on the SSE:
- Bright Dairy & Food Co., Ltd.
- Shanghai First Provisions Store Co., Ltd
- Shanghai Haibo Co., Ltd

- Shanghai Maling Aquarius Co., Ltd

The shares available to the public are A-shares, available only to Chinese residents.

Bright Food has a strategy to generate 20% of its revenues abroad and in recent years has made some significant investments overseas:

- July 2010 agreed to acquire a 51% stake in the New Zealand–based dairy producer Synlait for US$58 million, although it failed to obtain control;
- August 2011 acquired a 75% stake in Australia-based Manassen Foods for A$530 million;
- September 2010 entered into discussions for the acquisition of British snack food manufacturer United Biscuits but failed to make the acquisition;
- May 2012 acquired a 60% of the UK-based Weetabix breakfast cereal company for £1.2 billion, which was subsequently sold to US company Post Holdings for US$1.8 billion, in April 2017;
- May 2014 acquired a 56% stake in the Israel-based Dairy producer Truva for US$2.5 billion;
- October 2014 agreed to acquire a majority stake in Italian olive oil producer Salov;
- September 2015 Bright Food's subsidiary, Shanghai Maling Aquarius Co., Ltd. acquired 50% of New Zealand–based Silver Fern Farms dairy and meat company for NZ$261 million.

Rumors in the international finance world suggested that Bright Food might make an initial public offering to float one or more of its subsidiaries on the Hong Kong, New York, or London stock markets.

Questions for discussion

1. Why, do you think, Bright Food listed its four subsidiaries separately on the stock market, rather than listing the holding company?

2. Is the Bright Food strategy to generate 20% of its revenues overseas realistic?

3. What might be the implications for Bright Food if it floated one or more of its subsidiaries on the Hong Kong, New York, or London stock markets?

10

Corporate Governance in China in the Years Ahead

Bob Tricker

Gregg Li

In this chapter we consider:

- ❖ the context for change in corporate governance
- ❖ the basis of power in modern China
- ❖ the future control of Chinese enterprises
- ❖ drivers of change in corporate governance
    - ➢ the impact of changes in corporate financing
    - ➢ the impact of corporate restructuring
    - ➢ the impact of changes in the labor market
    - ➢ the impact of technological change
    - ➢ the impact of changes in societal expectations
- ❖ forces for change in Chinese corporate governance
- ❖ what the West might learn from Chinese corporate governance
    - ➢ let the bullets fly
    - ➢ The Chinese market is vast
    - ➢ explore, experiment, innovate
    - ➢ practical results not regulation in governance
    - ➢ enthusiasm but slow and consensual decisions
    - ➢ high-quality directors needed
    - ➢ treat CEOs as state employees
- ❖ corporate governance as a catalyst for economic growth
- ❖ the new "Xi" era of corporate governance

The context for change in corporate governance

For the first time in recent history, large and robust Chinese companies have the opportunity to extend their influence simultaneously eastward and westward: eastward into the North American markets, as Chinese companies become richer, stronger, and able to acquire multinational competitors; westward to Europe but also to the 65 other countries between China and Western Europe, now connected by China's One Belt, One Road Initiative.

The future of corporate governance in China depends, obviously, on the future of China itself, and there lie many uncertainties—economic, political, and cultural. As China is a land of experimentation in the realm of corporate governance, we expect to see major changes and innovation in corporate governance that other countries just talk about.

The economic future depends on levels of economic growth, productivity, and the balance of trade—all of which hinge not only on what China can achieve but also on economic factors around the world. In China, the availability of an educated labor force given an aging population, the use of robotics in production, and the need for continuing development of technology, will be important. As of 2017, China has earmarked more money to spend on artificial intelligence than has any other nation in the world.[1] According to Accenture, China has filed more than 8,000 AI patents in the five years leading up to 2015, which represented a growth rate of 190% and which outpaced all other leading markets. Plans are in place to predict crimes, lend money without banks, provide credit based on a person's travel patterns, install driverless cars, and track citizens better with more powerful facial recognition software.

The political future is likely to be even more significant. Economic success needs political stability. Maintaining China's centralized one-party system of national governance calls for a subtle balancing of the changing expectations of a populace which is increasingly educated, affluent, and informed. "Smart city" policies provide ready access to information and ideas even though strictly regulated. Overseas education and travel also expand the knowledge base.

Central Government policymakers also have to balance regional calls for more local influence, for example, in Hong Kong and Western border territories. The success of the new Belt and Road Initiative also depends on stable relations with neighboring countries to the west and in the seas of South China and Japan.

Underpinning both the economic and the political future of China lies its cultural context: the way people think, their beliefs and their values. These are changing. The underpinning set of beliefs affects the way businesses are perceived and the way they are run. This is the relevance for corporate governance.

Inherent in a culture are beliefs about human values and behavior. In the past, Western thinking tended to place more emphasis on individual rights and duties, whereas in Eastern countries greater emphasis was put on the responsibility to the family, the community, and society. More recently, Western thinking shows signs of shifting in the Eastern direction, with more emphasis on a socially responsible society, as seen in the growing emphasis on corporate social responsibility, sustainability, and business ethics.

---

1. Daugherty (2017, July 30).

The basis of power in modern China

The governance of companies and other corporate entities in a country must be consistent with and form part of the overall governance of that country. In the United States, corporate governance is rooted in law and regulation, reflecting the vital underpinning that law provides in the US Constitution. The UK, by contrast, has no written constitution and corporate governance involves voluntary adherence to a corporate governance code, which is consistent with company law and embedded in the stock market rules.

In China, the law serves the people, represented by the Communist Party. The underlying philosophy, reflecting Lenin's concept of "democratic centralism," holds that the leaders of the party should not seek to dictate or lead, rather to provide guidance, direction, and influence in responding to the needs of the people who are represented by the party. The aim of corporate governance is **not** really about enhancing "shareholders'" value but about enhancing "societal values." It is indeed capitalism with a Chinese social characteristic.

The head of the party and the state is Xi Jinping, general secretary of the Communist Party of China, president of the People's Republic of China, and chairman of the Central Military Commission. The president works with the Politburo, whose members are drawn from the Central Committee, which is elected by the large National Congress of the Chinese Communist Party.

Xi Jinping operates with a group of colleagues organized into "small groups" or committees. There are, for example, small groups covering economics and finance, cyber security, anti-corruption, party-building, and Hong Kong and Macau affairs. There is also a small working group for "comprehensively deepening reform." Subsets of the small groups operate at the provincial level. In his book, *The Governance of China*, Xi Jinping describes the governance of China to be a "work in progress."

Below this summit sit the heads of the provinces, the top brass of the PLA, the judiciary including the law courts, government ministries, and government regulatory agencies, such as the bodies overseeing corporate governance: CSRC and SASAC.

Early approaches to corporate governance in China sought to maintain the state's overall power through command of the political agenda and the economy, while facilitating markets, innovation, economic growth, and the acquisition of personal wealth. This was communism with a Chinese face.

The future control of Chinese enterprises

If we adopt a simple definition of corporate governance as the way power is exercised over corporate entities, how is power currently wielded over Chinese businesses? Independent companies incorporated under the Companies Act face regulation by the CSRC. SOEs are supervised by SASAC. Other organizations relevant to corporate governance in China include the Asset Management Association of China (AMAC), the China Association for Public Companies (CAPCO), and the China Institute of Finance and Capital Markets (CIFCM).

Companies listed on a stock market must also meet the listing rules of that exchange whether in China, Hong Kong, or abroad. Other laws and regulations, for example, on taxation, anti-corruption, and pollution, also affect business entities at the national, state, province, and local levels.

Owners of a business may also exercise considerable power; for example, in the case of a dominant founder owner. In SOEs, obviously, the state wields the ultimate power. When an SOE is listed, other investors, typically in a minority shareholder position, wield little influence. Powerful block holders or significant groups of institutional investors, frequently found in the West, do not yet exist in China.

In recent years, authorities in Beijing have felt that the corporate sector, though dramatically successful in building the economy and contributing to the restructuring of society, was increasingly running outside their control, which was not consistent with the country's underlying governance philosophy.

This was not surprising, given that China's companies acts and corporate governance procedures, including executive boards with independent directors and supervisory boards, were modeled on corporate governance practices in the US, the UK, and Germany, with advice given by the OECD.

The early days of corporate governance in China were influenced by Western practices. Those days are almost certainly over. Corporate governance in China is developing a distinctive Chinese face, reflecting the unique economic, political, and cultural situation. In the past, a company's allegiance to the state and the party were often maintained by having the local party secretary serve on the supervisory board, sometimes as its chairperson. But in practice, if the executive board was powerful and the company successful, the supervisory board may have had little influence.

An ongoing development is to give each company's Communist Party Committee (PC) a formal role in corporate governance. This is an attempt to re-exert state supervision of the corporate sector. In this model, each PC has a formal role in overseeing the performance of the company, to ensure that the state's needs as well as those of the shareholders are being met. The PC is appointed through the party's organization and is responsible upwards through the party hierarchy.

The PC represents the party within the company and monitors its activities. This broadens PCs' previous involvement in personnel matters and senior employee appointments. In SOEs the PC will be responsible for corporate governance matters.

The slogan "four meetings: one team" was coined to explain the workings of this new structure; the four meetings being: the PC, the executive board, the supervisory board, and the management team responsible for running the business. One significant policy suggestion was that board resolutions should be approved by the PC before being formally ratified by the board. But this idea was followed by the suggestion that the executive members of the executive board would also be members of the PC. These ideas are still evolving. The intention is for the state to exercise oversight and, if necessary, control for the benefit of the people, without adversely affecting the raising of capital, the successful operation of the business, or the generation of wealth.

This structure for the governance of companies differs from that in the present companies act, as described in Chapter 3. In this model, the executive board, with at least one-third independent non-executive directors, is elected by the shareholders and the supervisory board with input from the employee representatives' meeting. The supervisory board is elected by the shareholders and the employee representatives' meeting. The executive board is then responsible for running the business. The new structure returns power to the party.

An updated corporate governance code is likely to be written reflecting this new reality of Chinese corporate governance. In due course, there may be calls for a rewrite of the Chinese companies act. In the future, China's approach to corporate governance might influence other countries where the state wants to maintain control of the business sector and restrain unfettered market freedom.

Drivers of change in corporate governance

A number of factors can drive changes in corporate governance policies and practices.

The impact of changes in corporate financing

The next decade or two are likely to see some significant changes to the way Chinese companies are financed, with some interesting corporate governance implications. The new listing boards of the Shanghai and Hong Kong exchanges that cater more to growth companies in the Fourth Industrial Revolution will inevitably enrich the ecosystem.[2]

China's stock markets are emergent. Unlike developed markets, they are principally retail, with individuals as customers who have no governance ambitions. To many of them, investment is a gamble—a means to make money.

Institutional investors tend to dominate advanced stock markets. In the Chinese market they are not yet highly significant. There are some, such as Changjiang Pension Insurance, China Universal Asset Management, the Huaxia Fund, the National Social Security Fund, and other institutions in Shanghai and Shenzhen. But they do not wield the power of Western institutional investors on issues such as major strategic decisions, or directors' remuneration.

Private equity in the West has transformed corporate governance power. There are no significant hedge funds or private equity investors to put pressure on

---

2. Schwab, 2016.

boards in China. Consequently, there is little shareholder activism; but awareness is growing. Retail investors are no longer shy and have taken listed companies to court.[3] In the first-class action lawsuit, in 2015, 2,700 investors had won a judgment of RMB 180 million against the Foshan Electrical & Light Company for alleged misrepresentation.

However, the Chinese stock markets are becoming more mature, with retail customers more sophisticated, making decisions on a sober assessment of risk rather than gambling. The influence of institutional investors, based in mainland China, Hong Kong, and possibly overseas, is also likely to continue to increase. The growing closeness between the two Chinese stock exchanges and the HKSE will undoubtedly play an important role in this professionalization and market maturity.

Before 1997, much of the wealth came from abroad. By 2017, enormous wealth was coming from within China. Increasingly sophisticated Chinese investors with global ambitions are using Hong Kong to purchase companies and assets abroad. Similarly, Chinese domestic companies are increasingly using the HKSE to raise capital. Over 60% of the listed vehicles on the HKSE are now Chinese domestic firms. Before the handover in 1997, there were effectively none. Foreign capital coming into China has not dwindled either. In summary, the ecosystem has become much bigger, more sophisticated, and has more and diversified players.

New sources of finance are also likely to emerge, probably Internet-based and possibly from sources other than the stock markets and banks. The New Economy with its Fourth Industrial Revolution will need more capital and different forms of weighted voting rights, such as dual-class shares.

However, the state will continue to scrutinize and regulate cross-border monetary flows. The role of state-owned banks in providing finance for business is also likely to come under scrutiny from state regulators. At the other end of the spectrum, the China Investment Corporation (CIC), China's sovereign wealth fund, is slowly making an impact through its oversea purchases through its three subsidiaries: CIC International, CIC Capital, and Central Huijin. Large firms, those with hidden state ambition, will continue to push the boundaries. ChemChina bought Synenta; HNA (Hainan Air) is buying the whole world;[4] CNOOC bought Nexen, a Canadian oil firm, and was still writing off the purchase. Dalian Wanda, Fosun, and Anbang have bought hotels, a Portuguese bank, and a Russian gold mine. Overpaying for trophy assets, without any synergistic purpose, however, appeared to have been common.[5]

The next decade or so is likely to see consolidation and reorganization of existing companies, promoted by merger and acquisition activity but regulated and sometimes sponsored by the state.

---

3. Zhu, Fei, & Cheng, 2017.
4. Weinland, Massoudi, & Fontanella-Khan (2017, July 30).
5. Chinese companies' weak record on foreign deals (2017, June 8).

The impact of corporate restructuring

In recent years some Chinese companies have formed strategic alliances with overseas companies to use their manufacturing technologies. Others have entered JVs to market products or services. Chinese firms are buying American AI companies, for example. Predictably, not all of these ventures have been successful. Some have been closed; others have been restructured or acquired by other firms.

But merger and acquisition activity within China to date has been spasmodic. In some cases the take-over process has come under scrutiny. For example, Evergrande and Baoneng companies were both criticized for aggressive take-overs using investments in their insurance companies.

Acquisition activity outside China, however, has been striking. Some SOEs have made significant acquisitions abroad, presumably with party approval. As cited, some Chinese entrepreneurs have invested in a range of companies such as hotel chains, a gold mine, and football clubs, without apparent strategic logic other than the possibility of quick returns.

In Western corporate governance, there is a "market for control," which means that boards of listed companies know that predators constantly look for take-over opportunities. Consequently, these boards try to run successful companies and position themselves so that they are not prone to hostile bids. Regulators, meanwhile, try to prevent companies from taking measures that would protect them from such bids. No such market for control yet exists in China. The case of Vanke, described at the end of Chapter 5, is a vivid example of how the state is learning to mediate aggressive takeover activities.

The impact of changes in the labor market

China's enormous economic success in recent years has relied on a vast and inexpensive labor force. The move from countryside to city provided the workers for the manufacturing industries. Now that is changing.

The development of robotics and automation replaces routine jobs and needs better-educated, more knowledgeable workers. Similarly, new service industries need better-educated employees. But the population is aging. The cohort of young people is smaller than in the past because of the one-child policy. A new middle class has also emerged with more affluence, education, and information than their parents had. Travel to Hong Kong and abroad has widened their horizons. They are aware of alternatives; expectations are inevitably changing.

This could lead to growing dissatisfaction with existing corporate governance processes. A sense of impotence could lead to calls for genuine employee participation, a new focus on labor relations, workers' and women's rights, and calls for greater transparency in business. In other words, the traditional acceptance of authority might be questioned, which the party would undoubtedly counter.

The impact of technological change

Information technology provides new opportunities for corporate governance practices everywhere in the world but particularly in China, where electronic interaction, not the least in smart cities, is widespread. Given China's full-scale push towards artificial intelligence, having a full AI machine advising a board of directors may not be that far off. The first such machine may just set its foot on a Chinese board. Klaus Schwab, the founder and executive chairman of the World Economic Forum, predicted this will happen by 2025.[6]

Opportunities for employing IT and AI are immense; for example, the delivery of information to top management and the other participants.

Clearly the corporate regulators and others in the party hierarchy could be included in the loop. Oversight and regulation of the business sector is, obviously, vital for centralized state oversight and control. Internet technology provides the means for monitoring activities and accessing information.

As boards become more conscious and aware, through AI, IOT (Internet of things), cognitive engines, and dynamic filtering, virtually everything that is done by management will be visible.

There are strict controls on the movement of data over China's national borders. Overseas companies are required to run their China-based activities on information systems based in China and to hold information on Chinese subjects only within China. This has significant implications for international companies wanting to connect their Chinese operations with their global systems. Clearly, this also affects corporate governance systems for handling reporting to senior management and directors.

Information technology also raises the possibility of rethinking business boundaries. In corporate governance, companies are defined by their financial and ownership structures. New thinking might also define businesses by the structure and boundaries of their information networks. The democratization of information and expectations on transparency that come with digital assets will give more power to shareholders and, in China's case, power to its citizens, government agencies, or the party to hold companies to account.

The impact of changes in societal expectations

People growing up in China during the past 20 years will have seen amazing changes in their world. In the process, they will have acquired new expectations about the future. Traditionally, Chinese society respected authority, wisdom, and old age. New thinking is now needed, as Chinese society becomes more conscious of its roles and impact in this changing world.

---

6. Schwab, 2016, p. 26.

The Chinese have a greater awareness of their ancestors, history, and nature than do people in Western cultures. "Always remember the source of the Yangtze." Many Chinese families can trace their roots through many generations. Most can tell you the source and origin of their family name. The diaspora from mainland China to Hong Kong and other countries in Asia and further afield did not diminish this respect for past generations, nor did the dislocation of the Cultural Revolution, or the massive movement of populations from the countryside to the cities in recent years, as can be seen by the many millions who travel back to their family home-towns at Chinese New Year. Chinese culture has never been about the individual but about ancestral lineage, family, clan, and ultimately the emperor.

Belief systems in the underlying culture have not kept pace. Traditional religious beliefs—Daoism, Buddhism, and ancestor worship—were damaged by the Cultural Revolution and then the mass migration from the countryside villages to the massively growing cities. For some this has produced a sense of uncertainty, dissatisfaction, and possibly pressures for change. For many, this was a time of lost identity.

The acquisition of wealth is now acceptable in China, as it has been in Hong Kong for generations. To many, this is an honor. Indeed, some of Hong Kong's most successful (and richest) business leaders advise the Central Government in Beijing and are influential in the election of Hong Kong's Legislative Council (LegCo). Sir Li Ka-Shing, the richest man in Hong Kong, is revered. Prominent business leaders and some senior government officers are wealthy, even though some of their wealth may have been transferred abroad.

Forces for change in Chinese corporate governance

China is affected by developments in the rest of the world: changes, for example, in the balance between free trade and protectionism, free movement of capital and capital controls, free movement of people and immigration controls, free flow of ideas and censorship, balance of military power, and national ambition.

To identify possible changes to corporate governance principles and practice, consider what caused changes elsewhere in the world. Changes to corporate governance codes, company law, and corporate rules and regulations have typically been responses to perceived corporate collapses, excess, or corruption. The SEC in the US, the dominant regulator of American firms, was created, following the Great Depression, to control powerful company "barons." This produced a legal underpinning and a litigious culture for corporate governance in the US, which survives to this day. The US Sarbanes-Oxley Act followed the failure of the vast energy giant Enron and the subsequent collapse of its worldwide auditor, Arthur Anderson.

The first corporate governance code, the Cadbury Report in the UK, was a response to a string of company failures, following dubious board or dominant owner behavior, such as the Maxwell company failures. This code provided the underpinning for voluntary corporate governance, based on the principle of "comply with the code or explain why you have not." The Cadbury Report was quickly reflected in many other countries, including Hong Kong. The international financial crisis starting in 2007 brought another stream of corporate legislation and regulation around the world.

These developments in corporate governance were usually prompted by a government, regulator, or stock exchange concerned about adverse effects on the economy or the integrity of the stock market. They were sometimes prompted by media interest but hardly ever by the findings of academic research although academics might be involved in the development of the revised order.

So, what situations might prompt a review of corporate governance in China? It is not likely to be the public collapse of an SOE, because they are closely watched and supported when necessary. Their CEOs are changed frequently to reduce the possibility of complacency or corruption. The top management of companies incorporated by provinces is also monitored by their party committees, party state secretaries, and provincial governors, who are also replaced regularly by the central authorities.

But one or more of the newly created enterprises in media, communication, or the Internet could fail, perhaps by outstripping its ability to fund its growth or maintaining the growth momentum as competition increases or markets mature. Such a collapse would unnerve the stock market and the government. Consequently, the stock exchanges would probably require more information on whether companies were going concerns. Government regulators might exert more control. At the moment, senior officers of regulatory bodies rely on verbal advice or admonition ("window advice") or public criticism to police such situations that could change, or if investigations are launched and new rules enacted.

Political intervention could also change corporate governance practices. The state needs to encourage business development, innovation, and growth, while avoiding central regulation and control. Wealth creation that was thought by the authorities to be threatening or excessive could result in tighter governance controls and less freedom in business boardrooms. More state control might be applied to the creation of state strategies for key sectors in the economy, the regulation of acquisitions abroad, or for other controls in some business sectors, so that companies can be seen to be serving the people and the state as well as their owners.

What the West might learn from Chinese corporate governance

A corporate governance expert in the West, asked for his opinion on corporate governance in China, replied: "What corporate governance? I don't believe there is any in China." That remains the unspoken view of many Westerners. Forty years ago, before China's modernization drive, there clearly was no corporate governance, because there were no corporate entities: everything belonged to and was run by the state.

When SOEs were corporatized and, in some cases, listed on a stock exchange, corporate governance systems were needed. Subsequently, when independent private companies were created, the need was amplified. Western experience was used, with the help of the OECD and the World Bank, to create an infrastructure of company regulation and law, a corporate governance code, and listing rules for China's two stock exchanges.

But they have not been particularly effective, as we have seen in earlier chapters. Systems of checks and balances proved cumbersome or nonexistent. Lack of integrity and corruption were rife. Some ventures failed.

Yet today, a few of the largest and most successful companies in the world are Chinese. Key companies on the stock exchange boards in New York, London, Hong Kong, as well as on NASDAQ, are Chinese. Meanwhile the state-owned sector has been reorganized, reinvigorated, and is investing abroad. How has this happened? Does corporate governance in China have some unique attributes that have contributed to this recent success? More significantly, will these effects be maintained?

Researching and writing this book has given us some new insights. Thirty-five years ago, Ouchi[7] demonstrated the unique characteristics of Japanese management, including consensual decision-making, an emphasis on quality control and just-in-time supply chains, which challenged conventional Western management thinking. Drawing on the Chinese experience, a similar challenge now seems likely to conventional Western thinking on corporate governance.

In recent years, corporate governance in China has taken on a different direction from that of the West, which we believe offers a new approach to the subject. But to understand requires a different perspective.

The Chinese are intelligent and astute learners and have studied foreign corporate governance codes and regulations, keeping parts that would be relevant. Of course, corporate governance in China remains a work in progress, just as President Xi Jinping sees the governance of the country as an evolving activity. But thus far, some significant results are being delivered.

Everywhere in the world, sound corporate governance is recognized as important to ensure that the enterprise fulfills its objectives, by satisfying customers, motivating employees, providing opportunities for suppliers, meeting the expectations of shareholders, while being socially responsible, acting within the law, and growing over the long term. These objectives are, inevitably, in conflict. A sound corporate governance infrastructure needs to be in place if the enterprise is to succeed.

By contrast, during the research and writing of this book, we realized that China has developed a unique approach to corporate governance. Although initially building on Western experience, the Chinese see corporate governance as a

---

7. Dininni (2017, February 22).

means of improving the economy and building society in the interests of the people, the party, and the state.

Although these are early days, it is perhaps not too soon to suggest that there is more than one approach to corporate governance. Maybe the Western OECD-led mechanisms are not the only way to sound governance.

This book is not a defense of the Chinese model, as that model is still evolving, but more an inquiry into possible alternatives. However, success of the Chinese socialist way does raise questions about the universality of market-led capitalism and democratic norms.[8] A new insight into corporate governance in China is needed. China is different.

Although the list is not definitive, let us highlight a few of the approaches that China has adopted, giving each idea its own slogan, as the Chinese love to do (as in "let a thousand flowers bloom" by Mao Zedong or "The Belt and Road Initiative" by XI Jinping).

Let the bullets fly

This is the title of a popular movie in China and has a special following. The name of the movie suggested an attitude of reckless optimism. Just shoot and the bullets will eventually hit some targets. The state strategy of the Belt and Road Initiative is a fine example of this. In other words, according to corporate governance and business viability, as long as the Chinese company is in line with government policies and works within the permissible governance practices endorsed by the party, the state will become the administrator of the last resort. If nothing else works, the state will force-fit a square peg into a round hole if that's what's needed. As in Finland, public–private partnership is well developed in China. A good example is the case of Vanke,[9] where the state stepped in to correct governance failure at the last minute. Conversely, Wanda,[10] which is a private independent company not an SOE, was investing heavily in movie theaters in the US. But, when the Chinese government introduced tight controls on outbound investment to control the currency, Wanda had to adjust its strategy.

On the surface, the state sets the broad parameters, local government and businesses competing among themselves but generally keeping within the parameters. Unlike in Western democracies, the one-party Chinese Communist Party sets the tone for business.

---

8. Huang (2017, September 14).
9. See the Vanke case study at the end of Chapter 5.
10. See the Wanda case study at the end of Chapter 7.

The Chinese market is vast

The size of the Chinese retail market is a unique contributor that has created a crucial opportunity for the new companies. The Chinese middle class now has a massive disposable income. Moreover, the Chinese government can support a specific location attracting Chinese tourists and foreign visitors with their purchasing power.

Take the example of Tencent[11] and QQ Internet gaming. Gaming was a good but bounded market when each player played alone on his or her own electronic device. By connecting millions of users in China online through QQ, Tencent created a formidable expanding market. Tencent is now China's most valuable technology company with valuation over US$255 billion, also becoming the world's tenth-largest public corporation.[12]

Another interesting company is Mobike. Given China's market size, Mobike quickly became the world's first and largest bike-sharing platform, based on a simple idea and of course, backing from Tencent. One simply pays a small deposit, RMB 200 for example, using a mobile payment app. The large sums that were earned from the millions of deposit receipts proved the validity of the business model.

The size of the Chinese market in many fields provides overwhelming opportunities. For some companies, control mechanisms became secondary to the generation of revenue. When the stream of cash pouring into your bucket turns into a torrent, little hole in buckets can easily be ignored.

Explore, experiment, innovate

Experimentation in business model and corporate governance is another attribute that has contributed to the success of many Chinese firms.

In the corporate world, innovation and experimentation is generally rare. The likes of 3M, Google, Apple, and Amazon are the exceptions. There are many reasons for this. Executives do not like to fail or take risks that may undermine their careers. Innovators are often governed by the same set of short-term quarterly metrics for all subsidiaries (and the innovators are better off starting their own company, with fewer restrictions, albeit with added risks and a lack of funds.)

One of the most innovative business areas in China has been the so-called "shadow banking" sector. Traditional banking is heavily regulated and run through state-controlled banks dominated by the state-owned People's Bank of China. The government determines interest rates, encourages or discourages lending to certain industries, and controls the international flow of capital. The formal banking sector is heavily in debt, is risk-averse, and does not like to invest in emerging, uncertain,

---

11. See the case study at the end of Chapter 9.
12. See https://www.bloomberg.com/news/articles/2017-04-05/tencent-passes-wells-fargo-to-become-10th-biggest-company-chart.

and volatile markets. But the rapidly growing business sectors needed venture capital. Venture capital facilities are in a nascent stage in China.

The shadow banking sector spawned to meet the financial needs of the massive financial needs of the business sector. These "non-banks" are often subsidiaries of major organizations, acting as financial intermediaries in group transactions and offering a range of asset management services and financial products, which provide funding for a period and are, in effect, loans. But the shadow banking sector has not been sufficiently regulated by the government financial authorities. Moreover, it tends to have lower capital and liquidity requirements, has no limits placed on interest rates or the amounts involved, and is more risky, a factor that concerns the central banking authorities.

Facing the challenge to catch up to the economically advanced world, Chinese companies are willing to explore ideas and opportunities and to experiment in pursuing them. Fortuitously, the digital revolution offered opportunities, and many Chinese companies were prepared to explore new business models. Alipay (owned by Alibaba), WeChat Pay (owned by Tencent), and Ant Financial are changing the way customers pay for services and goods in China. Although it is illegal, some small businesses are now demanding payment through WeChat Pay rather than cash. The government permitted the experimentation of mobile peer-to-peer payment applications and did not issue any firm directives prematurely. As a result, thousands of applications emerged. Eventually the market is settling to a few: Alipay and WeChat Pay appear to hold the largest market shares in 2017. When the dust has settled, the Chinese authorities are likely to promulgate firm policies and mandates on mobile payments, but not before.

Practical results, not regulation in governance

Corporate governance in the West has a number of sacred cows; for example, "one share one vote," which produces the inequity of multi-class shares, or the demand on the genuinely independent directors, which means the more independent they are, the less they know about the company and its industry.

The Chinese have no such inhibitions. The early stage of corporate governance development allowed for a wide discussion of alternatives. Both the Chinese government and Chinese businesses are practical. If a corporate governance idea does not work, it is instantly replaced. There are no sacred cows. The Chinese authorities were bold in experimenting on governance practices, focusing on their real purpose and the desired outcome. The authorities see corporate governance as a vehicle: it doesn't matter how or where that vehicle was assembled. Perhaps this sense of uncertainty and freshness gave rise to the variety of options. Arrogance does not make a good student.

Enthusiasm but slow and consensual decisions

When we talk with businesspeople or teach students from mainland China, they exude an air of eager optimism in China that is pervasive. There is a yearning to catch up quickly, to jump at opportunities, and sometimes, unfortunately, to trade off on detail and quality. There's a general tendency on the part of businesspeople to keep legal contracts simple, then negotiate and adjust the contract along the way. In a world of disruption that is the norm in the Fourth Industrial Revolution, keeping legal contracts simple is preferred.

The need to keep agreements simple reflects the Chinese culture and the way companies make decisions. The US military has an acronym to describe extreme conditions: VUCA, standing for Volatile, Uncertain, Complex, and Ambiguous. This neatly covers the situation in many Chinese companies. Ambiguity works in such a world. In fact, the Fourth Industrial Revolution—the electronic digital age—was made *for* China and came at just the right time.

Decision-making in Chinese companies is generally by consensus. This means that by the time an action is executed, support is readily there. Everyone knows about the decision and people are committed. But this takes time and leaves an element of ambiguity.

Shared accountability for the outcome of decisions is encouraged. Holding a single individual to account, particularly if things go wrong, is more difficult. Lines of responsibility are often blurred and demarcation is difficult. But it can be done. Control systems can be introduced and people can be trained. Take, for example, the role of internal auditors. As well as identifying an audit problem, they are sometimes asked to provide the solution. They are expected to be both corporate watchdog and the corporate doctor at the same time, like teachers who are well respected and honored.

High-quality directors needed

Corporate governance discussions in the West recently have focused on board-level diversity—diversity of directors by gender, background, and experience. But at board level, ability is more important than diversity is. Competent directors are as vital in China as they are in the West.

Both the CSRC and SASAC have made major efforts to invite quality directors onto the board of their companies.

Of the many initiatives quietly introduced by the Chinese authorities, we have found their respect and resolve to find quality directors significant. Good directors are pampered and protected. Some boards forget that first-class directors are fundamental to governance effectiveness. The Chinese authorities have not.

Treat CEOs as state employees

Corporate governance in the West faces an unresolved problem: the control of excessive top management rewards. Remuneration committees of like-minded directors and shareholder votes that are only advisory have proved ineffective. This is not currently a problem in China.

Top managers of SOEs are government employees and are paid accordingly. They expect to be assessed by their government authorities and moved between enterprises according to their performance and the needs of the state.

Top management of independent private companies is still often the founders and their close associates. Consequently, their rewards are reflected in the rising worth of their companies and the value of their shareholdings, if the company is listed.

The overall cost of board-level and top management remuneration in Chinese companies is significantly lower than that of many Western companies. Of course, this provides a competitive benefit, particularly when competing with Western companies whose top management rewards are excessive. China may well face a challenge in future, as executives call for international parity.

But for the moment, China has a competitive advantage.

Corporate governance as a catalyst for economic growth

China has successfully leveraged corporate governance as a catalyst for economic development since the 1990s (along with political reform and the fight against corruption). Unlike the West, which has used corporate governance as a system for checks and balances, China has found this tool also timely to springboard their many private firms, namely start-ups and SMEs. China's economy has slowed down by 2017, forecast to grow at a mere 6.7% by the IMF.[13] Leveraging on private enterprises and entrepreneurism to spark the economy has been tried in many economies, but for China's socialist economy this is a unique challenge. Coupled with a huge and growing middle class which has often been the bedrock of entrepreneurial zeal, institutionalizing governance and ownership for private enterprises would seem sensible for China. We expect to see much more experimentation in this direction.

Another contributor of entrepreneurship is the rapidly rising number of those in the middle class, and this is particularly creating a critical mass. According to a McKinsey study, by the year 2022, China's middle-class ratio in urban areas will jump from a mere 4% in 2000 to over 76%.[14] China's middle class is around at 450 million, which is more than the population of the United States. By 2022, China's middle class is expected to grow to 550 million. Ironically, the American consumer was a driver of the global economy in previous decades. The new Chinese tourists,

---

13. Wong (2017, June 14).
14. Barton, Chen, & Jin, 2013.

made up mostly of China's middle class, are now the new driver of global economy. They bring a tremendous amount of spending power to retail markets worldwide and have pushed Hong Kong storefronts to their highest in the world by square footage.[15] The Chinese middle class is fast becoming a whole new generation of spenders.[16]

Leveraging on the energy of the SMEs and the middle class to spike the economy is not new, but unleashing start-ups, venture capital, and the whole mentality of co-working entrepreneurial spaces, outside ownership, and new listing platform like the N Board in Shanghai or the New Board in Hong Kong, do represent a concerted drive. We are noticing that past efforts to develop and refine corporate governance have been focused on SOEs, with the latest on mixing ownership structures that was announced in November 2013. In that measure, China would allow six large SOEs in a pilot program to attract private investment and improve corporate governance, under a so-called "mixed-ownership reform" and which was really a form of privatization.[17] The current and upcoming efforts appear to be about introducing stronger and more effective corporate governance into private enterprises.

Having studied some of the giants in the industry, we believe that China will begin to seed the start-ups and let loose a whole series of entrepreneurial measures in the next five years. We may see hybrids in preference shares, workers' shares, weighted voting shares, or maybe even shares that would be given only to innovators and inventors. Creating a more vibrant entrepreneurial ecosystem, fixing the shadow banking industry, and unlocking capital, deregulating onerous policies, and allowing exceptions for start-ups, and maybe even allowing more immigrants outside China but with entrepreneurial zeal to join the workforce would be possible areas of development.

There are many ways to develop and foster an economy, and these development measures have ranged from export-led to import substitution, to slash-and-burn techniques in agriculture that would free up laborers for a growing manufacturing base. But these have had limited success for developing economies. It would appear that one of the most interesting and evolving practices under experimentation in China is that of the catalytic power of corporate governance, in the sense of giving participating investors their due share in power, ownership, and control in the life of an organization. In other words, corporate governance is being used as a viable and supplementary method of economic development.

Over the next few years we should expect to see in China, especially in southern China's Shenzhen, coastal regions, and in smart cities in China, more experiments

---

15. Their visits saved Hong Kong during 1997, and tourist visits have now become a powerful negotiation for the Chinese government. It is interesting how the Chinese government has leveraged concessions from Taiwan and Japan in recent years.
16. Iskyan, 2016.
17. Developing Mixed Ownership Structures and Modern Enterprise Systems. Boston Consulting Group and the China Development Research Foundation. China Development Forum 2014, May 22–24, 2014. Beijing, China.

and policies to unleash the billions of start-ups and correspondingly ways to help make them grow into modern enterprises through more flexible and yet robust "unconventional" corporate governance practices[18] and architecture, including mixed ownership. Devolving authority of the SOEs to private investors is an attempt to meet this effort halfway, from the top down. The real challenge lies in designing new ownership and control structure for nascent organizations, from the bottom up, using perhaps a combination of Silicon Valley stock options, Hong Kong–style private equity models, with a bit of the old Hong Kong entrepreneurial "can-do" spirit, for example.

In the US, Finland, and Israel, where entrepreneurism has been strong, start-ups play an intricate and necessary role in their economic development. Silicon Valley, Tel Aviv, Helsinki, Austin, and other hubs of high-tech innovation have become synonymous with new economic growth, particularly in the New Digital Economy. (But even in the US, entrepreneurship is apparently on the decline. Start-up activities have slowed down, and according to a study at the Miller Center at the University of Virginia conducted in 2014, small businesses accounted for a staggering 60% of net job loss from 2007 to 2012.)[19] More importantly, the study also referenced how the middle class would lose from this, as many SMEs are in fact founded by those in the middle class. Such lessons, no doubt, will be studied very closely by the authorities in Beijing on how SMEs and start-ups are necessary for vibrant new growth.

Creating a vibrant entrepreneurial ecosystem has a good deal of parallels to the creation of smart cities. In China there are over 300 smart cities in development. We can begin to sense the direction of new policies in releasing entrepreneurship in helping to establish and sustain these new cities, or smart clusters. Ingredients for successful smart cities seem to be proximity, entrepreneurship, density, and diversity. All these ingredients are present in China's many smart cities, particularly in China's Silicon Valley, Shenzhen, and diversity more so if we bring in Hong Kong. Shenzhen, the birthplace of Tencent, Baidu, and many more start-ups, is loaded with the diversity of talents from throughout China, with proximity to various forms of capital in Hong Kong, is one location that is indeed worth monitoring. Interestingly, in Shenzhen we can see the three elements coming together quite nicely. What started as a town with 50,000 inhabitants has grown to house a population slightly larger than Hong Kong's own 7 million and now has GDP exceeding that of Hong Kong. Proximity to Hong Kong and the establishment of Qian Hai, just over the border of Hong Kong, will be a fascinating laboratory for the development

---

18. Unconventional corporate governance practice has been used to represent weight voting shares, for example. For a fuller description, see HKEx's new Concept Paper on the New Board, issued in June 2017. Retrieved August 30, 2017 from https://www.hkex.com.hk/eng/newsconsul/hkexnews/2017/170616news.htm; https://www.hkex.com.hk/eng/newsconsul/mktconsul/Documents/cp2017061.pdf.

19. Case and Fiorina, 2015.

of modern enterprise systems, including new corporate governance practices and architecture, in the world of the New Digital Economy.

The new "Xi" era of corporate governance

The year 2018 could prove to be a tipping point for years to come. The latest political and economic development could have pivotal implications for further changes to China's corporate governance system for SOEs, private companies, and listed firms. Xi Jinping's speeches at Davos in January 2017, later at the 19th Party Congress in October, and at Da Nang during the APEC Summit in November, reflected a China that is much more confident and assured. In essence, Xi spoke of building an inclusive society where more citizens can share in the riches of the society, opening and connecting with other parts of the world, encouraging innovation and experimentation with an aim towards growth, and equitable governance. The terms "innovation" and "development" were used profusely. Reading between the lines, we can sense this eagerness to experiment with governance at the corporate level.

The Party at the core

Xi's dominant influence in China after the 19th Congress was pivotal during the beginning of 2018. Some commentators even hinted that the party was trying to elevate his status to that of Mao and Deng.[20] Due to the removal of powerful figures like Zhou Yongkang, Sun Zhengcai, Guo Boxiong, Ling Jihua, and Xu Caihou, and the restructuring of a new power base, Xi's legacy and mark in the history of the Communist Party is now assured more than ever. A BBC study claimed that more than 170 ministers and deputy minister-level officials have been fired or purged, accused of corruption, misconduct, and violation of party discipline.[21] It would seem politically this tiger has started to pounce.

But party discipline isn't stopping at the individuals. It is now being extended into the boardrooms of domestic firms. Although earlier versions of the Company Law argued and stated the role of the party in an organization, the exact execution was vague and enforcement reportedly lax. That was before 2018. Earlier, the amended Company Law of 2013[22] cited the requirements that all companies (including a limited liability company or a joint-stock limited company) should establish an organization of the Chinese Communist Party to carry out activities of the party in the company and the company shall provide necessary conditions

---

20. Shambaugh, 2014.
21. Charting China's "great purge" under Xi (2017, October 23).
22. The Company Law was promulgated in 1993 and was amended three times, in 1999, 2006, and 2013. It was revised in 2013 for the third time on December 28, 2013, in accordance with the Decision on Amending Seven Laws Including the Marine Environment Protection Law of the People's Republic of China at the 6th Session of the Standing Committee of the 12th National People's Congress. Retrieved November 30, 2017 from http://www.fdi.org.cn/1800000121_39_4814_0_7.html.

for the activities of the Chinese Communist Party. (We touched on this earlier and gave some examples of how this practice had worked in some private companies.)

But starting 2018, the acceptance of a party influence inside all companies is looking to become a hard reality, and the core leadership role and influence of the Communist Party in corporate governance is to be unquestioned. The government recognizes the contributions of international corporate governance practices and standards but is mindful that corporate governance hasn't worked in all instances. Given China's unique cultural circumstances (euphemistically known as "Guoqing"), and socialism with Chinese characteristics, the party has specifically designed in its role in all such companies, at the board level. For state-owned domestic enterprises, the Party Committee is the leadership and political core of the business. For non-stated-owned listed companies,[23] their articles of association must in the future clearly outline and provide support for the activities of the party and to protect the legal rights of party members in their supervision within the company. Furthermore, to allow such interventions to be reviewed and understood by outsiders, the chair of CSRC reportedly had boldly accepted the invitation by OECD to join the international corporate governance development taskforce.[24]

A model of impermanence

Since 1978, experts from Hong Kong and OECD have helped to produce many sets of corporate governance guidelines in China. Inevitably, OECD drew on corporate governance practices in countries such as the US, the UK, and Germany. But these countries are democracies with independent judiciaries and a culture of business integrity. Individual accountability, transparency, and governance code have not been norms in China. The culture in China is one of collective and shared accountability. Opaqueness to outsiders has been the working norm for many SOEs. Although new governance codes and practices are being drafted, these practices, norms, and systems of corporate governance are all changing, each at its own pace and barely visible to outsiders.

Many writers have attempted to piece together a China economic development model and to a lesser extent, the China corporate governance model, with intent to make sense of this evolving complexity called China. Each writer paints a slightly different reality, and his or her wisdom has helped us better understand how rapidly China is changing. China is in fact changing extremely fast, and any "written" descriptions are at best temporal.

---

23. 刘士余主席在中国上市公司协会第二届会员代表大会上的致辞 [CSRC's Chairman Liu Shiyu's speech on meeting of the 2nd General Congress of China Association for Public Companies] (2017, April 8).
24. 证监会修订上市公司治理准则 进一步与国际标准接轨 [CSRC is amending the Guidelines for the Corporate Governance of Listed Companies and making it more in line with International standards] (2017, September 11).

Is there really a single Chinese model of corporate governance? We do not believe there is . . . yet. If it exists at all, it is very much an evolving working model, comprising many small models and whose interplay among the parts is literally changing the core. If it exists at all, any such a model would have to be grounded in its political and economic system. How the Chinese leadership had responded to the Washington Consensus[25] would be a good indication of this nuance.

The Washington Consensus focused on 10 points that would provide sustainable economic growth for any economy. This grand free market prescription was first raised by John Williamson in 1989 and endorsed by the IMF, World Bank, and the US Treasury Department. China, however, refused to believe that this was the only way. Then came 2008 and the Chinese saw and experienced the 2008 global financial crisis, underpinned by the best American model of corporate governance, in which giant and irresponsible American corporations nearly caused a global financial meltdown.[26] China continued to explore and experiment with its form of economic development along the line of a socialist economy with Chinese characteristics and believed substantial involvement in infrastructure and the public sector, an interventionist approach, could have a bigger return than could the free market.[27] By 2018, China had begun to assert these characteristics.

Paul Yip, an adviser to the former HKSAR government, saw this nuance this way (Yip, 2012). He believed that the Chinese Communist Party would never be so arrogant as to challenge the West by grandstanding its model of economic development or corporate governance. The Chinese would never say the Chinese model, if any, is the best model and everything else is subordinate to this.

Will there ever be such model? Perhaps. David Bell[28] suggested that there are three levels of governance in his China model. At the top of the pyramid where the party is in national control is meritocracy. In the middle where SOEs would be in enterprise control is experimentation. At the bottom where citizens would be in control is democracy. But most likely the Chinese authorities would be the last to admit this. In the past, the Chinese would learn, follow international standards, and adjust their local standards to fit. As innovation and new development began to take shape, led by China, the Chinese will probably be setting new standards based on their own constraints. If others want to play the game with the Chinese, they may have to play by Chinese rules. We believe this would also apply in the world of corporate governance. If foreign companies want to be established in China, they may have to invite party members onto their boards. Market rumors are hinting that, starting on January 1, 2021, the presence of party members may be a requirement.

---

25. Fischer (2018, February 9).
26. Stent, 2017.
27. Pettinger (2017, April 25).
28. Bell, 2015.

Is the Chinese framework of corporate governance working?

There are pockets of excellence particularly in large firms that are listed outside China. Some of the new non-SOEs like Alibaba and Tencent are pushing new and different standards in corporate governance, and so are a few SOEs. In the near future, probably by 2020, we should expect to see the inclusion of new committees such as the humanities and ethics committees in high-tech firms, purposely set up to ameliorate the excesses of AI, as not all technologies are beneficial to human-kind. Smaller family-run and independent businesses are progressing, but the sheer volume, broad diversity, old practices, and traditional business culture have damp-ened their pace of reform. Directors may include a robot with AI but whose role is only to provide suggestions and not for decision-making.

The Chinese are experimenting

The Chinese are experimenting. In their search, they have found new combinations of governance mechanics that seem to work better given their culture, their insti-tutions, and their timetable. Some of their inputs are different. Their processes of governance are not exactly the same. But for a few, we are beginning to see traces of the outputs of effective governance: higher sustained profit, sustainable growth, fair and open treatment to shareholders and workers, and mindful of their environment and their contribution to the society. We are beginning to see large Chinese firms reinvigorating their business model and repositioning to higher positions on the Fortune 500.[29] Increasingly, how the West has defined certain quality and mechanics of good corporate governance does not seem to apply consistently in China. Asians are generally much more positive and seem to understand how to find those hidden gems others would overlook. Many who are investing in companies in China are mindful of the limitations and potentials of these companies, and some of these investors are doing well. But for every China investor there are thousands more who have not invested. In fact, few have invested in China's leading domestic companies, mainly because these companies are difficult to fathom and understand. Thousands more investors have yet to invest, suspicious of the governance systems that Chinese companies have installed and the effectiveness of the local judiciary.

Some final thoughts

Undoubtedly, corporate governance in China is developing distinctive Chinese characteristics, reflecting China's unique economic, political, and cultural situation. The next phase may well see the influence of corporate governance with a Chinese face on the rest of the world.

---

29. Fuller, 2016.

In due course there may be calls for company law to be amended to maintain the state's overall command of the economy and political power, while facilitating markets, innovation, economic growth, and the acquisition of personal wealth. This would certainly be Communism with a Chinese face.

The Western world is still relying on a model of the joint-stock limited liability company that is, essentially, a nineteenth-century idea. China has the opportunity to develop a model of corporate entities that is based on twenty-first-century ideas and needs.

At the end of the day, corporate governance in China needs to contribute to a China that is prosperous, stable, and secure. There is still quite a road to travel.

References

Barton, D., Chen, Y., & Jin, A. (2013). Mapping China's middle class. *McKinsey Quarterly*. Retrieved March 30, 2017 from https://www.mckinsey.com/industries/retail/our-insights/mapping-chinas-middle-class.

Bell, D. (2015). *The China model, political meritocracy and the limits of democracy*. Princeton, NJ: Princeton University Press.

Case, Steve and Fiorina, Carly (2015). *Can start-ups save the American Dream?* Milstein Commission on Entrepreneurship and Middle-Class Jobs. Commission Co-Chairs, Steve Case and Carly Fiorina. January 2015, University of Virginia.

Chang, G. (2001). *The coming collapse of China*. New York. Random House.

Charting China's "great purge" under Xi. (2017, October 23). *BBC News*. Retrieved November 30, 2017 from http://www.bbc.com/news/world-asia-china-41670162.

Chen, J. (2004). *Corporate governance in China*. London. Routledge.

China 2030: Building a modern, harmonious, and creative society. [PDF version]. (2013). The World Bank and the Development Research Center of the State Council of the People's Republic of China. Retrieved November 30, 2017 from https://www.worldbank.org/content/dam/Worldbank/document/China-2030-complete.pdf.

Chinese companies' weak record on foreign deals (2017, June 8). *The Economist*. Retrieved August 30, 2017 from https://www.economist.com/news/business/21723164-overpaying-commodities-and-trophy-assets-has-become-norm-chinese-companies-weak-record.

证监会修订上市公司治理准则 进一步与国际标准接轨 [CSRC is amending the Guidelines for the Corporate Governance of Listed Companies and making it more in line with International standards]. (2017, September 11). *Sina*. Retrieved November 30, 2017 from http://news.sina.com.cn/o/2017-09-11/doc-ifykuftz6231839.shtml.

Daugherty, P. (2017, July 30). How China became an AI leader? *World Economic Forum*. Retrieved August 1, 2017 from https://www.weforum.org/agenda/2017/06/how-china-became-ai-leader/.

Dininni, J. (2017, February 22). Management theory of William Ouchi. Retrieved August 30, 2017 from https://www.business.com/articles/management-theory-of-william-ouchi/.

Developing Mixed Ownership Structures and Modern Enterprise Systems. Boston Consulting Group and the China Development Research Foundation. China Development Forum 2014, May 22–24, 2014. Beijing, China.

Fischer, S. (2018, February 9). The Washington Consensus. *Peterson Institute for International Economics*. Retrieved November 30, 2017 from https://piie.com/publications/chapters_preview/6628/02iie6628.pdf

Fuller, D. B. (2016). *Paper tigers, hidden dragons: Firms and the political economy of China's technological development*. Oxford: Oxford University Press.

Heilmann, S. (Ed.) (2017). *China's political system*. Lanham, MD: Rowman & Littlefield.

Huang, Y. (2017, September 14). What the west gets wrong about China's economy: debt, trade, and corruption. Retrieved November 30, 2017 from http://carnegieendowment.org/2017/09/14/what-west-gets-wrong-about-china-s-economy-pub-73109.

Ho, S. S. M., & Li, A. Y. S. (2010). *Corporate governance and institutions in China*. Hong Kong: Infolink Publishing Limited.

Iskyan, K. (2016). China's middle class is exploding. *Business Insider*. Retrieved March 30, 2018 from http://www.businessinsider.com/chinas-middle-class-is-exploding-2016-8.

Martin, J. (2009). *When China rules the world: The rise of the Middle Kingdom and the end of the western world*. Eastbourne: Gardners Books.

Lardy, N. R. (2014). *Markets over Mao: The rise of private business in China*. Washington, DC: Peterson Institute for International Economics.

Li, W. (2008). *Corporate governance in China: Research and evaluation*. Singapore: Wiley.

刘士余主席在中国上市公司协会第二届会员代表大会上的致辞 [CSRC's Chairman Liu Shiyu's speech on meeting of the 2nd General Congress of China Association for Public Companies]. (2017, April 8) *CSRC*. Retrieved November 30, 2017 from http://www.csrc.gov.cn/pub/newsite/zjhxwfb/xwdd/201704/t20170408_314862.html. See also 国有企业深化改革应注重政治治理 [To deepen the reform, SOEs should emphasize political governance]. (2017, July 1). CSRC. Retrieved November 30, 2017 from http://theory.people.com.cn/n1/2017/0712/c40531-29398523.html.

Nakamura, M. (Ed.). (2008). *Changing corporate governance practices in China and Japan: Adaptations of Anglo-American practices*. New York: Palgrave Macmillan.

Needham, J. (1954). *Science and civilization in China*. Cambridge: Cambridge University Press.

Pettinger, T. (2017, April 25). Washington consensus—definition and criticism. Retrieved November 30, 2017 from https://www.economicshelp.org/blog/7387/economics/washington-consensus-definition-and-criticism/.

Pisacane, G. (2017). *Corporate governance in China: The structure and management of foreign-invested enterprises under Chinese law*. Shanghai: Springer Verlag.

Saich, T. (2015). *Governance and politics of China*. Basingstoke, Hants: Palgrave.

Schwab, K. (2016). *The fourth industrial revolution*. London. UK: Penguin Random House.

Shambaugh, D. (2014). *China goes global: The partial power*. Oxford: Oxford University Press.

Shambaugh, D. (2017). Reform or repression: What will the next five years bring for China? *South China Morning Post*. Retrieved November 30, 2017 from http://www.scmp.com/comment/insight-opinion/article/2115025/under-xi-jinping-return-one-man-rule-china.

Stent, J. (2017). *China's banking transformation: The untold story*. New York: Oxford University Press.

Weinland, D. Massoudi, A., & Fontanella-Khan, J. (2017, July 30). HNA's buying spree surpasses $40bn with CWT deal. *Financial Times*. Retrieved August 30, 2017 from https://www.ft.com/content/fbd65e7a-1d35-11e7-a454-ab04428977f9.

Wong, S. L. (2017, June 14). IMF raises China 2017 growth forecast again, partly due to 'policy support'. *Business News*. Retrieved November 30, 2017 from http://www.reuters.com/article/us-china-economy-imf-idUSKBN1950KR.

Zhu, L. T., Fei, J., & Cheng, L. (2017, July 21). Investor activism on rise in China. *Caixin*. Retrieved August 1, 2017 from http://www.caixinglobal.com/2017-07-21/101120151.html.

Case study

Yum China Holdings

Kentucky-based Yum Brands Inc., owners of KFC (Kentucky Fried Chicken, Taco Bell, and Pizza Hut brands), opened its first restaurant in China in 1987. By the time the Chinese operations were spun off, on October 31, 2016, to Yum China Holdings Inc., it had become China's largest restaurant chain. Yum China owned the franchise for Pizza Hut in China with more than 1,500 restaurants in over 400 cities, and the franchise for KFC, with over 5,000 outlets in nearly 1,000 towns and cities. Taco Bell operations were also starting.

Primavera Capital Group, a China-based global investment firm, made a strategic investment in Yum China and the company was then listed on the NYSE (YUMC) in November 2016. Yum China Holdings Inc. is registered in Louisville, Kentucky with headquarters in Shanghai.

The board of directors of Yum China Holdings[30]

The board has nine members, seven of them independent according to the company.

Fred Hu is chairman and founder of Primavera Capital Group, a China-based global investment firm ("Dr. Hu has served as chairman of Primavera since its inception in 2010. Prior to Primavera, Dr. Hu served in various roles at Goldman Sachs.")

Peter A. Bassi served as president then chairman of Yum! International Restaurants. Prior to this, Mr. Bassi spent 25 years in a wide range of financial and general management positions at PepsiCo, Inc., Pepsi-Cola International, Pizza Hut (US and International), Frito-Lay, and Taco Bell.

Christian L. Campbell is currently owner of Christian L. Campbell Consulting LLC, specializing in global corporate governance and compliance. Mr. Campbell previously served as senior vice president, general counsel and secretary of Yum Brands from its formation in 1997 until his retirement in February 2016.

---

30. Source: Yum China press release.

Ed Chan Yiu-Cheong is currently a vice chairman of Charoen Pokphand Group Company Limited and has been an executive director and vice chairman of CP Lotus Corporation since April 2012. Mr. Chan was regional director of North Asia of the Dairy Farm Group.

Edouard Ettedgui currently serves as the non-executive chairman of Alliance Française, Hong Kong. Mr. Ettedgui also currently serves as a non-executive director of Mandarin Oriental International Limited, the company for which he was the group chief executive. Prior to that, Mr. Ettedgui was the chief financial officer for Dairy Farm International Holdings.

Louis T. Hsieh currently serves as a senior adviser to the chief executive officer and as a director of New Oriental Education & Technology Group.

Jonathan S. Linen is a member of the board of directors of Yum! Brands, a position he has held since 2005, and of Modern Bank, N.A. Mr. Linen is advisor to the chairman of American Express Company after serving as the vice chairman of American Express Company. Mr. Linen also served on the board of The Intercontinental Hotels Group.

Micky Pant is the chief executive officer of Yum China. Mr. Pant has served as CEO of Yum! Restaurants China since August 2015. Over the past decade, Mr. Pant has held a number of leadership positions at Yum! Brands, including CEO of the KFC Division, chief executive officer of Yum! Restaurants International, and president of Global Branding for Yum! Brands, and president of Taco Bell International.

Zili Shao has served as co-chairman of King & Wood Mallesons—China. Mr. Shao held various positions with JPMorgan Chase & Co., including chairman and CEO of JPMorgan China, vice chairman of JPMorgan Asia Pacific, and chairman of JPMorgan Chase Bank (China) Company Limited.

Yum China announces its chairman and CEO succession plans

On October 5, 2017, Yum China announced that its CEO, Mr. Micky Pant, would become vice chairman of the board and senior advisor to the company on March 1, 2018. Ms. Joey Wat, who currently serves as president and chief operating officer, would succeed Mr. Pant as CEO.

The company explained that Mr. Pant had served as CEO and a member of the board of Yum China since its spin-off from Yum! Brands, Inc. and, prior to that, he served as CEO of Yum! Restaurants (China), when it was a division of Yum Brands Inc.

"We are exceptionally grateful to Micky for leading the company through its spin-off and building a solid foundation as an independent company," said Dr. Fred Hu, chairman of the board of Yum China Holdings. "We thank Micky for his many significant contributions and are pleased that he will be vice chairman of the board and will also continue to serve the company as its senior advisor in order to ensure a seamless transition to Joey."

"Joey is an extraordinarily talented executive and the ideal leader to become our next CEO," Dr. Hu continued. "Joey has a strong track record of achieving results, and with her unique ability to translate vision and strategy into future world-class operations, I have no doubt that the Yum China business will continue to grow under her strong leadership.

Ms. Wat spent seven years in management consulting, including time with McKinsey & Company's Hong Kong office. From 2004 to 2014, she served in both management and strategy positions in the Hong Kong–based Hutchison Whampoa group, including time as managing director of their UK company, which operates the pharmacy chain Superdrug. Ms. Wat joined Yum China in September 2014, first as president of KFC China and then as CEO of KFC China in August 2015. She has been the president and chief operating officer of Yum China since February 2017 and was appointed as a member of the board in July 2017.

Yum China strategy

The company outlines its view of its potential on its website:

> Our brands are integrated into popular culture and consumers' daily lives.
>
> We are dedicated to serving our customers' evolving needs by enhancing the in-store experience, improving mobile connectivity, introducing innovative new products, and constantly delivering value. We also remain focused on driving shareholder value by growing sales and profits across our portfolio of brands through increased brand relevance, new store development and enhanced unit economics. With a rapidly growing consumer class and increasing urbanization, Yum China is well positioned for long-term growth.

Questions for discussion

1. What are the strengths and weaknesses of the Yum China board?

2. Why do you think Yum China announced its succession plans well in advance?

3. Should all listed companies be required to declare their chairperson and CEO succession plans?

Appendix I
Acquiring and Partnering with Local Entities

Gregg Li

Introduction

As China embarks on its path to the modernization of SOEs, one of the best means is to leverage on the expertise of foreign companies. By promoting foreign companies to join hands in the development of the corporate governance of local entities, China can effectively quicken the pace of reform. In the banking sector, where China has one of the largest non-performing loans in the world, finding clean assets is extremely difficult. Although the managerial and governance aspects of Chinese banks have changed considerably over the past two decades, and mostly in the positive direction, one has to understand how to navigate in this complex banking world.[1] In this extended case study, we consider a foreign banker's experiences and his stories in acquiring or just renting a local Chinese banking entity.

To buy or to rent

Mainland China is an increasingly important market, and many companies from abroad do not just want to be in China for a few weekends to establish a toehold. They want to stay and build a business empire. Eventually, whether to purchase through acquisition or simply to rent through partnering is a board-level decision that needs to be made.

The banking system in China has been undergoing rapid change leading up to and after the global financial crisis of 2008. Foreign expertise was needed to help strengthen the banking system. The government at the same time was recapitalizing the banks, listing some of them through IPOs, selling shares to foreign entities, and reportedly providing high interest rate spreads.[2] The CBRC has been encouraging local banks to partner with foreign entities, with the aim of improving the skills and expertise of the local banks. By 2008, of the 136 Chinese city commercial banks,

---

1. Stent, 2017.
2. Zhang, 2014, p. 122.

which collectively would form the third pillar in the Chinese banking system and were mostly owned by the state, 13 had foreign shareholders.[3]

For a CEO who is in China and has been tasked with growing a banking business through rapid acquisition, this is a hard question, hard because that CEO must also live with the consequences of this acquisition decision. The CEO will be put into a position to execute some tough missions through these new parties that have been spliced into the corporation. No CEO wants a B team. The CEOs of many acquirers would have to face tough questions from their boards, shareholders, and other stakeholders if their companies had minimal or, even worse, no gain in further business in the Middle Kingdom. The authors, however, would suggest they ask themselves first whether they are ready for China according to their understanding of local corporate governance practices and their expectations into splicing these homegrown practices into a completely different set of corporate governance architectures in the host company.

All markets are different and come with their unique set of challenges. Corporate governance is one of those things that in mainland China is not the same as in Western developed economies such as the US or the UK. It is our belief that the required depth of understanding would be largely determined by the closeness and structure of the relationship that one would get into. Each acquisition is an adventure because there's so much to learn on both sides. Each side requires a deep level of trust and mutual respect, so much so that both sides will have to stand ready to agree to disagree on certain nonnegotiable elements.

In this appendix, we have Mr. Richard Leung, a seasoned senior banker who has been tasked with building a stronger banking business in China, through acquisition. Richard started commuting to mainland China for business in 1989, when he was with Citibank N.A. in Hong Kong, and he lived in the Mainland during 2003 and 2011, when he was with UBS Wealth Management and DBS Bank as their China CEO. He has since retired and sits on several boards in the industry.

Acquisition of local entities

Richard was in charge of both organic and inorganic growth of the DBS Group's franchise in China, and he had researched extensively to identify targets, which are local financial institutions—including banks, securities companies, and asset management companies—for acquisition. The target company's corporate governance was one of areas that they scrutinized as an indicator of its structural integrity. The acquisition team attempted to understand the target's shareholders and background, board composition, and the membership of its various subcommittees, particularly the respective chairpersons, the frequency and management of the board and subcommittee meetings, particularly in relation to related-party transactions,

---

3. Tan, 2015, p. 99.

its goal-setting and monitoring processes, and the process of the appointment of senior management. Such information would shed light not only on the target's corporate governance practices but also its business strengths and weaknesses. Even more importantly, it would help the acquiring CEO to anticipate the future challenges that he or she would likely face when the acquisition materialized. This process was absolutely necessary, since the information would help determine how much play and flex there would be to structure into the new entity, before and after the acquisition.[4]

However, the above information was usually sketchy at best in public records in mainland China, and even reputable consultancy firms could not offer much help. When the acquirer's interest in certain targets came to light, interestingly some less known or unknown intermediaries or consultants or friends would appear claiming to have insight or even an inside track to help conclude the deal. As a general practice, the acquirer should always exercise utmost caution about these consultants' capability, legitimacy, representativeness, and compliance of such actions, not to mention a possibly hidden agenda or vested interest of his or her own or others whom he or she represents. In China, we just work on the assumption that everyone is connected, and we do not harbor any illusion that independence is a given. Such uninvited consultants are not unexpected even in the more developed Western markets, but we seem to see more of them in mainland China. In China, we have to remember that certain sensitive decisions must be sanctioned by the party and party members do not have nametags. Years back, the PLA didn't have visible ranks, and the only way one could tell who was more senior was by the number of pens in his pocket. The culture's consensual decision-making style (and lack of transparency) makes it difficult for rapid decision-making. It wasn't so long ago that any discussion of interest rate was tantamount to treason, as the authorities were nervous about interest rate manipulation by foreign entities.

While a firm rejection would be an easy decision to make and deliver if we were not comfortable with their capability or their ethical standard, it could be challenging if these operators represented a hidden agenda or vested interest of certain key stakeholders. Since these unsolicited consultants were always very eager to impress us, they would volunteer information willingly . . . until they got too eager and the buyer would have to show them the door. They usually would give us some ideas about the preference of certain stakeholder(s) in order to skew the acquisition. We, as buyers, without exception, would turn down all such offers but in a courteous way, hoping not to make enemies with the hidden stakeholders. If the stakeholders' preference happened to be in line with our thought, we would indicate, and have, on a few occasions indicated, it as one of the options under our consideration (after due consideration of possible outcome with such disclosure). We would think that our rejection should not be a big surprise to most, if not all, of these consultants,

4.   Fernandez & Underwood 2006.

because DBS Bank was known to uphold a very high standard in compliance and ethics.

The long list of required information about corporate governance mentioned in earlier paragraphs guided us through the process of acquisition. We tried to fill in the answers to each question as we went through desktop research, market research, dialogue with stakeholders, letters of understanding, due diligence, negotiation, and final assessment before making an offer. We would always ask ourselves about the target's corporate governance practices before we decided whether to advance to the next step.

Because information is often unstructured and opaque, getting at useful information is an art. Time and patience are key. Here, we would like to highlight that we had spent a tremendous amount of time and effort in having both official and casual dialogues with influential shareholders, board members, and key executives, individually and in a group. **While corporate governance might be well written on paper, it was the mindset and practices that determined its impact.** We needed to know how corporate governance was being practiced. Therefore, we learned to be excellent listeners, for both the trials of tribulation and the agonies of defeat. We listened closely as they aired their grievances and frustrations or when they shared their success stories and happiness at work.

The story that was told so far is not starkly different from those in the Western developed markets except for the prevalence and intensity of undesirable acts. Richard's experience told him that it was advisable not to assume best practices in corporate governance in mainland China were the norm. Every assertion needs to be investigated and confirmed.

Acquisition of SOEs

Distinct differences would be apparent when the target was an SOE, because there would be additional layers of stakeholders and their implications in the picture. An SOE would in many cases have other SOEs as its shareholders. Acquiring a behemoth like an SOE is a complicated undertaking. It is likely the SOE is already inefficient, having taken on heavy debt, and being staffed with unmotivated and insufficiently skilled employees. But somehow they have some special advantage such as market access, licenses, or customer bases that only through an acquisition would it be possible to gain.

First of all, each SOE, except the insignificant ones, would usually have a party secretary and a party committee, responsible for implementing the guidelines and policies handed down from their respective layer of government, central, provincial, or city. Major decisions like acquisition would need to be cleared and endorsed by them before their respective boards would make a decision. Therefore, they were among the most important stakeholders that we needed to understand, communicate with, and convince about our acquisition proposition. However, the more outside people know about any acquisition, the more complex the negotiation would become.

It was therefore very crucial to identify, and work with, those board and management members of the target SOE who were also members of the party committee. Knowing who these individuals are and understanding the power they represent requires special attention. They were the ones who could influence, if not determine or undermine, the acquisition at the highest hierarchy of the corporate structure of the target. They were probably the most reliable source of information when the deal was in progress, but subtly non-visible.

Knowing who the key decision-makers are is critical, but not often is this possible. According to Gary Yin, a partner with RPC Partners, which is a law firm that deals mainly with M&A with JVs, recalled that for many SOEs, a few bosses would call the final shots. Given the Chinese hierarchical system of command in many of these SOEs, the management and governance system in place might mostly be for show. Shared accountability and command is not and should not be a common expectation. The top power can bypass, and have bypassed, rules or procedures. The advantage is that a final decision can be quick, but the hidden disadvantage of such cultural rigidity would also hamper how much the top power is willing to create a new, shared power structure with a new board and board committees. The new entity cannot and should not be for show. To prevent this level of misunderstanding, Gary recommended that the acquirer spend time and effort to explain to the Chinese side the purpose and the functionality of the new board. To his surprise, it is rare the Chinese side fully appreciates or understands the art and complexity that foreign corporate governance practices would impose.

Additionally, the key personnel, including but not limited to the party secretary, board chairperson, and senior management, of the target SOE are government officials, and therefore they could be transferred out of the SOE at the government's discretion. Therefore, the continuity of key personnel, the succession issue, before and after acquisition, required particular attention and sensitivity.

Last but not least, the local government and central regulatory agencies could be key influencers or deal breakers. Generally speaking, the more significant the target, in view of size, industry, and government shareholding, the more important a role these regulatory agencies would play.

Richard's team, in one instance, had our eyes on an SOE bank in one of the southern provinces, which was to be sold to another local conglomerate in a private deal. We had a one-hour appointment with the provincial governor to express our interest and to present an idea to secure better terms for the province by inviting us and other selected parties to bid for the bank. The governor seemingly had been paying little attention to the target bank and was reluctant to intervene during the first half hour but finally agreed to our suggestion before our meeting concluded. With his endorsement, we immediately flew to Beijing to report the case to the central CBRC and requested it to instruct the provincial CBRC to facilitate the transaction. With the support of the regulatory agency and local government, the target bank was made available as we proposed.

Partnering with local partners

One of the authors was closely engaged with two Sino-foreign JV companies in mainland China with reasonably good results despite working through a very different structure of partnership. The foreign financial institutions had a minority equity stake in both cases due to regulations, but one had complete management control while the other did not, all for different good reasons. Their satisfactory outcome was due to the good mutual understanding among partners before the JV, which led to appropriate corporate governance structure in line with their future business development.

In one of the cases, the foreign minority shareholder assumed full responsibility of staffing and management, because the newly created JV would expand into business lines new to the local partners while playing to the expertise of the foreign one. The company shredded its SOE status so that the new JV would have its board but not the party committee, to facilitate the transfer of technical know-how and management knowledge.

The foreign partner also paid special attention and devoted enough resources to put in place proper corporate governance in the new JV, local shareholders being represented on the board. They preached best practices in corporate governance before the JV, and they persistently practiced it from day one of the partnership when the local shareholders were very open to changes. Establishing a high standard and conveying that expectation is an important practice.

In the other case, the JV remained an SOE entity with the foreign minority shareholder represented on the board. The foreign partner had the right to appoint selected senior positions, including finance, to make itself comfortable even though far short of full management control. The JV would continue to grow and earn a significant portion of its income from established businesses, while new business initiatives were developed as subsidiaries with the foreign partner in the driver's seat in management to facilitate transfer of expertise.

In our interview with Gary, he cautioned anyone not to go into any JV discussion without first understanding the cultural expectations over when and how to shape, and not control, a potential new business. He cited a case between a potential German acquirer and a mainland firm. The courtship took several years and finally when both sides felt a purchase could consummate the deal, the deal suddenly fell apart. The German side had demanded itemized entertainment expenses, which from all angles would represent a form of effective and meaningful internal control and oversight. But the Chinese side refused, as such a level of micro-management would put both sides at risk, they claimed. The Chinese side agreed to deliver the annual profit targets but disagreed on the high level of scrutiny to be paid over entertainment expenses. Obviously, had both sides had known about the practice of flex in the allowance of entertainment expenses that had been pervasive in some areas at the outset, both sides would have installed other elements to compensate. The smart acquirer should simply have demanded installing its own CFO and allowing the CFO to find ways to control potential abuses.

References

Fernandez, J. A., & Underwood, L. (2006). *China CEO: Voices of experience from 20 international business leaders.* Singapore: Wiley (Asia).

Stent, J. (2017). *China's banking transformation: The untold story.* New York: Oxford University Press.

Tan, M. (2015). *Corporate governance and banking in China.* London: Routledge.

Zhang, J. (2014). *Party man, company man: Is China's state capitalism doomed?* Honolulu, HI: Enrich Professional Publishing, Inc.

Appendix II

The Case of the MMMP Saudi Rail Project

Building Railroads along the Belt and Road

Gregg Li

This case has been pieced together from open websites, interviews with those involved, expert consultants and engineers familiar with the trade, and from newspaper clippings. The context is based on real history, but names have been purposely disguised, and if given at all, have been changed. In addition, in each of the short events described and the details noted, certain roles and positions have been duly adjusted. Any resemblance to persons living or dead resulting from changes to names or identifying details is entirely coincidental and unintentional.

Background

As China embarks on its grand Belt and Road Initiative, some of the first types of projects that will be put into place will be railroad and subway projects. These projects will link China with over 60 countries to the west of China. These massive infrastructural projects typically would involve multiple stakeholders, possibly the set-up of JV partnerships, and the coming together of investors, lenders, sponsors, regulators, and other professionals from around the world.

Building this particular railroad was a national priority for Saudi Arabia. President Hu Jintao and King Abdullah of Saudi Arabia had agreed to build this railroad and signed an agreement on February 10, 2009,[1] when the Chinese president visited. President Xi subsequently visited in January of 2016, under the banner of the Belt and Road Initiative in the Chinese news. Both countries as sponsors wanted this project to succeed.

But new construction projects are extremely risky, and in this case, once stations are completed, the train must run and the stations must be operational for only seven days, once a year. Idleness and non-use became an engineering challenge as well. Risk management, mandated reviews, frequent audits, and internal control

---

1. See "KSA Branch of China Railway Construction Corporation Limited" http://www.saudi-cocc.net/c35294/w225814.asp.

are critical at every stage of the project, but most importantly, a proper governance framework must be designed first and put in place, before any other action can begin. To deliver this project requires the coordination and management of many stakeholders, each coming with their own expectations and standards of corporate governance. At the core, how to work around the mismatch of corporate governance arrangements among the various stakeholders that within two national entities and economies is the backdrop of this story.

The rail industry is complicated enough where governance of the rail sector in the kingdom comprises multiple stakeholders such as the Ministry of Transport, the Ministry of Urban and Rural Affairs, the Saudi Electricity Company, the Public Investment Fund, the Saudi Railway Organization, and Saudi Railway companies. These are just the Saudi side of the story. This scenario created interesting and unique dynamics, given the context and the need for control by multiple stakeholders with varying levels of governance arrangements. To simplify the arrangement, the corporate governance of the new rail entity is essentially handed over to the manager as much as possible, with the Saudi owners worrying about the delivery of the new entity in the distant future.

In developing countries where the court and legal system are not as sophisticated or well developed, with corresponding company governance infrastructure that is incomplete (such as the availability of independent auditors), or where the project is so remote that key owners and developers would have to rely mostly on remote communication, responsibility must be designed or delegated as early as possible to a remote board of directors.[2] In fact, where the owners are less relevant during the initial building stages (except to ensure the availability of funds), much of the roles, power, and decision-making would need to be delegated to and would rest on a newly formed project governance team. To do this, it is typical to create a new management company with a new board of directors. Unless there is a clear dispute that needs the key shareholders to arbitrate at a shareholders' meeting, this remote board or project governance team in effect, runs the business. The work of governance for this story would be undertaken by the project management team which is to be called the Project Management Office (PMO).

Backdrop of corporate governance in Saudi Arabia

Corporate governance is a relatively new concept in Saudi Arabia, and given the political sensitivity of such visible projects like the building of subway and rail, the government would rather delegate any corporate governance requirements to some party, as much as possible, and use a contractual relationship to bind the delivery of the project. Like everyone else, Saudi Arabia was hit by the 2008 global financial

---

2. This is a fascinating project and how power is shared and risk managed through this governance arrangement would probably be replicated for future infrastructural projects along the Belt and Road.

crisis, and as a result, the government had introduced a barrage of corporate governance measures and regulations, many of which were still untested[3] and compliance was lax. Furthermore, Saudi Arabia is an Islamic law jurisdiction that generally enforces the Hanbali School of Jurisprudence. This means that any transaction involving usury or excessive risk will not be enforced by the court.[4] This means lenders that normally would provide the bulk of financing for such projects would only play a minority part. Even with insurance in place, damages cannot be claimed for indirect or consequential losses or any losses that are uncertain.

For some projects, the lenders acting as sponsors could provide the majority of the funds. These funders would probably be the World Bank, Asian Development Bank, the European Bank for Reconstruction and Development, or the Asian Infrastructural and Investment Bank. These lenders have the rights and power to replace the PMO or the board of directors. In some cases, there is a clause on limited recourse, and one party cannot go to the sponsor for extra money. This means the quality of the contract is critical to how power is actually shared.

Introduction to the governance arrangement

The new company to be formed by the winning bidder can be one of three types: a JV, a JV whose real work is the steering committee, and a JV purely for reporting purposes. The last one is to provide a mechanism to report to the major shareholders, since only shareholders should have privileged information. For this particular case, a JV steering committee was set up, whose steering committee is the PMO. The chair is the project director.

Under this steering committee, which effectively is the PMO, several committees could be set up. The first is for procurement purchases, as there are thousands of items to purchase. The second is for arbitration, since there will be claims and disagreement between the PMO and its suppliers. The third is probably the audit committee, but this committee would report into the client (in this case, the kingdom) and not to the PMO. For this project, the client or the owner requested his performance auditor be involved. Hence, hired at the owner's expense, an extra engineer was brought in to assess technical competency. This technical engineer would report directly to the owners.

For major projects such as this one, typically a BOT arrangement is used. BOT stands for build, operate, and transfer (of ownership back to the original owner). BOT projects are usually 20 to 30 years in length, and the owner would get the project back 20 or 30 years hence, after depreciation and refurbishment. For projects such as the MMMP, BOT would not work, since a faster turnaround was needed.

---

3. Alkahtani, A. W. (2016). Corporate governance standards in Saudi financial sector: Achievements and challenges. *International Journal of Business and Social Science, 7*(12), 124–136.
4. Husein, A. T. (2013, July 1). Construction and Projects in Saudi Arabia: An Overview. Retrieved May 1, 2018 from https://www.dentons.com/~/media/PDFs/Insights/2013/September/Saudi%20Arabiapdf.pdf.

Thus, an arrangement similar to BOT was more applicable, whereby the transfer to the owner was just three years, thereby eliminating the need for refurbishment. This arrangement used the EPC arrangement.[5]

Introduction to the MMMP case

This case is about the project governance of the Al Mashaaer Al Mugaddassah Metro (MMMP) Southern Line in Saudi Arabia.[6] Project governance here means effectively the development and operation of a governance structure to manage decisions and conflicts, allowing shareholders to apply, delegate, and dismiss controls within a preset governance arrangement. This arrangement was chosen in order to deliver the project on extremely tight timeframe, within budget, and at an agreeable level of quality. The output of the governance arrangement is just that: to deliver a working platform before the next Hajj in November 2010.

To build this railway in Saudi Arabia, starting in February 2009, and finishing within three years, required the participation of a number of parties, including:

- The China Railway Construction Corp (CRCC), an SOE and one of the largest contractors in China. They pitched and won the rights to exercise this EPC contract (effectively the EPC agent and main contractor);
- Changchun Railway Vehicles (CRRC), which provided the vehicle;
- The Kingdom of Saudi Arabia, the Ministry of Municipal and Rural Affairs, (effectively, the owner, client, and one of the sponsors);
- Thales, a multinational company that provided the signaling and automatic train control systems;
- Siemens, a multinational company, which provided the power, overhead catenary, and communication systems;
- Systra, the civil design consultant, that was responsible for the design of the civil engineering works;
- Atkins, the rail systems design consultant, that was responsible for preliminary design, specification, tender review, design approval, testing, and commissioning of all the rail M&E (mechanical and electrical) systems; and
- Various contractors and skilled workers from around the region, reportedly and according to official accounts, over 8,000 skilled and unskilled workers and over 5,000 engineers from a multitude of Chinese and foreign companies. According to the EPC office website, a number of Chinese parties were

---

5. EPC stands for Engineering Procurement and Construction, and the contract falls under the International Federation of Consulting Engineers (FIDIC) system. The EPC party is held responsible for all the activities from design, procurement, construction, to commissioning and handover to the owner. FIDIC issues standard forms of contracts.
6. Al Mashaaer Al Mugaddassah Metro Project, Saudi Arabia (2018, February). Retrieved May 1, 2018 from http://www.railway-technology.com/projects/al-mashaaer-al-mugad/

involved and were thrown in to help with the tight timeframe. These came from their respective Saudi divisions and from China, which included:

* Al Bokhari Shipping Trading
* Beijing Jangho Curtain Wall Company
* Changsha Construction Engineering Group
* China National Chemical Engineering
* China National Electronics Imp. and Exp. Corp.
* China North Industries Corporation, or NORINCO
* China Petroleum
* Jiangsu Huayi Decorate Engineering
* Sinopec
* Xuzhou Construction Machinery Group
* Various CRCC subsidiaries such as CCECC,[7] CR11 (e.g., China Rail Factory 11), CR12, CR14, CR15, CR16, CR17, CR18, CR19, and CR22

This line would have one of the highest capacities in the world but would operate just seven days out of a year. More than 3.5 million people would be transported on this line annually. This rail, with a length of 17.67 km, is mainly used as an exclusive shuttle train for Islamic pilgrims to Mecca during the Hajj. This particular line was actually partially operational by mid-November 2010 and had taken just 22 months to build. The project involved building the rail above the ground, creating nine stations and one depot along an 18-km stretch of barren land. Rolling on the rail will be multiple trains, each train consisting of a 12-car unit.

The project, sponsors, and governance architecture

Based on the best available information, the governance arrangement was based on FIDIC Conditions of Contract, and the model was EPC plus a three-year initial operation after commissioning. The contract was signed between the Kingdom of Saudi Arabia through their Ministry of Municipal of Urban and Rural Affairs and for the Chinese ministry through the CRCC.[8] The kingdom and the Chinese government were the "sponsors." The Chinese side, CRCC, won the project through a tendering exercise and was given the mandate to design, build, procure, deliver, install, test and commission the entire railroad plus an initial operation of three years. The contract price of the EPC was 6.65 billion Saudi Arabia riyals (about US$1.75 billion).[9]

---

7. China Civil Engineering Construction Corporation.
8. Public Transport Authority (June 2017). Railway sector in the Kingdom of Saudi Arabia—Express of Interest Document. Retrieved May 1, 2018 from http://saudiarabien.ahk.de/uploads/media/Expression_of_Interest_for_KSA_railway_market_01.pdf.
9. In the kingdom, the majority of the procurement arrangements are what contractors called an EPC agreement or where the Saudis have a planned design, engineering, procurement, and construction agreement.

To bring governance to the working level, the Chinese set up a new contract PMO, effectively the board of directors of this initiative.

The nominal project director was in fact the chairman, and he had the power of veto over deadlock. This had meant a deadlock mechanism had to be pre-agreed and installed at the outset, a vital step that had to be managed properly. The PMO was in effect the project governance team and had tremendous amount of authority and the responsibility to deliver the project. The project director would nominate three deputy project directors (DPDs). Each was held responsible for a key department and a critical success factor. These DPDs were all professionals with managerial, technical, and operational know-how. The three DPDs happened to be from Hong Kong: one was a systems engineer responsible for M&E Systems works, one was a contract engineer responsible for commercials (contracts and specs), and one was a civil engineer responsible for the civil works. The fourth DPD was hired later, responsible for maintaining the schedule of the program. These DPDs were effectively directors of this makeshift board.

Governance styles and legality

Lawyers who are experts in structured and project finance and who have worked on such large infrastructure projects in the Middle East and with Chinese SOEs noted that project transparency could be a huge issue and might become a hindrance and embarrassment for national ministries. Often the parties and their intentions are shrouded in mystery, because national policies and interests are involved. Lawyers often are the last to know.

Because of the history and legacy of infrastructural work along the Silk Road, English common law is commonly used in such contracts, and not Chinese law or Saudi Arabian law. Impartiality and adjudication of case laws over hundreds of years provide a special advantage in the use of English common law. Nonetheless, because all sides were not familiar with British legality and the role of the lawyers in international contracts and corporate governance, learning to work with lawyers did present a unique challenge, and typically this had meant a longer time was needed for education and discussion. But projects like these are inherently difficult due to a range of factors: trust among multiple parties, size, complexity, distance, climate (we often forget that due to the hot weather, work would commence in the evening with bright lights), skilled resources, language, culture, and, of course, urgency.

"Corporate governance is an art and mitigating the governance expectations of both sides in any large project usually would be unexpectedly difficult on all sides, at first, because art requires imagination and interpretation," cited these lawyers. Both sides had different governance and decision-making expectations, styles, and practices. Harmonizing these was a true challenge for the lawyers, other professionals, and institutions. For example, the speed of decision-making on the Chinese side could be heavily driven by policy directives. When a new directive was handed down from Beijing, the Chinese side would push for quick legal compliance or considerations into their project, regardless of costs. The Chinese side preferred less paper and less documentation, since such projects would have been agreed through diplomatic channels,[10] and too much paper and words would raise costs. But this lean concept could have added complications, particularly when insurance claims required a very clear set of exclusions and documentation procedures. When something goes wrong, the documentation is necessary for dispute resolution.

Authority matrix

Conversely, to ensure the success of this project, lawyers were requested by the Saudis and the working team to install governance and communication structure, veto mechanisms, and protocols; that is, during a crisis who from Party A shall speak with Party B, and so on.[11] Sometimes the phase "Authority Matrix" or "Approval Process" would be used. The standard approval process of the PMO had this structure:

- Approval in principle
- Approved
- Approved without comments
- Not approved and resubmission needed

There appeared two extremes when it comes to dealing with the Chinese mainlanders, said some lawyers. There are no hard and fast rules, and the culture of the institutions involved and time criticality would play a bigger role than would any assumed behaviors in making decisions. For example, because of their shared and collective responsibility, one assumption would be that it takes longer to reach any decision. To ensure accountability and rapid decision-making, one side would demand setting in this pecking protocol; the other side, the Chinese side typically, would not. Some Chinese did not want the decision matrix to be too explicit, but in other cases, some did and expected a clear decision protocol so decisions could be made rapidly. In the case of the MMMP however, the Chinese side was quite explicit and demanded rapid turnaround. Time was of the essence.

Critical success factors

The MMMP in Saudi Arabia was built in 22 months, a complete success for all the shareholders, and was built well on time. Both sides were proud of their commitment and mutual accomplishment. From those project leaders whom we had interviewed, it was evident that crucial and firm decisions during the formative

---

10. In this case, however, CRCC won this project through a tendering exercise.
11. This is sometimes known as a call-tree.

stage of project governance had contributed to this outcome. But there were other factors as well.

For this case, the critical success factors (CSFs) appeared to be the set-up and exercise of governance. The first was recognizing and designing the needed governance and authority into the project team, which lawyers would help set up. The project managers acted like directors. They held themselves accountable. A clear decision protocol also had eliminated many unnecessary dialogues. As there were many unexpected opportunities for losses and negotiation, a properly structured negotiation and arbitration process was vital.

Since acquiring and allocating resources belonged to the project managers, having readily and reliable suppliers, plus having the PMO acquire extra spare capacity to cover contingencies, was implicit.

This led to the second area of CSF, and that was having access and preparing a ready base of good suppliers. The closest supply hub was Dubai (and not Hong Kong), and what would have taken three months to acquire resources took only six weeks with MMMP. This was only possible because the experienced independent consultants, Atkins, knew exactly where and how to engage with thousands of suppliers. Granted, many suppliers had also reached out to MMMP, having heard of the size and challenge of this project. Nonetheless, familiarity with the suppliers also raised the possibility of collusion. Linking a system of procurement and supplier validation, which was a subset of the governance arrangement, made sure such collusion would not be given the light of day.

The third and probably the heart of all risks was system interfaces, namely, ensuring that the system interfaces were seamless and that all system couplings would match. With literally thousands of systems from thousands of independent suppliers, ensuring all systems can hum together under all conditions for those seven days was probably the biggest challenge to the EPC and the PMO. We will expand on this below, along with the discussion on how to minimize supplier collusion.

The fourth was having readily available knowledge and access to risk transfer, including risk management and having insurance experts on hand because risk mitigation and insurance claims were inevitable parts of such risky ventures. But this presupposed that blueprints were sufficiently detailed and that contracts were properly written and in line with generally accepted legal and insurance practices.

We will explore a few of the more interesting challenges below.

1. Designing in governance

According to those whom we had interviewed, it started with the creation of the board. Some of the most critical people to put in place during the inception were the project director and his DPDs, as this team's competency would make or break the project. The project director is the highest-ranked person in operations and technical engineering, but typically real expertise would rest with his deputy directors. The duty to locate and ready this person fell on the Chinese side, and a professional and seasoned engineer was eventually found after months of international search. The professional had years of solid experience building railroads and subways throughout Asia.

Once on the job, the project director suggested the disposal of the available sets of specifications and drawings, as they were incomplete and had critical errors. The initial draft was unexpectedly too rough and too high level. Sponsors balked, but the project director insisted, arguing that this 3D puzzle must fit and work at the first try. There was no second chance. Failure would mean a definite loss of face for all. Moreover, any variation from the previous blueprint would mean higher costs, and these would be inevitable and were unbudgeted. The sponsors eventually relented, and a new blueprint was immediately drafted by the project ream[12] with the assistance of an external and independent team of design consultants. In fact, to avoid similar embarrassment, from that point onward, the team insisted that any new contract must be drafted by certified professionals, since any insurance claims would be based on contractual disputes.

2. Spare capacity to manage massive uncertainties

Having a sufficient amount of cushion readily available has been a necessary condition for success. The cushion could be financial, human, or simply time, but unfortunately TIME was not what they had! Getting such cushions at the outset had required foresight and good negotiation skills on the part of the PMO. Since personnel was a constant problem, and those who did come would have to curtail their social life, management oversight was important. If the sponsors had been overly zealous on cost control, there wouldn't be any wiggle room to have the resources in place, to deal with a range of unexpected contingencies.

Given this was the second-biggest project in Saudi Arabia at that time, there simply were not sufficient professionals and skilled labor in the country. The other project had hired 70+ contract engineers, and the project director needed just as many if not more. The Chinese government sent their corps of engineers to assist, mostly skilled laborers. This helped but was still insufficient. A handful of engineers were finally negotiated, but most had never built this sort of rail under such conditions with such extreme temperature ranges (it gets extremely hot during the day and cold during the night). Because this was a national project and the Chinese must deliver on their promise, they had a lot of clout and were able to move the personnel into Saudi Arabia quickly. Subsequently, professional engineers throughout China were drafted onto this project. That administrative maneuver got the project director the engineers he needed, and these engineers ran parallel processing to save time. The lesson learned here was that the contracting party must be sufficiently resourceful and be able to pull in the needed parties. CRCC had that capacity.

---

12. Insurance will only pay out per written specs. Detailed documentation was a must.

In Saudi Arabia, social life is dry and absent. No alcohol is allowed. Cultural faux pas can get a foreigner in trouble. On one occasion, an Englishman was fined by the cultural police, as his wife touched the husband's hand in public. That is how different the culture norm was, and this incident had to be dealt with by senior management. Extra attention and time are always in short supply.

3. Managing and transferring risks

This railroad was unique. It would go from zero to full capacity during the Hajj. The rest of the year it would remain idle. Imagine a machine that is not used, said the project director, but expected to work the first time it is turned on again many months hence. Thus, the massive amount of pre-planning, contingency planning, and backup was unprecedented. "One station did catch fire, and that jacked up the costs, but time could not be extended. Some idiots had misplaced some kerosene and a welder set out the fire."

A key component that led to successful outcome of this project was a purposeful allocation of time, attention, and resources to risk management and insurance. Given the complexity, duration, and safety factors of this project for those working in a hostile environment, accidents are inevitable, and as a result, risk mitigation measures and insurance claims must be managed proactively.

Mitigating risks meant working with experienced professionals and international suppliers, on a set of agreed briefs. Because for many of the Chinese mainlanders English was not their mother tongue, they weren't able to contract out subsequent work to outsiders. Luckily, prior experience meant senior professionals had a wide network and were able to call upon outsiders such as Atkins, Systra, Hyder, Scott Wilson, and Mott McDonalds to participate in the selection of the design consultancy exercise. These professionals were quickly brought in and that eliminated a huge number of uncertainties. Experience, teamwork, and familiarity were key, said some of those involved in the project. Every management team was tasked with providing an updated project brief, and by linking and coordinating the briefs, the project team ensured screws would fit and rails would come together at the right time and at the right place. "In this business, a good engineer will know the importance of the performance of a single screw. An inexperienced one can't tell the difference between 10 brands of screws," said an engineer.

For risk transfer, key man insurance was purchased. Construction All Risks (CAR) insurance was also purchased. Typically for CAR, the entire premium is about 1% of the project sum and is paid upfront by the buyer. This covers both damage to a property and third-party injury or damage claims.[13]

But accidents happened. Despite strong enforcement and implementation of safety policy, incidents did occur, among them, sadly, a murder case. The

---

13. Damage to the property could include the structure not being properly constructed or receiving damage during a renovation. Third parties, including subcontractors, may become injured while working at the construction site.

complications that came afterwards were unimaginable, said those involved, and the carte blanche of the ministry or Chinese government saved the day. One involved the murder of a QA (quality assurance) engineer, killed by a local security guard. The QA engineer didn't like this young security guard and thought the guard was lazy and was frequently absent from his post. One day, the security guard allegedly got too excited and stuck a knife into the QA engineer.

The family of the QA engineer wanted to move the dead engineer out of Saudi Arabia as soon as was reasonable. But this was not possible due to local laws and investigative proceedings. One must remember the PMO had to deal with the remains of a dead body in a heated but dry environment.

Luckily, this corporate entity, with the PMO's insistence, had bought a range of insurance. Key man insurance was bought for all the deployed overseas staff, and in this case, the financial support was used to transfer a dead body out of Saudi Arabia. Because sophisticated insurance was needed, it had to be dealt with on a contractual basis. Other than CAR, it was fortunate he said that he anticipated and bought a range of risk-transfer instruments. Knowing which types of insurance to buy and at what capacity meant the difference between bringing the project within costs or beyond budget.

4. Setting in design and procurement systems and processes to manage quality, and deter fraud and collusion

In a project as large as this with so many suppliers involved and so much equipment and many parts required to be purchased, procurement needs to be managed rigorously. To minimize any problem of collusion or fraud, the PMO should and did engage outside independent design consultants to draw up the tender specifications, and the consultants must approve that the proper supplies have been received and are in good working order. Consultants designed the specs while the PMO conducted the tendering exercise. Although collusion among suppliers could still be hidden, the possibility of this happening was reduced because a good number of international suppliers were involved. The quantity, transparency, and availability of more suppliers should reduce the possibility of collusion. Besides, all suppliers had been prequalified, and this process was to weed out the unreliable ones.

To put even tighter control on the technical quality, the owner hired an independent engineer to audit the quality. On the EPC side, CRCC would audit the financial numbers. CRCC even further hired an independent safety engineer to verify operational readiness.

Engineers are risk aversive and typically add layers of extra oversight and control. Hence, all these safeguards reduced fraud and collision but could not eliminate it. All in all, active monitoring by the PMO would vastly deter any disruptor and minimize possibility of fraud and collusion.

Closing remarks

Building new projects along the Belt and Road will be a huge challenge for all parties. Probably the only outcome that is agreeable and acceptable by all the parties involved would be the successful completion of the project. This alignment of interests is critical, and the balance of power among the various parties is essential. The best governance system is one that can flex, rebalancing and rechecking itself whereby each part of the system has both a controlling and counterbalancing effect on another. Any party becoming too powerful can start the system toward a breakdown. But, if generally interests are aligned and checked, a properly constituted board of directors should be sufficient to handle distractions and noise in the system and bring the system back to normality. Indeed, a properly set up board of directors does and can allow for proper control, discussion, and allocation of authority and responsibility.

Corporate governance is about the exercise of power, but even the most powerful need to be restrained. Although the sponsors, typically the sovereign nation, can easily reclaim the project militarily, they usually would not. A nation can simply take away the concession and the project value will drop to nil. But doing so will weaken their international credibility and there are break clauses and a future stream of income that would not take place, and which would kill the project, should the government take possession prematurely. The PMO or the paper board thus created by the contracts may also become too powerful, but if this board is unable to perform, the sponsor (or lender in other cases) has the authority to replace the entire board. Conversely, the board or the EPC may purchase political risk insurance as an added safety net in case the government takes possession. The government can also take possession of the project if the PMO cannot perform. But if the project works, the government gains, and revenue produces dividends for the foreign tax authorities.

According to industry veterans, this project is considered a reasonable size but is a complex project by all dimensions because of the location, cultural challenges, logistics, and heat. The CSFs were the competency and capacity to manage contract administration, design, procurement, schedule, quality, safety, negotiation, and arbitration. But putting all these together and ensuring all systems can hum together, each adjusting as needed with some parameters, is the real art of system governance.

Questions for discussion

One of the many ways to simplify the governance arrangement between multiple stakeholders in a large project is to set up a new corporate entity whereby members of the board would each represent the shareholders. The spectrum of governance arrangement can range from ownership to leasing to service contract, for example.

Although popular, BOT is considered only an option. What other options are popular for such large-scale projects?

1. The Belt and Road Initiative undoubtedly would involve many more kilometers of rail, many tons of steel, and predefined governance architecture that would facilitate the delivery of stand-alone projects. If you were the Chinese authorities, how would you deal with future projects of this sort? What new governance arrangement would you introduce?

2. What are additional risk management and internal control elements needed for such projects? Recommend a few that have been used by your own organizations.

3. Building such an infrastructure in a distant land, headed by a team of professionals, is similar to sending out a billion-dollar cruise liner that you own, to Antarctica, with a captain and his team. Since miscommunication or cessation of communication is inevitable, how much decision protocol or authority would you delegate to your captain on the assumption that he would be offline for several days? How much power is too much for one person, the captain? How would you check the power of the captain (the PMO, that is)?

Appendix III
List of Acronyms, Organizations, and Websites

The websites of organizations involved with corporate governance matters contain a wealth of material and can provide valuable additional information.

ABC   Agricultural Bank of China
www.abchina.com/en

ADB   Asian Development Bank
www.adb.org

AIIB   Asia Infrastructure and Investment Bank

AMC   Asset Management Company

ANZ   Australia & New Zealand Banking Group
www.anz.com.au

A-shares   Shares only issued to domestic institutions or individuals in China

BCG   Boston Consulting Group
www.bcg.com

BOB   Bank of Beijing
www.bankofbeijing.com.cn/en2011/index.html

BOC   Bank of China
www.boc.cn/en

BOS   Bank of Shanghai
www.bosc.cn/en/index.shtml

B-shares   Shares issued only to foreign investors and traded on the Shanghai Stock Exchange or the Shenzhen Stock Exchange

CAPCO   China Association of Public Companies

CAR   Capital Adequacy Ratio or Construction All Risks

CAS   Chinese Accounting Standards

CASB   Chinese Auditing Standards Board
see www.ifac.org/news-events/2010-11/chinese-auditing-standards-board-and-international-auditing-and-assurance-standa

CBRC	China Banking Regulatory Commission
	www.cbrc.gov.cn/english/index.html
CC	Central Committee
CCB	City Commercial Bank
CCB	China Construction Bank
	en.ccb.com/en/home/indexv3.html
CSRC	China Securities Regulatory Commission
CDIC	Central Discipline Inspection Committee
CEO	Chief executive officer
CG	Corporate governance
CIAS	Chinese Independent Auditing Standards
CIC	China Investment Corporation
CICPA	The Chinese Institute of Certified Public Accountants
	www.cicpa.org.cn/introcicpa/
CIRC	China Insurance Regulatory Commission
	www.circ.gov.cn/web/site45/
COEs	Collectively-Owned Enterprises
COSCO	China Ocean Shipping (Group) Company
CPA	Certified public accountant
CPC	Communist Party of China
CPPCC	Central People's Political Consultative Conference
CMC	Certified Management Consultant
CRCC	China Railway Construction Corporation
CRRC	Changchun Railway Vehicles
CRV	China Resources Vanguard
CSF	Critical success factors
CSMAR	China Stock Market and Accounting Research
	blogs.ntu.edu.sg/lib-databases/subject/china-stock-market-account-
	ing-research-csmar-in-wharton-research-data-services-2 /
CSRC	China Securities Regulatory Commission
	www.csrc.gov.cn/pub/csrc_en/
DPD	Deputy project director
EAS	Enterprise Accounting Standard
EIU	Economist Intelligence Unit
	www.csrc.gov.cn/pub/csrc_en/
EPC	Engineering Procurement and Construction Contract

EPS	Earnings per share
ERM	Enterprise Risk Management
ESG	Environment, Sustainability, and Governance
FDI	Foreign Direct Investment
FIE	Foreign Invested Enterprise
GAAP	Generally Accepted Accounting Principles
GAC	General Administration of Customs
GAIC	General Administration of Industry and Commerce
GCI	General Competitiveness Index
GDP	Gross Domestic Product
HKICPA	Hong Kong Institute of Certified Public Accountants www.hkicpa.org.hk/en
HKICS	Hong Kong Institute of Chartered Secretaries www.hkics.org.hk
HKIoD	The Hong Kong Institute of Directors www.hkiod.com
HKSE	Hong Kong Stock Exchange (also SEHK) www.HKEx.com.hk
HSBC	The Hong Kong and Shanghai Banking Corporation www.hsbc.com
H-shares	China shares traded on the Hong Kong Stock Exchange
IAS	International Accounting Standards
IASB	International Accounting Standards Board www.iasplus.com
ICAC	Independent Commission Against Corruption (Hong Kong) www.icac.org.hk/en/home/index.html
ICBC	Industrial and Commercial Bank of China www.icbc-ltd.com/ICBCLtd/en
IFC	International Finance Corporation of the World Bank www.ifc.org
IFRS	International Financial Reporting Standards
IMF	International Monetary Fund www.imf.org
IPO	Initial public offering
ISA	International Standards on Auditing
JV	Joint venture
LBO	Leverage buy-out

LSE	London Stock Exchange
MBR	Market to book ratio
M&E	Mechanical and Electrical
MNC	Multinational Corporation
MMMP	The Al Mashaaer Al Mugaddassah Metro
MoF	Ministry of Finance PRC english.gov.cn/state_council/2014/09/09/content_ 281474986284115.htm
NAOPRC	National Audit Office of the People's Republic China www.audit.gov.cn/en/
NASDAQ	National Association of Securities Dealers Automated Quotations (USA)
NBS	National Bureau of Statistics www.stats.gov.cn/enGliSH
NDRC	National Development and Reform Commission en.ndrc.gov.cn
NGO	Non-governmental organization
NPC	National People's Congress
N-shares	Chinese companies listed on the New York Stock Exchange through ADRs; also Innovation Share
NYSE	New York Stock Exchange www.nyse.com/index
OBOR	One Belt One Road Initiative, also known as the Belt and Road Initiative
OCBC	Overseas Chinese Banking Corporation www.ocbc.com/group/group-home.html
OECD	Organisation for Economic Co-operation and Development www.oecd.org
OTC	Over-the-counter
PBOC	People's Bank of China www.pbc.gov.cn/english/130437/index.html
PC	Party Committee
PCAOB	Public Company Accounting Oversight Board (USA)
P/E ratio	Price/earnings ratio
PLA	People's Liberation Army
PPP	Purchasing Power Parity
PMO	Project Management Office

PRC	People's Republic of China
QA	Quality assurance
QDII	Qualified Domestic Institutional Investors
QFII	Qualified Foreign Institutional Investors
RCCs	Rural Credit Cooperative
RMB	Renminbi (Chinese currency)
ROA	Return on assets
ROE	Return on equity
SAC	Securities Association of China
	www.sac.net.cn/en
SAIC	State Administration for Industry and Commerce
	www.saic.gov.cn/english/
SAFE	State Administration of Foreign Exchange
SAMB	State Asset Management Bureau (local office of SASAC)
SASAC	State-Owned Assets Supervision and Administration Commission
	en.sasac.gov.cn/
SAT	State Administration of Taxation (PRC)
	www.chinatax.gov.cn/2013/n2925
SCMP	South China Morning Post
SEC	Securities and Exchange Commission (USA)
	www.sec.gov
SEHK	Stock Exchange of Hong Kong (also HKSE)
SERC	State Economic Reform Commission
	See NDRC
SETC	State Economic and Trade Commission (PRC); now known as Ministry of Commerce or MOFCOM
SEZs	Special economic zones
SFC	Securities and Futures Commission (Hong Kong)
	www.sfc.hk/web/EN/about-the-sfc/our-role
	english.sse.com.cn
SMEs	Small- and medium-sized enterprises
SPC	State Planning Commission
SOCBs	State-owned commercial banks
SOE	State-owned enterprise
SOX	Sarbanes Oxley Regulation
S&P	Standard & Poor's
	www.standardandpoors.com/en_US/web/guest/home

SSB	State Statistics Bureau, China
	See NBS
SSE	Shanghai Stock Exchange
STAQ	Securities Trading Automated Quotation System (China's version of NASDAQ)
SZSE	Shenzhen Stock Exchange
	www.szse.cn/main/en
TICs	Trust and Investment Corporations
TVEs	Town and village enterprises
UCCs	Urban credit cooperatives
WFOE	Wholly foreign-owned enterprise
WTO	World Trade Organization
	www.wto.org

Appendix IV
List of Interviewees

This list includes short biographical notes on those who have contributed to this book. Some interviewees asked to remain anonymous, and their wishes have been respected.

Jamie ALLEN. Founding secretary general of the Asian Corporate Governance Association (ACGA). From 2006 to 2010, Mr. Allen was appointed to the Listing Committee of the Stock Exchange of Hong Kong. From 2001 to 2007, he served on a new advisory committee, the Public Shareholders' Group, formed by the Hong Kong Securities and Futures Commission. In July 2013, Mr. Allen was appointed to the Financial Reporting Review Panel of the Financial Reporting Council (FRC) and served for three years. Later that year he was also appointed to the Operations Oversight Committee of the FRC.

Dr. Sari ARHO-HAVREN. Sinologist. Finnish Consul of Innovation at TEKES, the Finnish Funding Agency for Innovation.

Dr. Henry AU. Independent political risk analyst of China and the United States. Honorary CEO of Invotech.

Pru BENNETT. Director and head of BlackRock's Investment Stewardship team for the Asia Pacific Region. Member of the Australian Financial Services Council's ESG Working Group and Hong Kong's Securities and Futures Commission's Public Shareholder Group.

Benjamin CHANG. Regional managing director, Aon Global Insurance. Ben looks after the global multinationals doing businesses in China.

Moses Mo-Chi CHENG. GBM, GBS, OBE, JP. Formerly senior partner of PC Woo & Company. Chairman of the Hong Kong Insurance Authority. China-appointed attesting officer. INED of China Mobile and COSCO.

Prof. C. K. CHO (Barrister). Professor of Practice in Law at the Hong Kong Polytechnic University. Formerly senior inspector of the Independent Commission Against Corruption in Hong Kong.

Alice Qiu-Si CHA. Researcher. Engagement manager at G. Li & Company Ltd. Graduate of Hong Kong Polytechnic University (MA and BA).

Prof. Alfred Sai-Pak HO. FCMC. An editor of this book, who has extensive experience in corporate governance and management. He has held senior positions in the Hutchison Whampoa Group, Hong Kong Polytechnic University, The Management Development Centre of Hong Kong under the Vocational Training Council of Hong Kong, Poon Kam Kai Institute of Management at the Hong Kong University Business School, and the Hay Group.

Sir David AKERS-JONES. KBE. CMG. JP. Former chief secretary and acting governor of the HKSAR government. Akers-Jones was appointed a Hong Kong affairs adviser to the Chinese Central Government from 1992 to 1997, after he voluntarily relinquished his chairmanship of the Hong Kong Housing Authority, having served a five-year term.

Prof. Roger KING. Director of the Tanoto Center for Asian Family Business and Entrepreneurship Studies at the Hong Kong University of Sciences and Technology and the university's adjunct professor. Prof. King served as CEO of Sa International Holdings Limited, a retailer of cosmetics from August 1999 to May 2002, and served as its president, as managing director and chief operating officer of Orient Overseas (Holdings) Limited ("OOHL") from September 1985 to January 1987.

Kwok Chuen KWOK. Honorary senior research fellow at the School of Economics and Finance of the University of Hong Kong. Independent non-executive director of Sunevision Holdings Ltd. and of DBS Bank (Hong Kong) Ltd. Formerly, Hong Kong SAR government economist, and regional chief economist for Standard Chartered Bank–East Asia

Daryl LAI. Executive director and responsible officer of China Chengtong (HK) Asset Management Company Limited. Previously, managing director of CASH Wealth Management Company Ltd.

Dr. Charles LAM. CFA. Managing director of Real Estate for Baring Private Equity Asia.

Dr. Charles LAU. DBA, CA, CPA. CFO and company secretary of a Hong Kong listed company. A founding member of the Association of Certified Fraud Examiners (Hong Kong Chapter).

Francis Koon-Yum LEE. Specialist in corporate governance, internal audit, risk management and internal controls for both commercial and public sectors with Arthur Andersen and Coopers & Lybrand, in Southern China Shenzhen. Subsequently, deputy head of group internal audit with John Swire and Sons (Hong Kong) Limited and then general manager, Internal Audit of Urban Renewal Authority of Hong Kong.

Andy LEUNG. Managing director, Ronald Lu and Partners (RLP), professional architect, Hong Kong and China.

Richard Wai-Keung LEUNG. CEO in the financial sector, in Asia Pacific. Formerly managing director of UBS Securities Company in China.

Linlin LI. Researcher and analyst at G. Li & Company Ltd. Graduate of the Chinese University of Hong Kong (MSc) and Jinan University (BA).

Nana LI. Project manager. China and Hong Kong research analyst, Asian Corporate Governance Association.

Roger LUI. Partner, Allen and Overy. Graduate of the University of Oxford and the University of Sydney.

Roy LO. Managing director of Shine Wing and vice chairman of the HKINED Association.

May MAK. CPA. Chief financial officer and company secretary of listed company RM Group Holdings Ltd. She previously worked for Deloitte Touche Tohmatsu.

Francis MOK. PE. Professional engineer and consultant, with over 30 years' experience in the railroad industry in China and Hong Kong. Former Head of Human Resources at the Urban Renewal Authority. Formerly president of the HKIHRM.

Ludwig NG. Senior partner, ONC Lawyers (HK). Examiner, Overseas Lawyers Qualification Examination/APAA/Insolvency Law Committee; Practice Management Committee, Law Society of Hong Kong/Restructuring and Insolvency Faculty Executive Committee, HKICPA

Bill Koon-Kwai PANG. Banker with over 40 years of experience in China, with ICBC (Asia), Manufacturers Hanover, Deutsche Bank, and Citibank.

Edmund PANG. Professional civil engineer. Over 40 years of experience in construction and railways. Graduate of the University of Hong Kong.

Michael PANG. Managing director of the IT Consulting and Business Process Improvement practices of Protiviti Greater China. Previously with Boston Consulting Group, A. T. Kearney, and Kodak Services for Business.

REN Jiang. Held executive positions in consulting and construction companies in China, Canada, the UK, Australia, the Middle East, and East Asia. Professional engineer with experience in the transportation industry.

Nicholas TAN. Audit partner, Deloitte.

Gretchen TRICKER. An editor of this book. Co-author of *Shares in Hong Kong: The centennial history of the HKSE*, co-author of *Business Ethics: A stakeholder,* *governance, and risk approach,* co-editor of *Corporate Governance—an international review.* Researcher in the Carrian case. Previously editor of a Hong Kong style magazine.

Alec TSUI. Former chief executive of the HKSE. He was an advisor and a council member of the Shenzhen Stock Exchange from July 2001 to June 2002. Mr. Tsui is currently the director of WAG Worldsec Management Consultancy Limited, an independent non-executive director of a number of listed public companies including COSCO SHIPPING International (Hong Kong) Co., Ltd. (formerly known as COSCO International Holdings Limited) (stock code: 517), Kangda International Environmental Company Limited (stock code: 6136), Pacific Online Limited (stock code: 543), and Summit Ascent Holdings Limited (stock code: 102), all of which are listed in Hong Kong; Melco Crown Entertainment Limited (stock code: MPEL), a company listed on NASDAQ, and Melco Crown (Philippines) Resorts Corporation (stock code: MCP), a company listed in Philippines, and an independent director of ATA Inc. (stock code: ATAI), a company listed on NASDAQ. He is also an independent non-executive director of Industrial & Commercial Bank of China (Asia) Limited (ICBC (Asia)) starting in 2000. ICBC (Asia) was listed in Hong Kong until December 2010 when it was privatized.

Gary YIN. Partner with Smyth & Company, a law firm experienced in mergers and acquisitions and corporate law in China.

Christine ZHENG. An investment banker in China, as executive director of the Asset Management division at Shenwan Hongyuan Asset Mgt. Limited (SWS), a PRC-approved local investment bank.

Francis Yimin ZHU. Researcher. Graduate of the HKUST (MSc in Accounting) and Nanjing University (BA).

The authors much appreciate the valuable contribution of many other interviewees, who wished to remain anonymous.

Index

2002 Code of Corporate Governance, the, 120, 125

2006 Company Law and Securities Law, 104, 122

2008 Global Financial Crisis, 274

3M, 266

'A' Restricted Share, 112

'A' Share, 110–113, 172, 223, 253

Accenture, 255

Accounting Law (2000), 27, 125, 200

Administrative Measures on Information Disclosure by Listed Companies (2007), 125, 200

Agricultural Bank of China (ABC), 53

Al Mashaaer Al Mugaddassah Metro in Saudi Arabia (MMMP), 291

Alibaba, 14–19, 31, 35–39, 72, 174, 233, 234, 240, 251, 267, 275

AliPay, 15, 31, 32, 267

all non-executive board, 7

Anbang Insurance, 234, 235, 259

Anglo-American culture, 81

Ant Financial, 14, 18, 174, 267

Apple Computers, 102

Asia family-based model, the, 8, 10, 11

Asian Development Bank (ADB), 290

'B' Share, 107, 112, 113, 129, 172, 251

Baidu, 31, 37, 38, 39, 174, 271

Baoneng, 133–136, 139, 174, 260

Basic Standards for Enterprise Internal Control (2008), 200

Bo, Xilai, 33

board of supervisors. *See* supervisory board, 62, 65, 66, 68, 198, 224

board-level information, 243, 244, 228

Bossini, 187

Boston Consulting Group (BCG), 270

Bright Food, 252, 253

Buddhism, 31, 32, 81, 84, 92–96, 213, 262

Business ethics, 35, 61, 81, 83, 88, 89, 90, 93, 95, 96, 162, 255

BW Group, 187

Cadbury Report, 74, 152, 153, 262, 263

Caixin, 232

Capital Adequacy Ratio or Construction All Risks (CAR), 297, 298, 301

Carrian Investments, 150, 151

Cathay Financial, 187

CEIBS, 177

Central Committee (CC), 1, 54, 56, 61, 96, 256

Central People's Political Consultative Conference (CPPCC), 249

chaebol model, 8, 10, 12

Chan Buddhism, 213

Changchun Railway Vehicles (CRRC), 291

Changjiang Pension Insurance, 258

Cheng, Henry, 185, 186

Cheng, Yu-Tung, 185

China Aviation Oil, 35

China Banking Regulatory Commission (CBRC), 115, 125

China Baowu Steel Group, 52, 53, 55, 56, 58

China Insurance Regulatory Commission (CIRC), 115, 134, 136, 235

China Investment Corporation (CIC), 259
China Railway Construction Corporation
    (CRCC), 288, 291, 292, 294, 296, 298
China Resources Vanguard (CRV), 133, 136
China Securities Regulatory Commission
    (CSRC), 2, 65, 69, 75, 107, 108–110,
    113, 114, 118–120, 122, 125, 126, 152,
    200, 201, 206, 215, 216, 244, 251, 256,
    268, 273
China Universal Asset Management, 258
Chundu, 34
city commercial bank, 281
Code of Corporate Governance, 27, 65, 104,
    109, 110, 120, 199, 200
Code of Corporate Governance for Listed
    Companies (2002), the, 27, 65, 109,
    120, 200
Communist Party of China (CPC), 54, 56,
    57, 58, 59, 60, 69, 96, 256
Companies Act. See corporate law, 82, 85,
    148, 163, 215, 216, 256, 257, 258
company limited by shares, 61, 62
Confucianism, 31, 84, 93–97, 166, 180, 213
Continental European two-tier model, the,
    5, 8, 10
contract responsibility system, 108
Convergence of accounting and auditing
    standards with IFRS and ISA (2007),
    125, 200
corporate law, 44, 45, 71
Corporate Social Responsibility (CSR), 83,
    85–87, 163, 255
Criminal Law Amendment (2006), 200
critical success factors (CSFs), 294, 295,
    299, 302
Cultural Revolution, 25, 29, 31, 32, 40, 46,
    54, 60, 93–98, 174, 179, 183, 262

Ding, Lei, 174
Directive on Quarterly Reporting (2003),
    125, 200
Douban, 31
dual-class ownership, 18
dual-class shares, 18, 19, 37, 38, 52, 233, 259

Enterprise Risk Management (ERM), 110

Environment, Sustainability, and
    Governance (ESG), 21, 110, 243
Evergrande, 134–136, 138, 211, 235, 260
executive board, 7, 10, 67, 198, 206, 257, 258
executive directors, 7, 38, 137, 153, 156,
    157, 198, 203–205, 216, 224, 225

Foshan Electrical & Light Company, 259
Fosun International, 196, 230, 231, 259
Four Modernizations, 26, 40, 41, 54, 93, 95,
    104, 105, 167, 173, 185, 188
Fourth Industrial Revolution, 258, 259, 268
Foxconn, 102, 103

G. Li & Company (GliCo), 308, 309, 312
Geely, 236, 237
Generally Accepted Accounting Principles
    (GAAP), 109, 303
Gini coefficients, 38
Great Leap Forward, 29, 53, 60
group-wide governance, 241, 242
Growth Enterprise Market (GEM), 74, 144,
    145, 149
Guangdong Kelon Electrical Holdings Co.,
    35
Guangsha Holding Group, 180
guanxi, 30, 71, 84, 89, 99, 201, 210
Guidance on Listed Companies' Articles of
    Association (2006), 200
Guidelines on Independent Directors, 200
Guo, Boxiong, 33, 272

'H' Share, 3, 112, 113, 129, 223, 251
Hainan Air (HNA), 196, 259
Haixin Group, 176, 177
Hong Kong Bar Association (HKBA), 146,
    147
Hong Kong Companies Ordinances, 73,
    140, 152
Hong Kong Corporate Governance Code,
    74, 148, 152, 155, 246
Hong Kong Financial Reporting Council
    (FRC), 140, 159, 160, 307
Hong Kong Institute of Certified Public
    Accountants (HKICPA), 148, 159, 160,
    249, 250

Hong Kong Institute of Chartered
  Secretaries (HKICS), 148, 149
Hong Kong Institute of Directors (HKIoD),
  149, 160, 249
Hong Kong Land, 149, 150, 228
Hong Kong Stock Exchange (also SEHK),
  2, 18, 115, 140, 141, 142, 143, 152–154,
  159, 160, 164, 195, 201, 229, 245, 303,
  305
Hong Leong Group, 187
Hu Jiajia, 176
Huawei, 33, 37–39, 76–80, 231, 232
Huaxia Fund, 258
Huayi Group, 174
hukou system of control, 22

Independent Commission Against
  Corruption (ICAC), 140, 142, 145, 146,
  151, 303, 307
independent director, 17, 27, 65, 67, 74, 75,
  109, 120, 121, 125, 152, 153, 156, 157,
  199, 200, 201, 204, 206, 210, 219, 227,
  248, 257, 267, 310
independent non-executive director, 7, 10,
  11, 43, 73, 88, 126, 138, 153, 164, 219,
  225, 241, 242, 248–250, 258, 308, 310
Industrial and Commercial Bank of China
  (ICBC), 110, 222, 250, 303, 309, 310
International Accounting Standards (IAS),
  27, 109, 116, 303
International Financial Reporting Standards
  (IFRS), 109, 125, 200, 303
International Monetary Fund (IMF), 238,
  243, 244, 269, 274, 303
InTime, 32
ISA or the International Standards on
  Auditing (ISA), 125, 200, 303

'J' Share, 112
Jardines, 229
Jiang, Zemin, 25, 61, 65, 205, 231
joint venture or JV, 46, 73, 121, 179, 231,
  236, 239, 251, 303
joint stock company, 61, 110, 200, 239
Judiciary, the, 13, 82, 121, 126, 146, 147,
  239, 256, 275

Kanbox, 31
Kauide, 31
keiretsu, 5, 8, 10, 12, 92
Key Performance Indicators (KPI), 8, 210,
  211, 213, 219
King, Roger, 178, 308
Kwong, Siu-Hing, 186

'L' Share, 112
Law on the State-Owned Enterprises
  (2009), 200
Lee, Jean, 177
Lee, Shau Kee, 186
Lenovo Group, 230
Li, Chun-yuan, 177
Li, Haicang, 176, 177
Li, Ka-Shing, 150, 183, 185, 186, 262
Li, Kwok-Po, David, 186
Li, Robin, 39, 174
Li, Shek-Pang, 184
limited liability company, 5, 6, 61, 62, 200,
  272, 276
Ling, Jihua, 272
Liu, Chang, 176
Liu, Yonghao, 176
Lo, Vincent, 167, 185–187
Longsheng Group, 176
Lou, Zhongfu, 180
LSE or London Stock Exchange (LSE), 72,
  105, 112, 248, 304
Luen Thai Group of Companies, 187, 201

Ma, Huateng, 173, 234, 245, 247
Ma, Jack, 14, 15, 17, 39, 174, 233
majority executive director board, 7
majority non-executive board, 7
Mao, Zedong, 53, 60, 265
Maxwell Company Failure, 262
Maybank, 187
McKinsey, 23, 172, 238, 247, 269, 280, 312
Metersbonwe, 176
Ministry of Finance PRC (MoF), 115, 304
Minsheng Bank, 34, 234
Mobike, 266
Monkey King, 34

N Board, 111, 270
N Share, 112, 304
NASDAQ, 39, 105, 115, 121, 122, 143, 247, 248, 251, 264, 304, 306, 310
National Bureau of Statistics (NBS), 22, 23, 167, 171, 174, 304, 306
National Development and Reform Commission (NDRC), 40, 57, 59, 115, 304, 305
National People's Congress (NPC), 35, 63, 111, 122, 247, 272, 304
National Social Security Fund, 258
Nationalist, 33, 34, 42, 60, 183
NetEase, 174
New Hope Liuhe, 176
New York Stock Exchange (NYSE), 2, 16, 38, 105, 143, 229, 247, 248, 249, 278, 304
Ninebot, 31, 235
NOMAD, 140, 149
non-executive directors, 7, 138, 144, 156, 157, 225, 251
non-governmental organization (NGO), 74, 182, 304
non-outstanding shares, 111
Non-tradable Share Issue Reform, 108
non-tradable shares, 107, 108, 112

One Belt One Road Initiative, also known as the Belt and Road Initiative (OBOR), 239, 254, 255, 265, 288, 289, 299, 300, 304
One Country, Two Systems, 2, 60, 74, 76, 146
one share, one vote, 19, 37, 111, 240, 267
Organisation for Economic Co-operation and Development (OECD), 1, 13, 43, 61, 82, 116, 125, 199, 257, 264, 265, 273, 304
Ouchi, William, 264

'P' Share, 113
Pao, Y. K., 150, 183, 185
Pang, shiyi, 174
Party Committee (PC), 57, 75, 115, 203, 257, 273, 304

People's Liberation Army (PLA), 3, 304
Ping An, 130, 139, 221–227
PricewaterhouseCoopers (PWC) Study on Family Business, 173
principles-based model, 5, 9, 10
Provisions on Strengthening the Protection of the Rights and Interests of Public Shareholders (2004), 200

QQ, 250, 266
Qualified Domestic Institutional Investors (QDII), 122, 305
Qualified Foreign Institutional Investors (QFII), 111, 122, 305

Radio Frequency ID (RFID), 38
red chips, 112, 230, 251
Regulations on Major Asset Reorganization of Listed Companies (2008), 200
Regulations on the Administration of Company Registration (2005), 200
Regulations on the Takeover of Listed Companies (2006), 200
Ronald Lu & Partners, 187, 309
Ruan, Shuilong, 176
Ruan, Weixiang, 176
rule-based, 5, 8, 9, 91
Rules on Listed Companies' Shareholders' Meetings (2006), 200
Rules on Shareholders' Meetings of Listed Companies (2014), the, 27, 125

'S' Share, 112
Sarbanes-Oxley Regulation (SOX), 9, 122, 155, 262, 305
Schwab, Klaus, 261
Securities and Exchange Commission (SEC), 9, 15,16, 72, 82, 114, 118, 122, 233, 262, 305
Securities and Futures Commission (SFC), 37, 73, 114, 118, 141, 142, 143, 154, 155, 160, 163, 165, 208, 209, 305, 307
Securities and Futures Ordinance, 143, 154, 155, 247
Securities Law, 104, 110, 119, 122, 125, 200

Securities Trading Automated Quotation
  System (STAQ), 115, 306
Segway, 31, 235
SF Express, 174
shadow banking, 266, 267, 270
Shanghai Stock Exchange (SSE), 68, 69, 109,
  111, 115, 125, 196, 222, 250, 252, 301,
  306
Shanxi Haixin Iron and Steel Group Co.,
  Ltd., 177, 190
Shenzhen Stock Exchange (SZSE), 109, 111,
  115, 129, 133, 301, 302, 306, 310
Shuanghui International Holdings (now
  WH Group), 236
Shui On Group, 167, 187
SM Investment Corporation in the
  Philippines, 187
Small- and medium-sized enterprises
  (SMEs), 14, 29, 43, 53, 105, 269–271,
  305
Smart City, 38, 40, 255
Smithfield Foods, 236
SOE Reform, 27, 43, 56, 61, 66, 70
Soho China, 174
South China Morning Post (SCMP), 14, 33,
  69, 135, 185, 196, 233, 305
Standard & Poor's (S&P), 143, 144, 186, 305
State Administration of Foreign Exchange
  (SAFE), 115, 305
State Asset Management Bureau (SAMB),
  115, 305
State Council, 43, 54, 56, 61, 63, 64, 65, 114,
  115, 117, 118, 120, 121, 126, 145, 180
State Economic and Trade Commission
  (SETC); now known as Ministry of
  Commerce or MOFCOM, 65, 115, 305
State-Owned Assets Supervision and
  Administration Commission (SASAC),
  1, 52, 54, 56, 57, 59, 65, 68, 69,
  115–118, 126, 215, 217, 242, 244, 256,
  268, 305
state-owned enterprise or SOE, 1–3, 13, 26,
  27, 29, 33, 34, 35, 41–54, 56, 57, 59–70,
  73–75, 82, 85–87, 89, 90, 104–109, 112,
  114–118, 121, 122, 125, 126, 133, 138,
  194, 197–200, 203–207, 210–218, 220,

  228, 229, 236, 239, 242, 244, 256, 257,
  260, 263–265, 269–275, 277, 284–286,
  288, 291, 293, 305
Stock Exchange of Hong Kong (SEHK),
  141, 142, 152–154, 159, 160, 164, 195,
  201, 229, 245, 248, 249, 303, 305, 307
'ST' Share, 112
Sun, Yat Sen, 33
Sun, Zhengcai, 272
supervisory board, 1, 7, 10, 12, 43, 56, 57,
  59, 62, 66–68, 92, 124, 163, 198, 199,
  200, 206, 210, 212, 217, 227, 257, 258
Swire Pacific, 172

'T' Share, 112
Taobao, 31, 39, 233
Tan, George, 150
Teletronic Riches Ltd., 241, 251
Tencent, 31, 35, 37, 38, 173, 234, 245–247,
  249–251, 266, 267, 271, 275
Tiananmen Square incident of 1989, 26
Tmall, 31, 39
Toudu, 31
tradable shares, 107, 122
Trump, Donald, 25, 105, 235
TVEs or town and village enterprises, 46,
  168, 173, 306
two-tier model, 5, 8, 10

UK/Commonwealth principles model, the,
  8
Unirule Institute of Economics, the, 27
United Overseas Bank in Singapore, 187
United States rule-based model, the, 8
US Congress, 229

Vanke, 107, 129–139, 197, 215, 218, 260,
  265
Volvo, 236, 237

Wahaha, 174, 176, 179
Wanda, 174, 176, 188, 191–197, 231, 237,
  259, 265
Wang, Jianlin, 174, 176, 191, 192, 194–197,
  231, 237
Wang, Sicong, 174, 194–196

Wang, Wei, 174
Wang, Zhongjun, 174
Wang, Zhonglei, 174
Want Want China, 174
Wanxiang Group Corporation, the, 232
Washington Consensus, 274
WeChat, 31, 32, 177, 267
WeChat Pay, 267
Weibo, 31
wholly foreign-owned enterprise (WFOE),
    241, 306
World Trade Organization (WTO), 27, 46,
    65, 109, 121, 306

Xi, Jinping, 24, 33, 61, 69, 163, 230, 256,
    264, 265, 272
Xiami, 31
Xiaomi, 31, 39
Xu, Caihou, 33, 272

Yang, Marjorie, 186
Yang, Teresa, 186
Yanhuang, 27
Yao, Zhenhua, 174
Yin, Guangxia, 34
Youku, 31
Yum China Holdings, 278–280

Zen. *See also* Chan Buddhism, 31, 213
Zhang, Xin, 174
Zheng, Baiwen, 35
Zhou, Chengjian, 176
Zhou, Enlai, 25, 40, 42, 104
Zhou, Yongkang, 33, 272
Zhu, Rongji, 25
Zong, Qinghua, 174

About the Authors

Bob TRICKER

Bob Tricker was an officer in the Royal Navy and financial controller of the UK subsidiary of a US industrial company. Having then studied at Harvard and Oxford universities, he was professor of information systems at Warwick University (UK), and director of the Oxford Centre for Management Studies (forerunner of Oxford's Said Business School). He served on the councils of the both the UK Institute of Chartered Accountants and the UK Institute of Chartered Management Accountants. For many years, he was professor of finance at the University of Hong Kong and drafted Hong Kong's corporate governance code. In 1984, he wrote the first book to use "corporate governance" in the title and founded the research journal *Corporate Governance—an international review*. He is the author of the textbook *Corporate Governance* (Oxford University Press, 4th edition, 2018) and *Business Ethics* (with Gretchen Tricker, Routledge, 2014).

Gregg G. Ka-Lok LI FCMC

Gregg Li has been an industrial engineer and governance consultant and has designed and repaired governance and management systems for the last 30 years. Some of his most interesting assignments have been with boards in the NGO sector, family businesses, and in start-ups. He has served as a visiting professor in corporate governance, innovation, and leadership at universities such as Tsinghua and the University of Hawai'i at Manoa. He studied engineering (EngD) at Warwick (UK), has an MBA from UCLA, and studied liberal arts at Washington University in St. Louis. He is the founding chairman of G. Li & Company, Invotech, and the Institute of Management Consultants in Hong Kong. Currently, he is a board member of the Urban Renewal Authority, Cyberport, and a member of the Advisory Board of the Centre for Family Business at the Chinese University of Hong Kong. In finding solutions to dying boards, Gregg has worked with professionals at PwC, IBM, McKinsey, the World Bank, and Aon.